VENTURE CAPITAL DEVELOPMENT IN CHINA 2015

中国创业风险投资发展报告 2015

主 编 王 元 张晓原 张志宏 副主编 房汉廷 沈文京 李文雷 郭 戎

图书在版编目（CIP）数据

中国创业风险投资发展报告 2015/王元等主编. —北京：经济管理出版社，2015.10
ISBN 978-7-5096-3987-0

Ⅰ. ①中… Ⅱ. ①王… Ⅲ. ①风险投资—研究报告—中国—2015 Ⅳ. ①F832.48

中国版本图书馆 CIP 数据核字（2015）第 232638 号

组稿编辑：陈　力
责任编辑：陈　力　许　艳
责任印制：黄章平
责任校对：超　凡

出版发行：经济管理出版社
（北京市海淀区北蜂窝 8 号中雅大厦 A 座 11 层　100038）
网　　址：www. E-mp. com. cn
电　　话：(010) 51915602
印　　刷：北京易丰印捷科技股份有限公司
经　　销：新华书店
开　　本：880mm×1230mm/16
印　　张：13.75
字　　数：451 千字
版　　次：2015 年 11 月第 1 版　　2015 年 11 月第 1 次印刷
书　　号：ISBN 978-7-5096-3987-0
定　　价：150.00 元

中国创业风险投资发展报告 2015

编委会

参与和支持单位（排名不分先后）

科学技术部科研条件与财务司
中国科学技术发展战略研究院
科技部火炬高技术产业开发中心
科技部科技经费监督管理服务中心
国家科技风险事业开发中心
商务部外国投资管理司
国家开发银行投资业务局
中国进出口银行业务开发与创新部
中国社会科学院金融研究中心
中国科技金融促进会
中国台湾创业风险投资商业同业公会
亚洲创业基金期刊集团（中国香港）
中国风险投资研究院
《中国科技投资》杂志社
北京清科创业风险投资顾问有限公司
辽宁大学工商管理学院
北京创业投资协会
北京市科学技术委员会
北京首都科技发展集团公司
天津市创业投资协会
上海市创业投资行业协会
河北省科学技术厅
河北省科学技术情报研究院
河北石家庄高新技术产业开发区科技局
山西省科学技术厅
山西省风险投资协会
山西省科技基金发展总公司
内蒙古科技风险基金管理办公室
四川省绵阳高新技术产业开发区
四川成都创业投资协会
成都生产力促进中心
成都高新区经贸发展局
重庆市科委
重庆市科技创业投资协会
贵州省科学技术厅
贵阳高新技术创业服务中心
贵州省科技风险投资有限公司
云南省科学技术厅
云南省科技成果转化服务中心
辽宁省科技创业投资协会
辽宁科技创业投资有限公司
辽宁省沈阳市科学技术局
辽宁省沈阳科技风险开发事业中心
辽宁省大连市生产力促进中心
大连高新技术产业园区金融工作办公室
吉林省长春市科学技术局
吉林高技术创业服务中心
黑龙江省科学技术厅
黑龙江省科力高科技产业投资有限公司
哈尔滨市创业投资协会
湖北省科学技术厅
湖北省创业投资同业公会
湖北省高新技术发展促进中心
湖北省武汉市科技局
武汉市科技金融创新促进中心
湖北省襄樊高新技术创业服务中心
河南省科学技术厅
湖南省科学技术厅
湖南省科技交流交易中心
山东省科学技术厅
山东省科技统计分析研究中心
山东省青岛市科技局
青岛生产力促进中心
江苏省创业投资协会
无锡新区科技金融投资集团
江苏省南京市科技局
浙江省科学技术厅
浙江省风险投资协会
浙江省杭州市科技局
浙江省杭州市生产力促进中心
浙江省宁波市科学技术局
浙江省宁波市科学信息研究院
安徽省科学技术厅
安徽省科技成果转化服务中心
江西省科学技术厅
江西省科技金融促进会
福建省高新技术创业服务中心
福建省厦门市科技局
福建省厦门火炬高技术产业开发区管委会
厦门火炬高技术产业开发区管委会计划财政局
福建省高新技术产权交易所有限公司
广东省风险投资促进会

广东省佛山高新区管委会
广州风险投资促进会
广东省珠海高新技术创业服务中心
广东省佛山高新区经济发展和科技局
珠海高新区科经局
深圳市创业投资同业公会
海南省科学技术厅
甘肃省科技风险投资公司
甘肃省兰州高科创业投资担保有限公司
宁夏回族自治区科学技术厅
宁夏回族自治区科学技术厅生产力促进中心
陕西省科学技术厅
陕西省科技资源统筹中心科技金融部
陕西省宝鸡高新区高技术创业服务中心
陕西省杨凌农业高新技术产业示范区管委会金融办
陕西省西安高新技术产业开发区管理委员会金融服务办公室
新疆科技项目服务中心
新疆维吾尔自治区科学技术厅
新疆维吾尔自治区科技生产力促进中心
青海省国有科技资产经营管理有限公司
广西壮族自治区科学技术厅
广西壮族自治区科技情报所
广西分析测试协会

目 录

摘要　2014 年度中国创投的主要特征及发展 …… I

Abstract　The Features and Development of China's Venture Capital in 2014 …… I

1　中国创业风险投资机构与资本 …… 1

1.1　2014 年度调查概述 …… 1

1.2　创业风险投资机构和管理资本 …… 1

1.3　创业风险投资的资本来源 …… 3

1.4　创业风险投资机构的资本规模及分布 …… 5

1.5　中国创业风险投资累计投资情况 …… 6

2　中国创业风险投资的投资分析 …… 8

2.1　中国创业风险投资的行业特征 …… 8

2.1.1　中国创业风险投资的行业分布 …… 8

2.1.2　中国创业风险投资对高新技术产业与传统产业的投资比较 …… 14

2.2　中国创业风险投资的投资阶段 …… 15

2.2.1　中国创业风险投资所处阶段的总体分布 …… 15

2.2.2　中国创业风险投资在主要行业投资项目的阶段分布 …… 17

2.3　中国创业风险投资的投资强度 …… 19

2.3.1　中国创业风险投资强度的变化趋势与行业差异 …… 19

2.3.2　中国创业风险投资机构单项投资规模分布 …… 21

2.3.3　中国创业风险投资的投资策略（联合投资） …… 22

2.4　中国创业风险投资的首轮投资与后续投资 …… 24

2.5　中国创业风险投资机构持股结构 …… 24

2.6　中国创业风险投资项目的特征 …… 25

2.6.1　中国创业风险投资项目的资本规模 …… 25

2.6.2　中国创业风险投资项目的雇员规模 …… 26

2.6.3　中国创业风险投资项目的经营时间 …… 27

3　中国创业风险投资的退出 …… 29

3.1　中国创业风险投资退出的基本情况 …… 29

3.2　中国创业风险投资的退出方式 …… 30

3.2.1　中国创业风险投资的主要退出方式 …… 30

3.2.2　中国创业风险投资的 IPO 退出渠道 …… 31

3.3 中国创业风险投资退出项目的行业分布 …… 32
3.4 中国创业风险投资退出项目的地区分布 …… 34
3.5 中国创业风险投资项目的退出效果 …… 35
3.5.1 中国创业风险投资退出的总体绩效表现 …… 35
3.5.2 中国创业风险投资不同退出方式的绩效表现 …… 37
3.5.3 中国创业风险投资不同行业退出的绩效表现 …… 38

4 中国创业风险投资的绩效 …… 40

4.1 中国创业风险投资机构的收入 …… 40
4.1.1 中国创业风险投资机构的收入 …… 40
4.1.2 中国不同规模创业风险投资机构的收入特征 …… 40
4.1.3 中国创业风险投资机构的收入来源结构 …… 41
4.1.4 中国创业风险投资机构当年收入的最大来源 …… 42
4.2 中国创业风险投资项目的收益情况 …… 43
4.2.1 中国创业风险投资项目的主营业务收入 …… 43
4.2.2 中国创业风险投资项目的利润 …… 44
4.2.3 中国创业风险投资项目主营业务收入与利润的关系 …… 44
4.3 中国创业风险投资项目的总体运行与趋势 …… 46
4.3.1 中国创业风险投资项目总体运行情况 …… 46
4.3.2 中国创业风险投资项目总体运行趋势 …… 46
4.4 中国创业风险投资机构的总体运行情况评价 …… 47
4.4.1 中国创业风险投资机构对自身发展状况的评价 …… 47
4.4.2 中国创业风险投资机构对全行业发展情况的评价 …… 48
4.4.3 中国创业风险投资机构对 2015 年投资前景的预测 …… 49

5 中国创业风险投资的经营管理 …… 50

5.1 中国创业风险投资的项目来源 …… 50
5.2 中国创业风险投资的决策要素 …… 51
5.3 中国创业风险投资对被投资项目的监管方式 …… 52
5.4 与创业风险投资经营管理有关的人力资源因素 …… 53
5.5 投资效果不理想的主要原因 …… 55
5.6 中国创业风险投资机构的预期持股时间 …… 56
5.7 影响中国创业风险投资经营的外部因素 …… 56

6 中国创业风险投资区域运行情况 …… 58

6.1 创业风险投资机构数量和管理资本的地区分布 …… 58

6.2 各地区创业风险投资机构的规模分布 …… 60
6.3 各地区创业风险投资机构的资本来源 …… 62
6.4 各地区创业风险投资的投资特征 …… 63
6.4.1 创业风险投资项目的地区分布 …… 63
6.4.2 各地区创业风险投资的投资强度 …… 64
6.4.3 各地区创业风险投资机构的项目持股结构 …… 66
6.4.4 各地区创业风险投资项目的所处阶段 …… 68
6.4.5 部分地区创业风险投资对不同行业的投资 …… 69
6.5 各经济区域创业投资活动情况 …… 78
6.5.1 我国创业风险投资机构项目的区域分布 …… 78
6.5.2 我国不同区域创业风险投资的投资强度 …… 79
6.5.3 不同区域创业风险投资的持股结构 …… 79
6.5.4 不同经济区域创业风险投资项目所处阶段 …… 80
6.5.5 各经济区域创业风险投资项目的行业分布 …… 81
7 外资创业风险投资机构的运作 …… 85
7.1 外资创业风险投资项目的行业分布 …… 85
7.2 外资创业风险投资项目所处阶段 …… 88
7.3 外资创业风险投资的投资强度 …… 89
7.4 外资创业风险投资项目状况分析 …… 91
7.4.1 创业风险投资项目的实收资本情况 …… 91
7.4.2 创业风险投资项目的雇员情况 …… 92
7.5 外资创业风险投资项目的总体运作情况 …… 94
7.6 影响外资创业风险投资机构投资决策的因素 …… 95
7.7 外资创业风险投资机构获取信息的主要渠道 …… 96
7.8 外资创业风险投资项目的监管模式 …… 97
7.9 与外资创业风险投资机构经营有关的人力资源因素 …… 98
7.10 外资创业风险投资机构对总体发展环境的评价 …… 99
8 中国创业风险投资发展环境 …… 101
8.1 中国创业风险投资机构的政策环境 …… 101
8.1.1 中国创业风险投资机构可以享受到的政府扶持政策 …… 101
8.1.2 中国创业风险投资机构税收负担情况 …… 102
8.1.3 中国创业风险投资机构希望的政府激励政策 …… 102
8.2 国家科技计划支撑创业风险投资发展 …… 103

8.2.1 国家科技计划对创业风险投资项目的支持情况 …… 103
8.2.2 国家科技计划与创业风险投资项目对接的关键因素 …… 104
8.3 中国促进创业风险投资发展的主要政策 …… 105
9 中国创业风险投资引导基金发展情况 …… 107
9.1 中国创业风险投资引导基金发展现状 …… 107
9.2 中国创业风险投资引导基金投资项目的行业分布 …… 109
9.3 中国创业风险投资引导基金投资项目所处阶段 …… 111
9.4 中国创业风险投资引导基金投资项目运作状况 …… 112
附录 1 2014 年美国创业风险投资综述 …… 114
附录 2 2014 年欧洲创业风险投资回顾 …… 120
附录 3 2014 年韩国创业风险投资回顾 …… 129
附录 4 2015 硅谷指数解读 …… 133
附录 5 关于印发《中小企业发展专项资金管理暂行办法》的通知 …… 138
附录 6 科技部 财政部关于印发《国家科技成果转化引导基金设立创业投资子基金管理暂行办法》的通知 …… 143
附录 7 私募投资基金监督管理暂行办法 …… 147
附录 8 国务院关于进一步促进资本市场健康发展的若干意见 …… 151
附录 9 国务院办公厅关于多措并举着力缓解企业融资成本高问题的指导意见 …… 155
附录 10 中国创业风险投资机构名录 …… 157

摘 要

2014 年度中国创投的主要特征及发展

全国创业风险投资调查写作分析组①

创业风险投资作为一种新型的创新创业投融资机制，并不只简单地承载提供资金的功能，它还在创新项目孵化、创新成果转化、市场开拓、企业管理等方面发挥着重要作用。2012 年以来，受国内外宏观经济环境影响，资本市场低迷不振，行业的快速扩张带来的隐患开始显现，业内出现深度盘整，行业发展开始放缓，投资阶段开始前移。2014 年，我国经济发展步入“新常态”，经济结构转向“调存量”与“优增量”并举，经济发展动力转向新的增长点，更加注重科技进步和改革创新。A 股 IPO 重新开闸，多层次资本退出市场发展不断完善，再度激发了投资者的热情和信心。我国创投业进入了理性发展的扩张期，创投行业在募资、投资、退出方面均出现不同程度的增长。

1 2014 年中国创业风险投资发展的主要特征及趋势

1.1 机构数量与资本总量呈现明显增长态势

截至 2014 年底，中国创业风险投资各类机构数达到 1551 家②，增幅 10.2%。其中，创业风险投资企业（基金）1167 家，当年新募基金 216 家（见表 1、图 1）；相比而言，同期的美国基金为 1206 家，欧洲整个私募股权投资企业超过 1200 家，其中风险投资机构约占 40%，为 500 家左右。

表 1 中国创业风险投资企业（基金）总量、增量（2005~2014）③

项目 \ 年份	2005	2006	2007	2008	2009	2010	2011	2012	2013	2014
VC 基金（家）	277	312	331	410	495	720	860	942	1095	1167
较上年增长（%）	7.78	12.6	6.09	23.9	20.7	45.5	19.4	9.53	19.0	10.2
VC 管理机构（家）	42	33	52	54	81	147	236	241	313	384
当年新募集基金（数）④	14	35	76	88	99	189	177	152	185	216

① 中国科学技术发展战略研究院 2015 年“全国创业风险投资调查写作分析组”成员包括：郭戎、李希义、张明喜、张俊芳、魏世杰、付剑峰、朱欣乐、王秋颖等，写作组成员分别完成各章执笔。本摘要执笔：张俊芳、郭戎。

② 为实际存量机构数，主要包括：创业投资企业（基金）、创业投资管理企业以及少量从事创业投资业务的事业单位。该数据已剔除不再经营创投业务或注销的机构数。

③ 由于我国创投行业的迅猛发展，基金形态的日趋多样，从 2010 年起，按照国际惯例区分基金和基金管理公司，并对前期数据进行了追溯调整。

④ 在实际统计中当年新募基金数量存在一定偏差，存在当年进入统计而实际为前几年募集成立的基金，因此每年对前期新募基金数据进行调整。

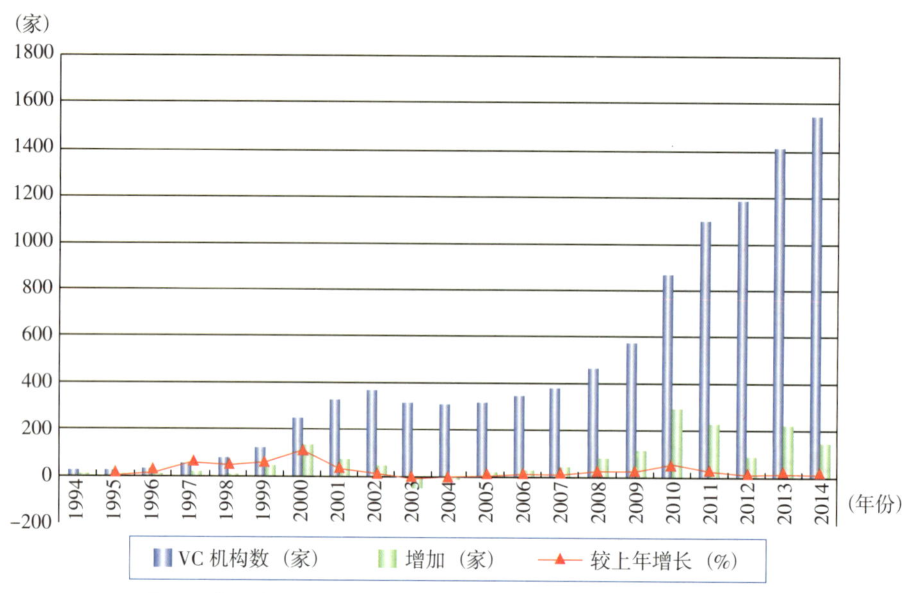

图 1 中国创业风险投资机构总量、增量（1994~2014）

从投资规模而言，2014 年，全国创业风险投资管理资本总量达到 5232.4 亿元，增幅为 31.7%，管理资本总量占全国 GDP 的 0.82%；基金平均管理资本规模为 4.48 亿元，较 2013 年大幅提高①（见表 2、图 2）。相比而言，同期美

表 2 中国创业风险管理资本总额（2005~2014）

项目 \ 年份	2005	2006	2007	2008	2009	2010	2011	2012	2013	2014
管理资本总额（亿元）	631.6	663.8	1112.9	1455.7	1605.1	2406.6	3198.0	3312.9	3573.9	5232.4
较上年增长（%）	2.3	5.1	67.7	30.8	10.3	49.9	32.9	3.6	7.9	31.7
基金平均管理资本规模（亿元）	2.28	2.13	3.36	3.55	3.24	3.34	3.72	3.52	3.26	4.48

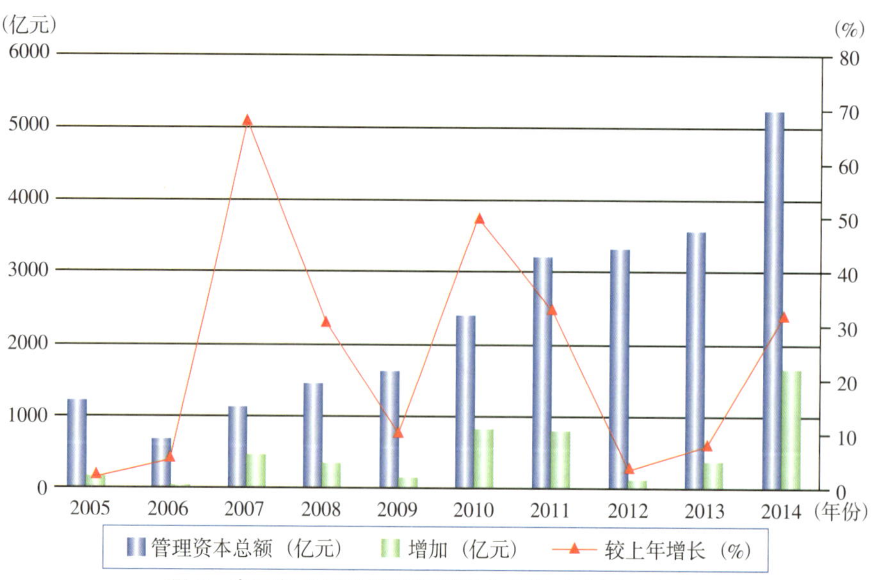

图 2 中国创业风险投资管理资本总额（2005~2014）

① 2014 年调查员针对北京地区做了全面统计，统计数据较往年大幅提升，由于北京地区的创投企业大多为大型创投企业，对管理资本总量和平均管理资本统计贡献度较大。

国创业风险投资的管理资本总额达到 1565 亿美元（约合一万亿元），占 GDP 的 0.93%；平均基金规模达到 194.9 百万美元（约合 12.48 亿元）；欧洲私募股权基金管理资本总额达到 5480 亿欧元，其中，风险投资的资本总量约占 10%（约合 4000 亿元），整个欧洲风险投资占 GDP 的比重为 0.024%，其中英国占比为 0.035%。可见，无论从创业风险投资的机构数量还是资本总量来讲，我国都已经成为名符其实的风险投资大国。

1.2 投资总量迅猛增加，投资标准日趋多元化

2014 年，新一代信息技术革命正在逐渐融合传统行业，创业机会增多，资本市场环境向好，当年投资项目数急剧增加至 2459 家，较上年增加 28.9%；投资金额增至 374.4 亿元，较上年增加 34.2%。截至 2014 年底，累计投资项目数达到 14118 项，其中投资高新技术企业项目数 7330 项，占比 51.9%；累计投资金额 2933.61 亿元，其中投资高新技术企业金额 1401.9 亿元，占比 47.8%。

从当年投资与累计投资情况来看，近年来我国创业风险当年投资项目集中在 1500~2500 项内，总投资金额在 280 亿~550 亿元区间，投资强度主要集中在 1500 万~3000 万元/项，具有几个明显的特征与趋势：一是投资情况与资本市场的发展密切相关，2009 年创业板的开闸促进了创投投资热潮，当年投资项目剧增，而 2012 年资本市场的低迷与 2013 年的 IPO 关停，无疑减缓了投资步伐。二是自 2011 年以来，高新技术企业的投资项目数呈现出逐年下降的趋势，占比从 2010 年的 60%左右下降到 2014 年的 30%左右，这在一定程度上表明投资标准日趋多元化。三是 2010 年以前，平均投资强度为 1716 万元/项，到 2011 年达到峰值 2879.1 万元/项，此后呈逐年下降趋势，这在一定程度上表明 2006 年以来的急剧扩张造成了机构短期化的后端逐利行为，从 2011 年起，投资行为更加理性，更趋于小规模、早前期企业，以及网络型等轻资产行业。

表 3 截至 2014 年底中国创业风险投资当年投资情况（2010~2014）

年度	投资项目数（项）	投资金额（亿元）	投资强度（万元/个）	其中：高新技术项目数（项）	占比（%）	其中：高新技术项目金额（亿元）	占比（%）	高新技术企业投资强度（万元/项）
2011	1894	545.3	2879.1	987	52.1	229.8	42.1	2328.3
2012	1502	318.5	2120.1	671	44.7	154.5	48.5	2301.7
2013	1501	279.0	1858.5	590	39.3	109.0	39.1	1846.9
2014	2459	374.4	1522	689	28.0	124.8	33.3	1811.0

1.3 新兴产业备受青睐，投资行业紧跟宏观热点

2014 年，中国创业风险投资年度投资项目主要集中在软件产业、网络产业、通信设备、其他设备和新材料工业等行业，这些行业集中了当年 40.6%以上的项目，且集中度较往年略有下降。

从历年投资趋势来看，主要呈现出以下几个特征：一是投资重点由过去的传统制造业逐步转向互联网、生物科技、新能源等新兴产业，特别是近年来互联网的兴起，涌现出大量投资机会，2014 年网络、IT 等信息服务业的投资项目数占比为 25.53%，位居首位；通信和其他电子设备制造业、新能源和环保业，以及医药生物业分别占比 14.63%、13.16%、9.39%。按投资金额划分，通信和其他电子设备制造业投资占比 21.15%，排在首位。二是投资行业热点轮动，如金融保险业、传播与娱乐业，以及农林牧副渔行业波动较大，在个别年份进入投资热点（见图 3）。

1.4 投资阶段经历了逐利的扩张期，逐步向理性回归

从我国创业风险投资历年投资的趋势来看，2011 年以前，急剧扩张的投资行为伴随着大量投资的短期逐利效应，投资阶段不断后移，成长期和成熟期的项目占比逐年提升；2011 年以后，我国创业风险投资业经历了竞争加剧的行业洗牌，投资行为也日趋理性，投资重心逐年前移，种子期和起步期的项目占比呈现出较为明显的上升态势；截至 2014 年底，初创期（种子期、起步期）项目占比达到 57.3%，远高于 2011 年的 39.4%（见图 4）。

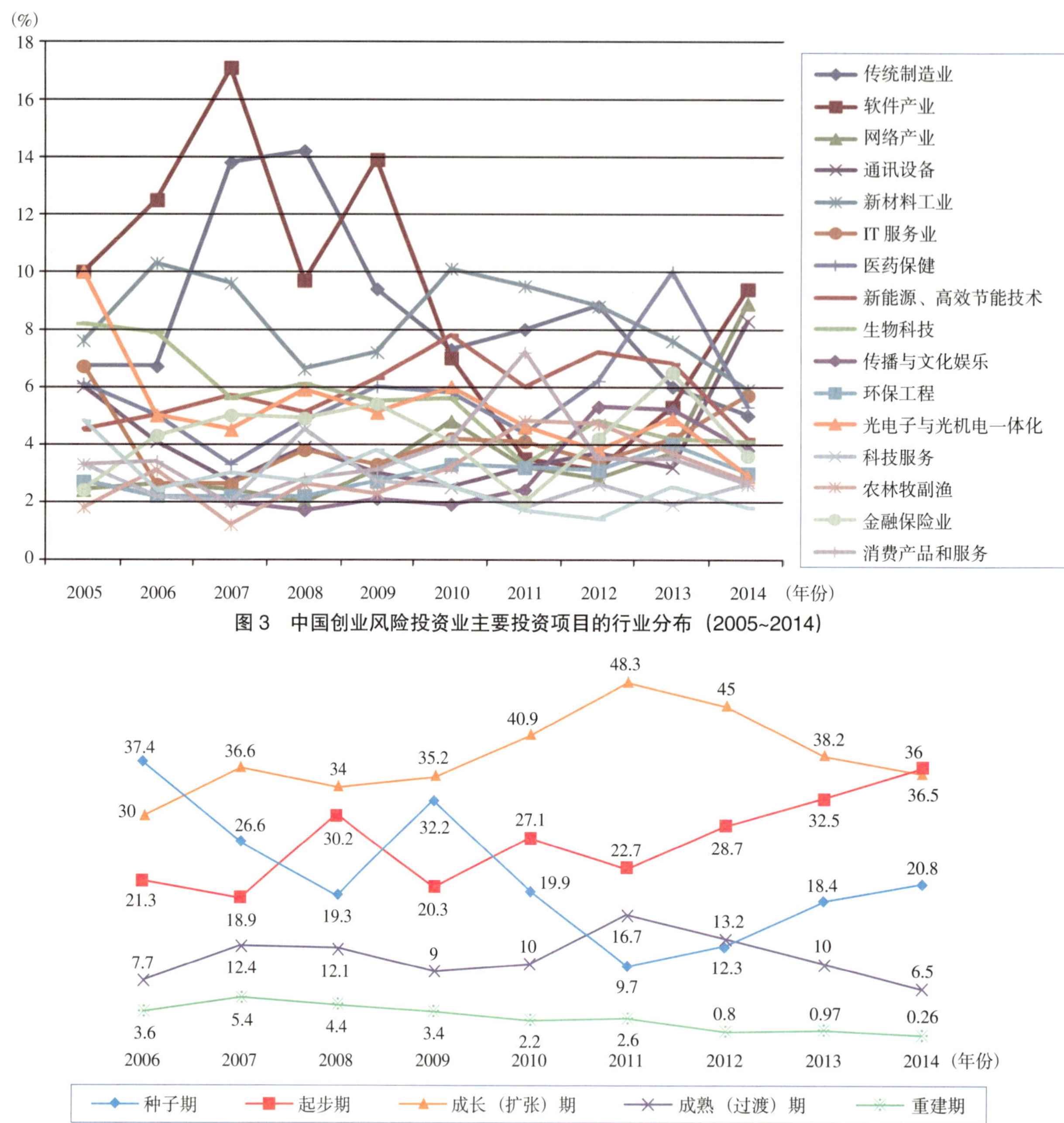

图 3 中国创业风险投资业主要投资项目的行业分布（2005~2014）

图 4 中国创业风险投资项目所处阶段的总体分布（按投资项目占比）（单位：%）

1.5 地区集聚效应明显，内陆欠发达地区以国有资本为主

整体看，我国创业风险投资的机构分布具有较为明显的区域特征，包括江苏、浙江、上海、广东在内的东部发达地区一直是国内创业风险投资机构最为集聚的地区，到 2014 年风险投资机构数量达到 892 家，占全国总量的 57.5%。从历年统计来看，风险投资的集聚效应非常明显，以江苏、浙江为首的风险投资在全国的占比从 2002 年的 18.2%持续增加到 2014 年的 48.4%。此外，安徽、重庆、湖北、山东等中西部地区的风险投资业在近年来呈现出比较明显的增长态势（见图 5）。

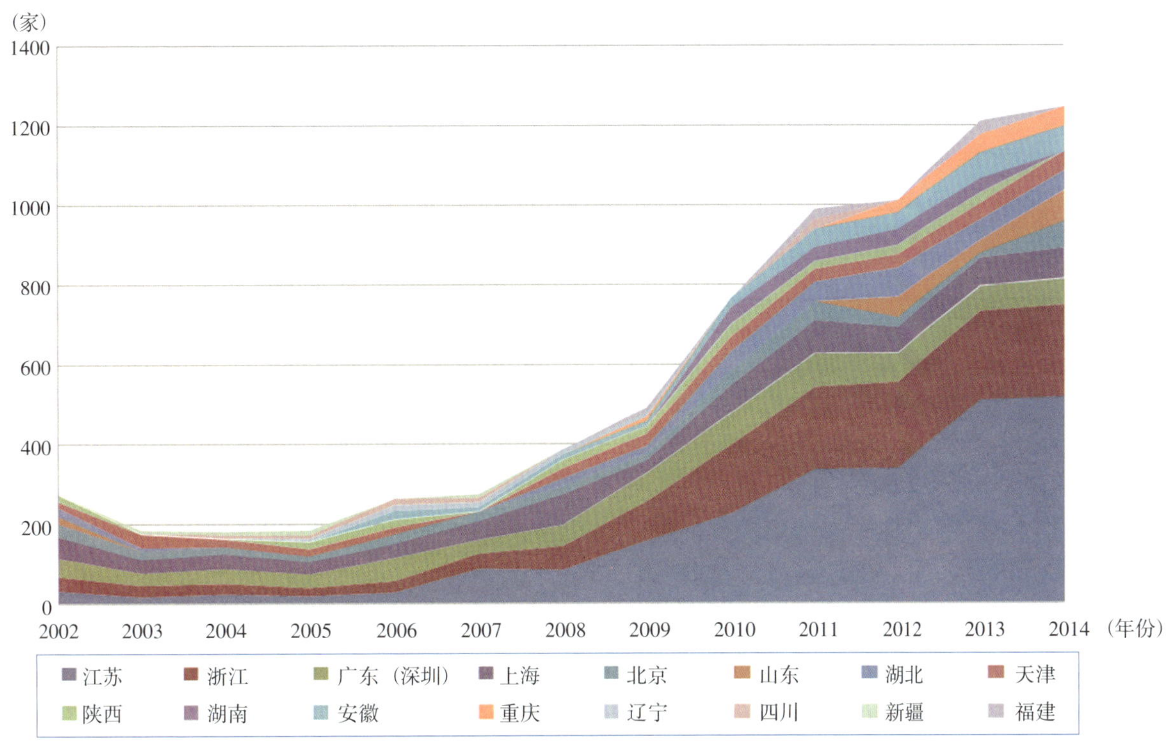

图 5 中国创业风险投资的主要地区分布（2002~2014）

从资金总量来看，2014 年，江苏、北京、广东、浙江、安徽的管理资本总量排在了全国前五名，合计占比 80.5%。其中，江苏、浙江地区的风险投资机构总量较小，约 80%的公司资金规模在 5000 万到 5 亿之间，而北京、广东地区的风险投资机构资金规模较大，大多集中在 5 亿以上。

从资本来源的结构来看，内陆经济欠发达地区的风险投资来源主要以政府和国有独资机构为主，山西、内蒙、甘肃、黑龙江、河北等地创业风险投资中政府和国有独资的资金占比一直保持在 50%以上。而北京、福建、浙江、江苏、广东湖北等地的市场化程度较高，主要通过企业行为募集资金。

1.6 行业退出渠道日趋完善，2014 年行业年均收益略有提升

目前，我国创业风险投资的退出方式仍然以并购和公司股权回购为主，但随着我国资本市场的逐步完善，上市退出的比例整体呈上升态势，在近两年 IPO 市场暂停期间，并购交易表现活跃 （见表 4）。据统计，2014 年，共有 103 个项目通过 IPO 市场实现退出收益，占总退出比例为 20.72%，披露并购交易 179 项，占比 36.02%。其中，境内创业板上市仍然是创业风险投资机构企业 IPO 退出的主要渠道，退出项目占比 42.72%。

表 4 中国创业风险投资的退出方式分布（2003~2014）

单位：%

年 份	上 市	并 购	回 购	清 算	其他（含新三板）
2003	5.40	40.40	36.30	14.90	3.00
2004	12.40	55.30	27.60	4.70	0.00
2005	11.90	44.40	33.30	10.40	0.00
2006	12.70	28.40	30.40	7.80	20.60
2007	24.20	29.00	27.40	5.60	13.70
2008	22.70	23.20	34.80	9.20	10.10

续表

年 份	上 市	并 购	回 购	清 算	其他（含新三板）
2009	25.30	33.00	35.3	6.30	0.00
2010	29.80	28.63	32.82	6.87	1.91
2011	29.40	29.97	32.28	3.17	5.19
2012	29.41	15.86	45.01	6.65	3.07
2013	24.33	23.75	44.83	4.60	2.49
2014	20.72	36.02	36.02	4.83	2.41

从历年退出的盈利表现来看，2014年，受中国资本市场IPO重启、股票市场活跃等利好政策影响，上市退出收益较前两年大幅提高，平均账面回报6.01倍；行业平均回报率为123.04%，平均投资退出时间6.83年，年均回报率为23.46%。

2 政府促进风险投资发展的主要举措

我国政府高度重视风险投资的发展，自1999年国务院办公厅转发科技部等七部门联合出台的《关于建立风险投资机制的若干意见》以来，各有关部门相继出台了支持创业风险投资发展的相关政策，涉及引导基金、监督管理、税收优惠、外商投资等方面，有效推动了我国创业风险投资事业的健康发展。大体而言，在扶持风险投资发展过程中，政府的主要举措分为以下几类：

2.1 设立政府引导基金

年度统计调查显示，从全国范围看，截至2014年底，获得各级政府创业风险投资引导基金参股支持的创业风险投资机构累计达322家，政府创业风险投资引导基金累计出资363.27亿元，引导带动创业风险投资管理资金规模超过1800亿元。

截至2014年，国家层面出台的基金主要有：①2007年科技部设立“科技型中小企业创业投资引导基金”，面向科技型中小企业，截至2014年底，累计投入财政资金49.93亿元；其中，通过阶段参股方式，共出资34.43亿元参股了100家重点投资于科技型中小企业的创业投资企业，累计注册资本约220亿元左右；通过风险补助和投资保障方式共立项1896项，累计安排补助资金15.5亿元。②2009年10月，发改委设立“国家新兴产业创投计划”，面向国家鼓励发展的高新技术产业，重点扶持处于初创期、成长期的创新型企业和高成长性企业。首期发起设立20只创业投资基金。中央财政出资10亿元，省级财政出资10亿元，面向社会募集资金不低于30亿元，总基金规模不低于50亿元。2011年8月，《新兴产业创投计划参股创业投资基金管理暂行办法》文件出台，新兴产业创投计划进入实质性运作阶段。③2011年7月，科技部设立“国家科技成果转化引导基金”，加速推动科技成果转化与应用，转化基金支持科技成果转化的方式包括设立创业投资子基金、贷款风险补偿和绩效奖励等。2014年8月，《国家科技成果转化引导基金设立创业投资子基金管理暂行办法》出台，基金进入实质性运作阶段。④2015年1月，国务院设立“新兴产业创投引导基金”，助力创业创新和产业升级，吸引有实力的企业、大型金融机构等社会、民间资本参与，预计形成总规模400亿元的新兴产业创投引导基金。

另据不完全统计，地方设立的引导基金超过百家，近年来设立的部分基金有：山东省2014年底出台《关于运用政府引导基金促进股权投资加快发展的意见》，提出将设立13只省级股权投资引导基金，到2017年，省级政府引导基金规模达到100亿元；安徽2014年12月组建了50亿元规模的高新技术产业政府引导基金；广东省财政2015年5月设立省级重大科技专项创业投资引导基金等。此外，近年来，各省市地区先后设立天使投资引导基金，包括江苏省天使投资引导资金、宁波市天使投资引导基金、扬州市天使投资引导资金、青岛市天使投资引导资金、中关村天使投资引导资金等。2013年2月，宁波市天使投资引导基金正式成立，规模为5年内总投资5亿元，这是国内首家政府设立的天使投资引导基金公司。2014年12月17日，上海市天使投资引导基金正式成立，该基金通过母基金（FOF）的形式，出资额上不封顶，一期到位约5亿元，采取股权投资的方式，撬动天使投资机构约20亿元。

2.2 制定相关税收优惠政策

我国目前针对股权投资的税收优惠政策主要集中在以下两方面：一是针对创业投资企业投资额的70%税前扣除优惠，2009年4月，《国家税务总局关于实施创业投资企业所得税优惠问题的通知》（国税发〔2009〕87 号）中明确规定，创业投资企业采取股权投资方式投资于未上市的中小高新技术企业 2 年以上的，可以按照其投资额的 70% 在股权持有满 2 年的当年抵扣该创业投资企业的应纳税所得额；当年不足抵扣的，可以在以后纳税年度结转抵扣。二是针对上市公司股权转让免税优惠和股息收入减半纳税。2014 年 12 月，国家税务总局发布《股权转让所得个人所得税管理办法（试行）》，明确了个人转让股权的税收征收政策。现行税收政策规定，个人从上海证券交易所、深圳证券交易所取得的上市公司股票转让所得，暂不征收个人所得税；个人转让上市公司限售股，依照相关规定征收个人所得税。

在地方层面，各地纷纷实践，大胆探索。经国务院批准，2012 年苏州工业园区开展了有限合伙制创业投资企业法人合伙人企业所得税政策试点工作，即注册在苏州工业园区内的有限合伙制创业投资企业的法人合伙人，可以享受创业投资企业的所得税优惠政策。[①] 2013 年 9 月，中关村也纳入到此项试点范围。[②] 规定在 2013~2015 年期间，对中关村有限合伙制创业投资企业采取股权投资方式投资于未上市中小高新技术企业 2 年以上的，该有限合伙制创业投资企业的法人合伙人可按其投资额的 70%，在股权持有满 2 年的当年抵扣该法人合伙人从有限合伙创业投资企业分得的应纳税所得额。此外，在个人所得税上，《关于中关村国家自主创新示范区企业转增股本个人所得税试点政策的通知》（财税〔2013〕73 号）中，对中关村中小高新技术企业以未分配利润、盈余公积、资本公积向个人股东转增股本有关个人所得税，可最长不超过 5 年分期缴纳；这比一般情况下，我国其他企业转增股本税收政策中，应按照“利息、股息、红利所得”项目适用 20%税率征收个人所得税，延长了征税时间，有利于促进企业进行股权投资等创新活动。在天使投资税收优惠方面，个别地方也进行了有效的探索实践，如《江苏省关于鼓励和引导天使投资支持科技型中小企业发展的意见》中明确了对天使投资发展的税收扶持。

2.3 营造有利于风险投资发展的政策环境

近年来，中央及地方出台了一系列政策措施支持风险投资发展。2015 年调查显示，约有 20.2%的创业风险投资机构享受到政府资金支持，22.9%的创业风险投资机构享受到所得税减免政策优惠，29.1%的创业风险投资机构在信息交流方面得到了政府支持，13.4%的创业风险投资机构在人员培训方面得到了政府帮助。总体上，政府对创投机构的直接支持在减少，间接服务在不断完善。政策投资环境逐年向好，行业发展由监管逐步走向自律。

2014 年 5 月，《国务院关于进一步促进资本市场健康发展的若干意见》（国发〔2014〕17 号）出台，明确提出要加快建设多渠道、广覆盖、严监管、高效率的股权市场，鼓励市场化并购重组，完善退市制度；建立健全私募发行制度，发展私募投资基金；壮大专业机构投资者。国家发改委发布《关于进一步做好支持创业投资企业发展相关工作的通知》，明确表示支持发展天使投资机构，鼓励符合条件的天使投资机构备案为创业投资企业，享受相应扶持政策。7 月，证监会发布《私募投资基金监督管理暂行办法》，对包括创投、证券投资基金等在内的以私募形式募集资金进行投资的基金行业进行了备案监管，进一步规范私募投资行为，促进资本市场健康发展；值得肯定的是，对创业投资基金采取区别于其他私募基金的差异化行业自律管理。8 月，《国务院办公厅关于多措并举着力缓解企业融资成本高问题的指导意见》（国办发〔2014〕39 号）提出要进一步促进私募股权和创投基金发展，逐步扩大各类长期资金投资资本市场的范围和规模，按照国家税收法律及有关规定，对各类长期投资资金予以税收优惠。此外，财政部、工信部、科技部、商务部联合发布了《中小企业发展专项资金管理办法》，整合开展了一系列面向中小企业创新发展的专项资金支持，让利市场机构，降低投资风险，引导社会资本参与政府计划，支持初创期科技型企业发展。

3 现阶段发展的主要障碍及建议

2000 年以来，我国创业风险投资发展迅猛，风险投资的组织与运营模式不断丰富，已成为名符其实的风险投资大国。在 VC 的快速发展与扩张中，也必然会面临一些问题，下面将结合创业风险投资行业的“行业自律为主，政策监管为辅”的发展趋势，浅析几点目前面临的不足及建议。

3.1 我国政府引导基金运营效率和市场化水平有待提升

目前，从国家发改委、科技部到各地发改委、经信委、开发区，层层设立的引导资金，无疑在促进行业发展

① 相关政策：《财政部、国家税务总局关于苏州工业园区有限合伙制创业投资企业法人合伙人企业所得税试点政策的通知》（财税〔2012〕67 号）。

② 相关政策：《财政部、国家税务总局关于中关村国家自主创新示范区有限合伙制创业投资企业法人合伙人企业所得税试点政策的通知》（财税〔2013〕71 号）。

中发挥了很重要的作用，调研中了解到，总体上，中小企业创投引导基金在一定程度上缓解了创投机构的融资问题，有利于引导投资方向，财政资金的引导放大作用超过6倍。但引导基金在设立与发展中，也暴露出一些问题：一是作为来源于政府财政资金的引导基金，资金使用往往带有很强的地方政策性色彩，运作效率较低。如地方政府要求与其合作投资的创业投资企业的管理团队在不同地方均设立管理公司，投资范围仅限于本地等，出现“择地不择优”的现象，不利于吸引和培养优秀的投资管理机构。二是引导基金的市场化运作机制尚不完善。目前我国设立的政府引导基金的管理模式主要分为两种，委托给公司或事业单位。部分委托给公司的政府引导基金强调了以“市场化运作，政府引导”为基本原则，但在的实践过程中，无论是从中央还是到地方，引导基金的市场化运作机制并不完善，依旧沿用传统的国有资产管理方式，各个地区的地方引导基金受到了主管部门管理运作水平和专业能力等各方面的制约，效果参差不齐，引导基金在基金设立与筛选能力、投资策略限制、投后管理、激励机制以及退出方式等多方面均与市场化的FOFs存在较大的差距。另一部分委托给事业单位的引导基金，仍然采用财政拨款的方式，按照国有资产“收支两条线”的方式管理，这使得引导基金不能按照市场化的规律运行，每次批复的基金审批时间长达半年左右，在很大程度上影响了基金运行效率，错过了初创企业的最佳投资期。引导基金的资金回流方式采用的是低息贷款的方式，尽管在一定程度上减少了企业融资成本，但对于引导基金本身而言，不能形成稳定的资金池，难以形成供血机制，不利于引导基金的长期发展。三是寻租问题显现，引导基金监管待补位。政府如何防止政府引导基金成为部分管理人员的寻租工具成为重中之重，严格、全面的监管与审批制度亟待补位。建议借鉴国际经验，按照公私合营方式，采用市场化的管理与运作机制，提高基金运营效率。

3.2 天使投资的发展远不足以支撑新兴产业创业发展

近年来，我国天使投资发展迅猛，但天使投资基金的总量不足VC基金的2%，与美国相比，更有显著差距。以美国硅谷与我国中关村作对比来看，近三年，硅谷公开披露的天使投资的首轮投资额逐年增多，2012年为7.26亿美元，2013年前三季度达到10.28亿美元，其投资额约占加利福尼亚州天使投资额的50%。[①] 而我国中关村地区，尽管天使投资市场约占全国的50%，但2014年上半年投资金额仅为5亿元左右，据粗略估算，其市场投资额大约为硅谷地区的5%。相比而言，硅谷地区2012年专利注册数为1.50万件（占加州地区的46.9%，占全美的12.4%），而中关村地区2012年专利授权数为2.26万件（占北京市的44.8%）；可见，我国天使投资的发展还远不足以支撑现有的新兴产业创业，大量的优质科技资源仍有待天使投资的开发与抚育。建议进一步扩大天使投资基金规模，增加杠杆比例。同时，引入国外联合投资的先进经验，建立多种形式的天使投资引导基金。进一步拓宽资金来源渠道，按照政府引导、市场运作的原则，引入“同股同权”、“利益共享”分配机制，形成天使投资基金的滚动式发展。

3.3 相关税收优惠政策有待完善

目前，我国创业风险投资的相关税收政策仍然有待进一步完善，主要表现在：一是现行的创业投资70%税前扣除优惠范围过窄。政策优惠对象仅包括备案的创业投资公司，且投资对象必须为中小高新技术企业。因此，有限合伙创投企业、未备案的创投企业和其他有相同投资行为的个人投资者都不在受惠范围之列，大量科技型中小企业也不在符合条件的投资范围之内。据国家税务总局统计，2012年享受优惠的创业风险投资企业仅134户，税前扣除的投资额仅6.8亿元。二是有限合伙创投合伙人所得税政策有失公平，急待理顺。建议借鉴国际经验，将对创业风险投资公司税前扣除优惠扩大到有限合伙风险投资企业、个人投资者和其他企业投资者，同时将投资对象由中小高新技术企业扩大到科技型中小企业。对于科技型中小企业标准，建议科技部联合财政部、国家税务总局共同制定。对有限合伙创投相关所得税政策单独发文，允许股息和股权转让收益在合伙企业环节从应纳税所得额中独立核算。

① 资料来源：《2014硅谷指数解读》，《中国创业风险投资发展报告2014》。

Abstract

The Features and Development of China's Venture Capital in 2014

National Venture Capital Survey Writing & Analysis Team①

As a new investment and financing mechanism for innovation and new business, venture capital does not simply possess the function of providing capital but also plays a very important role in the incubation of innovation program, the transformation of innovation results, the expansion of markets and the administration of enterprises.

Since 2012, affected by domestic and foreign macro-economic environment, capital market has slumped. The hidden hazards arising from the quick expansion of the industry began to emerge. Intensive consolidation started in the industry. Development of the industry slowed down, and the investment stage shifted forward. In 2014, the economic development in China entered "new norm". The economic structure shifted to equal emphasis on "stock adjustment" and "high quality growth". The motive force of economic development changed to new growth point, with greater emphasis on scientific and technological progress, reform and innovation. IPO of A-shares kicked off once again. Different levels of capital exit from market have been perfected, the enthusiasm and confidence of investors have been aroused. The venture capital industry in China has entered a period of rational development and expansion. The industry has seen different degrees of growth in fund raising, investment and withdrawal.

1 Major characteristics and trend of the development of venture capital in China

1.1 The amount of institutions and management capital showed rapid growth

By the end of 2014, the number of various venture capital institutions in China had reached 1551②, with an increase of 10.2% . Among them there were 1167 venture capital enterprises（funds）, 216 new funds were created（see Table 1, Fig. 1）. Comparatively, there were 1206 funds in the United States during this same period. The whole Europe has more than 1200 private equity investment enterprises, among which venture capital institutions account for 40%, about 500 funds.

① China Science and Technology Development Strategy Research Institute's 2015 "National Venture Capital Survey Writing & Analysis Team" members include: Guo Rong, Li Xiyi, Zhang Mingxi, Zhang Junfang, Fu Jianfeng, Wei Shijie, Zhu Xinyue, Wang Qiuying and so on. The authors of the report are Zhang Junfang and Guo Rong.

② Number of existing organizations, mainly including venture capital enterprises（funds）, venture capital management enterprises and a small number of institutions engaged in venture capital businesses. Organizations that no longer operate venture capital business or are cancelled are excluded from the data.

Table 1 The total number and increment of venture capital enterprises (funds) in China (2005~2014)①

Item \ Year	2005	2006	2007	2008	2009	2010	2011	2012	2013	2014
Number of venture capital funds	277	312	331	410	495	720	860	942	1095	1167
Year-on-year growth (%)	7.78	12.6	6.09	23.9	20.7	45.5	19.4	9.53	19.0	10.2
Number of venture capital management institutions	42	33	52	54	81	147	236	241	313	384
The amount of funds newly raised in the year②	14	35	76	88	99	189	177	152	185	216

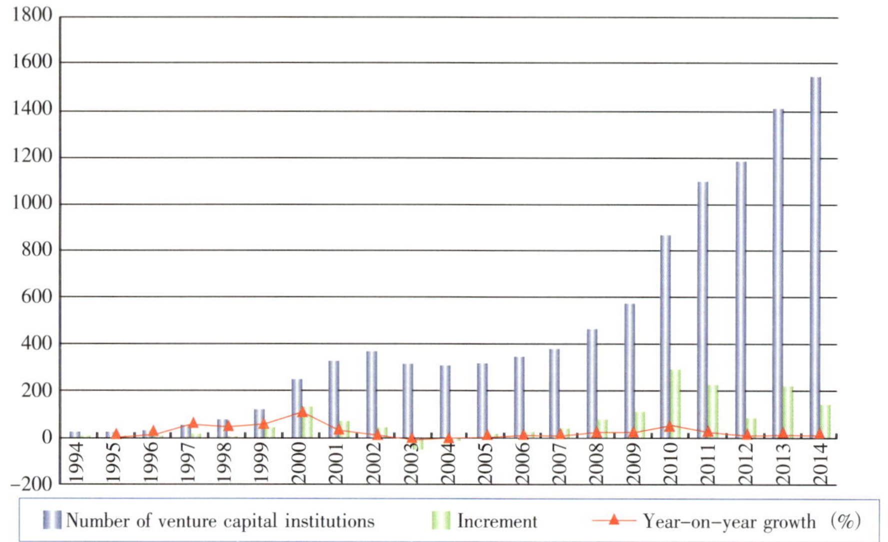

Fig. 1 The total number and increment of venture capital institutions in China (1994~2014)

As far as the scale of investment is concerned, in 2014, total management capital all over the country was 523.24 billion Yuan, an increase of 31.7%. The total management capital accounted for 0.82% of the country's GDP. On average, the management capital per fund is 448 million Yuan, a significant increase as compared with 2013③ (see Table 2, Fig. 2). Comparatively, during the same period, total management capital of the US was 156.5 billion dollars (approximately equivalent to 1000 billion Yuan), accounting for 0.93% of the America's GDP. On average, the management capital per fund is 194.9 million dollars (Approximately equivalent to 1.248 billion Yuan). In Europe, total management capital of private equity and fund was € 548 billion, among which total venture capital accounted for 10% (approximately equivalent to 400 billion Yuan), and total venture capital of Europe accounted for 0.024% of GDP. In Britain, the figure is 0.035%. Thus it can be seen that China has become a large country of venture capital, either in terms of the number of venture capital institutions or total capital.

① Because the venture capital industry has been developing very rapidly, the forms of funds have become increasingly diversified. Since 2010, funds and fund management companies have been separated according to international practices, and retroactive adjustment has been made to the former data.

② There existed a certain degree of deviation in the statistics of the newly raised funds in the year, because there are funds that are included in the year's statistics but were actually raised several years ago. Therefore the data of newly raised funds of former years are adjusted every year.

③ In 2014, the investigators made a full-range investigation of the area of Beijing. The statistical figures increased greatly as compared with those of the past years. Venture capital enterprises in Beijing are mostly large venture capital organizations, thus contributing greatly to the statistics of the total amount of management capital and average management capital.

Table 2 The total management capital of venture capital institutions in China (2005~2014)

Item \ Year	2005	2006	2007	2008	2009	2010	2011	2012	2013	2014
Total management capital (hundred million Yuan)	631.6	663.8	1112.9	1455.7	1605.1	2406.6	3198.0	3312.9	3573.9	5232.4
Year-on-year growth (%)	2.3	5.1	67.7	30.8	10.3	49.9	32.9	3.6	7.9	31.7
Average management capital per fund (hundred million Yuan)	2.28	2.13	3.36	3.55	3.24	3.34	3.72	3.52	3.26	4.48

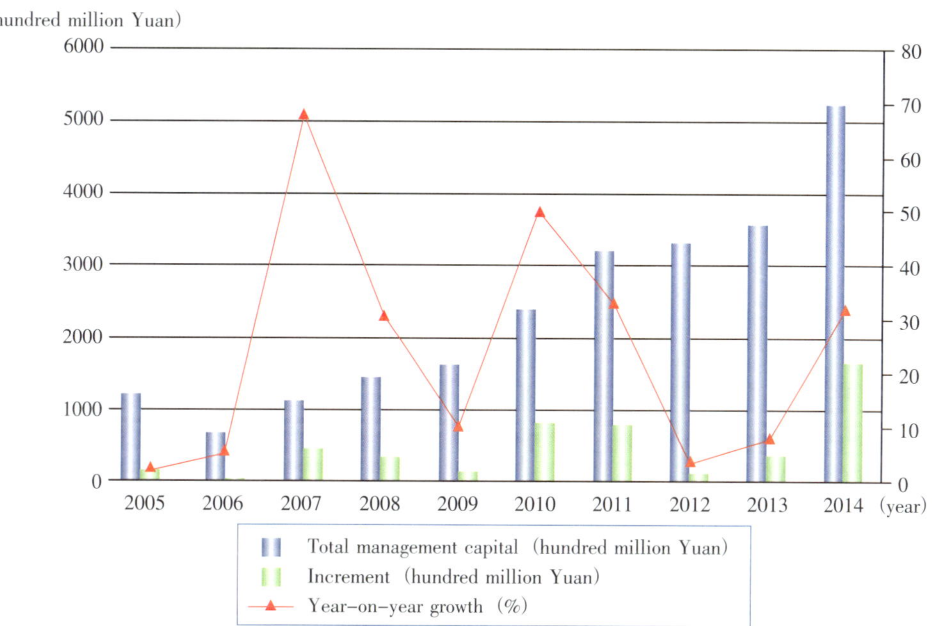

Fig. 2 Total management capital of venture capital institutions in China (2005~2014)

1.2 The amount of investment increase rapidly and the investment standard is being increasingly diversified

In 2014, a new generation of information technology revolution is blended in traditional industries, increased entrepreneurial opportunities, and good capital market environment, which promote the investment sharply increased to 2459, compared with last year increased by 28.9% ; Investment amount to 37.44 billion Yuan, a 34.2% increase last year.

By the end of 2014, the number of projects has added up to 14118, among which 7330 projects or 51.9% are high-tech enterprises. The total investment amount reached 293.361 billion Yuan, of which 140.19 billion Yuan or 47.8% has been invested in high-tech enterprises.

Judged from investment of the current year and the accumulated investment, the number of current-year venture capital projects in recent years ranges from 1500 to 2500, and the total investment amount ranges from 28 billion Yuan to 55 billion Yuan; the concentration of investments, from 15 million Yuan to 30 million Yuan. There are several obvious characteristics and trends: 1. Investment is closely related to the development of capital market. The opening of growth enterprise market in 2009 brought about the upsurge of venture capital. There was a dramatic increase of investment projects in that year. The depression of capital market in 2012 and the closure of IPO in 2013 have undoubtedly slowed down the pace of investment. 2. Since 2011, the number of investment projects in high-tech enterprises has been declining year by year, with the proportion declining from 60% in 2010 to 30% in 2014. This shows to some extent that the investment standards have been increasingly diversified. 3. Prior to 2010, the average investment was 17.16 million Yuan per project and peaked in 2011 at 28.791 million Yuan per project and since then has been declining year by year. In a way, this shows that the dramatic expansion since 2006 has caused the venture capital institutions to pursue short term profits. Since 2011, investment behavior has become more rational, and tends to focus on small-scale, early-stage enterprises, Internet-based enterprises, and industry with small capital needs.

Table 3 Current-year venture capital projects in China as of 2014（2010~2014）

Year	Number of investment projects	Amount of investment (Hundred million Yuan)	Concentration of investment (Ten thousand Yuan /project)	Among which:		Among which:		Concentration of investment in high-tech enterprises (Ten thousand Yuan /project)
				The number of high-tech projects	Proportion (%)	Amount of money invested in high-tech projects (Hundred million Yuan)	Proportion (%)	
2011	1894	545.3	2879.1	987	52.1	229.8	42.1	2328.3
2012	1502	318.5	2120.1	671	44.7	154.5	48.5	2301.7
2013	1501	279.0	1858.5	590	39.3	109.0	39.1	1846.9
2014	2459	374.4	1522	689	28.0	124.8	33.3	1811.0

1.3 The emerging industry has been especially favored, and the investment industry follows macroscopic hot spot closely

In 2014, the yearly venture capital projects in China are mainly concentrated in software industry, network industry, telecommunication equipment, other equipment, and new material industry, which accounted for more than 40.6% of investment projects for the year. The concentration of investment decreased slightly as compared with previous years.

The trend of investment over the years showed the following characteristics: 1. The focus of investment gradually shifted from traditional manufacturing industries in the past to emerging industries such as Internet, bio technology and new energy. Especially in recent years with the rise of Internet, a lot of investment opportunities have emerged. In 2014, information service industry like Internet and IT ranked first and accounted for 25.53% of investment projects. Telecommunication and other electronic equipment manufacturing, new energy and environment industry, and medicine and biology accounted for 14.63%, 13.16%, 9.39% respectively. In terms of investment amount, telecommunication and other electronic equipment manufacturing ranked first with a proportion of 21.15%. 2. Hot spot investment industry is changeable. For example, great fluctuations have been seen in financing and insurance, farming, forestry, animal husbandry, side-line production and fishery, communication and entertainment, which become investment hot spots in individual years.

1.4 After going through the period of expansion to pursue profit, the investment stage is now gradually returning to rationality

Judging by the trend of investment by venture capital companies, the dramatically expanding investment prior to 2011 was also accompanied by the pursuit of short term profits. Investment stage continuously retrocedes. The proportion of projects in the growth period and maturity period increases year by year. Since 2011, after going through the increasingly fierce industrial reshuffle, investment behavior becomes more and more rational. The focus of investment shifts forward year by year, the proportion of projects in the seed period and starting period rises significantly. By the end of 2014, projects in the seed period and starting period the accounted for 57.3%, which is far above 39.4% in 2011（see Fig. 4）.

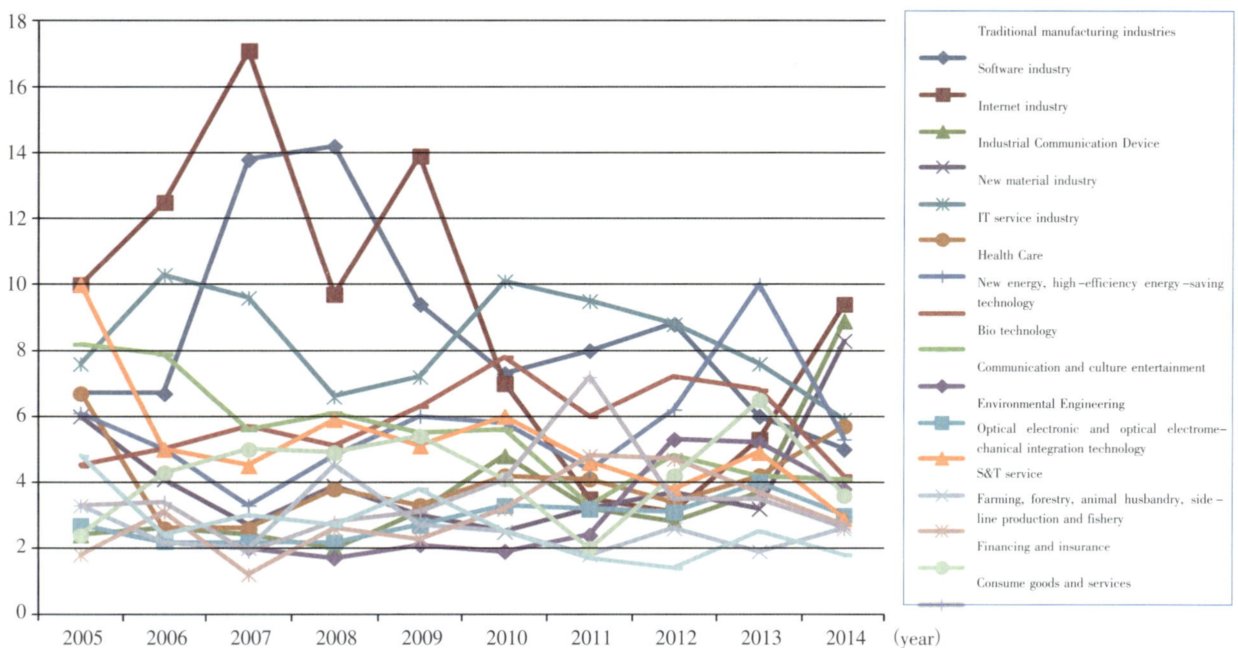

Fig. 3 Industry distribution of major investment projects by venture capital institutions in China (2005~2014), unit: %

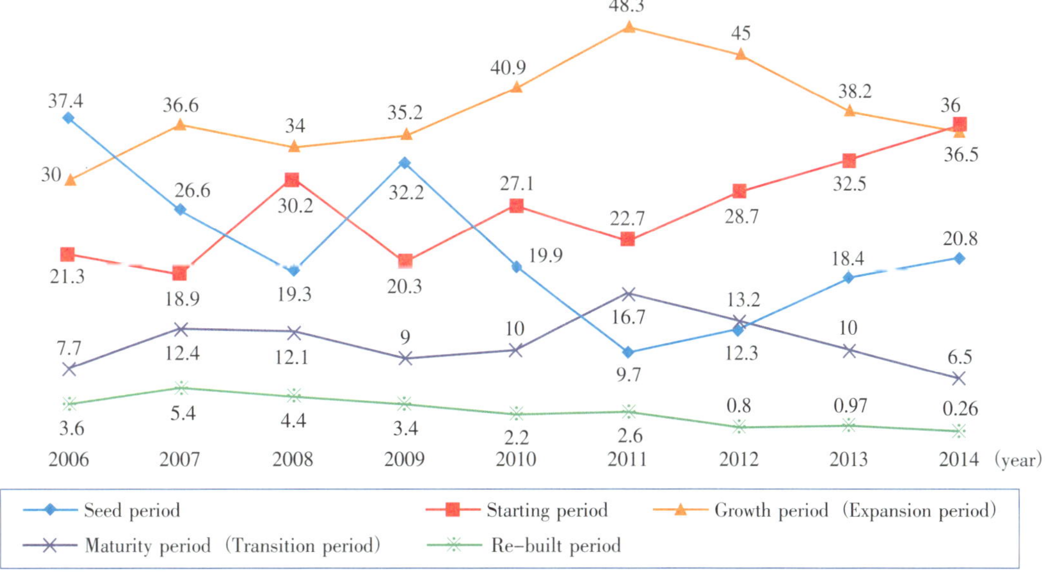

Fig. 4 General distribution of stages that venture capital projects currently belong to (as per the proportion of investment projects) unit: %

1.5 Regional concentration effect is obvious, in less developed inland areas, venture capital institutions are dominated by state owned capital

Overall, the distribution of venture capital institutions in China has distinct regional characteristics. The eastern devel oped area, including Jiangsu, Zhejiang, Shanghai and Guangdong, has long been the area with the greatest concentration of venture capital institutions in the country. By 2014, the number of venture capital institutions has reached 892, accounting for 57.5% of the country's total. From the perspective of statistics over the years, the concentration effect of venture capital has been very obvious. The proportion of venture capital in the area headed by Jiangsu and Zhejiang increased consecutively from 18.2% in 2002 to 48.4% in 2014. In addition, venture capital businesses in central and western region, including Anhui, Chongqing, Hubei and Shandong, has been increasing significantly in recent years (see Fig.5).

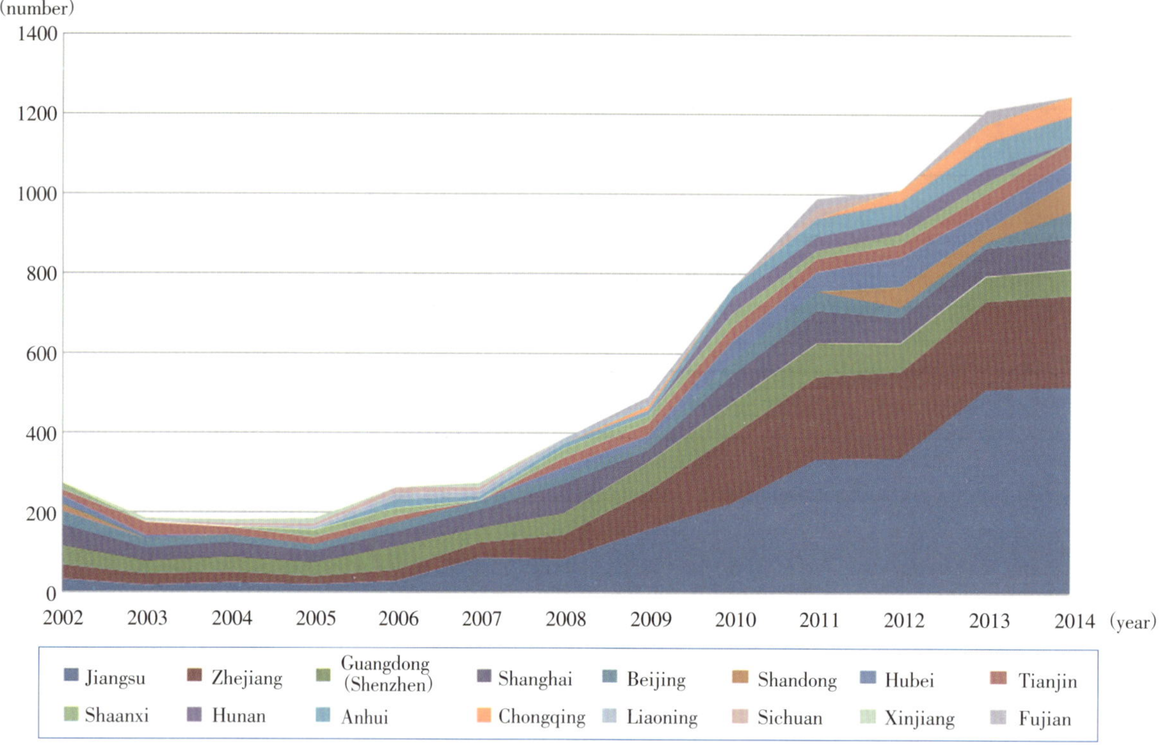

Fig. 5 The regional distribution of venture capital institutions in China (2002~2014)

From the perspective of the amount of capital, Jiangsu, Beijing, Guangdong, Zhejiang and Anhui were ranked among top five in the country. The total amount of management capital in these areas accounted for 80.5%. The scales of venture capital institutions in Jiangsu and Zhejiang are relatively small. The capital scale of 80% of the companies ranges between 50 million and 500 million Yuan. Venture capital institutions in Beijing and Guangdong have larger capital scales, mostly above 500 million Yuan.

From the perspective of capital source, the source of venture capital in less developed inland areas comes mainly from government or state owned organizations. In Shaanxi, Inner Mongolia, Gansu, Heilongjiang and Hebei, government capital and state owned capital have always accounted for more than 50% of venture capital. In contrast, venture capital institutions in Beijing, Fujian, Zhejiang, Jiangsu, Guangdong and Hubei are more market-oriented, and capital is raised mainly by enterprises.

1.6 The channel for exit from the industry is being perfected, the average yearly rate of return slightly ascending

Currently, the way of exit from venture capital in China is still mainly through merger and acquisition and stock buyback. However, with the perfection of capital market in China, the proportion of exit from venture capital is on the rise. In the recent two years, during which IPO market was suspended, merger and acquisition has been very active (see Table 4). The statistics show that in 2014 a total of 103 projects (20.72% of all exist) realized exit from profits through IPO market. Merger and acquisition of 179 (36.02%) projects were disclosed through IPO market. Growth enterprise market is still the main channel for venture capital institutions to exit from IPO, accounting for 42.72% of exit projects.

Table 4 Way of exit from venture capital in China (2003~2014)

unit: %

Year	Listing	Merger and acquisition	Buyback	Liquidation	Miscellaneous (including New Third Board)
2003	5.40	40.40	36.30	14.90	3.00
2004	12.40	55.30	27.60	4.70	0.00
2005	11.90	44.40	33.30	10.40	0.00
2006	12.70	28.40	30.40	7.80	20.60
2007	24.20	29.00	27.40	5.60	13.70
2008	22.70	23.20	34.80	9.20	10.10
2009	25.30	33.00	35.3	6.30	0.00
2010	29.80	28.63	32.82	6.87	1.91
2011	29.40	29.97	32.28	3.17	5.19
2012	29.41	15.86	45.01	6.65	3.07
2013	24.33	23.75	44.83	4.60	2.49
2014	20.72	36.02	36.02	4.83	2.41

Judging from profit performance of exit from listing over the years, In 2014, influenced by the restart of IPO in China's capital markets and the active stock market, the income on investment from listing exit was increased to a large extent as compared with the previous two years, the average book returns were 6.01 times. The average rate of return for the industry was 123.04%, The average time of investment exit is 6.83 years. The average yearly rate of return is 23.46%.

2 China's major measures to promote the development of venture capital

Chinese government attaches great importance to the development of venture capital. Since the General Office of the State Council's retransmission in 1999 of "Several Opinions Concerning the Establishment of Venture Capital Mechanism" jointly issued by the seven commissions and ministries including the Ministry of Science and Technology, relevant departments have successively introduced the relevant policies to support the development of venture capital. Involving fund of fund, supervision and management, preferential taxation and foreign investment, these policies have effectively pushed forward the healthy development of venture capital businesses in China. In general, the government has taken the following measures to support the development of venture capital.

2.1 Establish FOF

The yearly statistics and investigation shows that by the end of 2014 a total of 322 venture capital institutions in the country have obtained venture capital FOF of different levels. A total of 36.327 billion Yuan of venture capital FOF has been invested, which results in 180 billion Yuan of capital managed by venture capital institutions.

By far, national level funds mainly include: ① "Venture capital FOF for science and technology-based small and medium enterprises" founded in 2007 by the Ministry of Science and Technology to support mainly science and technology- based small and medium enterprises. By the end of 2014, a total of 4.993 billion Yuan financial fund has been invested. Of the total amount, 3.443 billion Yuan was invested by means of stage equity participation into 100 venture capital enterprises that focus on investing in science and technology-based small and medium enterprises. These venture capital enterprises have an accumulated registered capital of about 22 billion Yuan. A total of 1896 projects have been set up by means of risk subsidy and investment guarantee, and the assistance funds that have been arranged add up to 1.55 billion Yuan. ②In October, 2009, National Development and Reform Commission set up "National Venture Capital Program for Emerging Industries" to be geared to the needs of high-tech industries that the country encourages to develop. It focused on supporting innovation enterprises and high growth enterprises that are in the beginning and growth period. At the first phase, twenty venture capital funds were set up. With one billion Yuan from central finance, one billion Yuan from provincial finance and three billion Yuan from social fund raising, the total scale of the funds is no less than 5 billion Yuan. In August, 2011, "Interim Procedures for the Management of Equity Participation Venture Capital Fund in the Venture Capital Program for Emerging Industries" was issued, which marks the actual operation of Venture Capital Program for Emerging Industries. ③In July, 2011, the Ministry of Science and Technology set up "National FOF for the Transformation of Scientific Results" to accelerate the transformation and application of scientific achievements. The fund supports the transformation of scientific achievements by means of setting up sub funds for venture capital, loan risk reimbursement, and performance incentives. In August, 2014, "Interim Procedures for the Management of Venture Capital Sub-Fund Set up by National FOF for the Transformation of Science and Technology Achievements" was issued, which marks the actual operation of the fund. ④ In January, 2015, the State Council set up "FOF for emerging industries" to support the business innovation and industrial upgrading and attract the participation of social and private capital, for example, powerful enterprises and large financial institutions. It is predicted that a FOF for emerging industries worth 40 billion Yuan will be founded.

In addition, according to incomplete statistics, there are more than one hundred FOFs set up by local governments. The funds set up in recent years include: At the end of 2014, Shandong province issued "The Opinions Concerning the Use of FOF to Speed up the Development of Equity Investment", which stipulated that thirteen provincial FOFs for equity investment will be set up and that by 2017 the provincial FOF will reach 10 billion Yuan. In December, 2014, Anhui set up FOF of five billion Yuan for High-tech industries. In May 2015, Guangdong's financial department set up provincial special FOF for venture capital in major science and technology projects. In addition, in recent years, various provinces, municipalities and regions have set up Angel Investment FOFs, including Jiangsu Angel Investment FOF, Ningbo Angel Investment FOF, Yangzhou Angel Investment FOF, Qingdao Angel Investment FOF, Zhongguancun Angel Investment FOF, and so on. In February 2013, Ningbo Angel Investment FOF was officially founded. It aims to invest 500 million Yuan in 5 years. Ningbo Angel Investment FOF Company was officially registered. It is the first of its kind in the country. On December 17, 2014, Shanghai Angel Investment FOF was officially founded. It takes the form of FOF, with no upper limit of capital contribution. 500 million Yuan was put in place for the first phase. Equity investment was adopted to mobilize a total of 2 billion Yuan for Angel Investment organization.

2.2 Formulate relevant preferential taxation

Currently China's preferential taxation policies for equity investment are mainly concentrated in the following two aspects. One is the before-tax deduction of 70% of investment amount for venture capital enterprises. In April 2009, in "the Notice of State Administration of Taxation Concerning the Enforcement of Preferential Income Tax for Venture Capital Enterprises" (state taxation [2009] No. 87), it was stipulated in definite terms that, if a venture capital enterprise has been investing for more than two years in unlisted small and medium high-tech enterprises in the form of equity investment, then 70% of its investment amount can be used to deduct its taxable income tax in the year after it has held the equity right for two years. The balance can be carried over to the next taxation year. The second is tax-exempted equity transfer for listed company and halved tax for dividend income. In December 2014, State Administration of Taxation issued "Management Procedure for Income Tax from Equity Transfer (interim)", which definitely stipulated the tax levy policy for income from equity transfer by individuals. The current taxation policy stipulates that temporarily tax will not be levied from individuals on their income from transfer of stock of listed company at Shanghai Stock Exchange and Shenzhen Stock Exchange. Personal income tax will be levied according to relevant regulations from individuals on their income from transfer of non-tradable shares of listed company.

Local areas are active in putting this into practice and bold in exploration. In 2012, with the approval of the State Council, Suzhou Industrial Park carried out pilot work of business income tax policy for legal person and partner at limited partnership venture capital enterprises. That is to say, legal person and partner of limited partnership venture capital enterprises registered in Suzhou Industrial Park can enjoy preferential taxation policy① for venture capital enterprise. In September 2013, Zhongguancun was also included in this pilot work②. Is stipulated that, during 2013 and 2015, if a venture capital enterprise of limited partnership in Zhongguancun has been investing for more than two years in unlisted small and medium high-tech enterprises in the form of equity investment, then 70% of its investment amount can be used to deduct its taxable income tax in the year after it has held the equity right for two years. In addition, as for personal income tax, in the "Notice Concerning the Pilot Policy of Personal Income Tax for the Share Capital Increase from Accumulation Fund of Enterprises in Zhongguancun National Independent Innovation Area" (finance and taxation [2013] No.73), it is stipulated that installment payment over a maximum period of five years can be made for personal income tax levied on share capital increase to individual shareholder offered by small and medium high-tech enterprises in Zhongguancun in the form of undistributed profit, surplus reserves, and capital reserve. This policy has prolonged the time of tax levy and can stimulate enterprise to carry out equity investment, because generally the taxation policy stipulates that 20% of tax rate shall be levied on the interests, dividend and bonus of share capital increase to individual shareholder offered by enterprises. Some local areas have also carried out effective practice and exploration in preferential taxation for Angel Investment. For example, taxation support for the development of Angel Investment has been clearly laid out in "Jiangsu's Opinions on Encouraging and Guiding Angel Investment to Support the Development of Science and Technology-based a Small and Medium Enterprises".

2.3 Create policy environment favorable to the development of venture capital

In recent years, the central government and local authorities have introduced a series of policies and measures to support the development of venture capital. According to the investigation and survey in 2015, about 20.2% of venture capital institutions have enjoyed the capital support from the government, 22.9% of venture capital institutions have enjoyed the tax deduction and exemption, 29.1% of venture capital institutions have got the government support in exchange of information, and 13.4% of venture capital institutions have got help from government in personnel training. Generally, direct support from the government is decreasing, but indirect services is being continuously perfected. Policy environment for investment is becoming better and better year by year, and the development of the industry is shifting from supervision to self-discipline.

In May 2014, "Several opinions of the State Council on Further Promoting the Healthy Development of Capital Market" (State Council [2014] No. 17) was promulgated. It laid out in definite terms that we should speed up the building of multi-channel, wide-ranging, strictly supervised and efficient equity markets, encourage market-based acquisition and reorganization, perfect market exit system, build sound private placement system, develop private investment fund, and strengthen professional institutional investors. In National Development and Reform Commission's "Notice Concerning Further Effort to Support the Development of Venture Capital Enterprises", it is pointed out in definite terms that the development of Angel Investment organizations shall be supported, and that eligible Angel Investment organizations shall be recorded as venture capital enterprises to enjoy the corresponding support policy. In order to further standardize private investment behavior and promote the healthy development of capital market, China Securities Regulatory Commission issued in July "Interim Procedure for the Supervision and Management of Private Investment Fund",

① Relevant policy: Notice of the Ministry of Finance and the State Administration of Taxation Concerning the Pilot Policy of Income tax for Legal person and partner of limited partnership venture capital in Suzhou Industrial Park" (Finance and taxation [2012] No. 67).

② Relevant policy: "Notice of the Ministry of Finance and the State Administration of Taxation Concerning the Pilot Policy of business Income tax for Legal person and partner of limited partnership venture capital in Zhongguancun National Independent Innovation Model Area" (Finance and taxation [2013] No. 71).

which put on record for supervision the fund industry that raises fund for investment in the form of private placement, including venture capital and securities investment fund. In August, "Guiding Opinion of the General Office of the State Council on Various Measures to Relieve Enterprises' High Financing Cost" (State Council [2014] No.39) was promulgated. It calls for efforts to further promote the development of private equity and venture capital fund, gradually expand the range and scale of the capital market of various long-term capital investment, and offer preferential taxation for long-term investment capital according to the country's tax law and the relevant regulations. In addition, the Ministry of Finance, the Ministry of Industry and Information Technology, the Ministry of Science and Technology and the Ministry of Commerce jointly issued "Management Procedure for the Special Capital for Development of Small and Medium Enterprises", integrated a series of special capital support for small and medium enterprises' innovation and development, surrendered part of the profits to market organizations, lowered investment risk, guided social capital to participate in government program, and supported the development of science and technology-based enterprises in the developing period.

3 The obstacles to the development in the current period and suggestion

Since 2000, venture capital in China has been developing very quickly, and the organization and operation patterns of venture capital have been continuously enriched, China has become a really large country of venture capital. In the process of fast development and expansion of venture capital, some problems have unavoidably surfaced. In connection with the development trend of "self-discipline of the industry supplemented by policy supervision", the following is a tentative analysis of the shortcomings faced by the industry and suggestions for the improvement.

3.1 The operation efficiency and market level of China's FOF is to be promoted

Presently the FOF has been set up by National Development and Reform Commission, the Ministry of Science and Technology, and local development and reform commissions, economic information commissions, economic development zones. Undoubtedly, these capitals have played a very important role in the development of the industry. It is known from research and investigations that, as a whole, the FOF for small and medium venture capital institutions has in a way relieved the financing problem for venture capital institutions. It can help to guide the direction of investment. Financial capital can have sixfold amplification. However, some problems have also surfaced in the process of the FOF establishment and development. Firstly, FOF, which comes from government financial capital, has very strong local color in its use and the efficiency of operation is fairly low. For example, the local governments require the management team of venture capital enterprise cooperating with it to set up management companies in different places, all of which are limited to invest in the local areas. This results in the phenomenon of "selecting the area instead of selecting company that has the good quality and potential", which is to the disadvantage of attracting and fostering excellent investment management organizations. Secondly, the market-based operation mechanism of FOF is yet to be perfected. At present, the FOF management patterns in China mainly fall into two categories. That is, the management is either entrusted to the company or the institution. Some FOF entrusted to the companies put emphasis on the basic principle of "market based operation and government guidance". However, in the process of practice, neither at the central level nor at the local level does the FOF have a perfect market operation mechanism. The operation still follows the traditional management of state assets. The local FOFs of different areas are restricted by a lot of factors including the management and operation level and professional capacity of the competent departments. Therefore, the results are widely varied. And FOF is still a far cry from market-oriented based FOFs in many aspects, for example, in the capability to set up and sift funds, investment strategy limit, after-investment management, incentive mechanism and way of exit. Financial allocation is still adopted for the FOF entrusted to institutions. Separation between revenue and expenditure, a management pattern for state assets, makes it impossible for FOF to operate according to the law of markets. It often takes as long as half a year to get an official written reply to the application for examination and approval of the FOF, which greatly affects the efficiency of fund operation and misses the best period of investment for newly started enterprise. Low-interest loan is adopted to ensure capital backflow for FOF. This has in a way reduced the enterprises' financing cost, but for FOF itself, it is difficult to form steady capital pool and blood supply mechanism, which is not favorable to the long-term development of FOF. Thirdly, the problem of rent seeking has become obvious and the supervision of FOF should be perfected. The most important issue for the government is to prevent FOF from becoming rent seeking tools for some management personnel. Strict and comprehensive supervision and approval system needs to be set in place. It is recommended to learn from international experience, adopt public-private partnership and market-based management and operation to enhance the efficiency of fund operation.

3.2 Angel Investment is far from being capable of bolstering the creation and development of emerging industries

In recent years, Angel Investment in China has been developing very rapidly; however, the total amount of Angel Investment Fund accounts for less than 2% of venture capital fund. Compared with the United States, the difference is more significant. Taking Silicon Valley in the United States and Zhongguancun in China for an instance, in recent three years, the amount of first-round investment of Angel Investment, as disclosed by Silicon Valley, has been increasing year by year. In 2012, it was 726 million dollars, the figure for the first three quarters of 2013 reached 1.028 billion dollars. The investment amount accounts for about half of the total Angel Investment in California. [①] In contrast, although the market of Angel Investment in Zhongguancun accounts for half of Angel Investment in China, the amount of investment in the first half of 2014 was only 500 million Yuan. A rough estimate shows that its amount of market investment is only 5% that of Silicon Valley. In 2012, the number of patent registration in Silicon Valley was 15,000 (which accounts for 46.9% of California and 12.4% of America). In contrast, the number of patent registration in Zhongguancun was 22,600 (or 44.8% of Beijing). Thus it can be seen that the Angel Investment is far from being capable of bolstering the creation and development of emerging industries and a lot of high quality science and technology resources is still waiting to be developed and cultivated by Angel Investment. It is recommended that the scale of Angel Investment fund should be further expanded and the leverage be increased. At the same time, the advanced experience of joint investment shall be introduced from abroad, and diverse forms of FOF for Angel Investment shall be established. The source of capital shall be further expanded, the principle of government guidance and market operation shall be followed, and the distribution mechanism of "same share with the same right and profit sharing" shall be introduced so as to bring about the rolling development of Angel Investment Fund.

3.3 Relevant preferential taxation policy needs to be perfected

At present, the related taxation policy for venture capital in China still needs to be further perfected. First, currently, the coverage of before-tax deduction of 70% of venture capital is narrow. The preferential policy only aims at venture capital companies that have been put in record, and the investment should be made in small and medium high-tech enterprises. Therefore the policy has not included limited partnership venture capital enterprises, venture capital companies that have not been put in record, and the individual investors with the same investment behavior. A lot of science and technology-based small and medium enterprises are not included. According to the State Administration of Taxation, there were only 134 venture capital enterprises in 2012 that enjoyed the preferential taxation policy. The investment amount eligible for before-tax deduction was only 680 million Yuan. Second, the income tax policy for partners of limited partnership venture capital is unfair, and should be straightened out immediately. It is recommended that international experience should be learned from, and the preferential taxation policy should be extended to include limited partnership venture capital enterprises, individual investors and other enterprise investors. At the same time, the investment should aim at not only small and medium high-tech enterprises, but also science and technology-based small and medium enterprises. The Ministry of Science and Technology

① Source from: "Interpretation of Silicon Valley Indexes in 2014", "Report on the Development of Venture capital in China, 2014".

is recommended to collaborate with the Ministry of Finance and State Administration of Taxation to jointly formulate the standard for science and technology-based small and medium enterprises. Separate document shall be issued for income tax policies related to limited partnership venture capital, dividend and equity transfer proceeds shall be allowed to be independent from business accounting of taxable income tax in the partnership enterprise.

1 中国创业风险投资机构与资本

1.1 2014年度调查概述

2014年12月，按照工作部署，科技部、商务部、国家开发银行等部门联合开展了第13次全国创业风险投资年度调查工作，经国家统计局批准（国统制〔2014〕154号），组织全国30个省（市、自治区）、53个调查实施机构和132名调查员进行网上填报。从2010年起，本项调查为国家科技专项统计，统计数据正式编入《中国科技统计年鉴》。各类创业风险投资机构对调查工作给予了大力的配合，认真贯彻实施《统计法》。经过10余年努力，本项统计调查工作为我国许多重要政策的出台提供了有力支撑，也为科技部及地方创业风险投资年度评奖和引导基金的申报工作提供了有效的数据支持，成为我国科技金融工作的重要组成部分。

2014年度报告所调查的创业投资机构包括以下三类：①创业投资企业，即创业风险投资基金，也包括创业投资引导基金（俗称“母基金”）。②创业投资管理企业，其受创业投资企业委托，筛选投资项目，提出投资决策建议，并受托进行投资后管理。③少量从事政府创业风险投资业务的事业单位，有的直接以政府资金对项目进行投资，有的则具有创业风险投资引导基金的作用，参股创业风险投资企业，或对创业风险投资企业的投资给予某种形式的激励。

截至2014年底，“中国创业风险投资信息系统”（www.ivcc.cn）中共有3665家机构参加过调查（包括关停并转等注销企业）。根据创业风险投资的标准概念，我们对样本进行了剔除：①信托公司等不属于创业风险投资范畴的金融机构。②不属于创业风险投资的某些行业性和综合性投资公司，如电力投资、工交投资集团、投资主业模糊不清的投资类公司等，对以大项目为投资主业的产业投资基金也给予了剔除。③主要从事担保业务的担保公司，但持续地开展了创业风险投资业务的担保公司除外。④转业而不再从事创业风险投资业务的机构。⑤所填信息过少且所填报数据之间严重不匹配的机构。⑥在境外注册设立、在境内仅以办公室形式开展商业活动的私募股权机构。此外，随着我国创业风险投资的业态不断复杂化，很多大型创业风险投资机构以母基金（包括引导基金）的模式出现，简单相加则会带来管理资本的重复计算，因此，在调查过程中，对相关资本的重复计算部分进行了剔除。同样，对于创业风险投资企业与创业风险投资管理机构，当存在委托与受托关系时，对相关资本和项目的重复计算部分也进行了剔除。

1.2 创业风险投资机构和管理资本

2014年，我国经济发展步入“新常态”，经济发展方式转向质量效率型集约增长，经济结构转向“调存量”与“优增量”并举，经济发展动力转向新的增长点，更加注重科技进步和改革创新。2014年，A股IPO重新开闸，多层次资本退出市场发展不断完善，股票交易进入新一轮的牛市行情，极大地激发了投资者的热情和信心。在创新创业的大背景下，我国创投业发展进入投融资的黄金时代，且投资阶段不断前移，天使投资日益活跃，整个创投行业在募资、投资、退出方面均出现不同程度的增长。

2014 年，中国创业风险投资各类机构数达到 1551 家，[①] 较 2013 年增加 143 家，增长 10.2%。其中，创业风险投资企业（基金）1167 家，较 2013 年增加 72 家，增幅 6.6%；创业风险投资管理企业 384 家，较 2013 增加 71 家，增幅 22.7%；2014 年当年新募集基金 216 家（见表 1-1、图 1-1）。

表 1-1　中国创业风险投资企业（基金）总量、增量（2005~2014）[②]

项目 \ 年份	2005	2006	2007	2008	2009	2010	2011	2012	2013	2014
VC 基金（家）	277	312	331	410	495	720	860	942	1095	1167
较上年增长（%）	7.78	12.6	6.09	23.9	20.7	45.5	19.4	9.53	19.0	10.2
VC 管理机构（家）	42	33	52	54	81	147	236	241	313	384
当年新募集基金（数）[③]	14	35	76	88	99	189	177	152	185	216

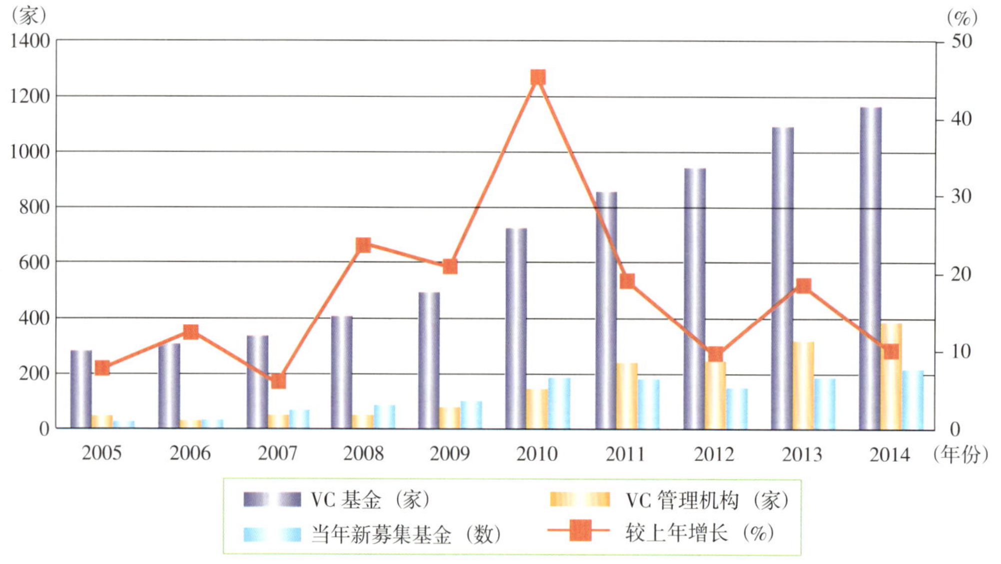

图 1-1　中国创业风险投资企业（基金）总量、增量（2005~2014）

2014 年，全国创业风险投资管理资本总量达到 5232.4 亿元，较 2013 年增加 1658.5 亿元，增幅为 31.7%；基金平均管理资本规模为 4.48 亿元，较 2013 年大幅提高[④]（见表 1-2、图 1-2）。

2014 年，全国市场母基金规模进一步扩大，据统计，最大母基金管理的子基金达 33 家，管理资金规模达 384 亿元。

① 为实际存量机构数，主要包括：创业投资企业（基金）、创业投资管理企业以及少量从事创业投资业务的事业单位。该数据已剔除不再经营创投业务或注销的机构数。

② 由于我国创投行业的迅猛发展，基金形态的日趋多样，从 2010 年起，按照国际惯例区分基金和基金管理公司，并对前期数据进行了追溯调整。

③ 在实际统计中当年新募基金数量存在一定偏差，存在当年进入统计而实际为前几年募集成立的基金，因此每年对前期新募基金数据进行调整。

④ 2014 年调查员针对北京地区做了全面统计，统计数据较往年大幅提升，由于北京地区的创投企业大多为大型创投企业，对管理资本总量和平均管理资本统计贡献度较大。

表 1-2 中国创业风险投资管理资本总额（2005~2014）

项目 \ 年份	2005	2006	2007	2008	2009	2010	2011	2012	2013	2014
管理资本总额（亿元）	631.6	663.8	1112.9	1455.7	1605.1	2406.6	3198.0	3312.9	3573.9	5232.4
较上年增长（%）	2.3	5.1	67.7	30.8	10.3	49.9	32.9	3.6	7.9	31.7
基金平均管理资本规模（亿元）	2.28	2.13	3.36	3.55	3.24	3.34	3.72	3.52	3.26	4.48

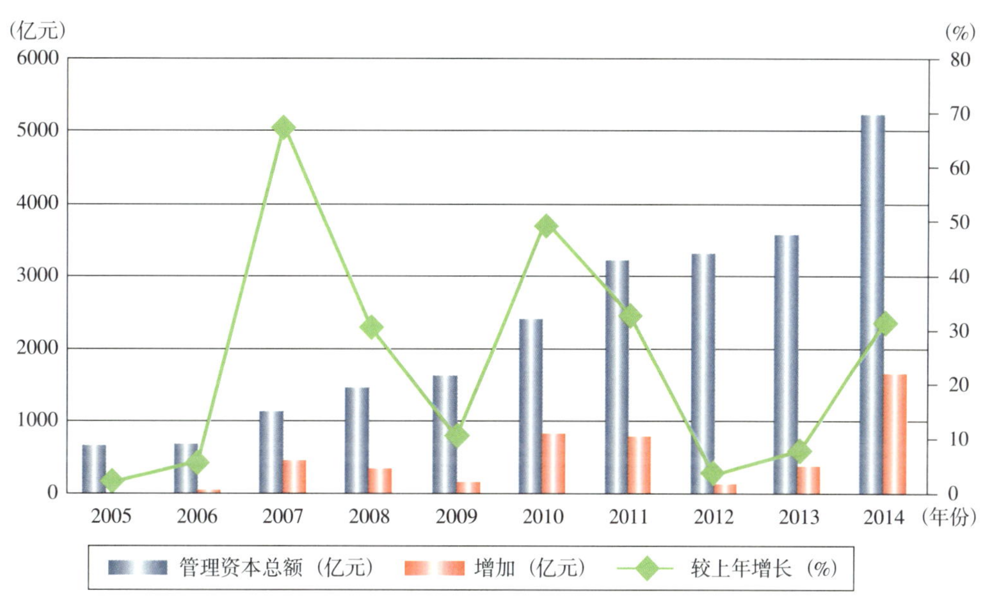

图 1-2 中国创业风险投资管理资本总额（2005~2014）

1.3 创业风险投资的资本来源

依据资本来源结构，可以将创业风险投资资本分为两大类：外资和内资。外资包括境内和境外两个部分。境内外资是指通过已在中国大陆境内注册并运作的外商独资（含港、澳、台地区）和合资合作企业取得的创业风险投资资本；境外资金是指境外机构获得的创业风险投资资本。本报告统计的外资资本主要是境外和境内外资机构向注册在中国大陆地区的创业风险投资企业所注入的资本额，不包括以离岸形式向中国大陆地区直接投资的外资量。

内资创业风险投资资本分类如下：①政府资金，包括各级政府（包括事业单位）对创业风险资本的直接资金支持。②国有独资公司资金，指国有独资公司直接提供的资金。③非上市公司资金，包括非上市股份有限公司和有限责任公司投入的创业风险投资资本。④上市公司资金，主要指在境内证券市场公开上市的公司投入创业风险投资的资本。⑤金融机构资金，包括银行业和保险业、证券业、信托业等金融机构的各类资金投入。⑥自然人及其他出资。

2014 年，中国创业风险投资的资本来源及变化如图 1-3、图 1-4 所示，资本来源结构仍以未上市公司为主体，占总资本的 38.04%，较 2013 年下降 4.17 个百分点；政府与国有独资投资机构合计占比 31.39%，较 2013 年上升

2.21 个百分点。与 2013 年相比，个人投资占比略有下降，外资资本下降明显，银行资本占比略有下降，但非银行金融机构占比明显提升。

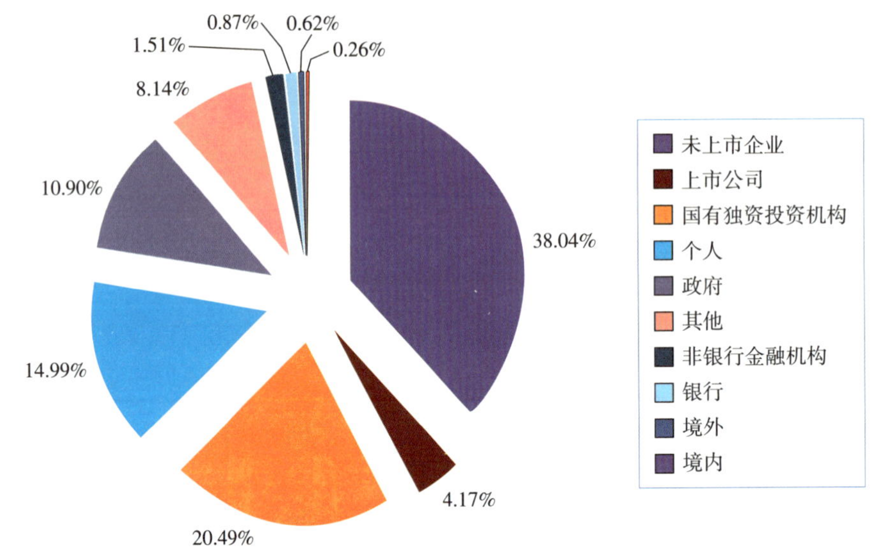

图 1-3 中国创业风险投资资本来源（2014）

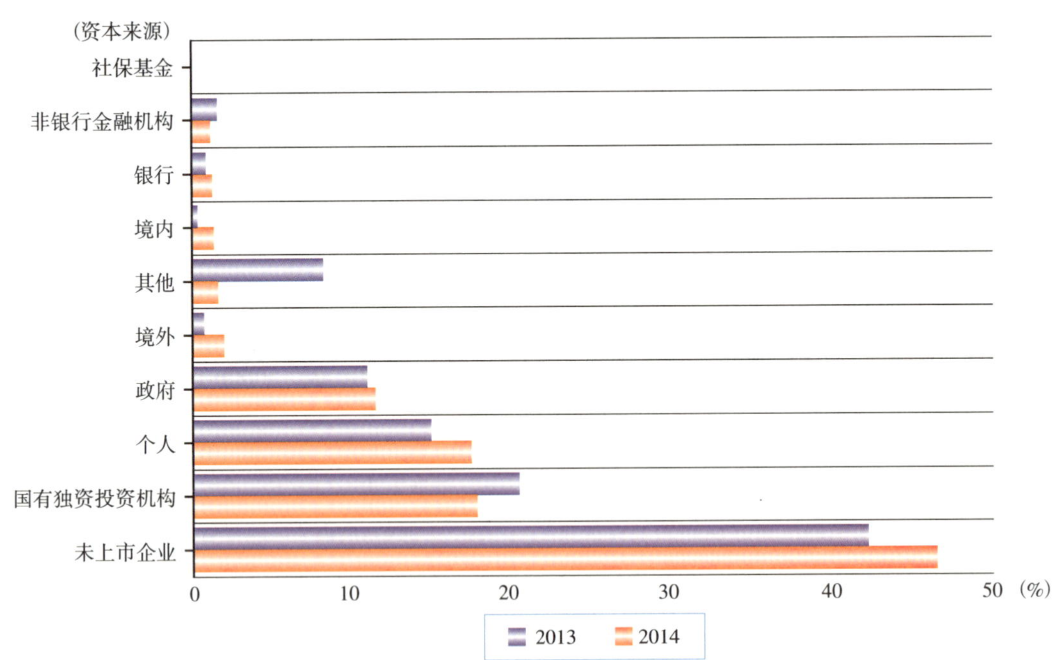

图 1-4 中国创业风险投资资本来源变化（2013~2014）

1.4 创业风险投资机构的资本规模及分布

总体而言，2014 年创业风险投资机构的管理规模较 2013 年大幅增加，尤其是大额管理资本的企业占比增加较为明显。从资金分布情况看，管理资金在 5000 万元以下的创业风险投资机构占机构总数的 25.2%，较 2013 年略有上升；管理资金在 5000 万~1 亿元的机构占比为 24.1%，管理资金在 1 亿~2 亿元的机构占比为 20.6%，管理资金在 2 亿~5 亿元的机构占比为 17.4%，均较 2013 年略有下降；而规模在 5 亿元以上的管理资金占比为 12.4%，较 2013 年提升了 2.3 个百分点（见图 1–5）。

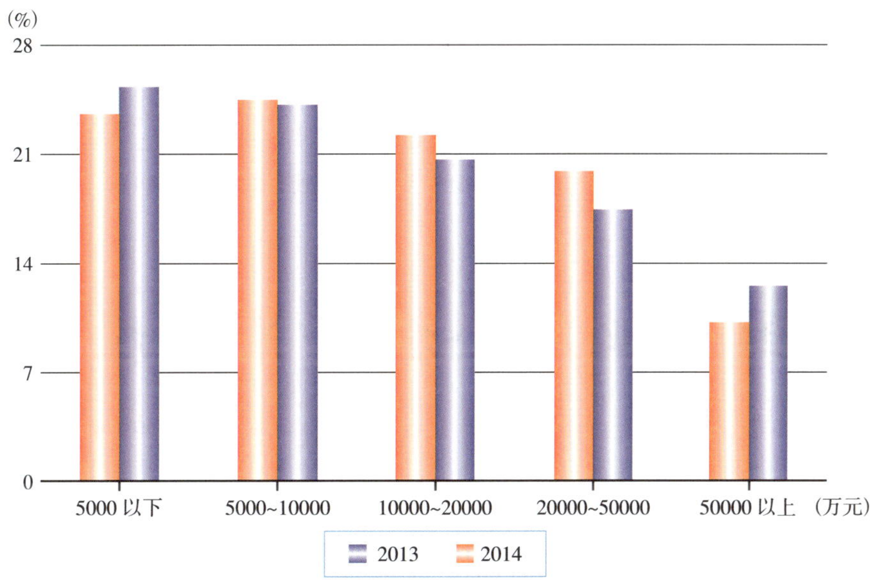

图 1–5 中国不同规模创业风险投资机构数分布（2014）

按管理资金规模划分，2014 年，创投公司管理资金规模有扩大的趋势，管理资金规模在 5000 万元以下的机构仅掌握着 1.4%的创业风险投资总资本，规模在 5000 万~1 亿元的机构掌握了 3.9%的份额，规模在 1 亿~2 亿元的机构掌握了 6.1%的总资金，规模在 2 亿~5 亿元的机构所占管理资本的份额为 10.2%，均比 2013 年有所下降；78.4%的管理资本掌握在规模在 5 亿元以上的机构手中（见图 1–6），资本集聚效应进一步凸显。

2014 年，国内创业风险投资管理机构中，最大管理资金为 211 亿元，超过 100 亿元的有 5 家，超过 50 亿元的有 13 家；在创业风险投资基金中，最大管理资金规模 277 亿元，超过 100 亿元的有 10 家，超过 50 亿元的有 18 家。

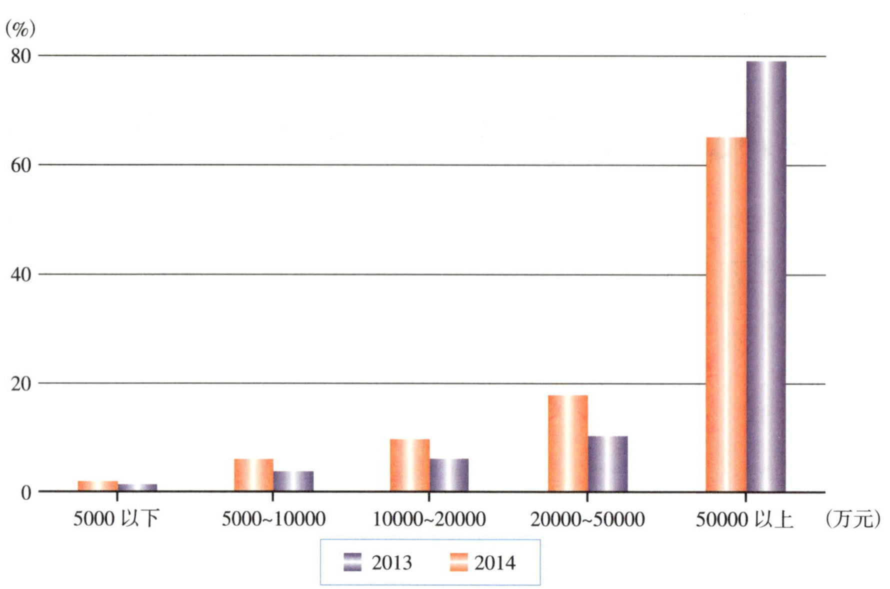

图 1-6 中国不同规模创业风险投资机构管理资本分布（2014）

1.5 中国创业风险投资累计投资情况

2014 年，投融资市场环境向好，中国创业风险投资机构当年投资项目达到 2459 项，较上年大幅提高；投资金额为 374.36 亿元，较 2013 年增加 34.2%，项目平均投资额为 1522 万元。其中，投资于高新技术企业项目数为 689 项，较 2013 年增加 16.8%；投资金额为 124.78 亿元，较上年增加 14.5%，项目平均投资额为 1811 万元（见表 1-3），与往年不同的是，尽管项目数额大幅提高，但总体项目的平均投资额却明显小于往年，而高新技术企业项目的平均投资额与往年基本持平，可能的原因之一是：2014 年有更多的互联网等轻资产项目，减小了项目平均投资额。

表 1-3 截至 2014 年底中国创业风险投资当年投资情况（2010~2014）

年　份	当年投资项目总数（项）	投资高新技术企业/项目数（项）	当年投资金额（亿元）	投资高新技术企业/项目金额（亿元）
2010	1901	1010	398.31	230.90
2011	2399	1250	545.28	229.76
2012	1903	850	356.00	172.63
2013	1501	590	278.96	108.97
2014	2459	689	374.36	124.78

截至 2014 年底，全国创业风险投资机构累计投资项目数 14118 项，其中投资高新技术企业项目数 7330 项，占比 51.9%；累计投资金额 2933.61 亿元，其中投资高新技术企业金额 1401.9 亿元，占比 47.8%（见表 1-4）。

表 1-4 截至 2014 年底中国创业风险投资累计投资情况（2010~2014）

年 份	累计投资项目总数（项）	投资高新技术企业/项目数（项）	累计投资金额（亿元）	投资高新技术企业/项目金额（亿元）
2010	8693	5160	1491.3	808.8
2011	9978	5940	2036.6	1038.6
2012	11112	6404	2355.1	1193.1
2013	12149	6779	2634.1	1302.1
2014	14118	7330	2933.6	1401.9

2 中国创业风险投资的投资分析

2.1 中国创业风险投资的行业特征

2.1.1 中国创业风险投资的行业分布

2014 年，中国创业风险投资年度投资金额主要集中在通信设备、其他行业、传统制造业、软件产业、医药保健五个行业，23.8%以上的资金投资在上述五个行业，其集中度较 2013 年下降了 5 个百分点。中国创业风险投资年度投资项目主要集中在软件产业、网络产业、通信设备、其他行业和新材料工业五个行业，集中了当年 40.6%以上的项目，集中度较 2013 年下降了 2.5 个百分点（见表 2-1、图 2-1、图 2-2）。

表 2-1 中国创业风险投资项目的行业分布：投资金额与投资项目（2013~2014）① 单位：%

行业	2014		2013	
	投资金额	投资项目	投资金额	投资项目
通信设备	13.8	8.3	3.1	3.2
其他行业	8.5	8.1	2.7	3.7
传统制造业	7.6	5.0	7.2	6.0
软件产业	7.4	9.4	2.0	5.3
医药保健	7.4	5.3	10.0	10.0
传播与文化娱乐	5.4	3.8	6.2	5.2
计算机硬件产业	4.2	1.7	0.7	1.2
网络产业	4.0	8.9	1.9	3.7
批发和零售业	3.8	1.9	0.5	0.4
新材料工业	3.7	5.9	7.1	7.6
生物科技	3.7	4.1	2.3	4.2
其他制造业	3.3	4.1	5.3	4.7
IT 服务业	3.0	5.7	3.6	4.2
新能源、高效节能技术	2.9	4.2	8.7	6.8
金融保险业	2.9	3.6	10.1	6.5
环保工程	2.8	3.0	2.9	4.0
社会服务	2.4	1.7	1.9	1.9

① 有效样本数为 2309 份。

续表

行　业	2014		2013	
	投资金额	投资项目	投资金额	投资项目
科技服务	2.2	2.6	1.0	1.9
农林牧副渔	2.0	2.7	6.3	3.7
房地产业	2.0	0.2	0.2	0.3
光电子与光机电一体化	1.9	2.9	4.6	4.9
消费产品和服务	1.6	2.6	5.0	3.5
半导体	1.4	1.8	1.4	2.5
其他 IT 产业	1.0	1.6	0.4	1.0
建筑业	0.6	0.6	1.3	1.2
水电煤气	0.4	0.2	0.3	0.3
交通运输仓储和邮政业	0.2	0.2	2.6	1.2
核应用技术	0.1	0.0	0.2	0.3
采掘业	0.0	0.0	0.5	0.6

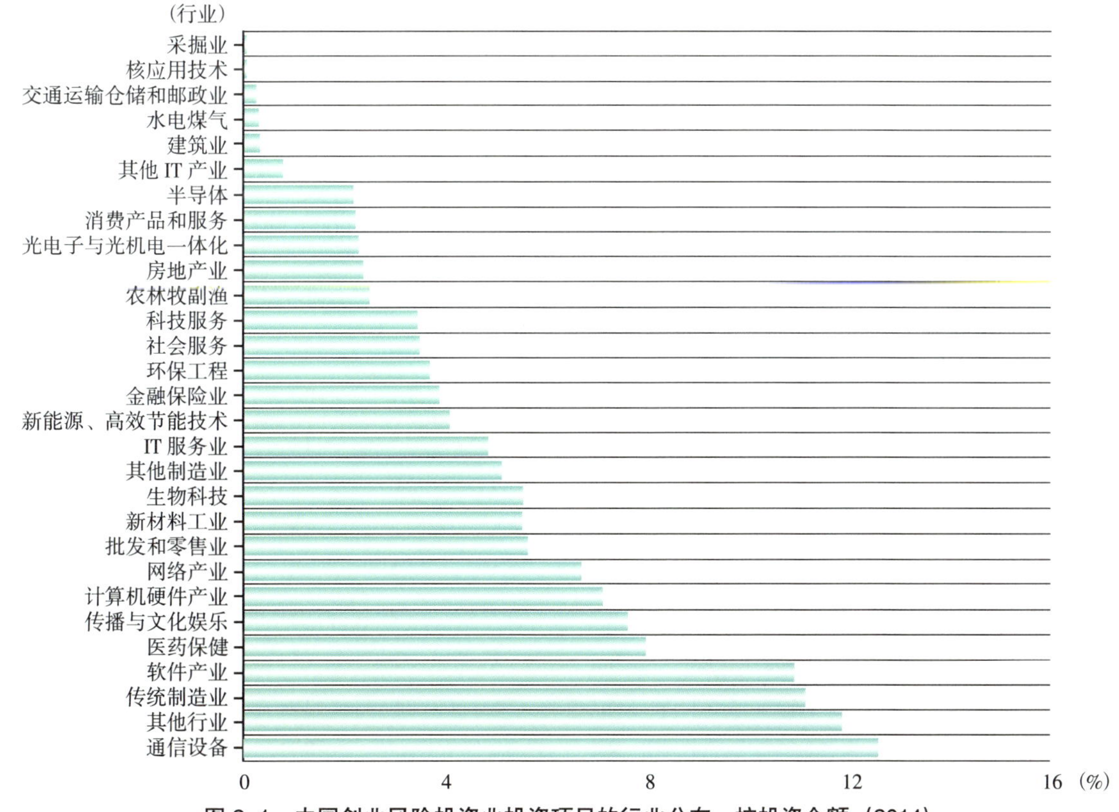

图 2-1　中国创业风险投资业投资项目的行业分布：按投资金额（2014）

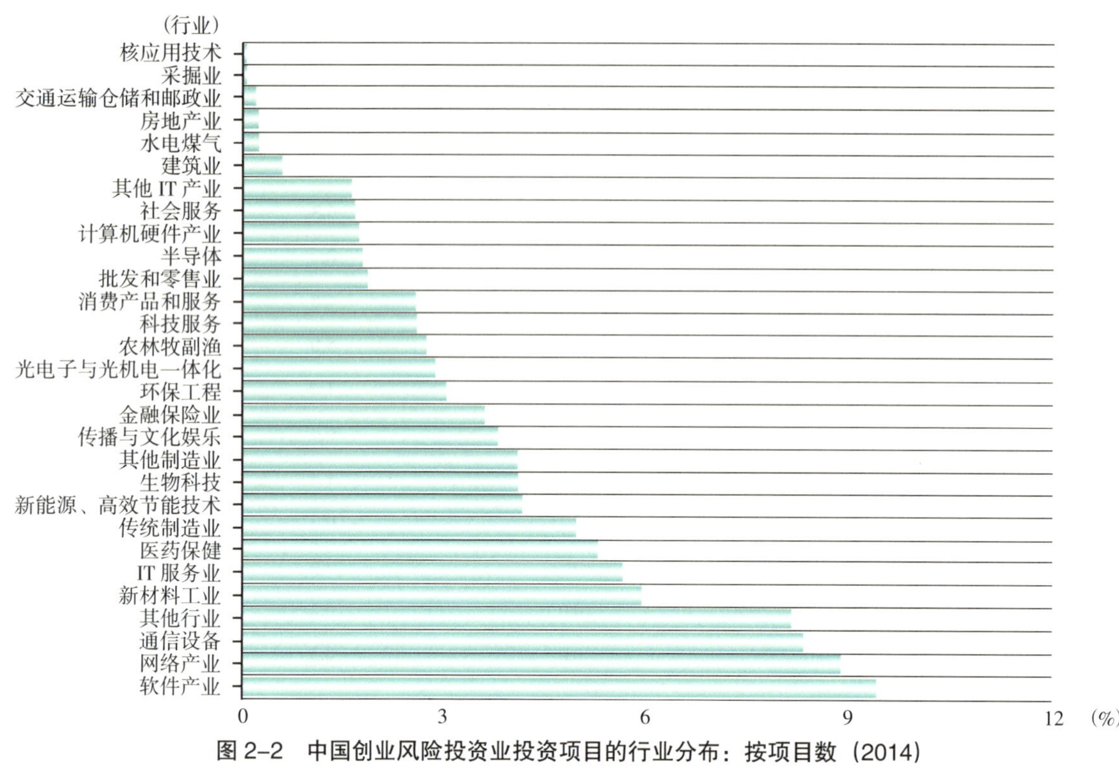

图 2-2 中国创业风险投资业投资项目的行业分布：按项目数（2014）

从近几年我国创业风险投资行业的变化趋势来看（见表 2-2、表 2-3），投资项目数和投资金额均由主要投资传统制造业向投资网络产业、通信设备等转移，同时，新材料工业、医药保健等不断获得创业风险投资青睐。

表 2-2 中国创业风险投资产业投资项目投资金额的行业分布（2005~2014） 单位：%

年份 投资行业	2005	2006	2007	2008	2009	2010	2011	2012	2013	2014
软件产业	3.5	14.6	16.0	6.2	10.9	2.9	2.1	2.4	2.0	7.4
计算机硬件产业	0.9	0.4	0.6	3.4	0.1	1.1	0.7	1.1	0.7	4.2
网络产业	2.7	1.5	0.5	2.7	1.8	2.8	2.5	2.1	1.9	4.0
通信设备	3.5	4.6	2.9	1.8	1.9	1.0	2.8	3.6	3.1	13.8
IT 服务业	7.1	3.1	1.0	4.6	1.5	3.2	2.8	3.1	3.6	3.0
半导体	16.5	2.1	1.3	2.9	2.3	1.2	1.3	1.4	1.4	1.4
其他 IT 产业	2.4	3.2	1.3	2.3	2.2	1.2	1.5	1.7	0.4	1.0
环保工程	3.1	1.3	1.5	1.3	1.8	3.3	2.6	2.8	2.9	2.8
生物科技	7.4	5.4	2.3	5.7	2.5	3.9	3.9	2.8	2.3	3.7
新材料工业	5.7	7.5	7.9	4.4	6.4	9.3	8.7	7.8	7.1	3.7
采掘业	4.5	3.7	1.9	3.6	1.5	2.5	0.6	1.3	0.5	0.0
光电子与光机电一体化	5.5	4.1	2.1	4.0	4.1	4.2	3.3	3.5	4.6	1.9

续表

投资行业＼年份	2005	2006	2007	2008	2009	2010	2011	2012	2013	2014
科技服务	2.1	1.2	4.9	2.1	2.0	2.3	1.6	1.6	1.0	2.2
新能源、高效节能技术	8.8	7.0	4.6	7.7	8.5	8.3	6.2	7.2	8.7	2.9
医药保健	4.3	2.7	2.0	2.5	4.9	5.3	3.8	4.9	10.0	7.4
消费产品和服务	1.7	4.1	1.4	3.9	4.3	7.1	9.4	6.3	5.0	1.6
传播与文化娱乐	3.2	1.1	2.2	1.8	2.5	2.1	2.2	6.4	6.2	5.4
传统制造业	8.9	11.3	12.6	15.6	11.9	10.1	7.7	10.1	7.2	7.6
农林牧副渔	0.5	9.4	1.2	2.6	3.5	4.1	4.1	6.1	6.3	2.0
金融保险业	3.4	3.8	22.1	8.2	15.2	7.8	2.4	5.4	10.1	2.9
批发和零售业	0.0	0.6	1.1	0.0	0.3	0.7	1.2	0.9	0.5	3.8
其他行业	4.0	7.6	8.3	12.7	10.0	15.7	11.2	7.6	2.7	8.5
核应用技术	0.3	0.0	0.0	0.0	0.1	0.0	0.4	0.2	0.2	0.1
房地产业	—	—	—	—	—	—	4.9	1.2	0.2	2.0
建筑业	—	—	—	—	—	—	1.6	1.9	1.3	0.6
交通运输仓储和邮政业	—	—	—	—	—	—	1.4	0.4	2.6	0.2
其他制造业	—	—	—	—	—	—	8.2	4.8	5.3	3.3
社会服务	—	—	—	—	—	—	0.7	1.1	1.9	2.4
水电煤气	—	—	—	—	—	—	0.1	0.3	0.3	0.4

表 2-3 中国创业风险投资产业投资项目数的行业分布（2005~2014） 单位：%

投资行业＼年份	2005	2006	2007	2008	2009	2010	2011	2012	2013	2014
软件产业	10.0	12.5	17.1	9.7	13.9	7.0	3.5	3.1	5.3	9.4
计算机硬件产业	1.2	1.0	1.1	1.3	0.4	1.4	1.3	1.5	1.2	1.7
网络产业	2.4	2.6	2.4	2.0	3.1	4.8	3.2	2.8	3.7	8.9
通信设备	6.0	4.1	2.7	3.9	3.0	2.5	3.2	3.7	3.2	8.3
IT 服务业	6.7	2.6	2.6	3.8	3.3	4.2	4.1	3.4	4.2	5.7
半导体	4.8	2.4	3.0	2.7	3.8	2.5	1.7	1.4	2.5	1.8
其他 IT 产业	2.1	3.8	2.6	3.2	3.7	2.3	2.4	1.9	1.0	1.6
环保工程	2.7	2.2	2.2	2.2	2.7	3.3	3.2	3.1	4.0	3.0
生物科技	8.2	7.9	5.6	6.1	5.5	5.6	3.3	4.8	4.2	4.1
新材料工业	7.6	10.3	9.6	6.6	7.2	10.1	9.5	8.8	7.6	5.9
采掘业	3.6	1.2	1.2	1.5	1.0	1.2	0.7	0.5	0.6	0.0
光电子与光机电一体化	10.0	5.0	4.5	5.9	5.1	6.0	4.6	3.8	4.9	2.9

续表

投资行业 \ 年份	2005	2006	2007	2008	2009	2010	2011	2012	2013	2014
科技服务	3.3	2.2	2.0	4.5	2.7	2.5	1.8	2.6	1.9	2.6
新能源、高效节能技术	4.5	5.0	5.7	5.1	6.3	7.8	6.0	7.2	6.8	4.2
医药保健	6.1	5.0	3.3	4.8	6.0	5.8	4.4	6.2	10.0	5.3
消费产品和服务	3.3	3.4	1.9	2.8	3.1	4.1	7.2	3.5	3.5	2.6
传播与文化娱乐	2.7	2.2	2.0	1.7	2.1	1.9	2.4	5.3	5.2	3.8
传统制造业	6.7	6.7	13.8	14.2	9.4	7.3	8.0	8.8	6.0	5.0
农林牧副渔	1.8	3.1	1.2	2.6	2.3	3.2	4.8	4.7	3.7	2.7
金融保险业	2.4	4.3	5.0	4.9	5.4	4.1	2.0	4.2	6.5	3.6
批发和零售业	0.0	1.9	1.2	0.2	0.3	0.7	1.2	0.7	0.4	1.9
其他行业	3.6	10.6	9.2	10.4	9.7	11.7	8.4	7.3	3.7	8.1
核应用技术	0.3	0.0	0.0	0.0	0.1	0.0	0.5	0.5	0.3	0.0
房地产业	—	—	—	—	—	—	0.3	0.5	0.3	0.2
建筑业	—	—	—	—	—	—	1.8	1.6	1.2	0.6
交通运输仓储和邮政业	—	—	—	—	—	—	0.8	0.2	1.2	0.2
其他制造业	—	—	—	—	—	—	8.3	5.0	4.7	4.1
社会服务	—	—	—	—	—	—	1.3	2.3	1.9	1.7
水电煤气	—	—	—	—	—	—	0.1	0.4	0.3	0.2

2011 年，国民经济行业分类（GB4754-2011）颁布实施，为与之接轨和便于分析，我们对行业分类进行了部分调整。计算机、通信和其他电子设备制造业，信息传输、软件和信息服务业是创业风险投资的热点领域（见表 2-4）。

表 2-4 中国创业风险投资产业投资项目的前十大行业分布（2013~2014） 单位：%

行业划分（代码）			2013		2014	
			投资金额	投资项目	投资金额	投资项目
C7	计算机、通信和其他电子设备制造业	计算机硬件产业 半导体 光电子与光机电一体化	9.81	11.78	21.15	14.63
I	信息传输、软件和信息服务业	网络产业 IT 服务业 软件产业 其他 IT 产业	7.86	14.24	15.41	25.53
C8	医药生物业	医药保健 生物科技	12.31	14.16	11.03	9.39

续表

行业划分（代码）			2013		2014	
			投资金额	投资项目	投资金额	投资项目
C9	新能源和环保业	新能源、高效节能技术 新材料工业 环保工程 核应用技术	18.88	18.60	9.55	13.16
O	其他行业		2.65	3.74	8.45	8.14
CA	传统制造业		7.19	6.03	7.64	4.98
N	文化、体育和娱乐业（传播与文化娱乐业）		6.16	5.24	5.44	3.81
J6	金融保险业		10.12	6.54	2.86	3.59
M	社会服务		1.86	1.87	2.36	1.65
L	科技服务		1.02	1.94	2.18	2.6

按照国际行业代码（VEIC）分类标准对中国创业风险投资业投资项目的行业调整后与美国创业风险投资行业划分进行对比，可以发现，我国创业风险投资行业集中在新材料工业、新能源/高效节能技术、通信设备、批发和零售业、软件，而美国创业风险投资中的资金集中在软件、媒体娱乐业、消费产品与服务等行业。和美国相比较而言，我国风险投资所投资行业的集中度较低（见表 2–5）。

表 2–5　中国与美国创业风险投资业投资项目的行业分布：投资金额与投资项目（2014）①　　单位：%

投资行业	中国		美国	
	投资金额	投资项目	投资金额	投资项目
软件	7.37	9.39	46.87	41.05
生物技术（生物科技）	3.68	4.11	13.60	10.75
工业/能源（新材料工业、新能源/高效节能技术）	6.66	10.09	5.41	5.66
医疗设备	—	—	0.81	7.22
IT 服务	3.00	5.67	7.42	7.52
媒体娱乐业（传播与文化娱乐）	5.44	3.81	13.34	10.96
消费产品与服务	1.57	2.55	5.00	4.49
半导体	1.35	1.77	1.73	2.11
通信（通信设备）	13.76	8.31	0.74	1.01
电子/仪器（光电子与光机电一体化）	1.89	2.86	1.61	1.22
零售（批发和零售业）	3.82	1.9	1.75	1.42
金融服务（金融保险业）	2.86	3.59	2.51	1.47
网络与设备（网络产业）	4.02	8.87	1.09	0.60
电脑与外设（计算机硬件产业）	4.15	1.69	3.32	1.44
健康护理服务	—	—	0.81	1.12
商业产品与服务	—	—	0.85	1.22
其他	—	—	5.44	0.73

① 此处行业中括号外为美国风险投资行业分类，括号内为我国风险投资行业分类，部分行业并无直接对等关系。

2.1.2 中国创业风险投资对高新技术产业与传统产业的投资比较①

将被投资项目按照高新技术产业和传统产业划分，2014 年，中国创业风险投资业对高新技术产业的投资项目和投资金额占比实现连续三年提高，但是仍然低于历史最高水平（见表 2-6、图 2-3、表 2-7、图 2-4）。

表 2-6 中国创业风险投资项目的年度行业分布：高新技术产业与传统产业（2004~2014） 单位：%

行业＼年份	2004	2005	2006	2007	2008	2009	2010	2011	2012	2013	2014
高新技术产业	76.70	78.30	67.90	65.50	63.20	67.70	67.00	53.40	55.30	61.30	65.40
传统产业	23.30	21.70	32.10	34.50	36.80	32.30	33.00	46.60	44.70	38.70	34.60

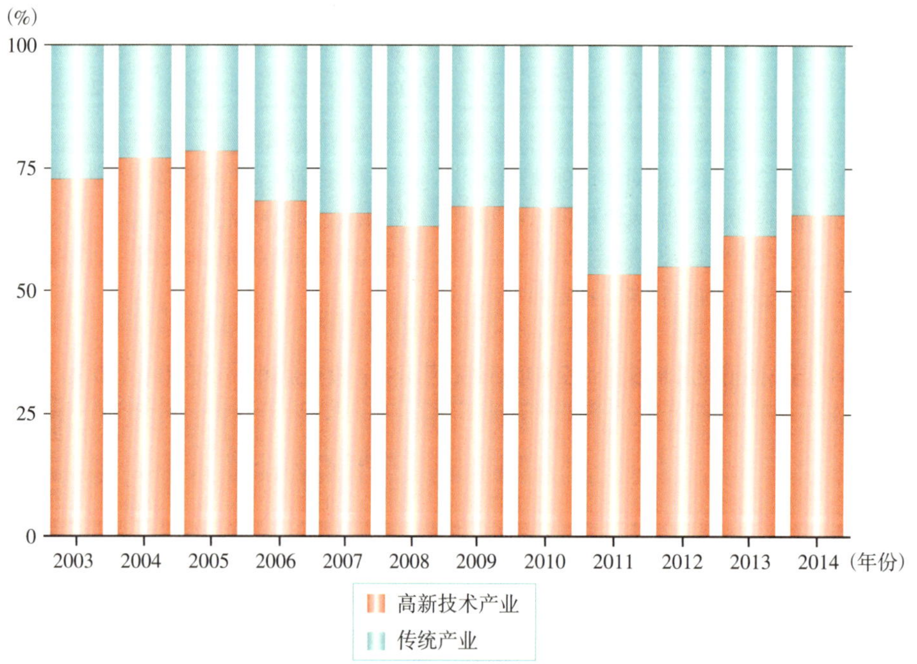

图 2-3 中国创业风险投资项目的年度行业分布：高新技术产业与传统产业

表 2-7 中国创业风险投资金额的年度行业分布：高技术产业与传统产业（2004~2014） 单位：%

行业＼年份	2004	2005	2006	2007	2008	2009	2010	2011	2012	2013	2014
高新技术产业	67.70	79.50	62.20	51.10	55.20	52.30	52.40	44.90	47.60	50.40	59.30
传统产业	32.20	20.50	37.80	48.90	44.80	47.70	47.60	55.10	52.40	49.60	40.70

① 有效样本数：高新项目样本数为 1510 份，传统项目样本数为 799 份。

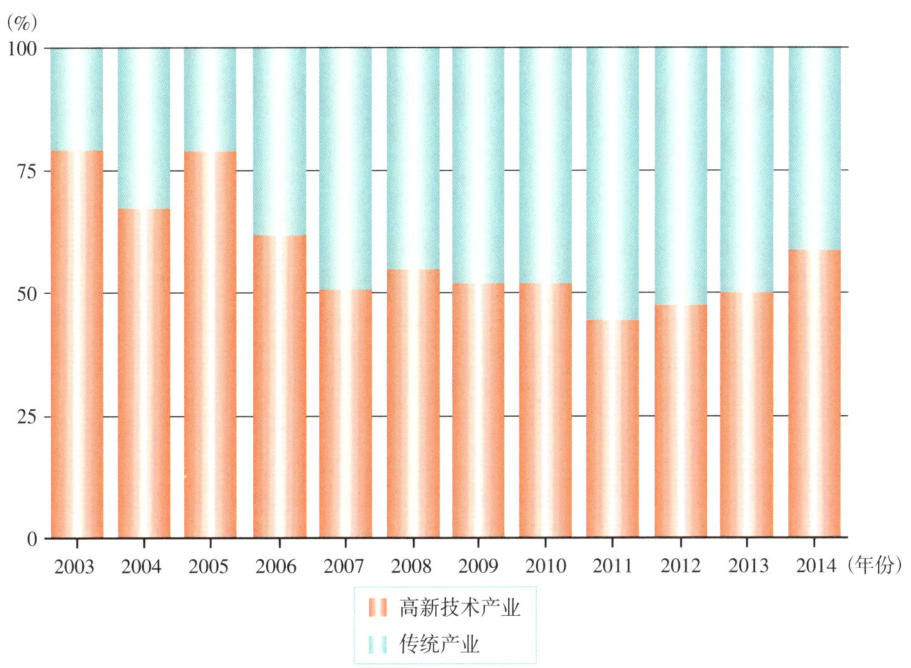

图 2-4 中国创业风险投资金额的年度行业分布：高新技术产业与传统产业

2.2 中国创业风险投资的投资阶段

2.2.1 中国创业风险投资所处阶段的总体分布①

2014 年，中国创业风险投资机构对种子期的投资金额占比降为 4.6%，但是投资项目占比增加至 20.8%；对起步期的投资金额略有下降，但是投资项目占比有所上升。投资机构对成长（扩张）期的投资金额依然保持最多，投资项目占比达 36.0%；与 2013 年相比，对成熟（过渡）期的投资金额和投资项目均有较大幅度的下滑（见表 2-8、图 2-5、表 2-9、图 2-6、表 2-10）。整体而言，中国创业风险投资呈现出关注早期项目，但是单个早期项目投资强度较低的局面。

表 2-8 中国创业风险投资项目所处阶段的总体分布：投资项目与投资金额（2014） 单位：%

成长阶段	投资金额	投资项目
种子期	4.6	20.8
起步期	20.7	36.5
成长（扩张）期	66.4	36.0
成熟（过渡）期	8.3	6.5
重建期	0.0	0.3

① 有效样本数为 2313 份。

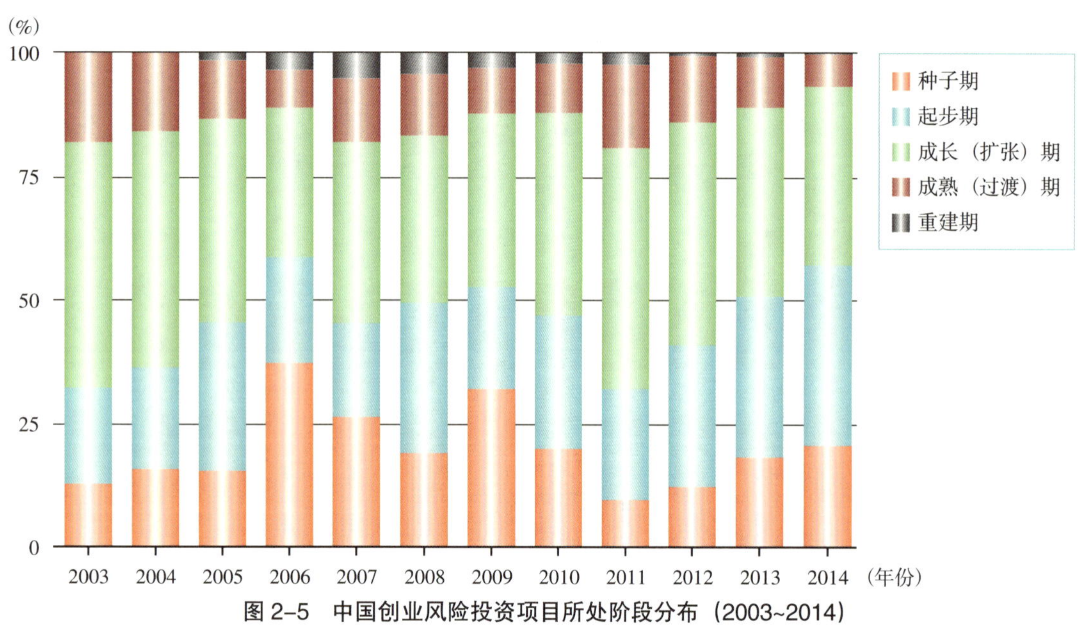

图 2-5 中国创业风险投资项目所处阶段分布（2003~2014）

表 2-9 中国创业风险投资项目所处阶段分布：投资项目（2004~2014） 单位：%

成长阶段 \ 年份	2004	2005	2006	2007	2008	2009	2010	2011	2012	2013	2014
种子期	15.80	15.40	37.40	26.60	19.30	32.20	19.90	9.70	12.33	18.36	20.75
起步期	20.60	30.10	21.30	18.90	30.20	20.30	27.0	22.70	28.66	32.46	36.53
成长（扩张）期	47.80	41.00	30.00	36.60	34.00	35.20	40.90	48.30	44.98	38.21	35.97
成熟（过渡）期	15.50	11.90	7.70	12.40	12.10	9.00	10.00	16.70	13.24	10.00	6.49
重建期	0.30	1.60	3.60	5.40	4.40	3.30	2.20	2.60	0.79	0.97	0.26

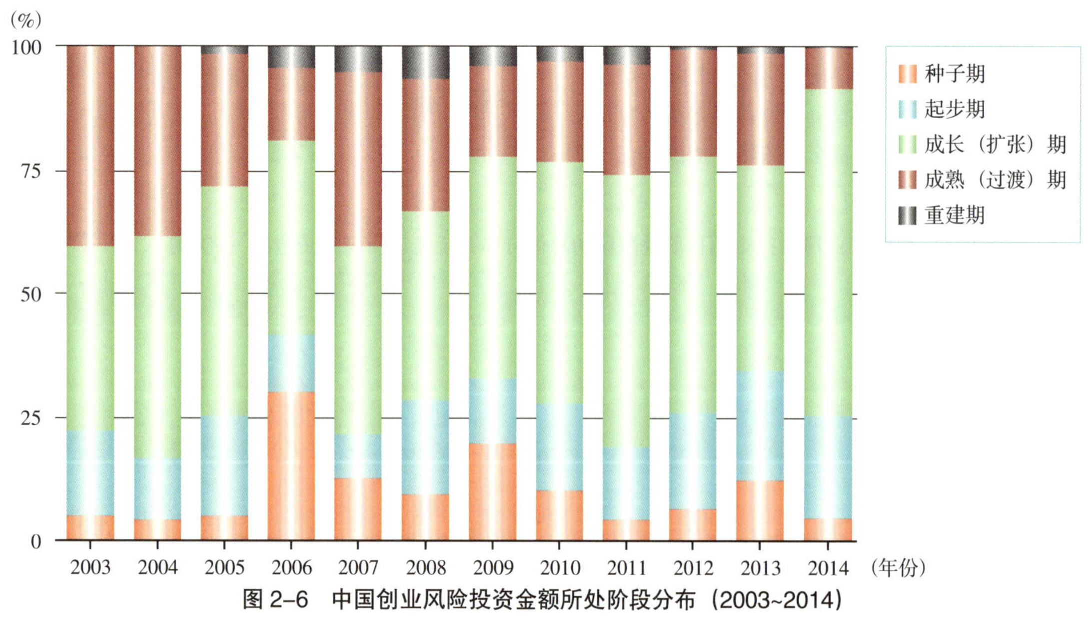

图 2-6 中国创业风险投资金额所处阶段分布（2003~2014）

表 2-10 中国创业风险投资项目所处阶段分布：投资金额（2004~2014） 单位：%

成长阶段 \ 年份	2004	2005	2006	2007	2008	2009	2010	2011	2012	2013	2014
种子期	4.50	5.20	30.20	12.70	9.40	19.90	10.20	4.30	6.55	12.22	4.62
起步期	12.30	20.00	11.50	8.90	19.00	12.80	17.40	14.80	19.32	22.38	20.72
成长（扩张）期	44.80	46.80	39.40	38.20	38.50	45.10	49.20	55.00	52.00	41.42	66.36
成熟（过渡）期	38.40	26.30	14.60	35.20	26.50	18.50	20.20	22.30	21.56	22.82	8.25
重建期	0.00	1.70	4.30	5.00	6.60	3.70	3.00	3.60	0.57	1.16	0.04

2.2.2 中国创业风险投资在主要行业投资项目的阶段分布①

2014 年，中国创业风险投资主要投资行业的阶段分布特点表现为：交通运输仓储和邮政业、房地产业、科技服务、其他行业、网络产业投资项目中种子期占比较高；采掘业、核应用技术、水电煤气、建筑业、其他行业投资金额中种子期占比较高。这一投资偏好说明，创业风险投资机构认为这些产业具有早期投资价值，值得在项目的初创期就开始进行投资。核应用技术、金融保险业、其他 IT 产业、网络产业、软件产业投资项目中起步期占比较高，水电煤气、交通运输仓储和邮政业、房地产业、核应用技术投资金额中起步期占比较高。建筑业、房地产业、水电煤气、传统制造业投资项目中成长（扩张）期占比较高，采掘业、核应用技术、房地产业投资金额中成长（扩张）期占比较高（见表 2-11、表 2-12），符合资金密集型产业的特征。

表 2-11 中国创业风险投资项目主要行业的投资阶段分布：投资项目（2014） 单位：%

投资行业	种子期	起步期	成长（扩张）期	成熟（过渡）期	重建期
传统制造业	2.65	23.89	58.41	15.04	0.00
消费产品和服务	22.03	40.68	20.34	16.95	0.00
软件产业	19.44	47.22	30.56	2.78	0.00
采掘业	0.00	0.00	0.00	100.00	0.00
其他行业	33.15	37.50	21.74	7.61	0.00
IT 服务业	30.53	37.40	25.19	6.11	0.76
批发和零售业	15.91	34.09	45.45	2.27	2.27
科技服务	33.33	28.33	35.00	3.33	0.00
交通运输仓储和邮政业	75.00	0.00	25.00	0.00	0.00
计算机硬件产业	30.77	23.08	46.15	0.00	0.00
网络产业	31.22	51.71	15.12	1.95	0.00
核应用技术	0.00	100.00	0.00	0.00	0.00
医药保健	16.81	27.73	49.58	5.88	0.00
水电煤气	0.00	0.00	60.00	40.00	0.00
房地产业	40.00	0.00	60.00	0.00	0.00
新材料工业	23.70	33.33	40.00	2.22	0.74
社会服务	21.05	36.84	28.95	13.16	0.00

① 有效样本数为 2288 份。

续表

投资行业	种子期	起步期	成长（扩张）期	成熟（过渡）期	重建期
传播与文化娱乐	27.27	26.14	31.82	14.77	0.00
其他制造业	9.57	29.79	51.06	9.57	0.00
半导体	12.20	31.71	53.66	2.44	0.00
其他 IT 产业	11.76	52.94	29.41	5.88	0.00
农林牧副渔	22.58	27.42	32.26	17.74	0.00
金融保险业	24.39	53.66	20.73	1.22	0.00
建筑业	0.00	7.69	69.23	23.08	0.00
环保工程	18.57	25.71	47.14	8.57	0.00
通信设备	6.81	41.36	51.83	0.00	0.00
光电子与光机电一体化	25.00	28.13	35.94	10.94	0.00
新能源、高效节能技术	13.68	29.47	47.37	7.37	2.11
生物科技	20.00	42.11	29.47	7.37	1.05

表 2-12 中国创业风险投资项目主要行业的投资阶段分布：投资金额（2014） 单位：%

投资行业	种子期	起步期	成长（扩张）期	成熟（过渡）期	重建期
传统制造业	0.36	13.21	71.92	14.51	—
消费产品和服务	5.04	26.85	21.33	46.77	—
软件产业	1.96	32.09	62.81	3.14	—
采掘业	—	—	—	100.00	—
其他行业	21.38	43.65	24.54	10.43	—
IT 服务业	6.97	37.96	42.34	12.64	0.08
批发和零售业	0.05	2.56	97.27	0.01	0.11
科技服务	6.24	24.83	66.44	2.48	—
交通运输仓储和邮政业	14.89	—	85.11	—	—
计算机硬件产业	2.96	4.92	92.12	—	—
网络产业	5.52	57.82	26.19	10.47	—
核应用技术	—	100.00	—	—	—
医药保健	11.99	11.83	63.91	12.27	—
水电煤气	—	—	16.71	83.29	—
房地产业	1.28	—	98.72		—
新材料工业	9.13	25.67	63.79	1.27	0.13
社会服务	6.99	17.85	71.31	3.86	—
传播与文化娱乐	2.18	10.96	75.37	11.50	—
其他制造业	1.89	26.87	61.14	10.10	—

续表

投资行业	种子期	起步期	成长（扩张）期	成熟（过渡）期	重建期
半导体	20.08	24.13	54.32	1.48	—
其他 IT 产业	6.84	42.84	43.43	6.88	—
农林牧副渔	2.30	38.37	45.64	13.69	—
金融保险业	12.48	38.37	49.06	0.09	—
建筑业	—	4.05	72.69	23.26	—
环保工程	0.24	17.87	60.93	20.96	—
通信设备	0.74	34.78	64.48	—	—
光电子与光机电一体化	4.63	16.95	32.35	46.06	—
新能源、高效节能技术	6.61	18.92	66.52	7.60	0.34
生物科技	6.32	18.61	58.38	16.49	0.20

2.3 中国创业风险投资的投资强度

2.3.1 中国创业风险投资强度的变化趋势与行业差异①

2014 年，我国经济发展进入新常态，中国创业风险投资强度持续下降，为 1129.53 万元/项。可能的原因在于软件产业、网络产业等投资强度低的行业获得投资较多。按行业划分，核应用技术、交通运输仓储和邮政业、批发和零售业、环保工程等行业的项目平均投资强度较大（见表 2–13、图 2–7、表 2–14、图 2–8）。

表 2–13　中国创业风险投资的投资强度（2005~2014）　单位：万元/项

年　份	2005	2006	2007	2008	2009	2010	2011	2012	2013	2014
投资强度	901.10	802.51	973.37	1041.25	1059.77	1356.53	1550.53	1322.66	1282.12	1129.53

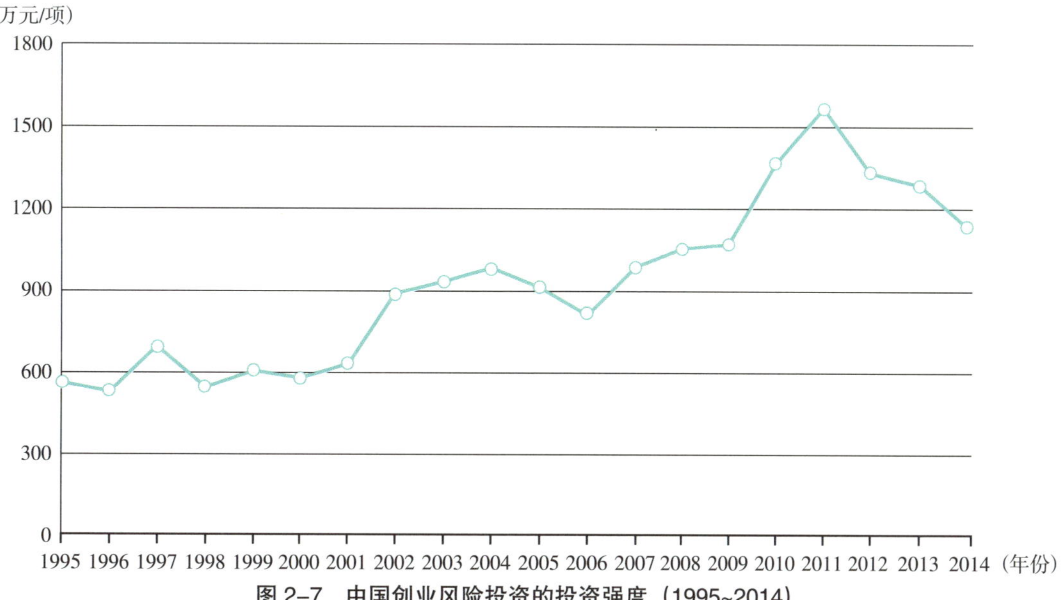

图 2–7　中国创业风险投资的投资强度（1995~2014）

① 有效样本数为 2159 份。

表 2-14 中国创业风险投资的投资强度平均投资额（2005~2014） 单位：万元/项

行业＼年份	2005	2006	2007	2008	2009	2010	2011	2012	2013	2014
医药保健	635.7	541.7	884.0	678.8	1052.5	1409.3	1444.5	1144.5	1351.0	1429.6
新能源、高效节能技术	1649.4	915.1	1152.4	1447.4	1156.6	1302.8	1647.8	1373.0	1420.2	1059.2
新材料工业	638.5	703.8	938.3	867.6	1212.9	1376.6	1639.7	1224.5	1444.0	1006.4
消费产品和服务	533.9	1190.5	1010.6	1774.1	1435.8	2463.2	2102.0	2036.9	1712.8	1053.3
网络产业	1077.4	559.3	309.0	1186.7	805.5	925.8	1487.4	1028.8	721.0	742.8
通信设备	486.8	1087.0	964.9	580.8	671.0	726.0	1791.6	1439.3	1704.3	1540.4
水电煤气	—	—	—	—	—	—	866.7	1050.0	1512.5	1232.5
生物科技	950.9	660.4	594.0	878.0	612.0	805.1	1369.0	904.5	960.5	1059.2
社会服务	—	—	—	—	—	—	1150.3	728.5	1370.1	1147.2
软件产业	315.0	763.1	979.1	732.4	788.4	756.2	976.3	1029.8	677.8	945.0
其他制造业	—	—	—	—	—	—	1825.3	1483.5	959.4	1181.2
其他行业	1124.0	701.7	1089.0	1155.6	1189.9	1542.2	1628.9	1110.4	1075.7	1400.5
其他 IT 产业	972.9	800.3	696.5	942.3	827.4	980.7	1297.0	1171.2	616.4	971.1
批发和零售业	—	304.6	1273.1	30.0	1673.3	1988.2	1642.8	1810.3	2410.0	1638.7
农林牧副渔	380.0	913.6	1411.2	1327.8	1580.6	2054.7	1505.4	1836.0	1516.6	1036.7
科技服务	531.8	529.7	456.4	600.8	785.9	1400.8	1391.7	842.4	944.0	903.1
金融保险业	1178.1	843.5	1498.1	1537.0	1964.0	1326.1	977.6	1653.0	1885.6	929.0
交通运输仓储和邮政业	—	—	—	—	—	—	2163.9	2244.7	1432.4	1762.5
建筑业	—	—	—	—	—	—	1466.7	1834.0	1989.3	1346.9
计算机硬件产业	642.5	365.0	840.4	782.1	495.0	997.3	1117.0	799.6	581.5	1225.9
环保工程	1095.8	567.8	982.2	760.8	893.7	1501.4	1368.9	1402.3	1268.6	1559.3
核应用技术	700.0	—	—	—	1200.0	—	1517.3	757.4	1008.3	2500.0
光电子与光机电一体化	466.1	788.8	670.3	898.9	879.1	1075.8	1420.0	1288.3	1294.2	863.4
房地产业	—	—	—	—	—	—	1492.2	1523.9	1237.5	511.0
传统制造业	1250.9	1316.0	1286.5	1320.7	1481.1	2057.8	1754.9	1390.3	1409.1	1032.4
传播与文化娱乐	1009.4	474.3	765.7	671.5	1437.6	1413.1	1458.1	1398.6	1441.9	1543.3
采掘业	1058.3	2979.2	1037.6	1850.5	1211.0	1633.2	1184.3	2130.4	1537.8	200.0
半导体	3100.6	861.7	626.4	1407.6	688.7	895.4	1608.3	1312.6	963.9	1322.8
IT 服务业	1002.2	506.0	607.3	791.0	609.1	1002.1	1208.5	1216.5	963.0	843.4

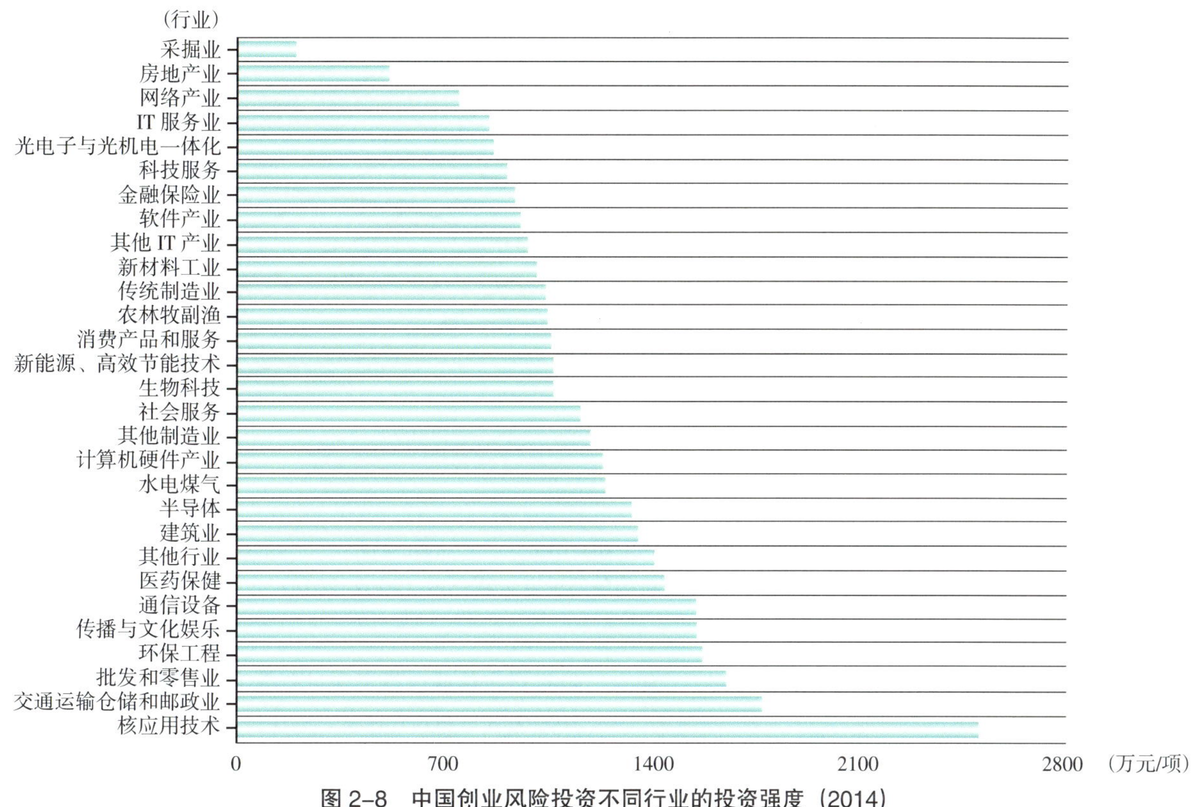

图 2-8 中国创业风险投资不同行业的投资强度（2014）

2.3.2 中国创业风险投资机构单项投资规模分布①

2014 年，中国创业风险投资机构单项投资金额 100 万元以下的项目占比有所上升，单项投资金额分别为 300 万~500 万元、500 万~1000 万元的项目占比都有不同程度的下降。1000 万~2000 万元的投资项目所占比例最大，达 20.40%；其次为 100 万~300 万元的投资项目。300 万元以下的投资项目较 2013 年有较大幅度上升（见表 2-15、图 2-9）。

表 2-15 中国创业风险投资机构单项投资金额分布（2005~2014） 单位：%

年份 \ 金额（万元）	100 以下	100~300	300~500	500~1000	1000~2000	2000 以上
2005	23.90	19.70	15.50	20.00	11.00	9.00
2006	24.10	25.10	9.00	19.30	12.00	10.50
2007	16.10	17.60	18.30	18.10	17.40	12.50
2008	17.10	22.00	11.70	15.00	18.90	15.20
2009	11.70	22.40	12.60	20.30	17.30	15.70
2010	13.40	15.50	8.90	17.50	21.50	23.20
2011	6.80	10.60	10.20	20.60	25.70	26.20
2012	10.20	13.10	11.30	21.20	24.70	19.50
2013	8.40	17.60	14.60	20.00	20.10	19.30
2014	12.30	19.10	13.90	18.30	20.40	15.90

① 有效样本数为 2159 份。

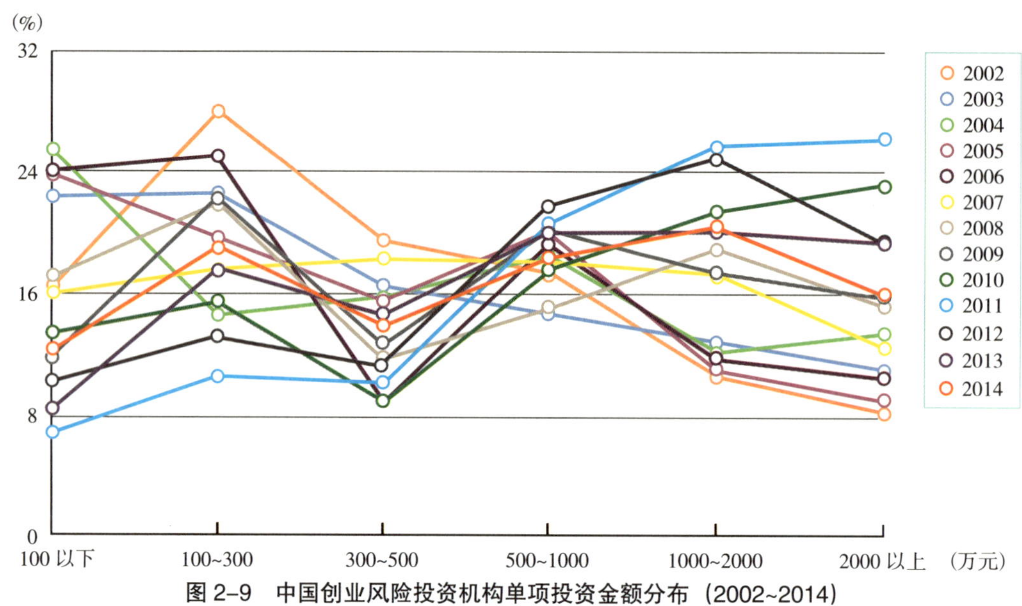

图 2-9 中国创业风险投资机构单项投资金额分布（2002~2014）

2.3.3 中国创业风险投资的投资策略（联合投资）

联合投资可有效分散创业风险投资公司风险，通过合作分享其他联合投资伙伴的专业知识和技能，实现资金使用效率的最大化，从而最终实现优化项目选择和提升整体投资组合价值的目标。2014 年，由创业风险投资机构和其他投资主体联合投资项目总数为 163 项。其中 100 万~1000 万元项目占比降低，其他投资金额项目占比均上升；100 万~500 万元项目中，有 27.60%的项目为联合投资，是各投资规模项目中占比最高的（见表 2-16、图 2-10、表 2-17、图 2-11）。

表 2-16 中国创业风险投资联合投资的单项投资金额分布（2005~2014）[①] 单位：%

年份 \ 金额（万元）	100 以下	100~500	500~1000	1000~2000	2000 以上
2005	16.50	24.10	19.50	15.00	24.90
2006	13.60	50.00	15.90	11.40	9.10
2007	9.10	39.40	9.10	30.30	12.10
2008	19.00	31.60	13.90	20.30	15.20
2009	13.00	28.00	21.00	19.00	19.00
2010	10.30	15.40	24.10	23.10	27.20
2011	6.10	22.00	18.30	25.60	28.00
2012	13.00	28.70	20.90	20.00	17.40
2013	12.00	32.00	28.00	12.00	16.00
2014	16.00	27.60	10.40	23.30	22.70

① 有效样本数为 163 份。

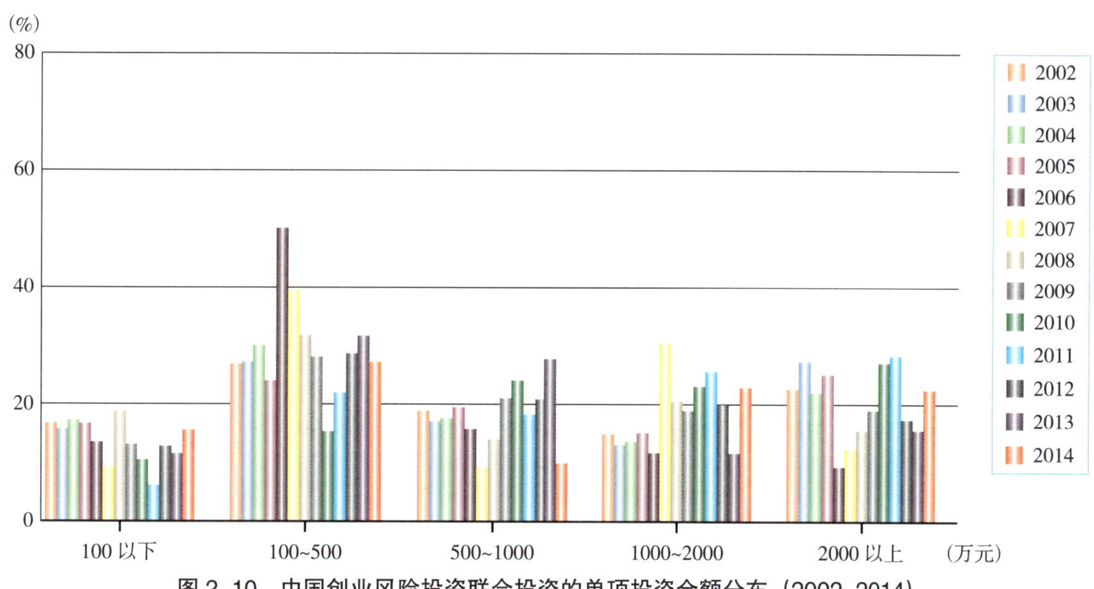

图 2-10 中国创业风险投资联合投资的单项投资金额分布（2002~2014）

表 2-17 中国创业风险投资机构与其他类型投资机构的联合投资（2014）[①] 单位：%

金额（万元） 投资额分布	100 以下	100~300	300~500	500~1000	1000~2000	2000 以上
创业风险投资机构的投资额	0.61	4.11	5.83	14.56	29.31	45.58
其他类型投资机构的投资额	0.51	1.89	4.78	6.63	26.56	59.63

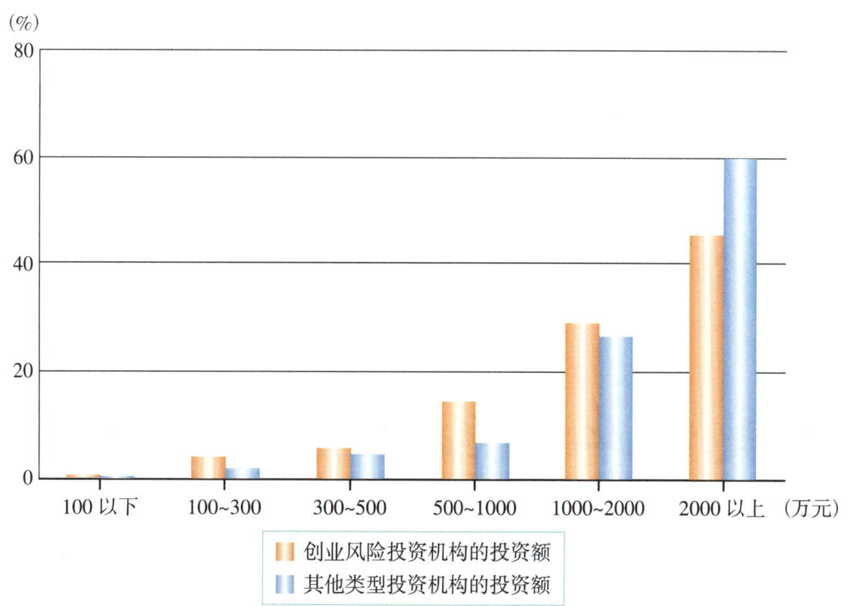

图 2-11 中国创业风险投资机构与其他类型投资机构的联合投资（2014）

① 创业风险投资机构有效样本数为 1878 份；其他类型投资机构有效样本数为 163 份。

2.4 中国创业风险投资的首轮投资与后续投资

2014 年，中国创业风险投资项目的首轮投资和后续投资分别占 68.1%和 31.9%，首轮投资仍然占主导地位，但后续投资的比例不断上升，基本延续了前几年投资轮次的格局（见表 2-18、图 2-12）。

表 2-18 中国创业风险投资的首轮投资和后续投资（2005~2014）① 单位：%

年份 项目	2005	2006	2007	2008	2009	2010	2011	2012	2013	2014
首轮投资	70.80	77.00	83.10	84.50	82.70	86.20	83.40	80.10	77.50	68.10
后续投资	29.20	23.00	16.90	15.50	17.30	13.80	16.60	19.90	22.50	31.90

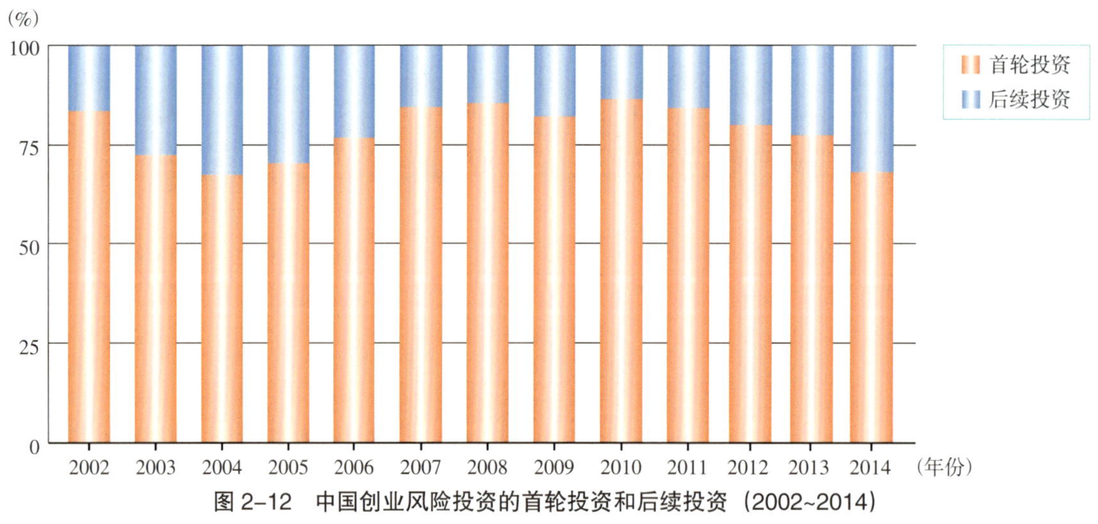

图 2-12 中国创业风险投资的首轮投资和后续投资（2002~2014）

2.5 中国创业风险投资机构持股结构

中国创业风险投资机构的股权结构仍然保持多元化趋势，其中参股和相对控股仍然是主要的投资方式。2014 年，持股比例在 20%以下的项目所占比例较上年有所上升（见表 2-19、图 2-13）。这一持股的趋势表明：不谋求控股的创业风险投资经营策略仍然占主导地位。与往年相比，尽管中国创业风险投资机构的投资强度总体呈上升趋势，其所占股权比例在 20%~30%以及 50%以上区间的比重有下降趋势，而其他股权比例所占的比重则在上升。

① 有效样本数为 2034 份。

表 2-19 中国创业风险投资机构持股结构分布（2005~2014）[①] 单位：%

年份 \ 股权比例（%）	10 以下	10~20	20~30	30~40	40~50	50 以上
2005	16.70	26.40	14.50	20.30	6.90	15.20
2006	25.00	25.00	20.35	12.50	6.10	11.05
2007	43.33	20.32	14.44	8.41	4.92	8.57
2008	42.92	23.65	10.95	8.61	6.13	7.74
2009	44.60	22.77	13.64	5.98	5.14	7.87
2010	50.99	25.15	10.85	6.17	3.14	3.70
2011	61.04	20.46	7.08	4.38	2.24	4.80
2012	56.29	22.57	9.07	4.70	3.00	4.37
2013	50.32	25.60	11.60	4.40	2.88	5.20
2014	50.82	26.41	9.30	5.55	4.60	3.33

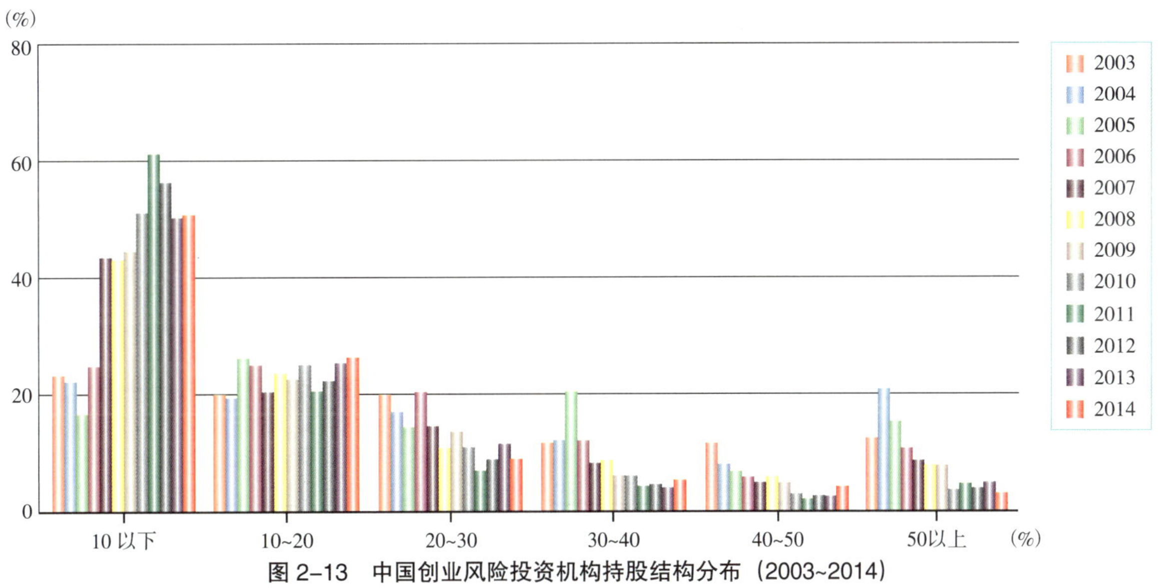

图 2-13 中国创业风险投资机构持股结构分布（2003~2014）

2.6 中国创业风险投资项目的特征

2.6.1 中国创业风险投资项目的资本规模

从被投资项目的实收资本而言，2014 年，规模在 500 万元以下和 5000 万元以上的项目是中国创业风险投资的重点对象。500 万元以下的中小投资项目的占比较 2013 年增加了 15.89 个百分点；5000 万元以上的投资项目占比与 2013 年相比下降了 5.1 个百分点。总体而言，中国创业风险投资项目规模分布的基本趋势表现为，对中小项目投资有所上升，对大型项目的投资略有下降，其他规模项目的比例大致稳定（见表 2-20、图 2-14）。

① 有效样本数为 1893 份。

表 2-20 中国创业风险投资项目的实收资本规模分布（2005~2014）[①] 单位：%

年份＼资本规模（万元）	500 以下	500~1000	1000~3000	3000~5000	5000 以上
2005	34.40	12.80	26.10	8.90	17.80
2006	28.20	13.20	27.80	14.10	16.70
2007	26.82	12.83	20.41	13.12	26.82
2008	18.90	15.70	26.50	12.20	26.70
2009	21.60	13.90	23.50	15.40	25.60
2010	26.40	12.43	23.42	13.06	24.68
2011	15.23	11.50	24.23	13.56	35.48
2012	16.93	14.49	26.09	13.18	29.32
2013	19.49	15.25	23.74	14.44	27.07
2014	35.38	12.07	20.82	9.77	21.97

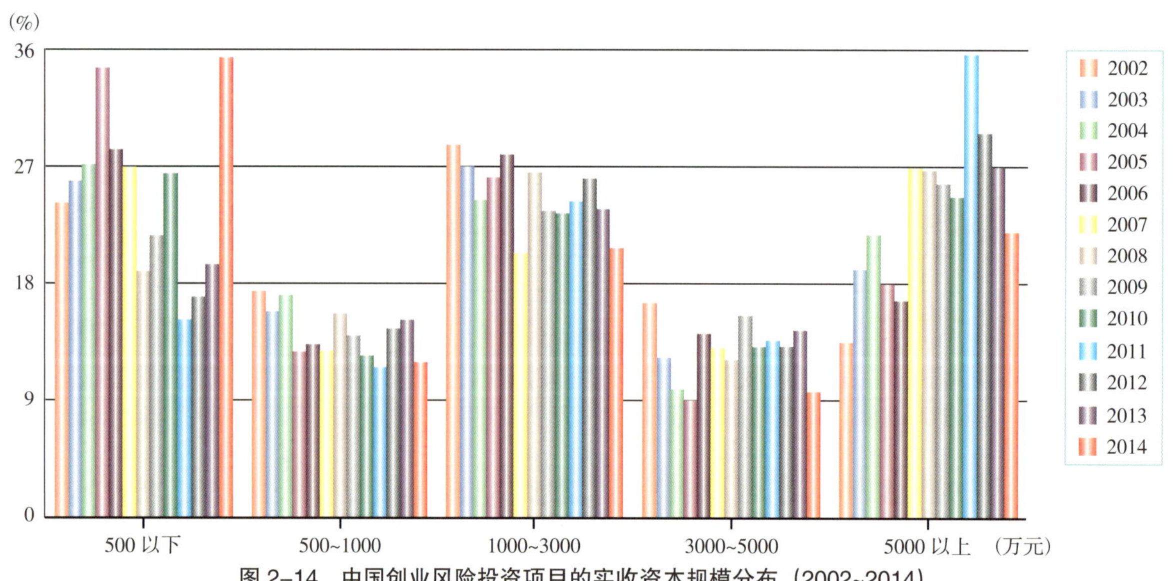

图 2-14 中国创业风险投资项目的实收资本规模分布（2002~2014）

2.6.2 中国创业风险投资项目的雇员规模

以项目雇员划分被投资项目的规模，2014 年，中国创业风险投资机构投资项目的规模与 2013 年相比大体一致。创业风险投资机构首选拥有雇员 10~50 人的项目，占比达到 32.43%；其次为拥有雇员 200 人以上的项目，占比达 20.37%（见表 2-21、图 2-15）。

表 2-21 中国创业风险投资项目雇员规模分布（2005~2014）[②] 单位：%

年份＼雇员规模（人）	10 以下	10~50	50~100	100~150	150~200	200 以上
2005	17.70	37.10	13.70	7.40	7.40	16.70
2006	14.10	36.40	13.00	7.10	7.60	20.70

① 有效样本数为 1566 份。
② 有效样本数为 1178 份。

续表

年份 \ 雇员规模（人）	10 以下	10~50	50~100	100~150	150~200	200 以上
2007	14.70	26.10	12.90	8.50	7.00	30.10
2008	14.60	29.90	14.40	7.50	3.40	29.90
2009	21.80	36.70	9.80	6.20	4.80	19.90
2010	14.60	28.90	13.90	8.20	5.90	27.50
2011	11.30	24.30	13.30	8.90	6.90	34.10
2012	12.88	25.96	13.39	11.76	8.62	27.38
2013	13.75	30.38	13.97	10.20	7.43	24.28
2014	18.51	32.43	14.77	8.83	5.09	20.37

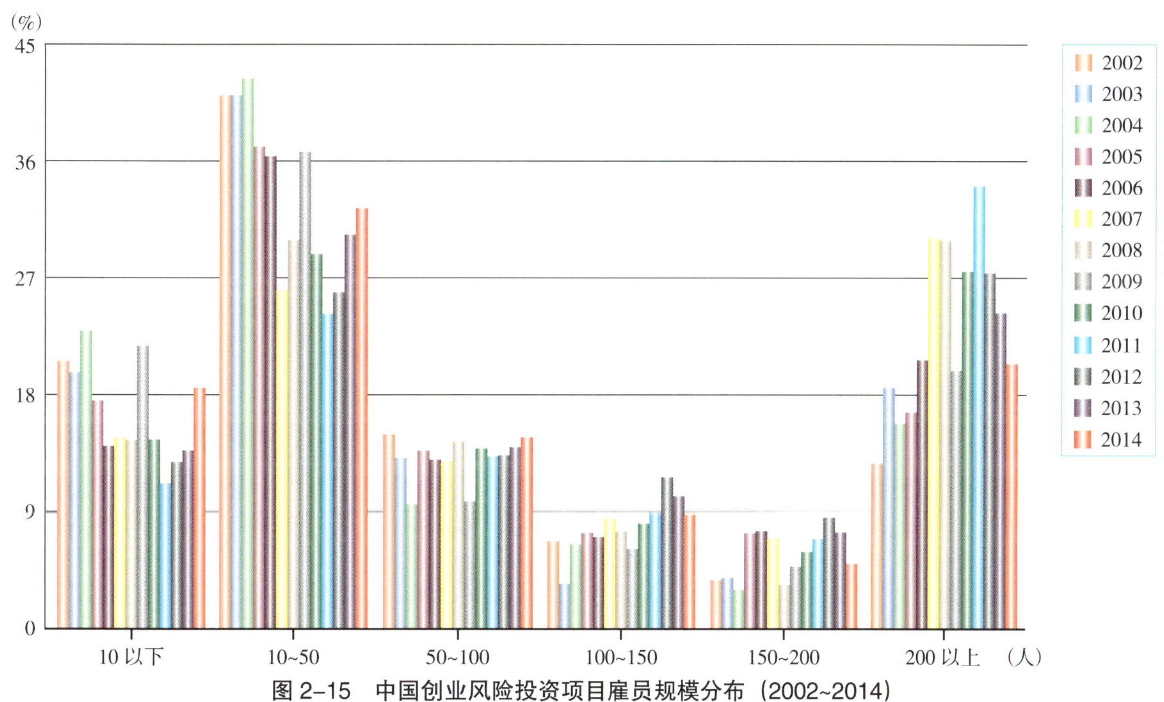

图 2-15 中国创业风险投资项目雇员规模分布（2002~2014）

2.6.3 中国创业风险投资项目的经营时间

从被投资项目的经营时间看，一方面，创业风险投资机构仍然偏好比较稳健的成熟项目，成立时间在 5 年以上的企业占比最高，达到 32.35%，但近年来持续下降；另一方面，也有较多成立时间在 1 年以下的初创期企业获得投资机构青睐，占比为 29.29%，连续三年上升（见表 2-22、图 2-16）。结合投资项目的注册资本金额、雇员分布情况可以发现，这三组数据与 2013 年中国创业风险投资行为的描述大体一致。

表 2–22　中国创业风险投资项目经营时间分布（2005~2014）[①]　　单位：%

年份 \ 经营时间（年）	1 以下	1~3	3~5	5 以上
2005	32.00	33.70	16.30	18.00
2006	18.80	32.10	16.50	32.60
2007	24.20	17.40	15.80	42.70
2008	17.30	24.30	19.00	39.40
2009	40.20	16.70	12.30	30.80
2010	13.60	28.80	13.60	43.90
2011	11.80	20.10	16.30	51.80
2012	14.25	20.51	15.19	50.05
2013	19.54	21.54	17.21	41.71
2014	29.29	22.21	16.14	32.35

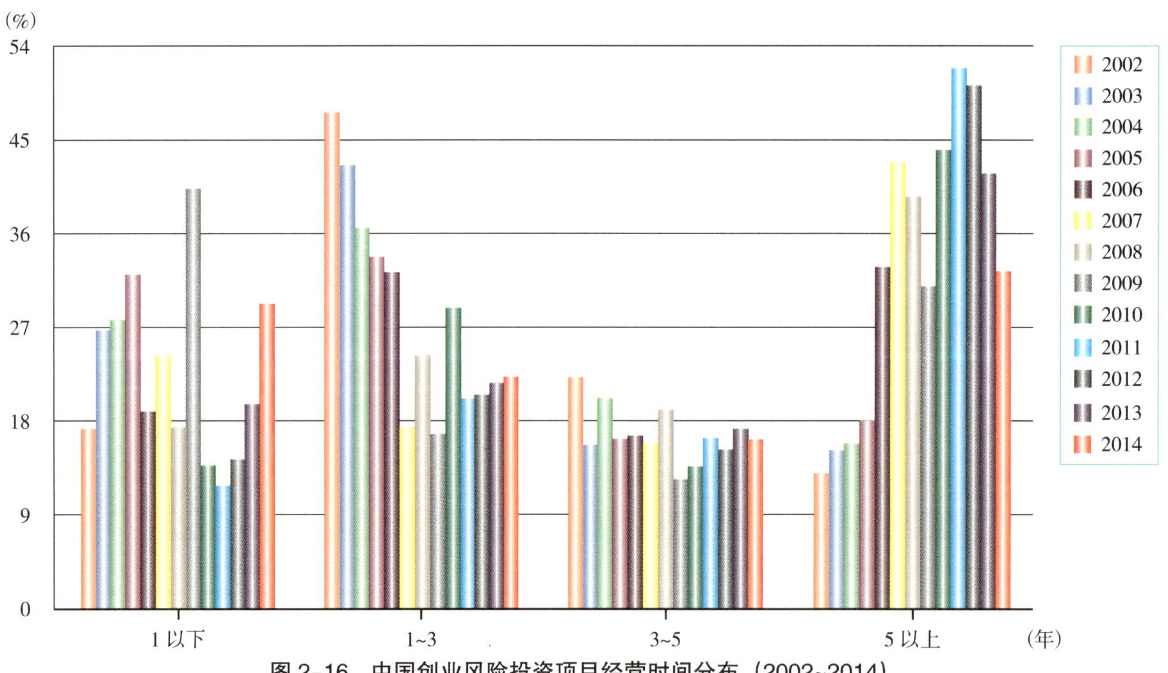

图 2–16　中国创业风险投资项目经营时间分布（2002~2014）

① 有效样本数为 1499 份。

3 中国创业风险投资的退出

3.1 中国创业风险投资退出的基本情况[①]

2013年11月30日，中国证监会发布《中国证监会关于进一步推进新股发行体制改革的意见》，标志着境内IPO开闸。2014年以来，全国共有125家中国企业在境内上市，合计融资130.87亿美元，平均融资104.69亿美元；96家中国企业在境外资本市场上市，合计融资492.59亿美元，上市数量及融资规模较2013年同期分别上升2.35倍和2.28倍。[②]

受市场环境利好因素影响，中国创业风险投资市场全年退出的项目收入规模总体上有所增加，收入规模在100万~2000万元的项目比例均较2013年显著提高，收入规模在100万元以下和2000万元以上项目的比例较2013年有所下降（见表3-1、图3-1）。

表3-1 中国创业风险投资项目退出的收入分布（2008~2014） 单位：%

收入规模（万元）/年份	100以下	100~500	500~1000	1000~2000	2000以上
2008	36.5	24.6	11.1	9.5	18.3
2009	26.8	27.5	15.7	12.4	17.6
2010	27.3	19.7	13.7	13.7	25.7
2011	22.9	24.1	11.0	10.6	31.4
2012	19.2	17.1	10.5	17.4	35.8
2013	21.8	19.8	10.6	11.8	35.9
2014	15.7	24.7	14.4	12.7	32.4

① 有效样本数为362份。
② 清科数据库。

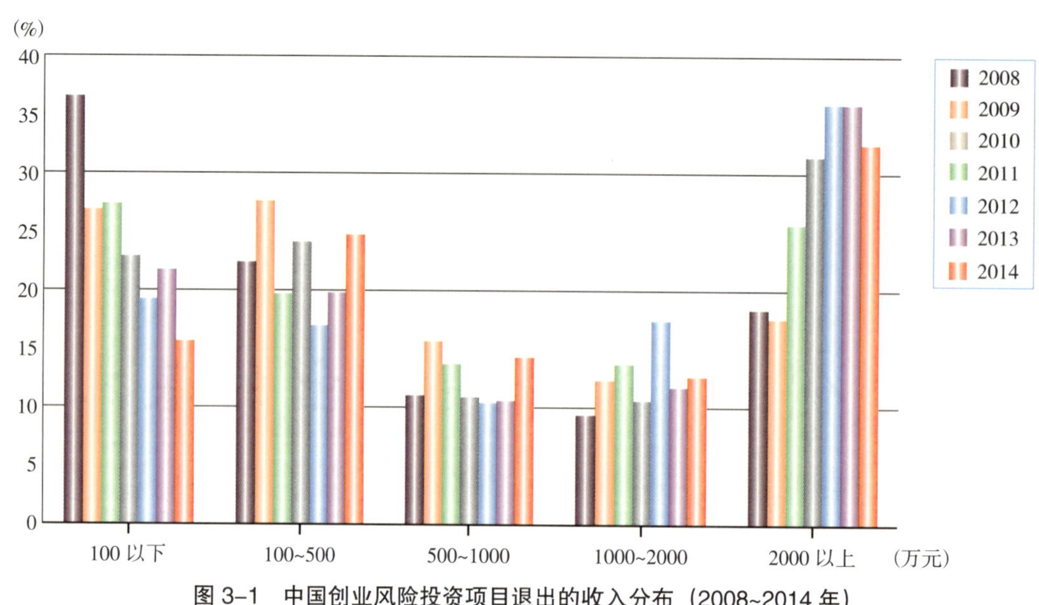

图 3-1 中国创业风险投资项目退出的收入分布（2008~2014 年）

3.2 中国创业风险投资的退出方式[①]

3.2.1 中国创业风险投资的主要退出方式

据统计数据显示，2014 年全年共发生 497 笔退出交易。按照退出渠道划分，创业风险投资孵化的企业中共有 103 个项目通过 IPO 方式退出，较 2013 年的 27 家大幅提升，但相对占比有所回落，为 20.72%；与此同时，并购市场在 2014 年持续发展，退出占比达到了 36.02%，成为创业风险投资机构主要的退出渠道。此外，全年有 12 个项目通过新三板挂牌进行交易，回购退出的占比也少于往年，退出的总体环境向好（见表 3-2、图 3-2）。

表 3-2 中国创业风险投资的退出方式分布（2008~2014）

单位：%

年份 \ 退出方式	上市（IPO）	并购	回购	清算	其他（含新三板）
2008	22.70	23.20	34.80	9.20	10.10
2009	25.30	33.00	35.30	6.30	0.00
2010	29.80	28.63	32.82	6.87	1.91
2011	29.40	29.97	32.28	3.17	5.19
2012	29.41	15.86	45.01	6.65	3.07
2013	24.33	23.75	44.83	4.60	2.49
2014	20.72	36.02	36.02	4.83	2.41

① 有效样本数为 497 份。

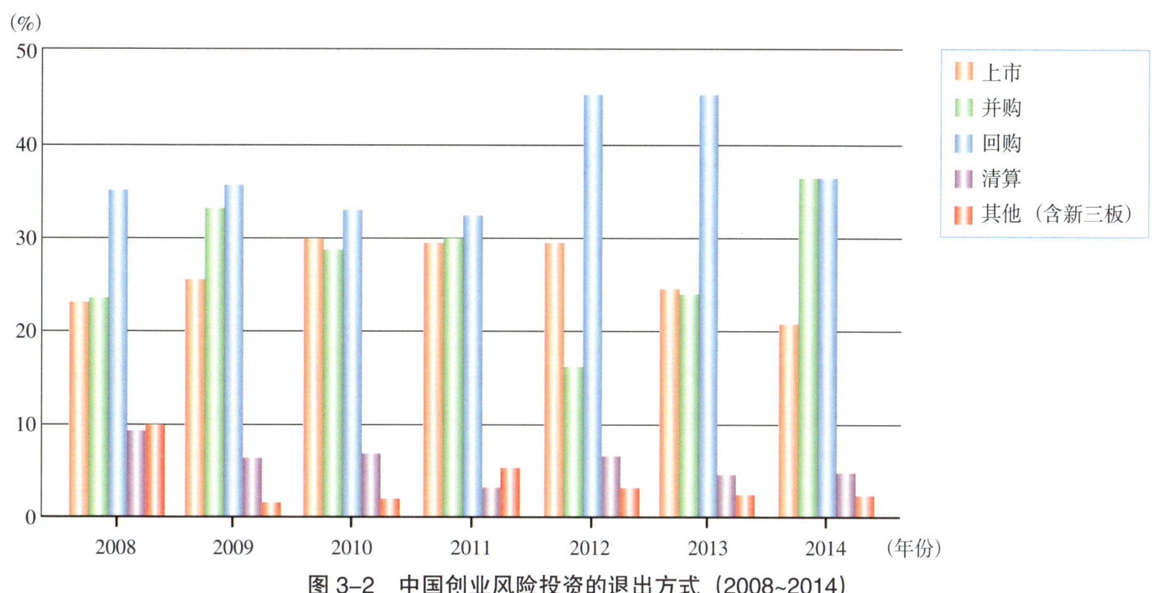

图 3-2 中国创业风险投资的退出方式（2008~2014）

3.2.2 中国创业风险投资的 IPO 退出渠道

目前，我国多层次资本市场已初步形成主板、中小板、创业板以及新三板市场的构架。据统计，2014 年，共有 103 个项目通过 IPO 市场实现退出收益，其中，境内创业板上市仍然是创业风险投资机构企业退出的主要渠道，42.72%的项目通过境内创业板上市；受 A 股市场 IPO 开闸利好，22.33%的企业通过境内主板市场退出，21.36%的企业通过境内中小板市场退出，另有 13.59%的企业通过境外市场退出（见表 3-3、图 3-3）。

表 3-3 中国创业风险投资 IPO 分布（2010~2014）①

单位：%

年份 \ 退出方式	境内主板上市	境内创业板上市	境内中小板上市	境外上市
2010	16.67	35.90	44.87	2.56
2011	14.71	30.39	49.02	5.88
2012	21.74	38.26	36.52	3.48
2013	21.26	40.94	30.71	7.09
2014	22.33	42.72	21.36	13.59

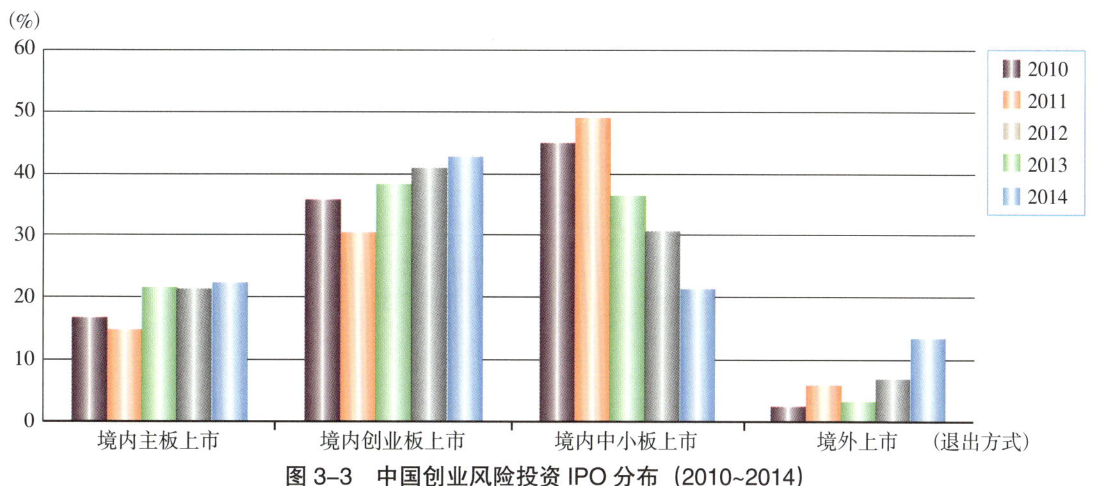

图 3-3 中国创业风险投资 IPO 分布（2010~2014）

① 有效样本数为 2778 个。

3.3 中国创业风险投资退出项目的行业分布①

从二级行业划分的情况来看，2014 年，中国创业风险投资实现项目退出最多的行业依然是传统制造业，但较 2013 年占比大幅下降。排名前十的行业依次为传统制造业（12.17%），其他行业（8.72%），医药保健（6.69%），新材料工业（6.29%），软件产业（5.88%），传播与文化娱乐（5.48%），通信设备（5.27%），新能源、高效节能技术（4.67%），网络产业（4.67%），农林牧副渔（4.26%），10 个行业合计实现退出的项目占全部退出项目的 64.1%，集中度较 2013 年下降 13.7 个百分点（见图 3-4）。

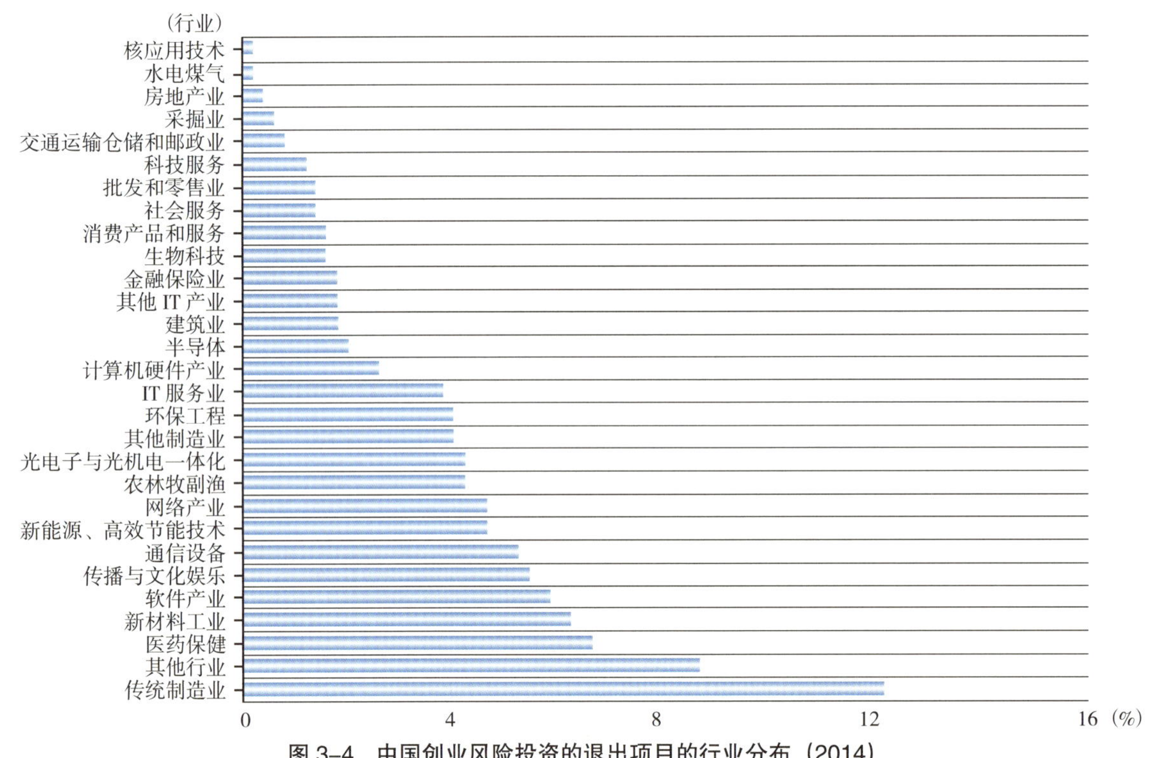

图 3-4 中国创业风险投资的退出项目的行业分布（2014）

从一级行业划分情况来看，2014 年，新能源和环保业、计算机、传统制造业、软件和信息服务业依然是项目退出较为集中的领域。从占比排名来看，传统制造业、医药生物业的退出占比出现大幅下滑，传播与文化娱乐产业及其他行业占比有较大提升，其他行业与上年基本持平（见表 3-4、图 3-5）。

① 有效样本数为 493 份。

表 3-4 中国创业风险投资的退出项目的行业分布（2005~2014）①　单位：%

行业 \ 年份	2005	2006	2007	2008	2009	2010	2011	2012	2013	2014
新能源和环保业②	6.90	15.70	12.90	10.10	12.70	24.50	16.70	22.20	16.20	15.22
计算机、通信设备制造业③	13.80	18.60	8.80	16.00	18.10	14.20	14.40	10.60	14.00	14.20
传统制造业	12.90	6.90	8.10	13.00	12.20	7.90	11.30	14.30	17.50	12.17
软件和信息服务业④	18.10	13.70	32.20	24.50	26.70	15.90	12.90	9.40	11.50	11.56
其他行业	6.90	16.70	14.50	10.60	9.50	11.40	5.00	6.20	3.90	8.72
医药生物业⑤	18.10	15.60	18.60	15.50	9.00	11.00	13.50	11.10	12.50	8.31
传播与文化娱乐	0.00	1.00	0.80	0.50	0.90	1.60	1.90	3.00	2.70	5.48
农林牧渔业	0.00	1.00	0.00	2.40	1.40	4.70	6.00	6.50	3.70	4.26
其他制造业	0.00	0.00	0.00	0.00	0.00	0.00	5.30	6.20	8.20	4.06
金融保险业	0.00	4.90	0.80	2.40	2.70	3.10	2.20	2.20	3.90	1.83
社会服务	0.00	0.00	0.00	0.00	0.00	0.00	0.60	1.60	0.80	1.42
科技服务	0.00	2.90	1.60	3.40	2.70	1.60	0.60	2.20	0.60	1.22

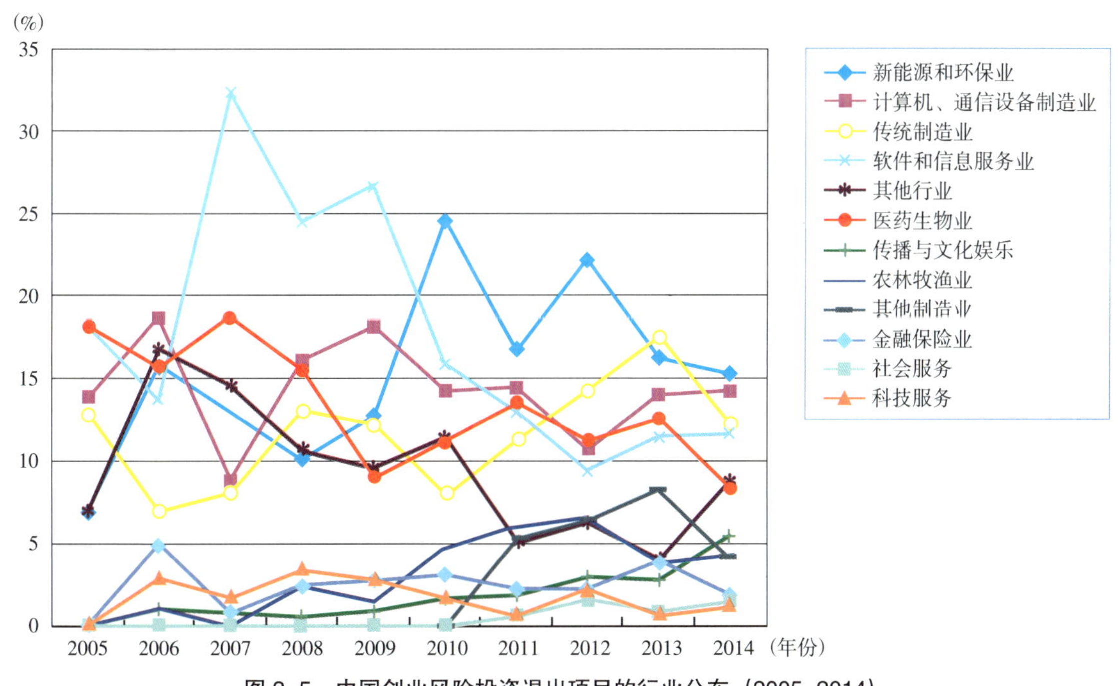

图 3-5 中国创业风险投资退出项目的行业分布（2005~2014）

① 有效样本数为 493 份。
② 包括原有的新材料工业、新能源/高效节能技术、核应用技术、环保工程四个细分的二级行业。
③ 包括原有的通信设备、半导体、计算机硬件产业、光电子与光机电一体化四个细分的二级行业。
④ 包括原有的网络产业、IT 产业、软件产业、其他 IT 产业四个细分的二级行业。
⑤ 包括原有的医药保健、生物科技两个细分的二级行业。

3.4 中国创业风险投资退出项目的地区分布①

2014 年，中国创业风险投资退出项目的地区分布总体上与创业风险投资机构分布情况较为一致，东部地区因创业风险投资发展相对成熟，江苏、浙江、广东、上海等地区在项目退出方面长期处于领先地位，尤其是江苏仍然继续保持退出第一的地位，但退出占比较往年大幅下降，2014 年退出占比仅为 20.4%。

从 2006~2014 年的总体趋势来看，退出项目数占比排名前十的地区历年合计占比依次为 85.2%、79.2%、86.0%、86.3%、85.7%、85.7%、89.0%、83.85%、82.93%，区域集聚效应仍然较为明显（见表 3-5、图 3-6）。

表 3-5 中国创业风险投资退出项目的地区分布前 10 名（2006~2014） 单位：%

年份											
2006 年	地区	广东	江苏	浙江	上海	北京	黑龙江	深圳	陕西	安徽	四川
	比例	16.00	11.70	11.70	9.60	8.50	7.40	6.40	5.30	4.30	4.30
2007 年	地区	江苏	上海	广东	浙江	山东	湖北	安徽	云南	山西	辽宁
	比例	24.20	11.00	9.90	5.50	5.50	5.50	4.40	4.40	4.40	4.40
2008 年	地区	江苏	广东	上海	浙江	山东	安徽	湖南	北京	湖北	四川
	比例	15.90	14.00	13.40	10.80	6.40	6.40	5.70	5.10	4.50	3.80
2009 年	地区	江苏	广东	浙江	北京	陕西	安徽	上海	四川	湖北	天津
	比例	26.40	17.40	10.00	7.50	5.50	5.00	4.00	4.00	3.50	3.00
2010 年	地区	江苏	湖北	广东	浙江	上海	山东	北京	新疆	湖南	天津
	比例	26.60	16.70	12.40	9.00	6.40	3.40	3.00	3.00	2.60	2.60
2011 年	地区	江苏	上海	浙江	广东	天津	北京	河南	山东	湖北	福建
	比例	27.60	11.50	11.20	9.60	8.10	6.50	3.40	2.80	2.80	2.20
2012 年	地区	江苏	浙江	广东	湖北	北京	上海	河北	天津	安徽	湖南
	比例	35.60	9.80	8.40	7.60	7.30	5.40	3.80	3.80	3.80	3.50
2013 年	地区	江苏	浙江	上海	广东	北京	天津	安徽	山东	湖北	重庆
	比例	34.99	10.56	8.07	7.66	5.38	5.18	3.31	3.11	2.90	2.69
2014 年	地区	江苏	浙江	广东	上海	北京	湖北	辽宁	湖南	山东	天津
	比例	20.40	13.53	13.30	10.20	9.76	3.77	3.33	3.10	2.88	2.66

① 有效样本数为 451 份。

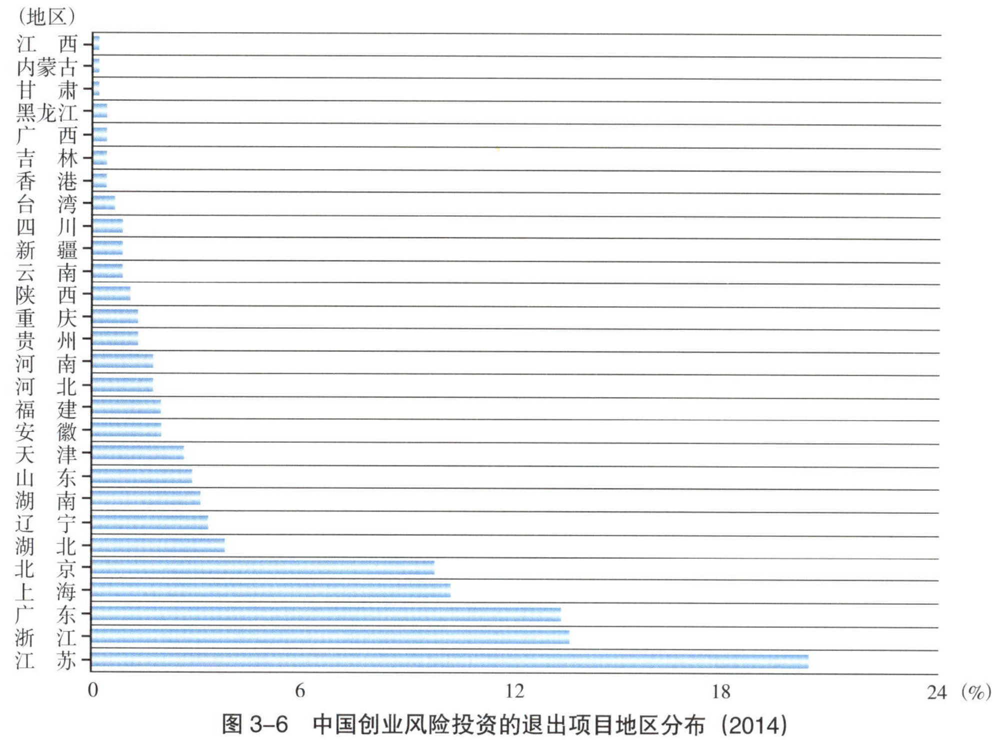

图 3-6　中国创业风险投资的退出项目地区分布（2014）

3.5 中国创业风险投资项目的退出效果

3.5.1　中国创业风险投资退出的总体绩效表现

2014 年，受资本市场利好、货币宽松政策等积极影响，创业风险投资项目退出收益率明显好转，全行业的项目退出收益率达到 123.04%，整个行业投资进一步前移，项目投资时间明显增加，平均投资退出时间达到 6.83 年，整体行业平均收益率达到 23.46%（见表 3-6、图 3-7）。

根据退出项目的投资收益分布的趋势情况显示（见表 3-7、图 3-8）：2014 年，受资本市场 IPO 重启影响，中国创业风险投资退出的项目收益较 2013 年有所提高。亏损项目较 2013 年下降了 10.2 个百分点，占比 56.9%，退出收益率在 0~100%的项目占比均明显高于往年，但收益在 100%以上的项目占比进一步下滑。这在一定程度上表明，中国创业风险投资市场更加趋于理性，盲目扩张的高收益现象减少了。

表 3-6　中国创业风险投资退出的投资收益率（2005~2014）①　　单位：%

年份	2005	2006	2007	2008	2009	2010	2011	2012	2013	2014
年度收益率	58.80	56.62	77.12	240.36	144.89	221.87	193.71	196.35	117.70	123.04
年度平均收益率	45.49	4.66	4.32	32.68	19.33	37.82	45.62	44.01	13.85	23.46

① 有效样本数为 1468 份。

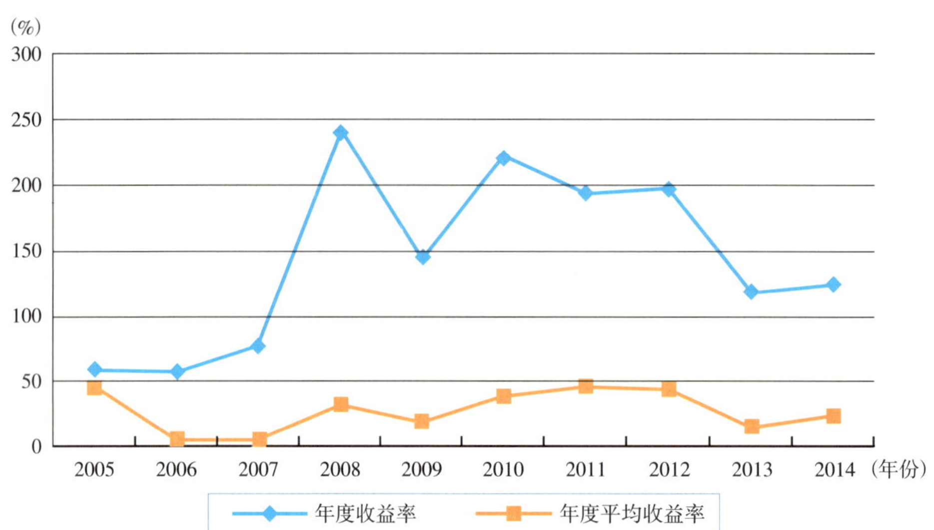

图 3-7 中国创业风险投资退出收益率（2005~2014）

表 3-7 中国创业风险投资退出收益率分布（2005~2014）①

单位：%

退出收益率（%） 年份	亏损	0~15	15~20	20~50	50~100	100 以上
2005	58.1	4.3	5.4	5.4	8.6	18.3
2006	73.8	6.0	0.0	3.6	2.4	14.2
2007	61.2	9.2	5.1	6.1	8.2	10.2
2008	65.1	3.4	1.4	4.1	8.9	17.1
2009	63.0	4.8	3.2	10.6	4.2	14.3
2010	63.2	8.0	1.9	4.7	4.2	17.9
2011	47.9	9.9	3.0	10.6	6.5	22.1
2012	47.0	8.6	3.5	10.5	4.5	25.9
2013	67.1	2.4	2.7	8.7	2.2	16.9
2014	56.9	4.7	4.1	9.4	11.6	13.3

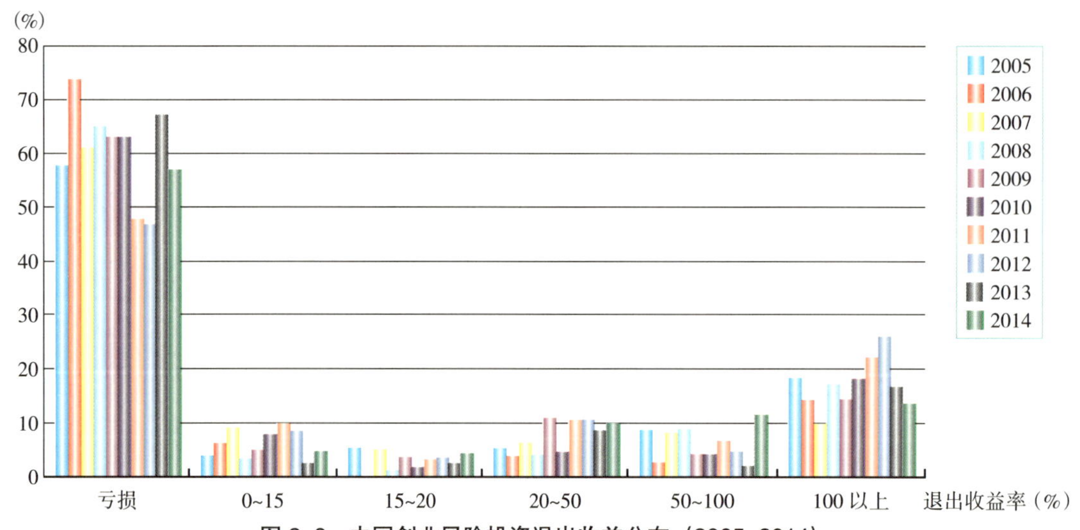

图 3-8 中国创业风险投资退出收益分布（2005~2014）

① 有效样本数为 362 份。

3.5.2 中国创业风险投资不同退出方式的绩效表现

从历年不同退出渠道的绩效表现来看，一般而言，上市退出的收益最为可观，投资收益约为投资总额的 5 倍，最高实现收益高达 9 倍；并购退出收益其次，由于存在并购企业价值被低估的情况，部分年份并购退出未能获得收益；在大部分情况下，股份回购未能实现收益，投资收入存在部分损失；而清算退出则存在较大投资损失。因而，创业风险投资行业的投资收益主要由少数成功上市退出项目来弥补多数项目的损失（见表 3-8、图 3-9）。

表 3-8 不同渠道的创业风险投资退出项目盈亏情况（2005~2014）① 单位：%

年份＼退出渠道	上市	并购	回购	清算	新三板挂牌交易
2005	419.25	-20.56	20.53	-61.40	—
2006	491.45	27.35	-30.81	-53.63	—
2007	436.07	-15.37	-26.80	-42.63	—
2008	916.66	28.35	-41.98	-29.13	—
2009	327.75	4.74	-29.47	-42.66	—
2010	736.68	44.71	-21.19	-24.43	48.85
2011	799.38	41.47	-30.51	-65.37	63.19
2012	486.10	198.29	29.18	-15.34	32.48
2013	448.03	15.27	-34.28	-43.47	89.79
2014	601.66	63.55	-34.43	-34.43	27.23

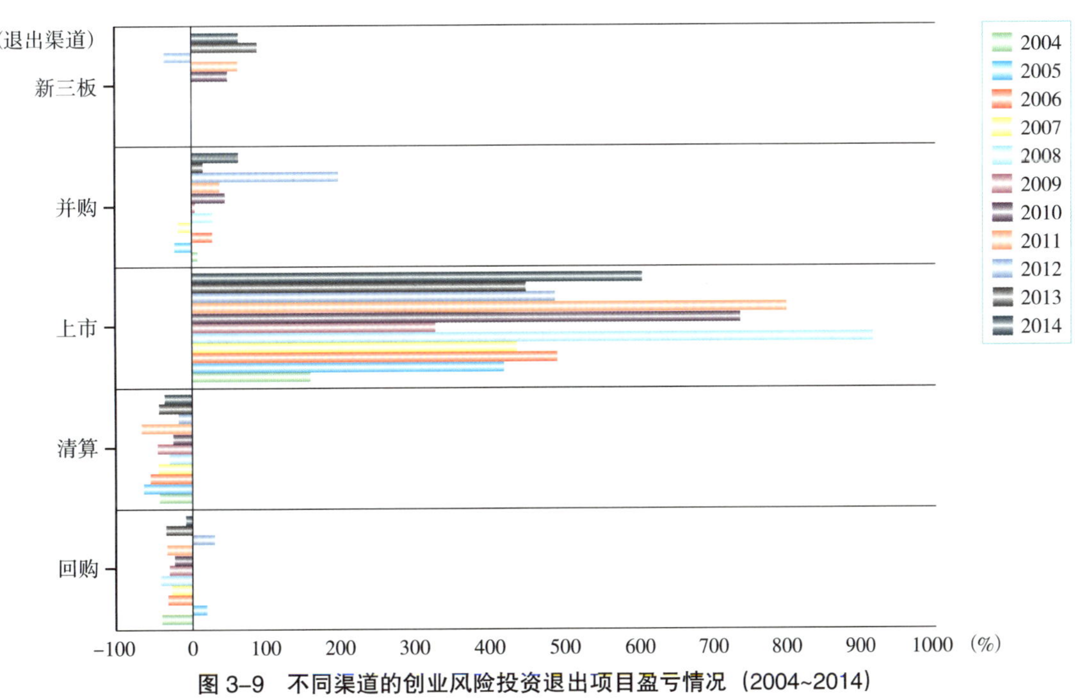

图 3-9 不同渠道的创业风险投资退出项目盈亏情况（2004~2014）

① 有效样本数为 1882 份。

2014 年，受中国资本市场 IPO 重启、股票市场活跃等利好政策影响，上市退出收益较往年大幅提高，达到 601.66%，即平均账目回报 6.01 倍；通过并购退出的项目收益率有较大幅度提高，收益率达 63.55%。此外，新三板市场的快速发展也为部分项目退出提供了良好的通道，实现了 27.23%的收益水平。

3.5.3 中国创业风险投资不同行业退出的绩效表现

一般而言，创业风险投资行业的退出绩效呈现出“成三败七”的特点，往往需要用少数成功的投资项目来弥补多数的损失。但近年来，随着我国创业风险投资行业投资管理能力的逐步提升，项目的总体收益率呈上升趋势。尽管经历了 2013 年的较大下滑，但 2014 年无论是高新技术行业还是传统行业，项目退出的盈利水平均有较大提升。

比较传统行业与高新技术行业的退出绩效可以看出，大部分情况下高新技术行业尽管面临着更高的投资风险，但投资盈利比例明显高于传统行业（见表 3-9、图 3-10、表 3-10、图 3-11）。

表 3-9 高新技术行业创业风险投资退出项目盈亏状况（2006~2014）① 单位：%

盈亏状况 \ 年份	2006	2007	2008	2009	2010	2011	2012	2013	2014
盈利	25	40.58	35.35	37.17	37.3	52.87	55.62	32.12	47.76
亏损	75	59.42	64.65	62.83	62.7	47.13	44.38	67.87	52.24

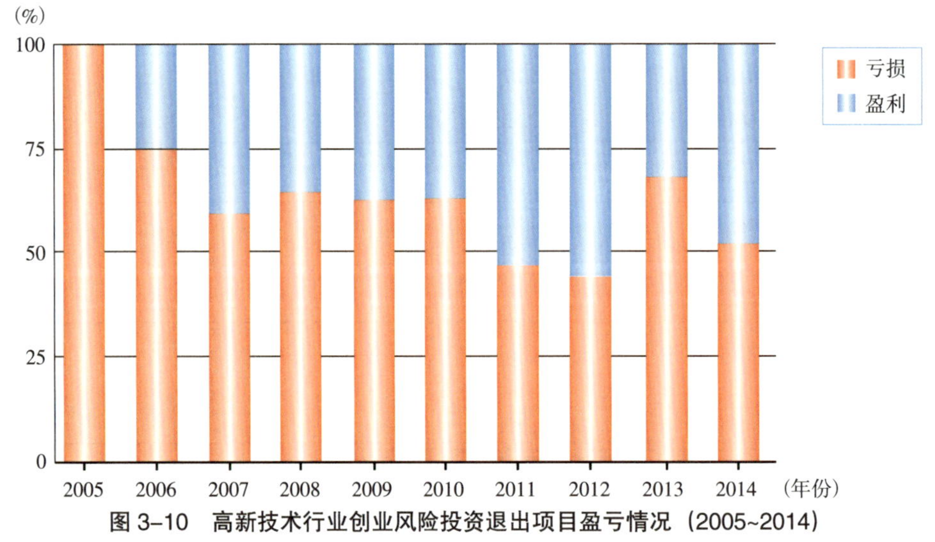

图 3-10 高新技术行业创业风险投资退出项目盈亏情况（2005~2014）

表 3-10 传统行业创业风险投资退出项目盈亏状况（2006~2014）② 单位：%

盈亏状况 \ 年份	2006	2007	2008	2009	2010	2011	2012	2013	2014
盈利	25	20	15	39.29	36.36	48.48	50	35.45	38.56
亏损	75	80	85	60.71	63.64	51.52	50	64.55	61.44

① 有效样本数为 201 份。
② 有效样本数为 153 份。

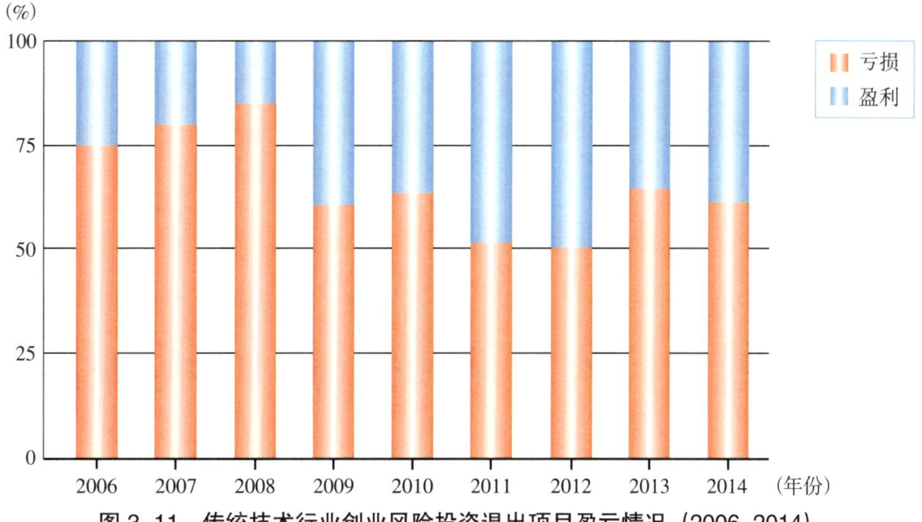

图 3-11　传统技术行业创业风险投资退出项目盈亏情况（2006~2014）

4 中国创业风险投资的绩效

4.1 中国创业风险投资机构的收入

4.1.1 中国创业风险投资机构的收入

2014 年，披露信息的 942 家创业风险投资机构的主营业务总收入达到 144.18 亿元；平均收入为 1678.23 万元，较 2013 年下降 15.55%，与 2012 年持平（见表 4–1）。

表 4–1 中国创业风险投资机构的收入状况（2010~2014）

年 份	总收入（亿元）	披露信息机构数量（家）	平均收入（万元）
2010	173.58	569	3050.58
2011	106.89	581	1839.75
2012	120.97	727	1664.01
2013	172.88	870	1987.16
2014	144.18	942	1678.23

其中，16 家股份有限公司的平均收入最高，达到 3675.00 万元，合伙企业平均收入最低，214 家合伙企业的平均收入仅为 365.89 万元，约为股份有限公司的 1/10；事业单位、有限责任公司的平均收入与全部机构平均收入接近，分别为 1927.27 万元和 1852.88 万元。与 2013 年相比，事业单位机构的平均收入明显增加，而股份有限公司的平均收入则明显下降，可能的原因：一方面，样本量较小，单一机构的数据对样本数据影响较大；另一方面，同一类型机构在不同年份的退出项目数量和收益并不平稳。

此外，政府资助对于机构的平均收入有显著的影响，331 家获得政府资助的机构平均收入达到 2611.28 万元，是未获得政府资金资助机构的 2.75 倍，与 2013 年相比，政府资助对机构平均收入的影响明显增加。

4.1.2 中国不同规模创业风险投资机构的收入特征[①]

2014 年，按机构管理资本规模从低到高，将创业风险投资机构划分为 5 组，统计不同规模创业风险投资机构的平均收入及不同规模机构收入占总收入的比重（见表 4–2）。

表 4–2 中国创业风险投资机构收入的规模分布（2010~2014）

年 份 \ 机构规模（亿元）		≤0.5	0.5~1	1~2	2~5	≥5
2010	平均收入（万元）	1096.4	6361.3	4134.2	14877.4	6578.8
	占总收入比重（%）	3.1	25.1	10.9	40.8	20.1

① 有效样本数为 1009 份。

续表

年份 \ 机构规模（亿元）		≤0.5	0.5~1	1~2	2~5	≥5
2011	平均收入（万元）	694.4	486.7	983.9	2777.6	5577.4
	占总收入比重（%）	8.7	6.4	9.8	28.6	46.4
2012	平均收入（万元）	916.0	593.1	1224.9	1190.6	6794.9
	占总收入比重（%）	10.8	7.9	13.7	14.8	52.8
2013	平均收入（万元）	443.4	945.4	1406.6	3150.7	7896.3
	占总收入比重（%）	4.7	10.1	12.3	31.9	41.1
2014	平均收入（万元）[①]	319.8	1205.3	779.7	1299.7	7383.7
	占总收入比重（%）[②]	4.8	17.5	9.6	16.5	51.5

2014年，中国创业风险投资机构收入分布具有如下特征：

首先，机构平均收入与机构规模正相关。管理资本5000万元以下的机构平均收入最低，为319.8万元，管理资本超过5亿元的机构平均收入最高，达到7383.7万元，是前者二十多倍；大型机构收入占比保持较高水平，管理资本5亿元以上的机构收入占总收入的比重超过50%，而管理资本5000万元以下的机构收入占比仅为4.8%。

其次，管理资本在5000万元以下的机构平均收入近年来持续下降，从2012年的916.0万元下降到2014年的319.8万元；管理资本5000万~1亿元的机构平均收入近年来稳步增加，从2012年的593.1万元增长到2014年的1205.3万元。

最后，中等规模创业风险投资机构的平均收入和收入占比波动较大，其中管理资本2亿~5亿元的机构平均收入波动最大，2012年平均收入是上年的1/2，2013年平均收入则是上年的2倍多，2014年又再次出现大幅下降。

4.1.3 中国创业风险投资机构的收入来源结构

2014年，510家[③]创业风险投资机构披露主营业务收入，其中股权转让增值收入占全部收入的57.0%，分红收入占9.0%，管理费、咨询费收入占11.0%，其他收入占23.0%（见图4-1）。与2013年相比，股权转让增值收入占比明显提高，增加了6个百分点，分红收入和管理费、咨询费收入占比分别下降了9.6个百分点和5个百分点，其他收入占比增长了8.6个百分点。

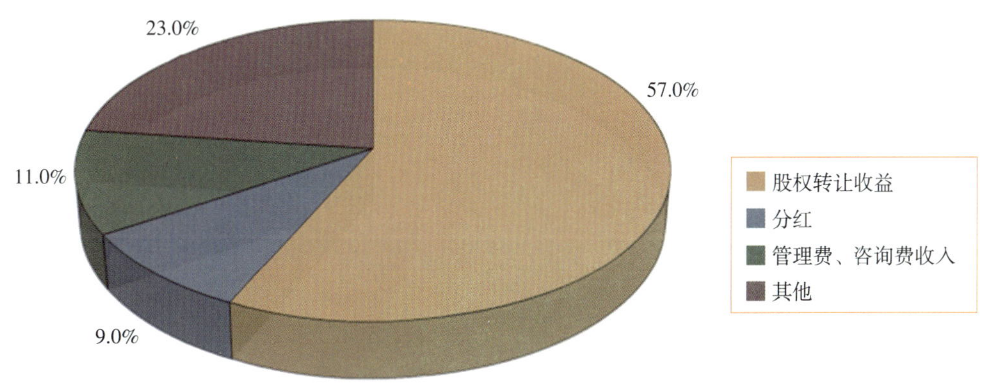

图4-1 中国创业风险投资机构收入来源比例（2014）

① 有效样本数为857份。
② 有效样本数为857份。
③ 仅包括收入大于0且各项收入占比之和等于100%的机构。

近年来，股权转让增值和分红收入对创业风险投资机构收入的贡献逐年增加，在一定程度上说明，随着资本市场的建设和完善、退出渠道的不断拓宽，创业风险投资机构从长期的投资中获得的回报增长。2014 年，股权转让增值收入比重反弹，与 2013 年的情况形成了鲜明的对比，侧面反映了退出渠道对创业风险投资机构收入结构的影响。IPO 重启、新三板加速扩容以及区域股权交易市场的发展，为创业风险投资机构退出拓宽渠道，因而股权转让增值收入占比明显提高，分红收入占比相对下降。

4.1.4 中国创业风险投资机构当年收入的最大来源①

2014 年统计调查显示，中国创业风险投资机构最大收入来源分布与往年相比，未发生显著的结构变化。其中，以股权转让为最大收入来源的创业风险投资机构占 26.9%，较上年有所下降，是近年来比重最低的年份；以分红为最大收入来源的创业风险投资机构占 19.1%，上升幅度较大；以管理（顾问）费为最大收入来源的创业风险投资机构比例为 24.1%，为历年最高水平；以咨询服务收入为最大收入来源的创业风险投资机构占比为 6.4%，在连续下降后出现微弱上升；以其他收入为最大收入来源的创业风险投资机构占比为 23.5%，较上年有小幅增长（见图 4-2、表 4-3）。2014 年，创业投资机构的核心主营业务保持在较重要位置，连续三年有一半以上的创业风险投资机构的最大收入来源于股权收益和分红两个主要项目，但是，以股权转让收益为最大收入来源的机构占比下降导致两者占比之和明显降低，为近 5 年来最低。

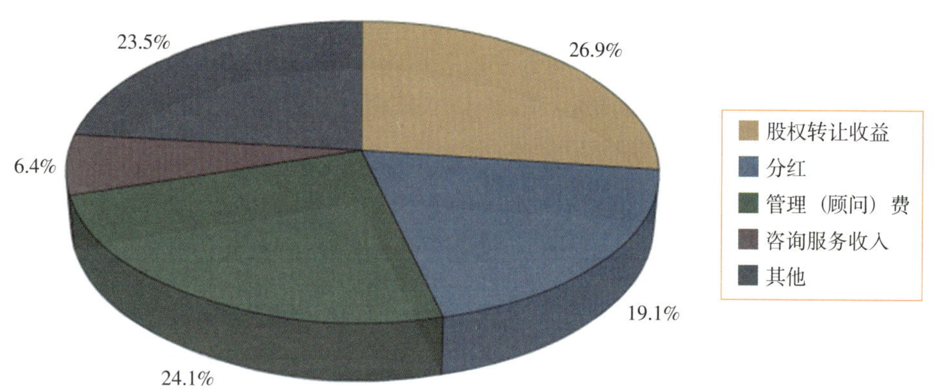

图 4-2 中国创业风险投资机构的最大收入来源（2014）

表 4-3 中国创业风险投资机构的最大收入来源（2010~2014） 单位：%

年份 \ 收入来源	股权转让收益	分红	管理（顾问）费	咨询服务收入	其他
2010	34.4	14.1	21.1	11.4	19.0
2011	36.8	15.5	21.6	8.7	17.3
2012	34.1	16.5	21.6	7.3	20.5
2013	37.1	15.0	21.2	6.2	20.5
2014	26.9	19.1	24.1	6.4	23.5

近年来，中国创业风险投资机构的收入来源已经趋于稳定，越来越多的机构通过创业风险投资的核心业务，即股权收益和分红收益获得其最大的营收，从侧面反映了行业发展已经日趋成熟。

① 有效样本数为 1138 份。

4.2 中国创业风险投资项目的收益情况

4.2.1 中国创业风险投资项目的主营业务收入①

据统计，2014 年中国创业风险投资机构当年新增投资项目 2459 个，披露主营业务收入情况的项目 1716 个。在"大众创业、万众创新"的背景下，中国创业风险投资机构投资项目选择发生较大变化（见表 4-4、图 4-3）：

表 4-4　创业风险投资项目的主营业务收入分布（2010~2014）　单位：%

年份 \ 收入（万元）	<100	100~500	500~1000	1000~3000	3000~5000	>5000
2010	29.1	6.8	5.0	12.3	4.8	41.9
2011	14.9	6.7	4.7	10.0	5.4	58.3
2012	20.3	7.7	5.5	9.8	6.7	49.9
2013	29.9	10.7	4.6	10.4	5.9	38.6
2014	54.0	5.8	3.4	8.7	4.8	23.3

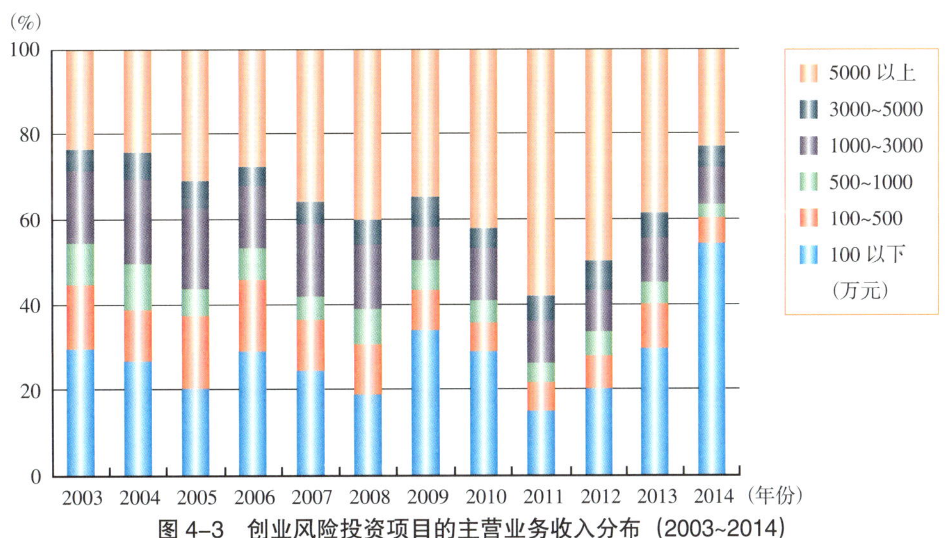

图 4-3　创业风险投资项目的主营业务收入分布（2003~2014）

（1）2014 年，中国创业风险投资项目的主营业务收入的"W 形"分布并未发生改变，其中，主营业务收入 100 万元以下和 5000 万元以上的项目占比较高，其他组别的项目分布相对平均。

（2）2014 年，主营业务收入 100 万元以下项目占比延续了近年来的上升趋势，且首次高于主营业务收入 5000 万元以上项目；其他所有组别的项目占比均出现不同程度的下降，其中主营业务收入 5000 万元以上的项目下降了 15.3 个百分点，但仍然处于第二；主营业务收入 500 万~1000 万元和 3000 万~5000 万元的项目比重始终是最低的两类，2014 年两类项目合计占比仅为 8.2%，是历年来最低水平。

① 有效样本数为 1716 份。

4.2.2 中国创业风险投资项目的利润[①]

2014 年，中国创业风险投资项目的利润分布总体依然呈现为 U 形，利润超过 1000 万元和亏损的项目占比较高，分别为 18.6%和 61.4%，其他项目占比均未超过 10%（见表 4-5、图 4-4）。

表 4-5 中国创业风险投资项目的利润分布（2010~2014） 单位：%

年份 \ 利润（万元）	亏损	0~100	100~300	300~500	500~1000	>1000
2010	31.2	10.4	7.4	5.1	7.4	38.6
2011	19.6	8.1	7.3	4.2	7.6	53.2
2012	27.2	8.9	8.1	5.8	7.5	42.6
2013	39.1	9.7	8.0	5.7	5.5	32.1
2014	61.4	7.8	4.7	3.1	4.4	18.6

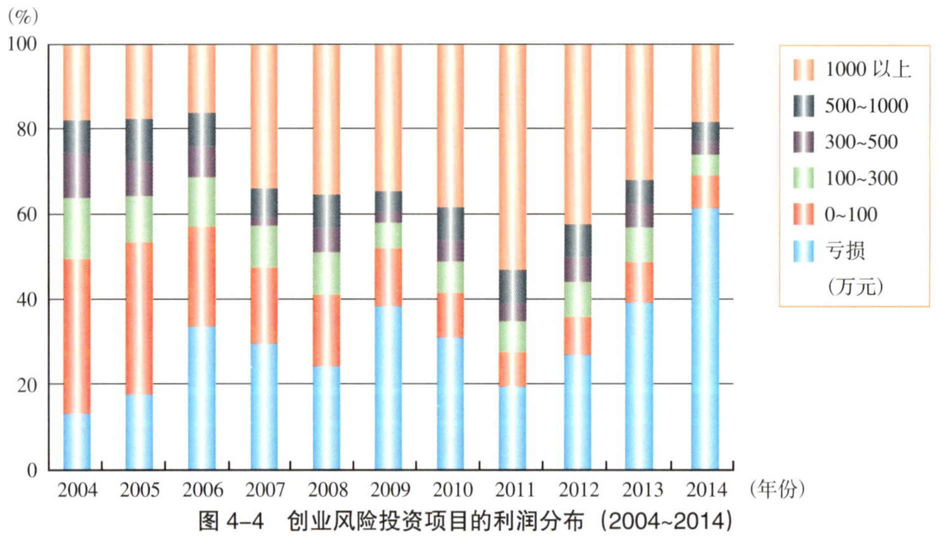

图 4-4 创业风险投资项目的利润分布（2004~2014）

其中，非盈利项目比重连续三年大幅提高，与 2011 年相比增长了 40 个百分点，其中 2014 年贡献了一半以上的增幅；非盈利项目数量的大幅增加导致其他所有类别项目比重均出现不同程度的下降，其中利润不超过 100 万元的项目比重连续两年提高后再次下降，2014 年达到 7.8%；利润在 100 万~300 万元、300 万~500 万元和 500 万~1000 万元的项目比重也均出现了不同程度的下降；利润超过 1000 万元的项目比重则大幅下降了 13.5 个百分点，回归到 10 年前的水平。

2013 年以来，我国创业氛围日趋热烈，各类孵化机构大量涌现，为创业者和创业风险投资机构提供了对接的平台，而资金的大量增加使得非盈利项目获得融资的可能性提高。此外，非盈利项目比重提高也与中国创业风险投资机构的投资行为日趋成熟有关，机构从追逐短期盈利向追逐长期成长转变，因此在项目选择方面，也会提高对非盈利项目的宽容度。

4.2.3 中国创业风险投资项目主营业务收入与利润的关系

2014 年，中国创业风险投资机构投资项目[②]的平均利润率延续了 2013 年的下降趋势。其中，主营业务收入超过 5000 万元的项目规模巨大，且平均利润率下降明显，因此拖累整体利润率下降。主营业务收入 1000 万元以下的项目的平均利润率也出现了明显下降，所有组别平均利润率均小于 0。

① 有效样本数为 1687 份。
② 有效样本数为 891 份。

2014 年，中国创业风险投资机构投资项目的平均利润率随着项目规模的提高而提高，主营业务收入 100 万元以下的项目平均利润率接近-700%，主营业务收入上升到 3000 万~5000 万元时，平均利润率达到 13.08%，但是当项目规模超过 5000 万元时，项目平均利润率反而出现下滑（见图 4-5）。

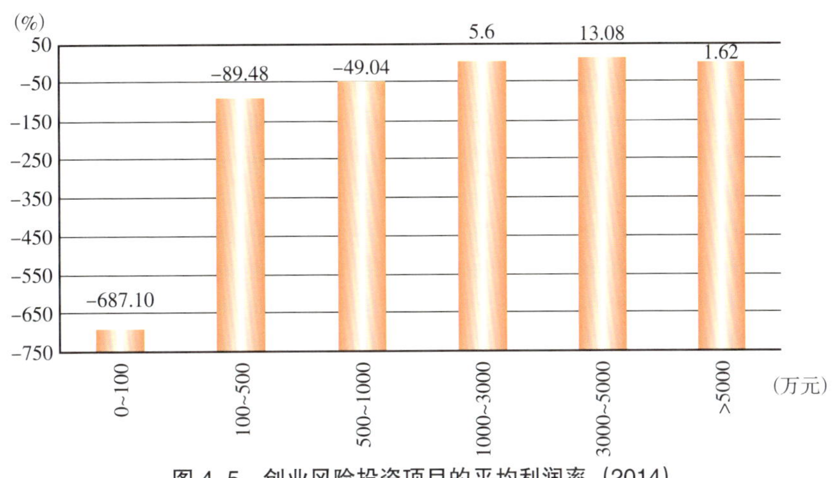

图 4-5 创业风险投资项目的平均利润率（2014）

2010~2014 年，不同主营业务收入规模的创业风险投资项目的平均主营业务收入和平均利润关系具有如下特点（见表 4-6）：

表 4-6 不同主营业务收入的创业风险投资项目的平均主营业务收入和平均利润（2010~2014） 单位：万元

主营业务收入（万元）		<100	100~500	500~1000	1000~3000	3000~5000	>5000
2010 年	平均销售收入	11	249	751	1884	4200	51994
	平均利润	-39	-62	108	342	1109	7060
2011 年	平均主营业务收入	13	281	759	1971	3951	62777
	平均利润	-123	-15	114	270	593	5739
2012 年	平均主营业务收入	13	281	729	2170	4030	37292
	平均利润	58	-135	-52	316	497	4192
2013 年	平均主营业务收入	13	253	776	1915	4040	64047
	平均利润	-477	-99	-48	130	121	5266
2014 年	平均主营业务收入①	33.02	290	725	1871	4028	775370
	平均利润②	-226.89	-259.80	-355.68	105	527	12579

（1）规模较小的项目出现亏损的可能性更大，其中，主营业务收入在 1000 万元以下的项目平均利润均为负，且项目规模越小，亏损越严重；主营业务收入 100 万~500 万元的项目连续五年为负平均利润，而主营业务收入在 500 万~1000 万元的项目平均利润连续三年为负，1000 万元以上的项目平均利润继续保持正值。

（2）主营业务收入规模中等的项目与宏观经济环境的关系最密切，金融危机对这部分项目的影响最大，这部分项目的平均利润总体上均随着金融危机爆发而出现下滑，在全球经济逐步复苏过程中有所提升，但近两年中国经济疲软又导致了这部分项目平均利润再次出现连续下滑。2014 年，主营业务收入 1000 万~3000 万元的项目平均利

① 有效样本数为 892 份。
② 有效样本数为 892 份。

润继续下降，从上年的 130 万元下降到 105 万元。

（3）2014 年，主营业务收入在 3000 万元以上的项目平均利润有所上升，特别是主营业务收入 3000 万~5000 万元的项目平均利润止跌回升，从上年的 121 万元增长到 527 万元。

（4）主营业务收入 5000 万元以上的项目盈利能力相对较强，平均利润连续两年上升，从 2012 年的 4192 万元上升到 2014 年的 12579 万元，其中主营业务收入 1 亿元以上的项目平均利润达 1.8 亿元。

4.3 中国创业风险投资项目的总体运行与趋势

4.3.1 中国创业风险投资项目总体运行情况

截至 2014 年底，中国创业风险投资机构[①] 累计投资项目达到 14118 项，其中，69.7%继续运行；已上市和准备上市的项目合计占比 16.9%；原股东（创业者）回购和管理层收购项目合计占比 7.3%；被其他机构收购项目比重为 4.7%；清算的项目比重为 1.4%（见图 4–6）。

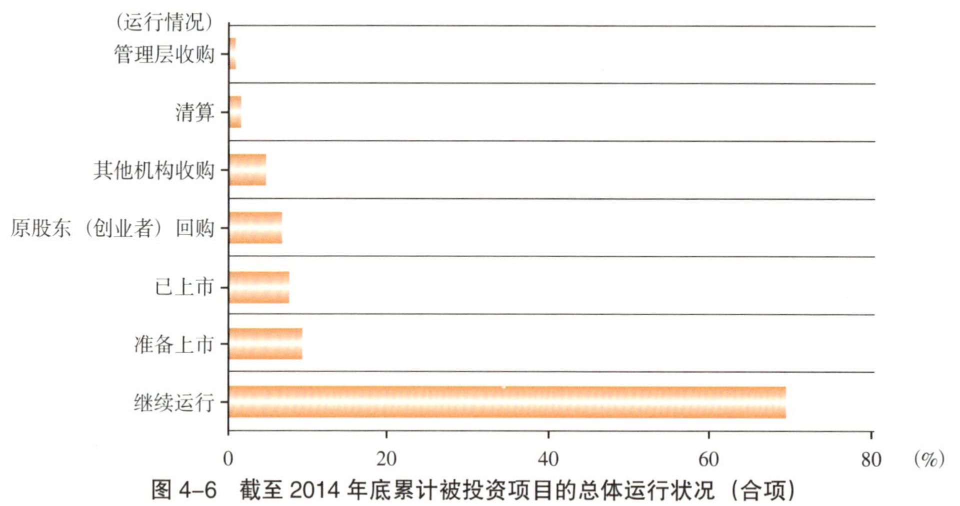

图 4–6 截至 2014 年底累计被投资项目的总体运行状况（合项）

4.3.2 中国创业风险投资项目总体运行趋势

2014 年，中国创业风险投资机构累计投资项目的运行趋势表现出如下特征（见表 4–7、图 4–7）：

（1）受新增投资项目数增加影响，继续运行项目比重有所提高，较 2013 年提高了近 4 个百分点，是各类运行状况中上升幅度最大的；准备上市项目占比连续三年下降，其中准备境内上市项目占比下降到 9.08%，准备境外上市的项目占比下降到 0.24%。

（2）国内外资本市场的持续回暖促进了成功上市比例的提高，其中境内上市（含全国中小企业股份转让系统挂牌）项目占比 5.99%，较 2013 年有微弱提高，境外上市项目占比则增幅明显，从 0.88%提高到 1.62%。

（3）五种不同类型的收购占比增减不一，管理层收购和原股东（创业者）回购均出现约 2 个百分点的下降，特别是管理层收购下降到不足 1%，出现近五年来的最低水平；近两年 A 股的回暖支持了境内上市公司收购，因此境内上市公司收购占比增幅明显，达到近年来的最高点。

（4）被清算的项目占比再次出现下降，甚至低于 2012 年的水平。

① 有效样本数为 1041 份。

表 4-7 截至 2014 年底累计被投资项目的总体运行状况（2010~2014） 单位：%

被投资项目运行情况 / 年份	已上市		准备上市		被收购			原股东（创业者）回购	管理层收购	继续运行	清算
	境内	境外	境内	境外	境内上市公司	境内非上市公司或自然人	境外收购				
2010	5.86	1.66	16.39	0.95	0.61	4.05	0.37	10.56	0.94	56.14	2.47
2011	6.74	1.53	15.70	0.43	0.32	3.34	0.22	7.96	1.42	60.62	1.72
2012	6.66	1.37	12.37	0.39	0.32	3.04	0.12	7.19	0.96	66.18	1.38
2013	5.71	0.88	10.19	0.38	0.55	3.20	0.11	8.66	2.73	65.93	1.66
2014	5.99	1.62	9.08	0.24	1.64	2.82	0.28	6.60	0.67	69.70	1.36

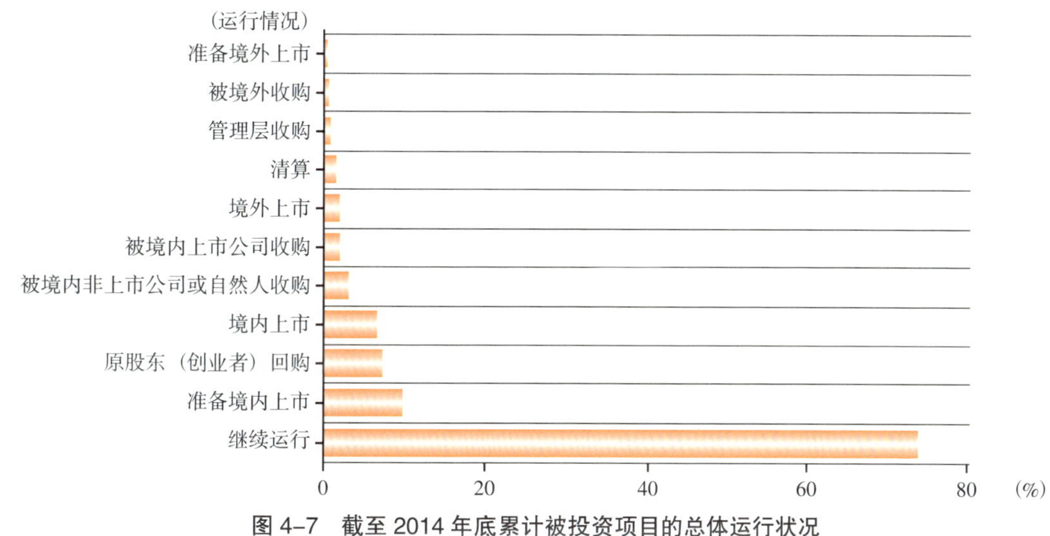

图 4-7 截至 2014 年底累计被投资项目的总体运行状况

2014 年，125 家公司在 A 股首发融资，1193 家公司在新三板挂牌，这为创业风险投资机构通过上市方式退出提供了近年来最好的机遇，大量准备上市的项目顺利挂牌，境内外上市项目占比与上年准备境内外上市项目占比之间的差距从 2011 年的 9 个百分点缩小为 2014 年的 3 个百分点。

4.4 中国创业风险投资机构的总体运行情况评价

4.4.1 中国创业风险投资机构对自身发展状况的评价[①]

2014 年，1156 家创业风险投资机构对自身发展情况进行了评价，总体上持乐观评价的机构比重明显提高。

调查显示，2014 年有超过一半的创业风险投资机构认为自身发展较为乐观，且持乐观评价的机构分布较上年向左偏移，说明整体上行业的乐观情绪有所提升；其中包括 5.10%认为自身发展状况非常好，16.70%认为自身发展状况好，35.64%认为自身发展状况较好，合计达到 57.44%，实现连续两年增长（见表 4-8、图 4-8）。

① 有效样本数为 1156 份。

表 4-8 创业风险投资机构对自身发展状况的评价（2013~2014） 单位：%

年份＼评价	非常好	好	较好	一般	较差	差	非常差
2013	3.31	11.79	36.06	42.30	3.90	2.14	0.49
2014	5.10	16.70	35.64	38.58	3.03	0.52	0.43

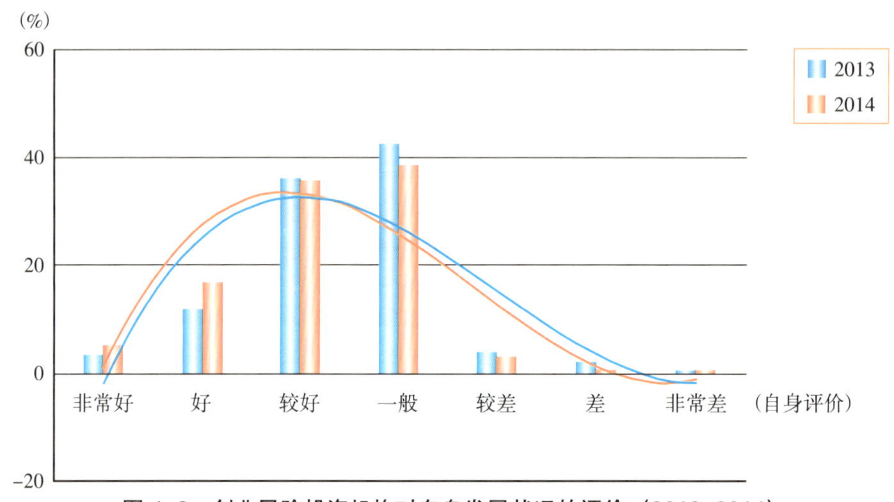

图 4-8 创业风险投资机构对自身发展状况的评价（2013~2014）

国内外资本市场的持续回暖及对创业创新的扶持有效激励了创业风险投资机构。2014 年，对自身发展状况评价悲观的机构占比不到 4%，其中认为非常差的机构仅为 0.43%，较 2013 年略有下降，而认为差的机构占比则下降了 1.5 个百分点。

4.4.2 中国创业风险投资机构对全行业发展情况的评价①

2014 年，1156 家创业风险投资机构对全行业发展情况给出自己的评价，与 2013 年相比，中国创业风险投资机构对全行业的评价更加积极，对全行业的整体评价分布较上年明显左移，认为全行业整体发展非常好、好以及较好的机构占比达到 54.93%，首次超过半数，各分项占比均大幅提升，其中认为非常好和好的比重提高了一倍以上，认为较好的比重也提高了一半以上；而认为全行业发展非常差、差和较差的机构占比仅为 7.09%，各分项占比均下降了 1/2 以上，其中认为非常差的比重仅为 0.35%（见表 4-9、图 4-9）。

表 4-9 中国创业风险投资机构对全行业的整体评价（2013~2014） 单位：%

年份＼整体评价	非常好	好	较好	一般	较差	差	非常差
2013	1.27	5.45	23.95	48.10	12.56	7.40	1.27
2014	3.37	13.93	37.63	37.98	5.28	1.46	0.35

① 有效样本数为 1156 份。

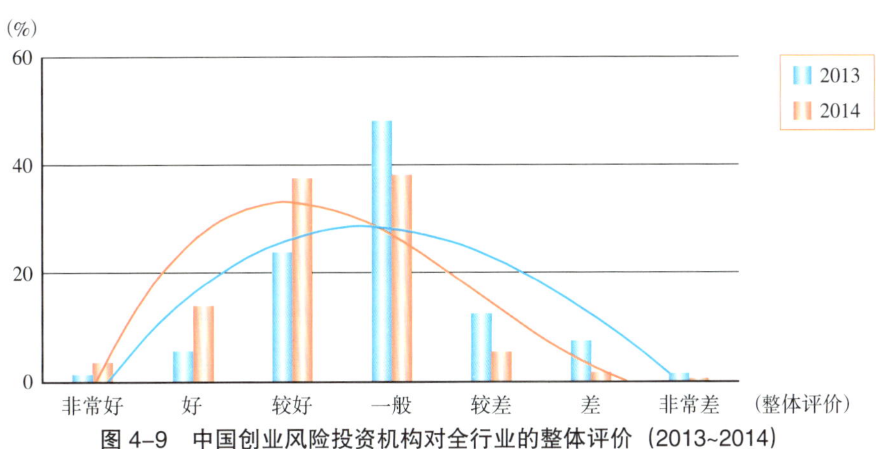

图 4-9　中国创业风险投资机构对全行业的整体评价（2013~2014）

政策体系和市场环境的完善为行业的整体向好奠定了坚实基础，为创业风险投资机构提供了更多的投资标的，而资本市场的快速升温提供了较好的退出机遇。

4.4.3　中国创业风险投资机构对 2015 年投资前景的预测①

对于 2015 年投资前景，1153 家中国创业风险投资机构给出了较为乐观的预测。近七成机构看好未来前景，认为下一年投资前景非常好、好、较好的机构分别达到 5.6%、21.8%和 43.5%，其中认为非常好和好的机构占比均上升一倍左右；对 2015 年前景持悲观情绪的机构占比仅为 1.5%，较上年下降一半以上（见表 4-10、图 4-10）。

表 4-10　创业风险投资机构投资前景的预测（2014~2015）　单位：%

前景预测 年份	非常好	好	较好	一般	较为不好	不好	非常不好
2014	2.0	11.3	43.3	37.9	3.3	1.9	0.3
2015	5.6	21.8	43.5	27.7	1.1	0.2	0.2

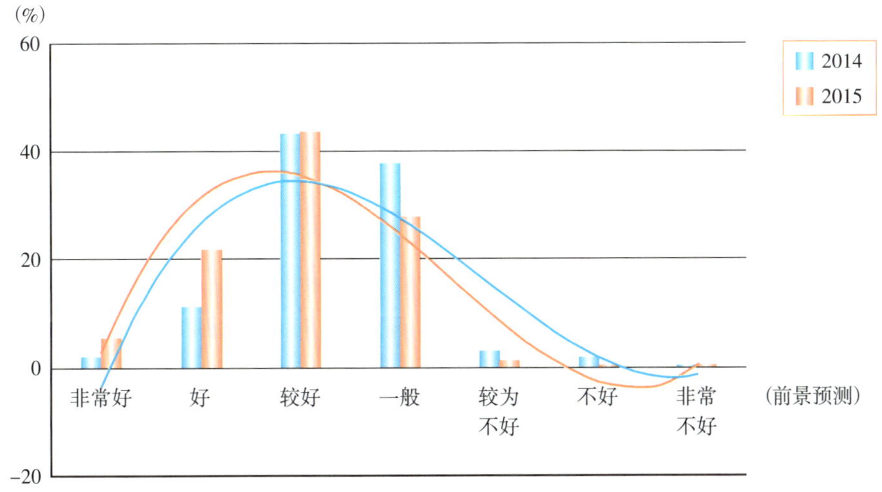

图 4-10　创业风险投资机构投资前景的预测（2014~2015）

① 有效样本数为 1153 份。

5 中国创业风险投资的经营管理

5.1 中国创业风险投资的项目来源

通过对 2014 年中国创业风险投资信息渠道调查发现，[①] 信息获取渠道虽然并不存在实质性改变，但仍有一些新特点（见表 5-1、图 5-1）。

（1）三大主要信息来源之和占比五年来首次出现下降。自 2008 年以来，“政府推荐”、“朋友介绍”和“项目中介机构”长期是创业风险投资机构获取项目信息的三大主要来源，但是 2014 年三者之和占比下降至 59.7%（见图 5-1）。相较于“政府部门推荐”占比的下降幅度而言，通过“朋友介绍”和“项目中介机构”获得的信息占比下降幅度更为显著。

表 5-1　创业风险投资机构获取项目信息来源渠道（2008~2014）　单位：%

信息渠道 / 年份	政府部门推荐	朋友介绍	项目中介机构	股东推荐	项目业主	银行介绍	媒体宣传	其他
2008	25.7	17.7	16.1	13.6	15.5	5.6	2.9	2.8
2009	25.9	19.1	16.1	13.4	13.0	6.6	3.0	2.9
2010	26.2	17.9	18.5	13.2	11.3	7.2	2.9	2.7
2011	25.4	18.7	18.5	13.3	11.7	7.4	2.8	2.1
2012	25.2	19.2	18.6	13.2	11.5	6.9	2.2	3.2
2013	25.5	19.9	19.1	13.2	10.1	6.0	2.6	3.6
2014	24.9	17.7	17.1	14.3	11.0	7.4	3.9	3.6

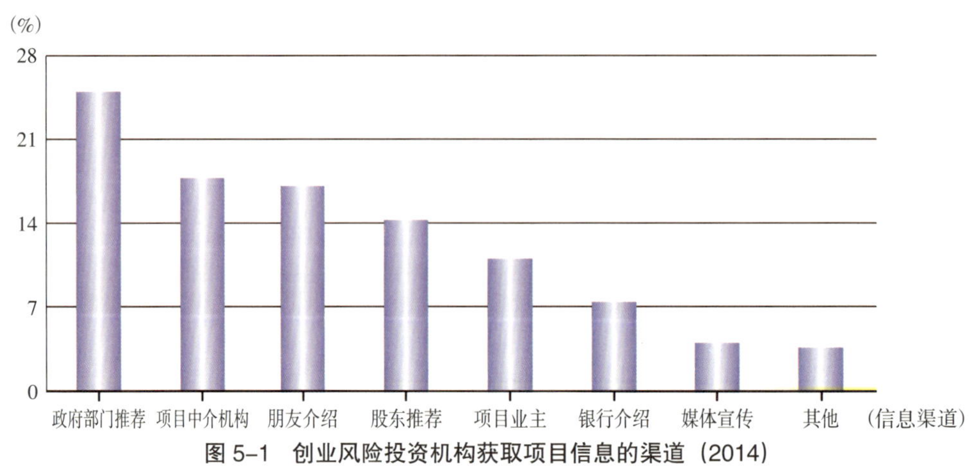

图 5-1　创业风险投资机构获取项目信息的渠道（2014）

① 有效样本数为 1172 份。

（2）信息来源逐渐趋于多样化。2014年的调查数据显示，通过“股东推荐”、“项目业主”、“银行介绍”、“媒体宣传”以及“其他”途径获取信息的占比都有所上升，说明信息来源正在走向多元化。其中，相较于2013年，“银行介绍”占比略有上升，可能是由于各大银行纷纷推出专门针对消费企业的计划。

5.2 中国创业风险投资的决策要素

对2014年影响创业风险投资机构进行投资决策的因素进行调查，结果显示[①]（见图5-2）：“市场前景”、“管理团队”延续了2013年的调查结果，是创业风险投资机构进行投资决策的两个最主要因素，比重分别为24.3%和21.4%，在被调查的八个因素中累计占比45.7%。这说明被投资项目的市场前景以及投资项目所在的管理团队一直是创业风险投资机构最看重的两个决策要素。

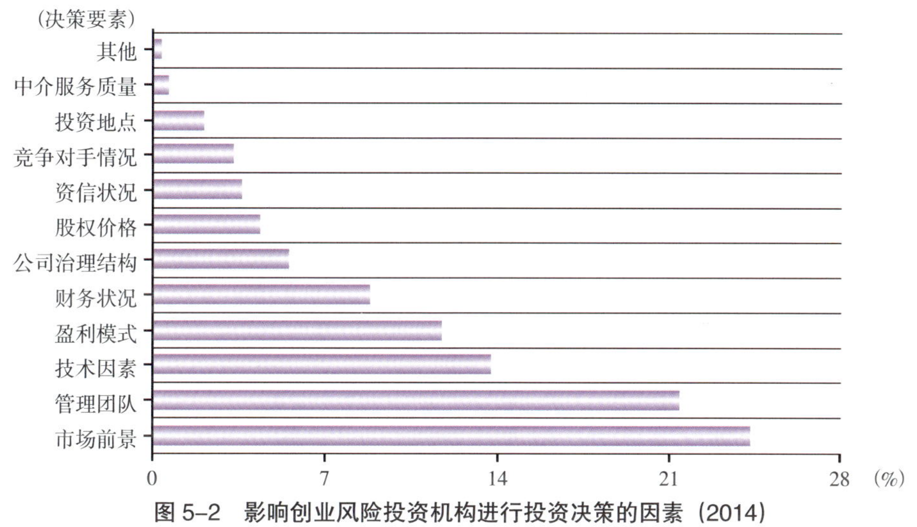

图5-2 影响创业风险投资机构进行投资决策的因素（2014）

与2013年相比，2014年的“技术因素”、“盈利模式”和“财务状况”并没有发生排序变化。其中，“技术因素”所占比重较2013年略有上升，达到13.7%；“盈利模式”的要素影响力继续下降，占比11.7%；“财务状况”占比由2013年的9.9%下降至8.8%。

与2013年相比，“公司治理结构”对于创业风险投资机构的影响要明显高于“股权价格”的影响，比例分别是5.6%和4.4%。其中，“公司治理结构”占比要明显高于2013年的4.5%。这说明创业风险投资机构在进行投资决策时，更加重视公司的内部控制、管理团队等内部原因。

另外，“竞争对手”占比较2013年略有上升，达到3.3%，而“投资地点”对创业风险投资机构的决策作用并无变化，依然保持在2.1%。“中介服务质量”和“其他”分别占比0.7%和0.4%，较2013年略有上升。

① 有效样本数为1173份。

5.3 中国创业风险投资对被投资项目的监管方式

调查显示①：2014 年创业风险投资机构对被投资项目的监管方式并没有出现明显变化（见图 5-3），“提供管理咨询”、“董事会席位”和“财务咨询”依然是最主要的三种监管方式，合计占比达到 88.8%。其中，“提供管理咨询”仍然是创业风险投资机构监管投资项目的最主要方式，占比为 34.5%，较 2013 年的 33.2%略有提高；通过“董事会席位”和“财务咨询”对被投资企业进行监管的监管方式占比与 2013 年基本一致，依然位于监管方式中的第二、第三位；“只限监管”略有下降，占比从 2013 年的 10.1%下降至 2014 年的 8.3%。相比较而言，创业风险投资机构直接进入被投资企业内部进行直接监管的方式正在逐渐弱化，更倾向于采用间接监管的方式。

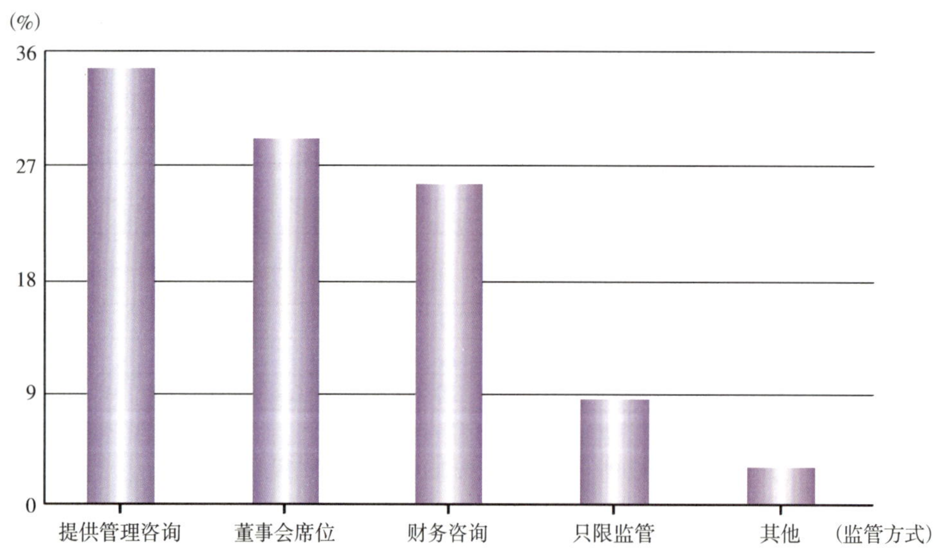

图 5-3 创业风险投资机构对被投资企业的监管方式（2014）

2014 年，创业风险投资机构依旧以“一般参股”为重点方式②（见表 5-2、图 5-4），与 2013 年相比，2014 年创业风险投资机构股权参与程度在“绝对控股”和“相对控股”两方面的变化较为明显。其中，“绝对控股权”从 2013 年的 5.20%下降至 2014 年的 3.36%，是近三年首次出现下降；“相对控股权”相比 2013 年略有上升，达到 12.30%。这说明我国的创业风险投资机构越来越倾向于成为战略投资人。

表 5-2 创业风险投资机构股权参与程度（2008~2014） 单位：%

股权参与程度 / 年份	绝对控股	相对控股	一般参股
2008	3.90	15.70	80.00
2009	7.70	16.10	76.30
2010	3.70	12.10	84.20

① 有效样本数为 1170 份。
② 有效样本数为 1902 份。

续表

年份 \ 股权参与程度	绝对控股	相对控股	一般参股
2011	4.90	8.60	86.50
2012	4.37	11.02	84.61
2013	5.20	10.16	84.64
2014	3.36	12.30	84.33

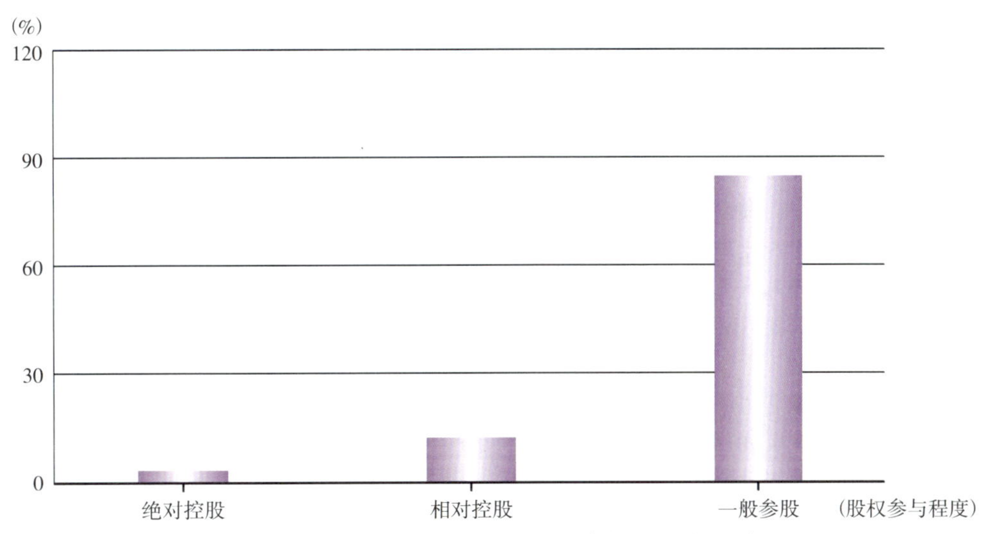

图 5-4 创业风险投资机构的股权参与程度（2014）

5.4 与创业风险投资经营管理有关的人力资源因素

通过对 2014 年从事创业风险投资人员的基本素质进行调查发现[①]（见图 5-5）："资本运作能力"与"判断力和洞察力"是一名合格的创业风险投资人员最应该具备的两个素质。与 2013 年相比没有出现明显变化，总体排名仍然是"资本运作能力"、"判断力和洞察力"、"商务谈判能力"、"财务管理能力"、"人际关系网络和协调能力"、"技术背景"以及"其他"。

具体而言，"资本运作能力"、"判断力和洞察力"以及专业人员的"技术背景"占比都较 2013 年有所上升，分别从 20.2%、18.3% 和 11.6% 上升至 22.7%、18.8% 和 13.2%。

另外，"商务谈判能力"、"财务管理能力"与"人际关系网络和协调能力"都比 2013 年有明显下降，分别从 16.5%、16.1%和 15.2%下降到 15.5%、15.3%和 13.8%。

综上所述，一名合格的创业风险投资人员既应该注重提升自身的技术能力，同时也应该提升对资本运作和对项目研判的能力，并且也应该具有对国家宏观政策等问题的敏感性。

① 有效样本数为 1169 份。

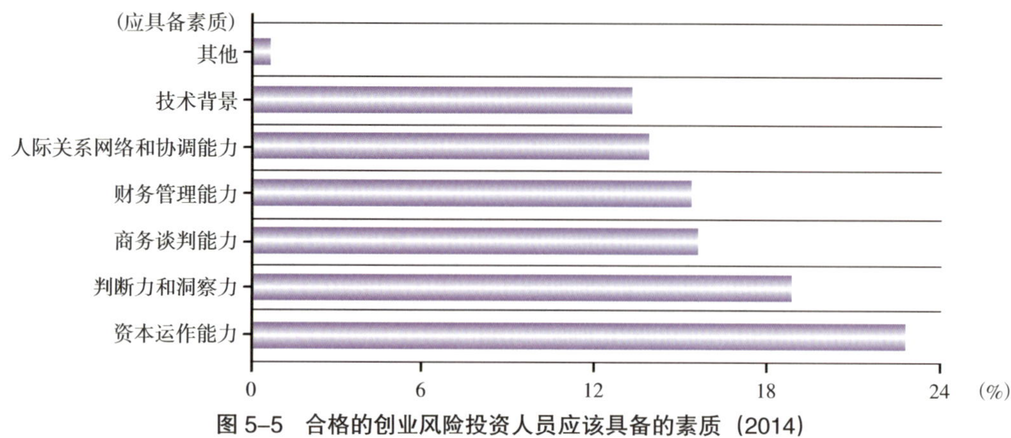

图 5-5 合格的创业风险投资人员应该具备的素质（2014）

图 5-6 给出 2014 年创业风险投资人员相对缺乏的专业知识的统计情况①："技术评估"和"资本运作"依然是创业风险投资人员最缺乏的两个专业知识。但是，相较于 2013 年，"技术评估"所占比重略有下降，从 18.4%下降至 17.9%，而缺乏"资本运作"能力所占比重则较上年有所上升。

此外，创业风险投资人员缺乏"企业管理"能力超过了"项目识别"能力，所占比重从 2013 年的 15.0%上升至 2014 年的 15.3%。与此同时，缺乏"项目识别"的能力所占比重下降了 1 个百分点，从 2013 年的 15.1%下降至 2014 年的 14.1%。

"技术背景"、"法律知识"、"财务管理能力"和"商务谈判能力"的排名与 2013 年相同。其中"技术背景"和"法律知识"所占比重均有所下降，从 2013 年的 12.8%和 9.2%下降至 2014 年的 12.2%和 8.8%；"财务管理能力"与 2013 年持平；而"商务谈判能力"与 2013 年相比略有上升，达到 6.5%。

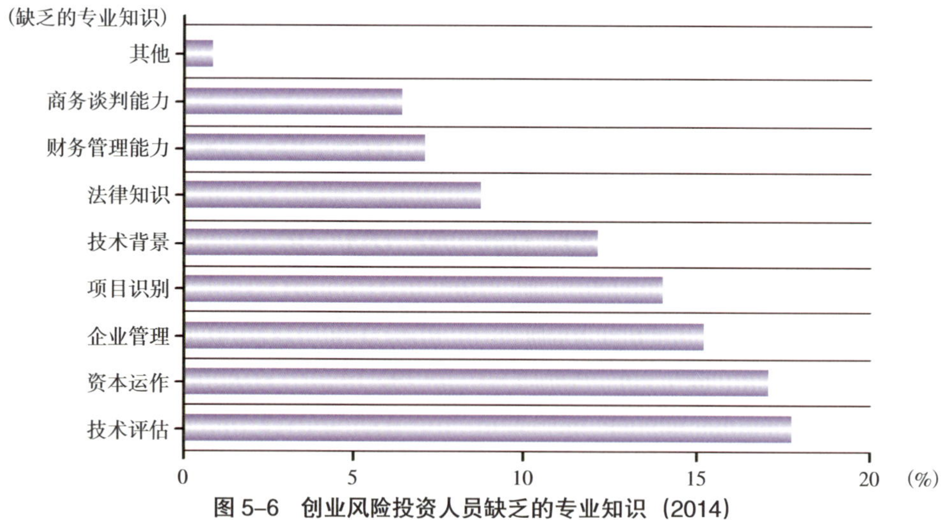

图 5-6 创业风险投资人员缺乏的专业知识（2014）

① 有效样本数为 1163 份。

5.5 投资效果不理想的主要原因

我国创业风险投资机构投资效果不理想的主要原因依然集中在“退出渠道不畅”、“政策环境变化”、“市场竞争”、“内部管理水平有限”、“后续融资不力”、“技术不成熟”、“其他”以及“缺乏诚信”[①]（见图 5-7）。与 2013 年相比，出现了一些比较明显的变化：

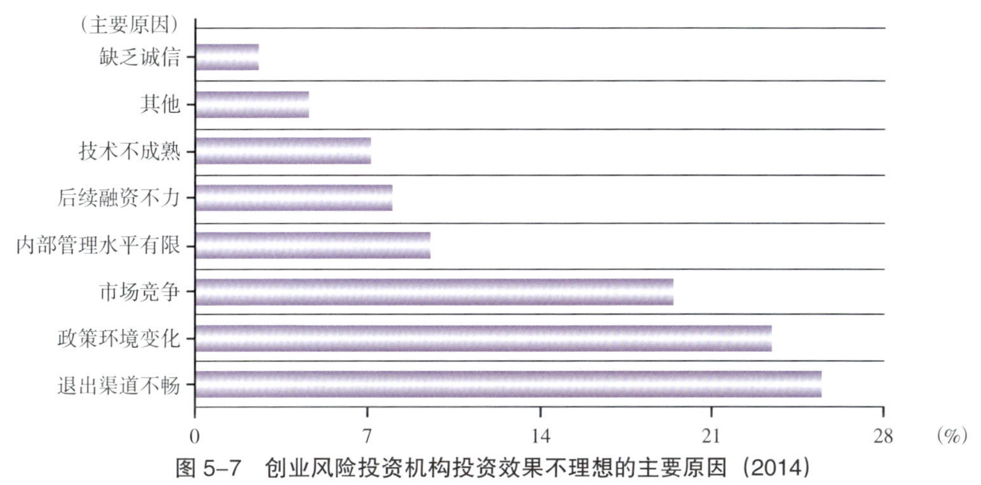

图 5-7　创业风险投资机构投资效果不理想的主要原因（2014）

（1）“政策环境变化”首次不再作为导致创业风险投资效果不理想的主要原因。自 2011 年起，“政策环境变化”一直是导致创业风险投资效果不理想的最主要原因，且所占比重呈连年上升趋势，从 2011 年的 17.4%、2012 年的 18.9%骤升至 2013 年的 26.7%。2014 年，“政策环境变化”下跌至 23.4%。这说明了我国对创业风险投资业的体制改革和政策制定正在逐渐走向成熟和完善，创业风险投资机构的良好生态环境正在逐渐形成。

（2）“退出渠道不畅”所占比重连续三年上升，2014 年成为导致创业风险投资机构投资效果不理想的第一原因，这主要源于 2013 年底以来的 IPO 市场限制，投资项目难以退出。“内部管理水平”、“技术不成熟”、“后续融资不力”所占比重都较 2013 年有所上升，比重分别由 2013 年的 8.2%、6.8%和 7.0%上升至 9.5%、7.1%和 8.0%。这说明内部管理、技术等因素导致的创业风险投资机构投资效果不理想进一步加剧。

（3）“市场竞争”所占比例连续上升。“市场竞争”作为影响创业风险投资机构投资效果不理想的第三个主要原因，其所占比重自 2012 年以来连续三年上升，比重从 2012 年的 17.4%、2013 年的 17.9%上升至 2014 年的 19.4%，且在政策影响逐渐减弱的环境下，创业风险投资机构的市场竞争愈加激烈，市场对创业风险投资的调节作用日益显现。

（4）“缺乏诚信”所占比重连续下降。自 2011 年以来，我国整体信用环境不断优化，“缺乏诚信”对创业风险投资机构投资效果的影响逐渐减小，由 2011 年的 10%、2012 年的 8.4%下降至 2013 年 3.1%。2014 年该项原因所占比重继续下降了 0.5 个百分点。这说明我国投资行业的诚信状况逐渐改善。

① 有效样本数为 1152 份。

5.6 中国创业风险投资机构的预期持股时间

调查显示[①]（见图 5-8）：2014 年创业风险投资行业发展总体较为平稳，以往对于退出时间的消极态度有所缓解，整体形势较 2012 年和 2013 年均有所好转。其中，预期持股时间 5 年以上和时间在 2~3 年的所占比重较 2013 年稍有上升，分别由 2013 年的 14.9%和 19.4%上升至 17.0%和 21.1%。但是，预期持股时间在 3~5 年的所占比重与 2013 年的 64.1%相比降幅较大，降低了 4.4 个百分点。

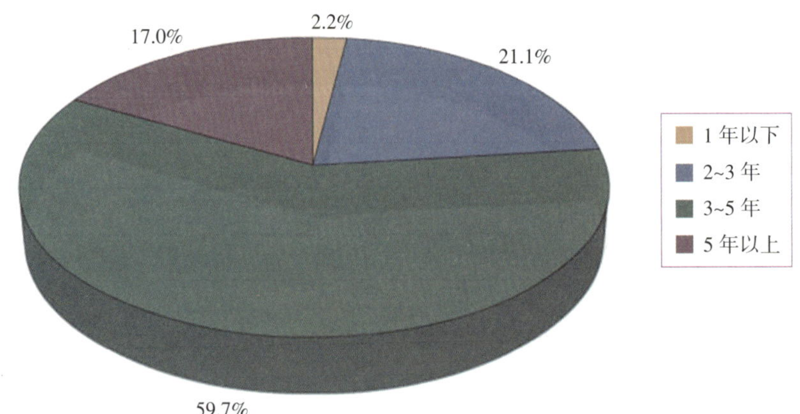

图 5-8 创业风险投资机构对被投资企业的预期持股时间（2014）

5.7 影响中国创业风险投资经营的外部因素

对影响中国创业风险投资经营的外部因素进行调查统计发现[②]（见图 5-9）：2014 年影响创业风险投资发展的主要困难依然集中在“多层次资本市场不完善”、“政策不明朗”以及“缺乏好项目”三大因素。

（1）“多层次资本市场不完善”依然是我国创业风险投资发展的主要障碍。2014 年“多层次资本市场不完善”因素虽然较 2013 年有了小幅下降，但仍然是我国创业风险投资发展的主要障碍，所占比例由 2013 年的 51.4%下降至 47.9%。2014 年我国经济发展逐渐步入新常态，面临经济增速放缓、改革步入“深水区”等不利因素，资本市场依然延续调整状态。与此相对应，多层次资本市场虽然从内部改革和外部支撑等多方面有了进一步改善，但仍然是现阶段我国创业风险投资发展的主要障碍。

（2）“政策不明朗”占比下降。相较于 2013 年，“政策不明朗”所占比例由 19.7%下降至 17.7%。我国在支持创业风险投资发展的政策方面不断优化，不断完善相关政策，为创业风险投资行为和机构发展扫除了部分障碍。但是，由于我国资本市场起步较晚，许多问题仍处于摸索阶段，因此，“政策不明朗”依然是我国创业风险投资发展的第二大障碍。

① 有效样本数为 1151 份。
② 有效样本数为 1150 份。

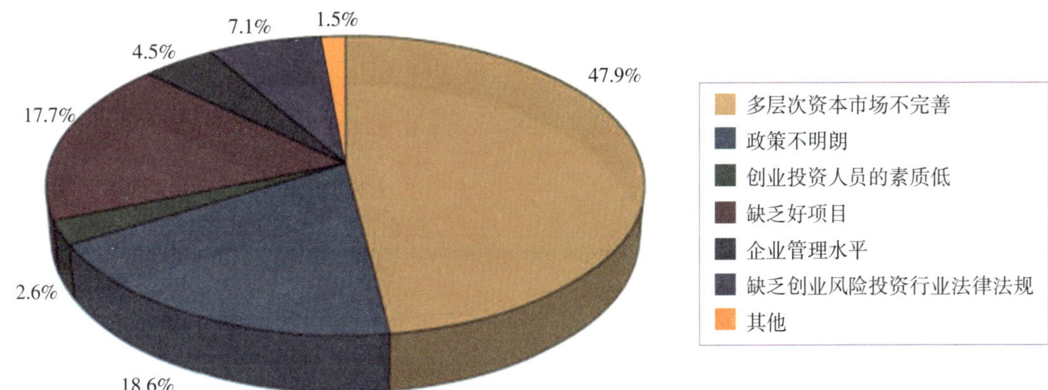

图 5–9 影响创业风险投资发展的主要困难（2014）

（3）“缺乏好项目”所占比重略有上升。与 2013 年相比，“缺乏好项目”所占比重由 17.3%上升至 17.7%。这表明在 2014 年我国宏观经济增速持续放缓的背景下，风险投资机构数量急剧攀升，加剧了行业内的竞争态势，缺乏优质的投资项目。

与 2013 年相比，“缺乏创业风险投资行业法律法规”、“企业管理水平”和“创业投资人员的素质低”三者所占比重都有所上升，分别从 5.3%、3.7%和 1.7%上升至 2014 年的 7.1%、4.5%和 2.6%。

6 中国创业风险投资区域运行情况

6.1 创业风险投资机构数量和管理资本的地区分布

根据调查统计，2014 年创业风险投资机构总数达 1551 家，比上一年度增加 143 家，仍然保持了近几年的增长态势，增幅 10.2%。其中，创业风险投资企业（基金）1167 家，比 2013 年增加 72 家，增幅 6.6%；创业风险投资管理企业 384 家，较 2013 增加 71 家，增幅 22.7%；创业风险投资管理企业保持了增长比例持续高于创业风险投资企业（基金）的趋势（见表 6-1、图 6-1）。

从地域分布看，2014 年 1551 家创业风险投资公司分布在 30 个省、直辖市和自治区行政区划内，创业风险投资在全国的分布具有以下几个特点：

（1）整体看，全国创业风险投资机构呈现“两超多强”的局面，包括上海、北京、广东在内的东部发达地区仍然是国内创业风险投资机构发展较多的地区，其中以江苏、浙江尤为明显。西部地区创业风险投资机构数量仍相对较少，大部分地区的机构数量为个位数。创业风险投资管理机构主要集中在经济发达地区，西部地区主要是直接投资的企业，管理类机构很少。

（2）江浙一带仍然是我国创业风险投资最多的地区。江苏持续 4 年保持全国创业风险投资机构数量最多地区的地位，机构数量达 518 家，占全国机构总数的 34.05%，超过全国的 1/3；浙江机构数是 232 家，继续位居全国第二，占全国总数的 15.25%，两者合计占比为 49.3%，占全国机构总量的近一半。至于创业风险投资企业（基金），江苏的数量仍高居第一，有 408 家，占全国总数的 35.48%，浙江排名第二，有 187 家，占全国总数的 16.26%，两者合计占比 51.73%，占全国总数的比重超过一半。

表 6-1 中国各地区创业风险投资机构数量（2014）

单位：家

地区	江苏	浙江	山东	上海	北京	安徽	广东	重庆	湖北	天津	湖南	辽宁	福建	陕西	新疆
创投机构总量	518	232	78	77	68	66	65	50	48	48	42	25	23	23	23
创投基金	408	187	69	52	30	58	47	24	32	40	29	17	15	14	19
创投管理机构	110	45	9	25	38	8	18	26	16	8	13	8	8	9	4

地区	云南	河北	四川	贵州	河南	黑龙江	甘肃	宁夏	江西	海南	吉林	广西	青海	山西	内蒙古
创投机构总量	22	21	18	17	14	9	6	6	5	4	4	3	3	2	1
创投基金	16	20	14	14	14	6	5	2	5	1	4	3	3	2	0
创投管理机构	6	1	4	3	0	3	1	4	0	3	0	0	0	0	1

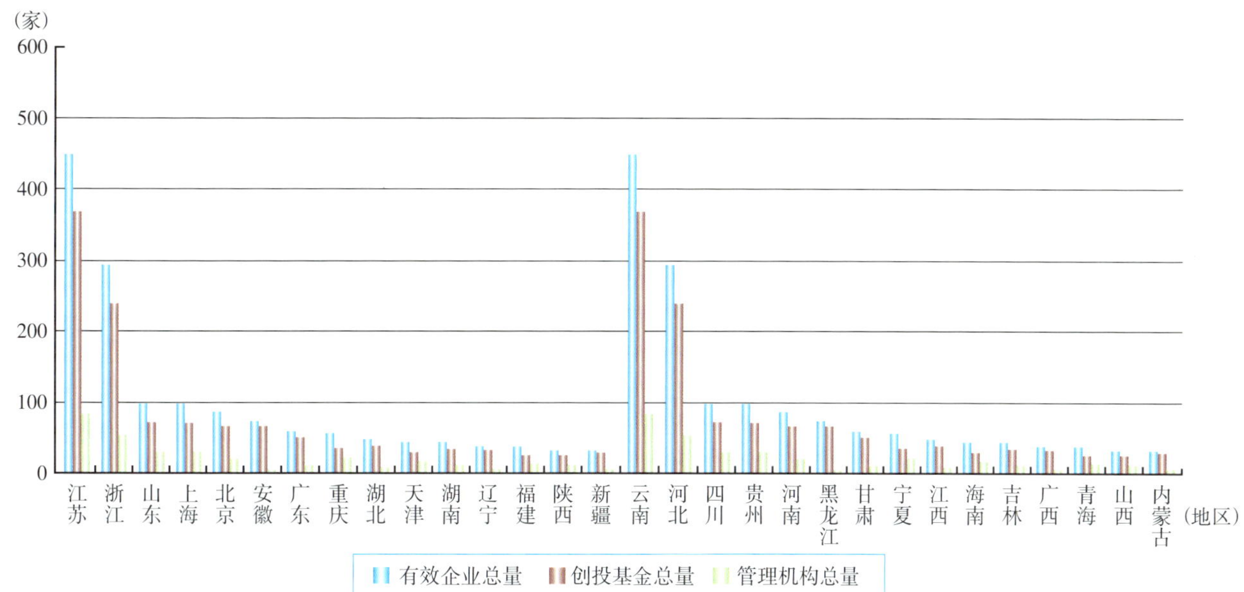

图 6-1 中国各地区的创业风险投资机构数量（2014）

（3）上海、北京、广东等地仍然是国内创业风险投资发展较好的地区，但是在全国的排名有所变化。其中，上海排名比 2013 年下降一位，机构数量是 77 家。广东排名从 2013 年的第五位下降到 2014 年的第七位，机构数量是 65 家。北京的机构数量是 68 家，排名第五位。

（4）2014 年东部部分地区创业风险投资发展迅速。典型的是山东和安徽，其 2014 年创业风险投资机构数量在国内排名前列，其中山东进步明显，机构数量排名为全国第三，数量是 78 家，其中创业风险投资企业（基金）数是 69 家。山东创业风险投资企业（基金）数量上升的原因主要是省内各级政府日益重视创投在发展经济中的重要作用，采用政府出资、引导基金方式来推动各地创业风险投资机构的设立和发展。安徽的创业风险投资机构数是 66 家，比上年增加了 1 家，处于稳步发展水平。

（5）湖北、湖南等中部地区的创业风险投资稳步发展。2014 年，湖北省创业风险投资机构数 48 家，比 2013 年减少 2 家；湖南省则是 42 家，比 2013 年增加 5 家。

（6）2014 年很明显的一个特点是：一些西部地区创投发展迅速，机构数量增加较多，西部部分地区的创业风险投资快速发展。2014 年，云南、贵州的创业风险投资机构增加较多，云南从 2013 年的 8 家增长到 2014 年的 22 家，贵州增加了 2 家，达到了 17 家。

表 6-2 和图 6-2 显示了 2014 年我国不同地区创业风险投资公司的管理资本规模。

表 6-2 部分地区创业风险投资的管理资本分布（2014）

地　区	创投基金（公司）（家）	管理资本总量（亿元）
江　苏	408	1729.23
北　京	30	1229.03
广　东	47	830.82
浙　江	187	294.28
安　徽	58	128.52
上　海	52	125.90
湖　北	32	104.74
山　东	69	86.55
天　津	40	83.95
湖　南	29	67.98
重　庆	24	56.71
四　川	14	42.01

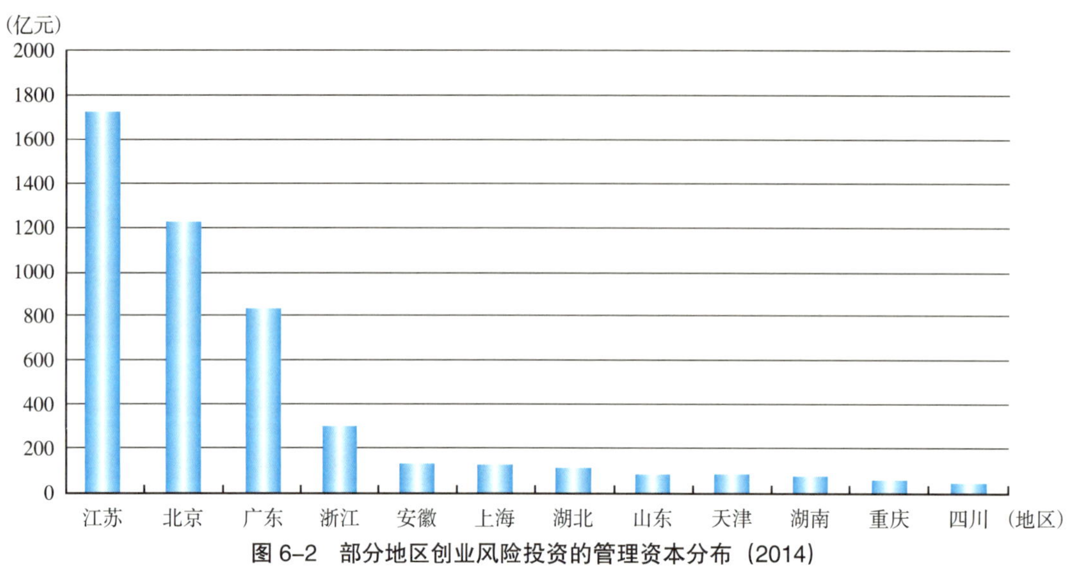

图 6–2 部分地区创业风险投资的管理资本分布(2014)

2014 年,全国创业风险投资公司管理资金规模达 5232.4 亿元,较 2013 年增加 1658.5 亿元,增幅达 46.4%;而管理机构代为管理的资金是 2370.1 亿元。2014 年,全国创业风险投资公司管理资金的地区特点如下:

(1)整体上,与 2013 年一样,全国创业风险投资的资本地区差异很大。东部经济发达地区创业风险投资管理资金规模非常大,有的地区超过千亿,而西部地区创业风险投资管理资金规模在 1 亿元以下。

(2)江苏继续保持国内创业风险投资管理资本最多的位置。2014 年,江苏不但创业风险投资机构数量连续排名全国第一,而且管理资本总量也连续稳居国内榜首地位,管理资金达到了 1729.23 亿元,占全国总数的 33.05%;比 2013 年增加了 321.71 亿元,增长 23%。

(3)北京 2014 年的创业风险投资资本跃升至第二位,资本规模是 1229.03 亿元,占全国的 23.49%。北京创业风险投资的资本大幅度提高的原因之一是北京参与调查工作的创业风险投资机构数量大幅增加,同时北京的很多机构管理资金很多,这也非常符合北京金融中心的地位。

(4)广东、浙江、安徽、上海和湖北是全国创业风险投资公司资本较多的地区,资本规模都在 100 亿元以上。2014 年,广东省创业风险投资公司虽然数量排名只占第七位,但是资本总量的排名占第三位,资本规模是 830.82 亿元,这表明广东创业风险投资公司的规模较大。浙江的创业风险投资机构虽然数量排第二位,但是机构规模都相对较小,2014 年资本总量是 294.28 亿元,排名第四位。安徽的创业风险投资不但机构数量发展迅速,且资本总量也上升很快,2014 年的资本规模是 128.52 亿元,排名第五位。上海创业风险投资机构的资本总量是 125.9 亿元,湖北则达到了 104.74 亿元。

(5)部分地区的创业风险投资的资本规模较小。2014 年,江西、山西、吉林、海南、青海、广西、宁夏、内蒙古等地区的资本规模都在 10 亿元以下,西部地区的宁夏、内蒙古都在 1 亿元以下。

6.2 各地区创业风险投资机构的规模分布

表 6–3 和图 6–3 显示了 2014 年我国不同地区创业风险投资管理资本的规模分布。

表 6-3 各地区不同规模创业风险投资机构的数量分布（2014）

单位：%

地 区	5000 万元以下	5000 万~1 亿元	1 亿~2 亿元	2 亿~5 亿元	5 亿元以上
安 徽	11.11	18.52	25.93	33.33	11.11
北 京	4.69	4.69	9.38	10.94	70.31
福 建	20.00	25.00	35.00	15.00	5.00
甘 肃	20.00	20.00	—	40.00	20.00
广 东	21.82	7.27	18.18	12.73	40.00
广 西	66.67	—	33.33	—	—
贵 州	29.41	29.41	17.65	23.53	—
海 南	—	50.00	25.00	25.00	—
河 北	47.06	17.65	17.65	11.76	5.88
河 南	22.22	—	33.33	44.44	—
黑龙江	12.50	12.50	12.50	37.50	25.00
湖 北	12.50	17.50	25.00	40.00	5.00
湖 南	16.13	9.68	41.94	16.13	16.13
吉 林	—	33.33	—	66.67	—
江 苏	20.39	20.83	29.39	20.18	9.21
江 西	—	—	75.00	25.00	—
辽 宁	23.81	14.29	28.57	23.81	9.52
内蒙古	—	100.00	—	—	—
宁 夏	66.67	—	—	33.33	—
青 海	—	33.33	66.67	—	—
山 东	28.30	13.21	37.74	20.75	—
山 西	50.00	—	—	—	50.00
陕 西	23.53	29.41	23.53	17.65	5.88
上 海	20.51	—	33.33	25.64	20.51
四 川	30.77	15.38	23.08	7.69	23.08
天 津	24.00	36.00	16.00	12.00	12.00
新 疆	28.57	28.57	21.43	14.29	7.14
云 南	30.00	20.00	20.00	20.00	10.00
浙 江	19.63	20.55	28.77	22.37	8.68
重 庆	21.74	19.57	13.04	30.43	15.22

总体而言，2014 年国内大部分地区创业风险投资机构的规模未发生较大变化，经济发达地区创业风险投资规模增长迅速，且不同规模的创业风险投资机构分布相对分散，而经济欠发达地区的创业风险投资机构的规模则相对集中，如宁夏、海南、江西、青海、内蒙古等，内蒙古地区均在 5000 万~1 亿元之间，青海则分布在 5000 万~1 亿元和 1 亿~2 亿元，宁夏主要在 5000 万元以下，占比为 66.7%，其余则在 2 亿~5 亿元之间。

值得注意的是，2014 年北京的创业风险投资机构，其辖内机构的管理资本规模比较大，拥有管理资本 5 亿元以上的机构数量占比在 70%以上，显示北京作为中国的经济和金融中心，机构可以募集到较多的资金。江苏的管理资本规模在 5 亿元以上的机构比例只有 9.21%，在其他规模区间上的机构数量基本呈现均匀分布。浙江的特点与江苏非常相似，管理资本规模在 5 亿元以上的机构比例为 8.68%，其他几个规模区间的机构占比基本持平。另外，管理资本规模在 5 亿元以上的机构比例比较高的地区还有广东，比例为 40%。

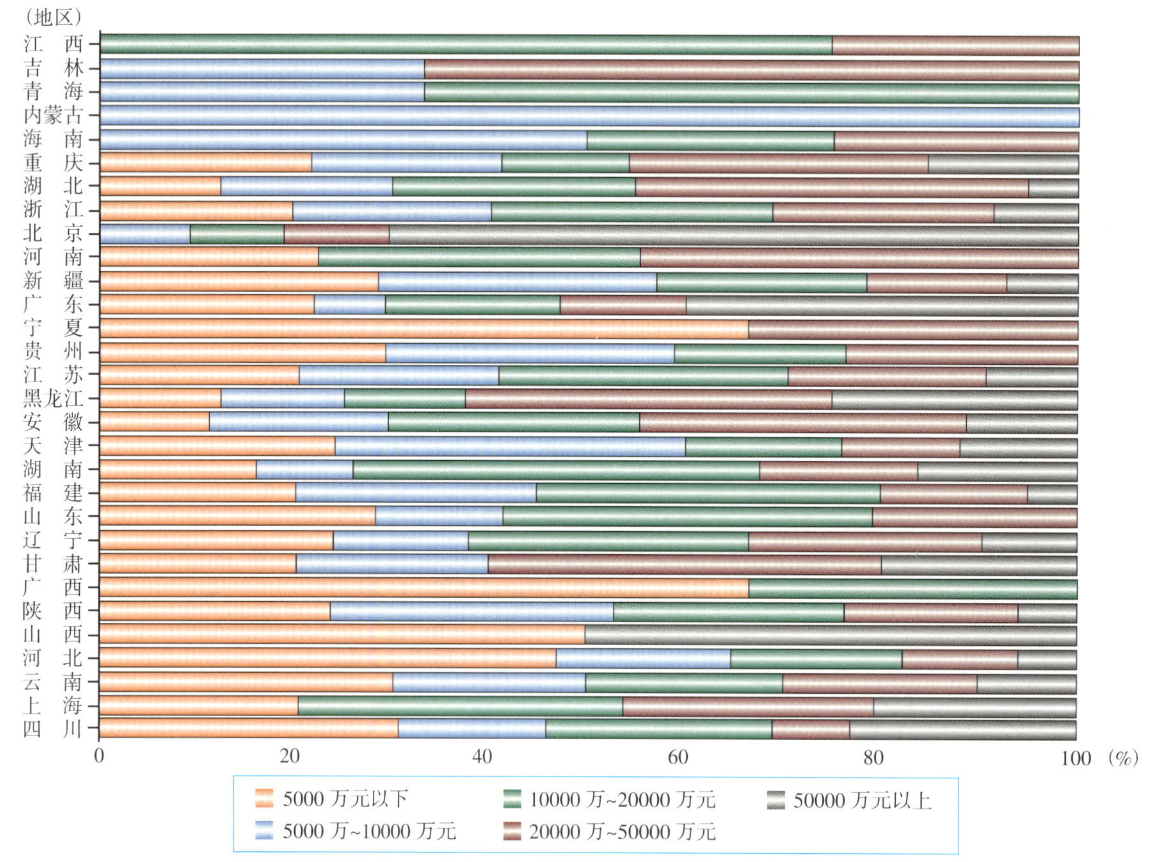

图 6-3 各地区不同规模创业风险投资机构的数量分布（2014）

6.3 各地区创业风险投资机构的资本来源

2014 年，全国各地区创业风险投资机构的资本来源未发生较大变化，以政府财政资金、国有独立投资机构资金、企业资金和个人资金为主（见图 6-4）。

（1）企业资金成为国内大部分地区创业风险投资机构的主要资本来源。2014 年，企业资金占比超过 50%的有北京、福建、湖北、江西、宁夏、云南和浙江 7 个地区，较 2013 年多 1 家，其中，比例最高的福建占比达 61.8%，其次是浙江，比例为 61.1%。另外，广东、河南、湖南、吉林、江苏、山东和重庆 7 个地区的企业资金占比也都超过了 40%。

（2）政府财政资金仍然是国内某些地区创业风险投资机构的主要资金来源。2014 年，内蒙古和山西与 2011~2013 年情况相同，仍然完全是由政府出资。政府直接出资超过 50%的地区有甘肃、海南、广西、黑龙江、河北。政

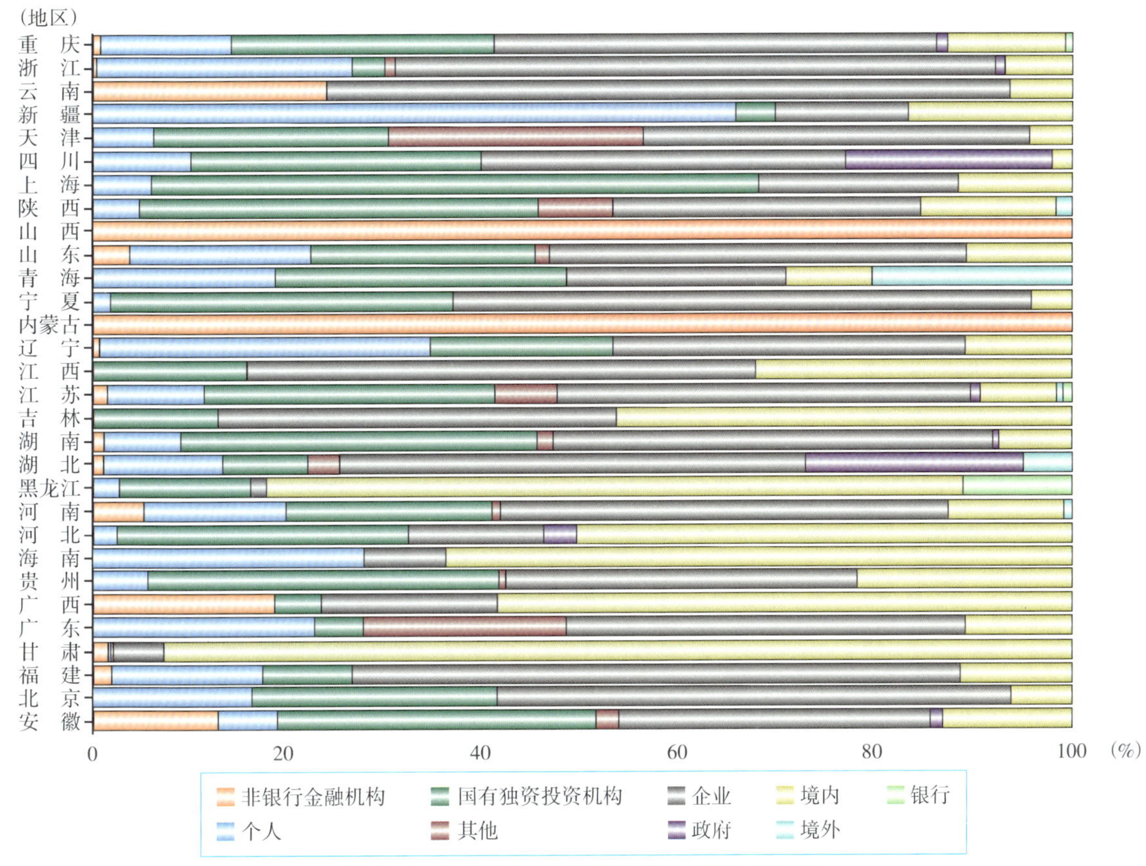

图 6-4 各地区创业风险投资资本来源（2014）

府直接出资和国有独资投资机构出资的资金比例之和超过50%的地区有贵州、吉林、上海和陕西，其中上海的国有性质的资金占比达到了73.2%。

（3）个人资金出资设立创业风险投资机构的比例也越来越高。2014 年，个人资本占机构管理资本比例 10%以上的地区有 13 个，较 2013 年多 11 个，分别是北京、福建、广东、海南、河南、湖北、辽宁、青海、山东、四川、新疆、浙江、重庆。其中，新疆占比最高，达 65.5%，较第二位的浙江省高出 39 个百分点。

（4）个别地方创业风险投资机构的资金来源特征明显。2014 年，黑龙江的境外资金来源占比较高，达 11.2%。云南、安徽和广西三个地区的非银行金融机构资金占比均超过 10%，其中云南为 24.1%。

6.4 各地区创业风险投资的投资特征

6.4.1 创业风险投资项目的地区分布

表 6-4 显示了 2014 年我国不同地区创业风险投资机构所投资项目的情况。

根据调查统计，2014 年，全国 26 个地区的创业风险投资机构，共投资 2438 个项目，比 2013 年增加近 1000 个，显示 2014 年国内创业投资机构的投资更加活跃。其中，投资项目最多的三个地区是江苏、北京和浙江，江苏的创业风险投资机构所投资的项目依然最多，占比 32.2%，比 2013 年略有下降。北京的投资项目占比上升幅度较高，从 2013 的 1.2%提高到 16.6%，排在第二位。近两年排在

表 6–4 2014 年我国创业风险投资机构所投资项目的地区分布 单位：%

地　区	项目占比
江　苏	32.2
北　京	16.6
浙　江	10.9
广　东	10.0
上　海	4.6
山　东	3.5
重　庆	3.3
安　徽	3.1
湖　北	2.8
湖　南	2.1
黑龙江	1.7
河　南	1.4
贵　州	1.0
新　疆	0.9
云　南	0.9
河　北	0.9
陕　西	0.8
福　建	0.8
辽　宁	0.7
天　津	0.7
四　川	0.4
青　海	0.3
甘　肃	0.2
广　西	0.1
宁　夏	0.1
江　西	0.1

第二位和第三位的广东和浙江分别排在了第四位和第三位。整体上看，创业投资项目的地域集中性比较明显，上述四个地区的项目合计占比 69.7%。另外，投资项目较多的地区还有上海、山东、重庆、安徽、湖北等。中西部地区开展的创业投资项目相对较少。

6.4.2 各地区创业风险投资的投资强度

2014 年，全国 28 个地区的创业风险投资机构都进行了投资，各地区创业风险投资所投资项目的投资强度见表 6–5 和图 6–5。

表 6-5　2014 年各地区创业风险投资的投资强度　　单位：万元/项

地　区	投资强度
北　京	5740.87
辽　宁	3541.18
宁　夏	2750.00
广　东	2720.18
四　川	2393.89
安　徽	1896.20
河　北	1855.76
黑龙江	1708.47
湖　南	1629.67
江　西	1600.00
青　海	1587.50
湖　北	1456.15
上　海	1266.06
浙　江	1199.69
江　苏	1174.16
甘　肃	1132.00
山　东	1079.35
云　南	1069.20
陕　西	1041.26
天　津	1021.57
广　西	956.00
贵　州	852.41
重　庆	805.41
河　南	724.76
福　建	686.02
新　疆	684.77
吉　林	500.00
山　西	300.00

2014 年，全国各地创业风险投资的项目投资强度差距比 2013 年小，最高的是北京市的 5740.87 万元，远低于 2013 年海南的 1 亿元的平均投资规模，最低的山西省，只有 300 万元，高于 2013 年山西的 86.67 万元。总体上看，2014 年全国创业风险投资的项目投资强度低于 2013 年，大部分地区项目投资金额在 1000 万~3000 万元，低于 2013 年的 1000 万~4000 万元。

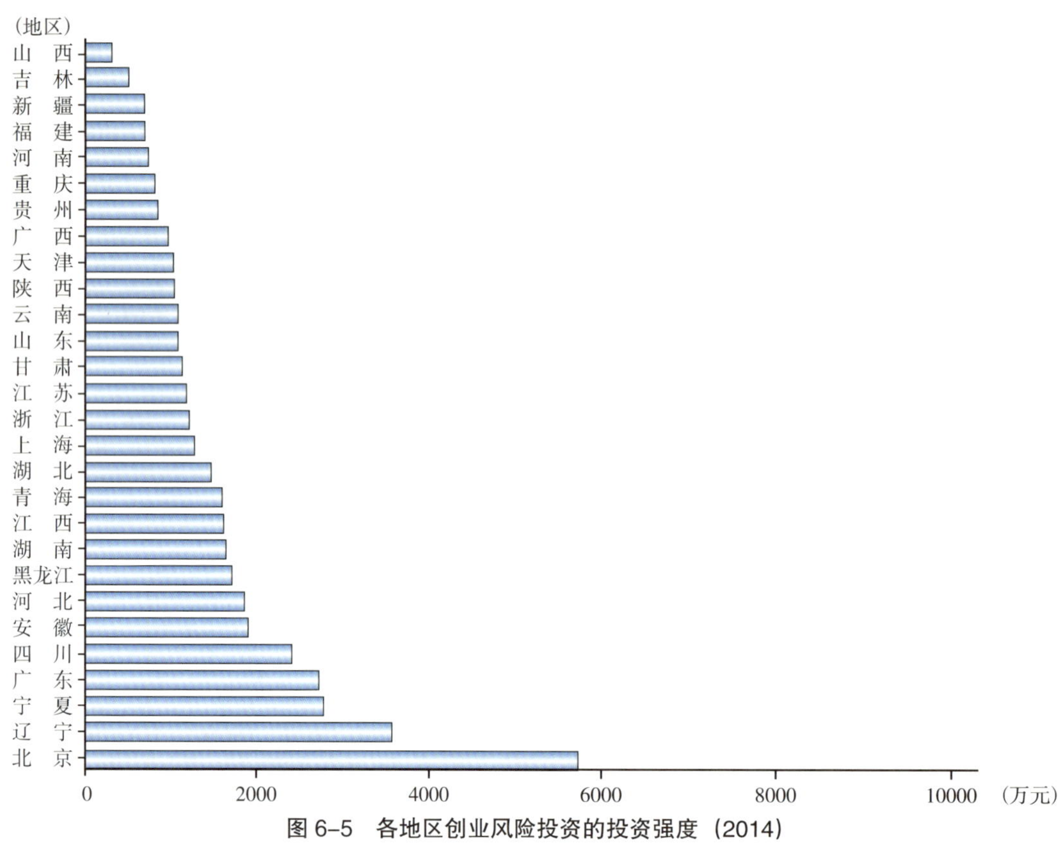

图 6-5　各地区创业风险投资的投资强度（2014）

6.4.3　各地区创业风险投资机构的项目持股结构

2014 年，不追求绝对控股的创业风险投资机构有所增加，有 10 个地区的项目持股比例全部在 50%以下。全国各地区持股比例≥50%项目占比明显下降，最高的天津只有 12.5%，远远低于 2013 年最高地区辽宁 36%的比例（见表 6-6、图 6-6）。

表 6-6　2014 年中国创业风险投资机构所投资项目持股结构的地区分布　　单位：%

地　区	持股比例≥50%	持股比例<50%
天　津	12.5	87.5
云　南	12.5	87.5
辽　宁	11.8	88.2
黑龙江	9.8	90.2
河　南	9.7	90.3
湖　北	9.0	91.0
安　徽	6.9	93.1
上　海	5.5	94.5
福　建	5.3	94.7
新　疆	4.5	95.5
贵　州	4.2	95.8

续表

地　区	持股比例≥50%	持股比例<50%
湖　南	4.1	95.9
江　苏	3.4	96.6
北　京	3.2	96.8
浙　江	2.7	97.3
重　庆	2.5	97.5
山　东	2.5	97.5
广　东	2.1	97.9
吉　林	0.0	100.0
青　海	0.0	100.0
河　北	0.0	100.0
陕　西	0.0	100.0
江　西	0.0	100.0
甘　肃	0.0	100.0
山　西	0.0	100.0
广　西	0.0	100.0
宁　夏	0.0	100.0
四　川	0.0	100.0

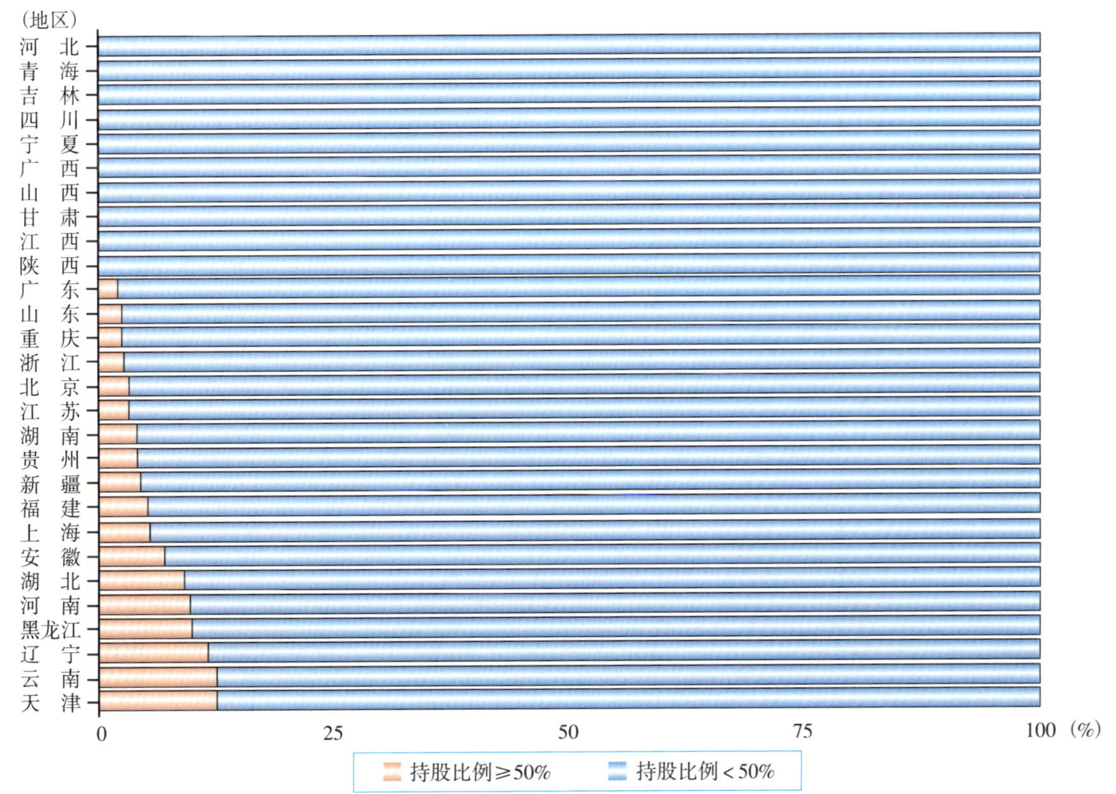

图 6–6　各地区创业风险投资机构的持股结构（2014）

6.4.4 各地区创业风险投资项目的所处阶段

表 6-7 和图 6-7 显示了 2014 年我国各地区创业风险投资机构所投资项目的所处阶段。

2014 年，我国各地区创业风险投资项目所处阶段呈现以下特点：

（1）与往年一样，成长（扩张）期的项目仍然是 2014 年我国大部分地区创业风险投资机构投资最多的项目。其中，部分地区投资于成长（扩张）期的项目比例超过 50%，如黑龙江、广西、四川、陕西、青海和江西。

（2）起步期的项目越来越受到全国各地创业风险投资机构的青睐。2014 年，有 7 个地区的创业风险投资机构在起步期的项目占比超过 50%，分别是天津、山西、辽宁、

表 6-7 2014 年各地区创业风险投资项目的所处阶段

单位：%

地 区	种子期	起步期	成长（扩张）期	成熟（过渡）期	重建期
北 京	5.0	44.3	49.3	1.5	0.0
天 津	0.0	50.0	33.3	16.7	0.0
河 北	9.1	36.4	40.9	13.6	0.0
山 西	0.0	100.0	0.0	0.0	0.0
辽 宁	0.0	66.7	25.0	8.3	0.0
吉 林	100.0	0.0	0.0	0.0	0.0
黑龙江	2.4	39.0	58.5	0.0	0.0
上 海	8.1	47.7	34.2	7.2	2.7
江 苏	36.2	25.3	32.4	5.9	0.1
浙 江	21.7	42.2	27.8	8.4	0.0
安 徽	9.5	37.8	44.6	8.1	0.0
福 建	5.3	52.6	36.8	5.3	0.0
江 西	0.0	50.0	50.0	0.0	0.0
山 东	21.0	44.4	32.1	1.2	1.2
河 南	33.3	36.4	24.2	6.1	0.0
湖 北	45.6	26.5	19.1	8.8	0.0
湖 南	11.8	49.0	37.3	2.0	0.0
广 东	13.4	45.2	33.5	7.9	0.0
广 西	50.0	0.0	50.0	0.0	0.0
四 川	25.0	12.5	50.0	12.5	0.0
贵 州	13.0	30.4	34.8	21.7	0.0
云 南	9.1	13.6	9.1	68.2	0.0
重 庆	15.4	25.6	46.2	12.8	0.0
陕 西	10.5	26.3	57.9	5.3	0.0
甘 肃	0.0	80.0	20.0	0.0	0.0
青 海	0.0	25.0	62.5	12.5	0.0
宁 夏	0.0	50.0	50.0	0.0	0.0
新 疆	31.6	26.3	36.8	0.0	5.3

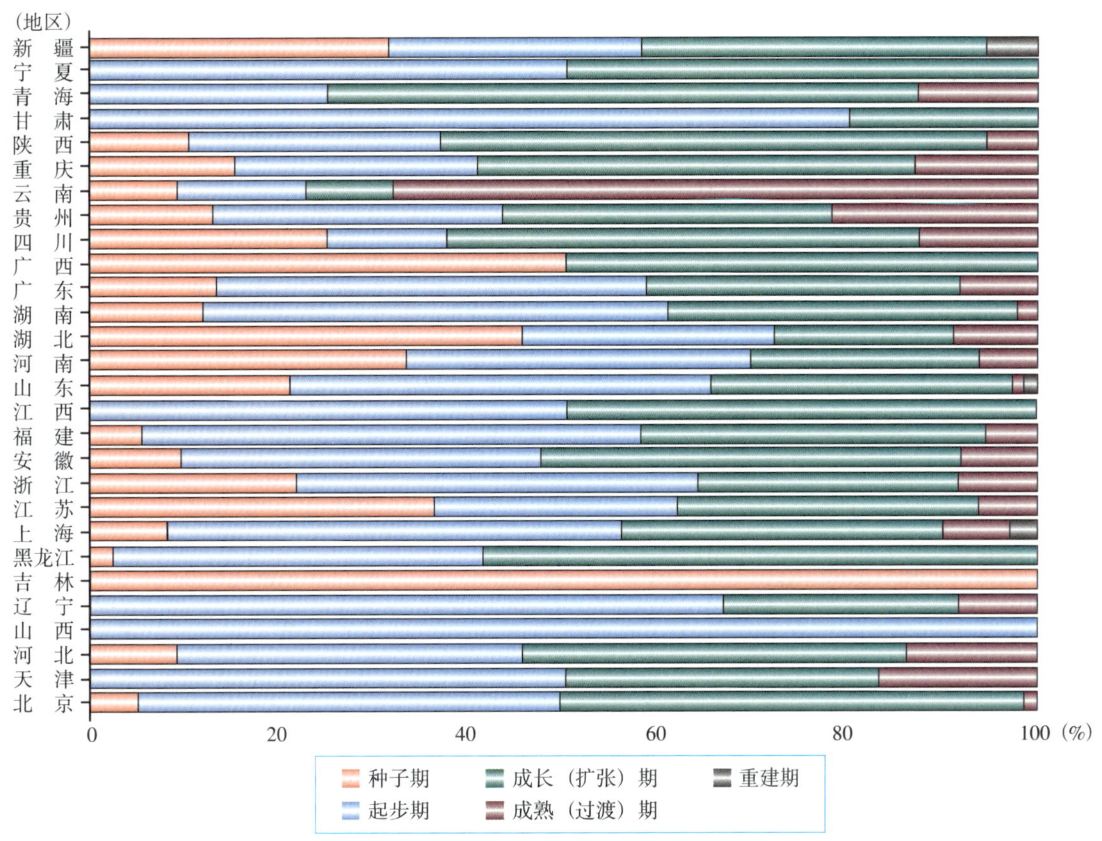

图 6-7 各地区创业风险投资项目所处阶段（2014）

福建、江西、甘肃、宁夏。超过 30%的地区有 18 个，占全部地区的 60%。

（3）越来越多地区的创业风险投资重视种子期的项目。2014 年，有 9 个地区的创业风险投资，在种子期的项目占比超过 20%，分别是吉林、江苏、浙江、山东、河南、湖北、广西、新疆、四川，其中最高的吉林达到了 100%。

（4）发达地区创投机构投资项目阶段的分布差异较大。北京、浙江和广东三地基本以中间阶段的项目为主，侧重起步期和成长（扩张）期，两头比例少；而江苏省则是种子期的项目占比最高，达到了 36.2%，显示江苏省内的创业风险投资机构对种子期项目的重视程度。

6.4.5 部分地区创业风险投资对不同行业的投资

根据 2014 年全国创业风险投资调查统计，本小节重点分析 2014 年我国创业风险投资较为活跃的地区，以掌握和了解这些地区投资项目的行业分布和资金情况（见表 6-8 至表 6-17）。

表 6-8 2014 年北京市创业风险投资的行业特点 单位：%

项目数		投资强度	
行 业	百分比（%）	行 业	行业投资强度（万元）
通信设备	35.7	批发和零售业	33727.5
软件产业	26.0	医药保健	15500.0
批发和零售业	7.9	水电煤气	12600.0
传统制造业	6.1	计算机硬件产业	10473.0
IT 服务业	5.4	其他制造业	6066.7

续表

项目数		投资强度	
行　业	百分比（%）	行　业	行业投资强度（万元）
社会服务	3.6	传统制造业	5002.2
计算机硬件产业	3.6	社会服务	4694.6
科技服务	3.3	通信设备	3373.2
消费产品和服务	1.3	科技服务	2961.9
金融保险业	1.3	金融保险业	2202.0
新材料工业	1.0	软件产业	2136.8
其他制造业	0.8	光电子与光机电一体化	1466.0
传播与文化娱乐	0.8	半导体	1446.0
生物科技	0.8	网络产业	1200.0
医药保健	0.5	生物科技	1200.0
新能源、高效节能技术	0.5	传播与文化娱乐	1018.0
光电子与光机电一体化	0.3	农林牧副渔	1001.1
半导体	0.3	环保工程	1000.0
网络产业	0.3	IT 服务业	735.4
环保工程	0.3	消费产品和服务	726.0
农林牧副渔	0.3	新能源、高效节能技术	700.0
水电煤气	0.3	新材料工业	455.0

2014 年，北京市的创业风险投资项目分布在 22 个行业，其中关注度最高的是通信设备和软件产业，最高的通信设备占比达 35.7%，第二位的软件产业占比 26.0%，二者合计达 61.7%。

从行业的投资强度看，2014 年北京市创业风险投资项目的投资强度比较大，最高的批发和零售业达到 3 亿元以上，医药保健、水电煤气、计算机硬件产业的平均投资规模都在 1 亿元以上；在 22 个行业中，投资强度在 1000 万元以上的行业有 18 个。

表 6–9　2014 年天津市创业风险投资的行业特点

项目数		投资强度	
行　业	百分比（%）	行　业	行业投资强度（万元）
传统制造业	27.8	金融保险业	1700.0
传播与文化娱乐	22.2	生物科技	1500.0
其他制造业	11.1	传播与文化娱乐	1200.5
半导体	11.1	传统制造业	1006.4
金融保险业	5.6	其他制造业	1000.0
软件产业	5.6	半导体	1000.0
生物科技	5.6	网络产业	800.0
新材料工业	5.6	新材料工业	483.4
网络产业	5.6	软件产业	71.0

2014 年，天津市创业风险投资相对上年而言并不活跃，投资项目分布在 9 个行业，比 2013 年减少了 10 个，主要集中在传统制造业、传播与文化娱乐。2013 年投资的重点行业——软件产业和新能源/高效节能技术已不是投资机构关注的重点。

至于行业的投资强度，2014 年天津市创业风险投资的行业项目平均投资资金差距不大，而且与 2013 年相比下降幅度非常明显：最高的金融保险业是 1700 万元，远远低于 2013 年最高的 25520 万元；最低的软件产业是 71 万元，与 2013 年最低的半导体行业 76.6 万元很接近。

表 6–10　2014 年上海市创业风险投资的行业特点

项目数		投资强度	
行　业	百分比（%）	行　业	行业投资强度（万元）
网络产业	22.3	通信设备	9000.0
其他行业	11.6	科技服务	3325.0
IT 服务业	10.7	其他行业	2249.6
软件产业	7.1	传播与文化娱乐	2079.4
医药保健	7.1	医药保健	1484.3
新材料工业	7.1	其他制造业	1333.3
传播与文化娱乐	4.5	社会服务	1304.0
新能源、高效节能技术	3.6	半导体	1239.4
半导体	3.6	消费产品和服务	1125.0
科技服务	3.6	新材料工业	902.6
消费产品和服务	3.6	IT 服务业	791.2
其他制造业	2.7	生物科技	766.7
生物科技	2.7	网络产业	627.6
光电子与光机电一体化	1.8	农林牧副渔	600.0
社会服务	1.8	新能源、高效节能技术	587.5
通信设备	1.8	软件产业	473.9
其他 IT 产业	1.8	金融保险业	450.0
金融保险业	0.9	光电子与光机电一体化	400.0
农林牧副渔	0.9	批发和零售业	80.0
批发和零售业	0.9	其他 IT 产业	70.0

2014 年，上海市创业风险投资的投资行业有 20 个，比 2013 年减少 4 个；投资行业最多的是网络产业，占比为 22.3%，IT 服务业投资比例也很高，占比为 10.7%；另外，软件产业、医药保健和新材料工业的项目也相对较多。与 2013 年相比，2014 年上海市的创业风险投资机构，对金融保险行业的投资项目数量下降明显，而对网络产业和 IT 服务业的关注度则明显上升。

从投资强度上看，2014 年上海市的创业风险投资行业平均投资资金差距很大，最高的是通信设备，高达 9000 万元，最低的其他 IT 产业，只有 70 万元。与 2013 年相比，上海市创业风险投资的行业整体上投资强度略有下降，超过 1000 万元的只有 9 个行业，而 2013 年则有 19 个行业。

表 6–11　2014 年广东省创业风险投资的行业特点

项目数		投资强度	
行　业	百分比（%）	行　业	行业投资强度（万元）
网络产业	18.6	房地产业	25351.1
其他行业	11.0	传统制造业	8708.9
IT 服务业	8.9	医药保健	5948.1
环保工程	7.2	光电子与光机电一体化	4599.9
医药保健	6.8	生物科技	4515.5
消费产品和服务	5.5	通信设备	3156.7
传播与文化娱乐	5.1	环保工程	3153.5
新材料工业	4.6	其他行业	2838.0
传统制造业	4.2	社会服务	2400.0
软件产业	3.8	传播与文化娱乐	2268.0
通信设备	3.8	消费产品和服务	2185.7
光电子与光机电一体化	3.4	其他 IT 产业	1952.0
其他制造业	3.4	半导体	1833.5
新能源、高效节能技术	2.5	农林牧副渔	1500.0
生物科技	2.5	其他制造业	1436.7
其他 IT 产业	2.1	金融保险业	1400.0
科技服务	1.3	新材料工业	1220.0
半导体	1.3	网络产业	1154.3
农林牧副渔	0.8	建筑业	1150.0
社会服务	0.8	IT 服务业	1078.3
金融保险业	0.8	计算机硬件产业	1000.0
房地产业	0.8	科技服务	983.7
建筑业	0.4	新能源、高效节能技术	957.8
计算机硬件产业	0.4	软件产业	909.0

2014 年，广东省的创业风险投资所投资项目，分布在 24 个行业，总数比 2013 年少 2 个，其中投资最多的行业是网络产业，占比为 18.6%，另外，IT 服务业、环保工程和医药保健行业也是广东省创业风险投资机构投资较多的行业。与 2013 年相比，2013 年投资最多的金融保险业占比下降明显，从 2013 年的 14.7%下降到 2014 年的 0.8%。网络产业则从 2013 年的 7.1%上升到 2014 年最高的 18.6%。医药保健行业则是创业风险投资机构持续关注度比较高的行业。

至于投资强度，2014 年广东省创业风险投资的行业投资强度比 2013 年增幅很大，最高的行业是房地产业，达到了 25351.1 万元，排名第二的传统制造业也有 8708.9 万元，远远高于 2013 年最高的其他制造业的 4810.8 万元；最低的软件产业为 909 万元，远高于 2013 年最低的交通运输仓储和邮政业的 167 万元。另外，24 个行业中，有 21 个行业的平均投资规模超过 1000 万元，高于 2013 年的 20 个。

表 6-12 2014 年江苏省创业风险投资的行业特点

项目数		投资强度	
行　业	百分比（%）	行　业	行业投资强度（万元）
其他行业	10.8	房地产业	28100.0
新材料工业	8.8	传播与文化娱乐	3193.6
软件产业	7.9	社会服务	2016.0
医药保健	6.9	新能源、高效节能技术	1649.0
生物科技	6.0	医药保健	1511.0
传播与文化娱乐	6.0	建筑业	1414.1
网络产业	5.8	其他制造业	1269.1
其他制造业	5.1	金融保险业	1167.0
新能源、高效节能技术	4.6	生物科技	1156.3
传统制造业	4.1	新材料工业	1029.3
IT 服务业	4.1	其他行业	1014.6
环保工程	3.9	环保工程	967.4
金融保险业	3.5	IT 服务业	958.0
光电子与光机电一体化	3.5	半导体	849.9
农林牧副渔	2.8	光电子与光机电一体化	761.8
通信设备	2.8	其他 IT 产业	736.6
科技服务	2.7	通信设备	728.0
其他 IT 产业	2.2	消费产品和服务	684.5
半导体	2.2	软件产业	635.7
消费产品和服务	1.9	传统制造业	616.2
计算机硬件产业	1.4	科技服务	607.8
建筑业	1.1	农林牧副渔	384.6
批发和零售业	1.1	计算机硬件产业	379.6
社会服务	0.7	网络产业	304.8
房地产业	0.1	批发和零售业	132.2

2014 年，江苏省创业风险投资所投资的行业有 25 个，总数比 2013 年减少 2 个，其中投资最多的行业是其他行业，占比为 10.8%，投资较多的行业还有新材料工业、软件产业、医药保健、生物科技、传播与文化娱乐。整体上看，2014 年江苏创业风险投资比较关注高科技行业。

与 2013 年相比，2014 年江苏省创业风险投资机构重点投资的行业基本保持了连续性。医药保健、新材料工业、软件产业在 2014 年的比例有所下降，但仍然是江苏省创业风险投资关注度较高的行业，传播与文化娱乐行业的占比基本保持不变。

2014 年，江苏省创业风险投资的行业投资强度最高的是房地产业，达到了 28100 万元，除了这个特殊行业外，其他行业的投资强度在 3200 万元以下，排名第二的行业是传播与文化娱乐，只有 3193.6 万元，最低的是批发和零售业，只有 132.2 万元。整体上看，2014 年江苏省创业风险投资的行业投资强度比 2013 年有所下降，投资强度在

1000 万元以上的行业只有 11 个，比 2013 年少 6 个。

表 6–13 2014 年浙江省创业风险投资项目的行业特点

项目数		投资强度	
行　业	百分比（%）	行　业	行业投资强度（万元）
网络产业	24.0	建筑业	5150.0
IT 服务业	7.6	农林牧副渔	3931.2
金融保险业	7.2	传统制造业	3885.3
其他行业	6.5	其他行业	2215.1
消费产品和服务	5.7	医药保健	1653.1
其他制造业	5.3	新材料工业	1471.8
软件产业	4.6	环保工程	1428.6
新材料工业	3.8	新能源、高效节能技术	1424.6
生物科技	3.8	其他 IT 产业	1308.3
医药保健	3.8	计算机硬件产业	1136.0
通信设备	3.4	其他制造业	1102.6
传播与文化娱乐	3.4	传播与文化娱乐	1049.8
新能源/高效节能技术	3.4	网络产业	1047.7
环保工程	2.7	生物科技	987.4
其他 IT 产业	2.3	通信设备	959.3
社会服务	2.3	软件产业	936.7
计算机硬件产业	1.9	IT 服务业	917.7
农林牧副渔	1.9	消费产品和服务	732.0
光电子与光机电一体化	1.5	社会服务	691.7
传统制造业	1.5	光电子与光机电一体化	565.3
科技服务	1.5	批发和零售业	500.0
建筑业	0.8	科技服务	416.5
水电煤气	0.4	金融保险业	278.4
交通运输仓储和邮政业	0.4	交通运输仓储和邮政业	250.0
批发和零售业	0.4	水电煤气	180.0

2014 年，浙江省创业风险投资涉及的行业有 25 个，比 2013 年减少 1 个。与 2013 年关注领域相对分散不同，2014 年浙江省创业风险投资关注的行业相对集中，最高的网络产业占比达到了 24%，远远高于其他行业的占比；另外，IT 服务业和金融保险业的占比也相对较高，都在 7% 以上。与 2013 年相比，IT 服务业、软件产业是浙江省创业风险投资持续投资的重点。

2014 年，浙江省创业风险投资的行业投资强度差距比较大，最高的是建筑业，达 5150 万元，最低的是水电煤气，只有 180 万元。与 2013 年相比，建筑业、农林牧副渔、传统制造业的行业平均投资额大幅增加，而医药保健等行业则下降幅度明显。与 2013 年相比，2014 年平均投资金额在 1000 万元以上的行业数量有所下降，只有 13 个，减少了 5 个。

表 6–14　2014 年湖北省创业风险投资项目的行业特点

项目数		投资强度	
行　业	百分比（%）	行　业	行业投资强度（万元）
金融保险业	20.6	金融保险业	3517.9
光电子与光机电一体化	10.3	半导体	3000.0
医药保健	10.3	IT 服务业	2000.0
其他行业	8.8	新材料工业	1716.7
传统制造业	8.8	医药保健	1608.9
新能源/高效节能技术	7.4	传播与文化娱乐	1430.0
软件产业	7.4	新能源/高效节能技术	1393.6
网络产业	5.9	其他制造业	1200.0
新材料工业	4.4	房地产业	1000.0
传播与文化娱乐	2.9	传统制造业	785.3
生物科技	2.9	其他行业	622.5
IT 服务业	1.5	软件产业	510.0
消费产品和服务	1.5	光电子与光机电一体化	414.3
农林牧副渔	1.5	生物科技	350.0
房地产业	1.5	农林牧副渔	320.0
其他制造业	1.5	消费产品和服务	260.0
半导体	1.5	网络产业	250.0
社会服务	1.5	社会服务	150.0

2014 年，湖北省创业风险投资的项目分布在 18 个行业，比 2013 年增加了 5 个，投资领域更加宽泛；主要集中在金融保险业、光电子与光机电一体化、医药保健、其他行业和传统制造业，其中，金融保险业最高，占比达 20.6%。与 2013 相比，光电子与光机电一体化、医药保健和新能源/高效节能技术行业一直是湖北省创业风险投资的投资重点，而农林牧副渔的投资比例则下降较多，金融保险业成为新的投资热点。

至于行业投资强度，2014 年湖北省创业风险投资的行业投资强度最高的是金融保险业，达 3517.9 万元，最低的是社会服务业，只有 150 万元。与 2013 年相比，金融保险业的投资强度明显提高，比 2013 年平均增加了 1500 多万元，光电子与光机电一体化、农林牧副渔和医药保健等的投资强度下降明显，新能源/高效节能技术的投资强度略有下降。

表 6–15　2014 年山东省创业风险投资项目的行业特点

项目数		投资强度	
行　业	百分比（%）	行　业	行业投资强度（万元）
传统制造业	14.6	传播与文化娱乐	2734.0
网络产业	9.8	农林牧副渔	2033.3
新材料工业	7.3	其他行业	2032.5

续表

项目数		投资强度	
行　业	百分比（%）	行　业	行业投资强度（万元）
金融保险业	6.1	社会服务	2000.0
其他制造业	6.1	软件产业	1326.7
新能源/高效节能技术	6.1	其他制造业	1288.0
IT 服务业	4.9	通信设备	1265.3
生物科技	4.9	新材料工业	1250.0
其他行业	4.9	环保工程	1107.2
医药保健	4.9	传统制造业	1098.1
环保工程	4.9	生物科技	927.0
光电子与光机电一体化	4.9	金融保险业	766.6
软件产业	3.7	医药保健	647.5
通信设备	3.7	网络产业	568.0
农林牧副渔	3.7	新能源/高效节能技术	402.0
交通运输仓储和邮政业	2.4	交通运输仓储和邮政业	400.0
社会服务	2.4	光电子与光机电一体化	377.7
科技服务	1.2	IT 服务业	323.3
半导体	1.2	消费产品和服务	300.0
消费产品和服务	1.2	科技服务	200.0
传播与文化娱乐	1.2	半导体	100.0

2014 年，山东省成为国内创业风险投资比较活跃的地区，投资分布在 21 个行业，比 2013 年增加了 8 个；主要集中在传统制造业、网络产业、新材料工业、金融保险业、其他制造业、新能源/高效节能技术 6 个行业，其中传统制造业最高，占比为 14.6%。与 2013 年相比，传统制造业一直是山东省创业风险投资的重点行业，网络产业则成为新的投资热点。

2014 年，山东省创业风险投资的行业投资强度差别较大，最高的是传播与文化娱乐，达 2734 万元，最低的是半导体，只有 100 万元。21 个行业中，有接近一半行业的投资强度在 1000 万元以上。

表 6–16　2014 年安徽省创业风险投资项目的行业特点

项目数		投资强度	
行　业	百分比（%）	行　业	行业投资强度（万元）
其他行业	12.3	传统制造业	6142.7
新能源/高效节能技术	9.6	其他行业	4594.2
计算机硬件产业	8.2	农林牧副渔	2103.3
新材料工业	8.2	医药保健	2017.3
其他制造业	6.8	新材料工业	1997.8

续表

项目数		投资强度	
行　业	百分比（%）	行　业	行业投资强度（万元）
软件产业	5.5	生物科技	1872.5
环保工程	5.5	计算机硬件产业	1443.5
科技服务	5.5	IT 服务业	1300.3
生物科技	5.5	科技服务	1292.5
传统制造业	5.5	新能源/高效节能技术	1102.1
网络产业	5.5	环保工程	1022.5
金融保险业	4.1	其他制造业	1003.6
IT 服务业	4.1	光电子与光机电一体化	1000.0
医药保健	4.1	软件产业	726.5
农林牧副渔	2.7	其他 IT 产业	650.0
其他 IT 产业	2.7	网络产业	647.5
通信设备	1.4	通信设备	600.0
半导体	1.4	半导体	250.0
光电子与光机电一体化	1.4	金融保险业	120.0

2014 年，安徽省的创业风险投资项目分布在 19 个行业，比上年减少 2 个；投资较多的行业是其他行业、新能源/高效节能技术、计算机硬件产业、新材料工业，其中最多的是其他行业。与 2013 年相比，新能源/高效节能技术和新材料工业一直是安徽省创业风险投资机构投资较多的行业，光电子与光机电一体化的项目占比下降幅度很大，计算机硬件产业则成为新的关注重点。

从行业投资强度来看，2014 年安徽创业风险投资的行业投资强度差距非常大，最高的传统制造业为 6142.7 万元，而最低的金融保险业则只有 120 万元。与往年相比，2014 年安徽的传统制造业、农林牧副渔业的投资强度提高较大，而新材料工业、新能源/高效节能技术、生物科技等行业投资强度则下降较大。

表 6–17　2014 年重庆市创业风险投资项目的行业特点

项目数		投资强度	
行　业	百分比（%）	行　业	行业投资强度（万元）
新能源/高效节能技术	12.8	农林牧副渔	2816.7
科技服务	12.8	医药保健	2120.0
IT 服务业	10.3	新能源/高效节能技术	1786.4
其他行业	10.3	IT 服务业	1314.0
医药保健	10.3	软件产业	1100.0
其他制造业	10.3	建筑业	1000.0
农林牧副渔	7.7	网络产业	1000.0
传播与文化娱乐	2.6	传播与文化娱乐	1000.0

续表

项目数		投资强度	
行　业	百分比（%）	行　业	行业投资强度（万元）
软件产业	2.6	环保工程	1000.0
其他 IT 产业	2.6	其他行业	906.8
消费产品和服务	2.6	消费产品和服务	800.0
传统制造业	2.6	传统制造业	798.4
网络产业	2.6	其他制造业	754.8
通信设备	2.6	科技服务	600.0
环保工程	2.6	光电子与光机电一体化	500.0
光电子与光机电一体化	2.6	其他 IT 产业	400.0
建筑业	2.6	通信设备	300.0

2014 年，重庆市的创业风险投资活动比较活跃，投资项目最多的行业是新能源/高效节能技术和科技服务，两者并列最高，占比为 12.8%，IT 服务业、医药保健和其他制造业的项目也相对较多。

从投资强度看，投资强度最高的是农林牧副渔，达 2816.7 万元，其次是医药保健，投资强度为 2120 万元，最低的是通信设备，只有 300 万元。整体看，2014 年重庆市创业风险投资机构的行业投资强度还比较高，投资金额在 1000 万元（含）以上的行业有 9 个，超过行业总数的 50%。

6.5 各经济区域创业投资活动情况

本节从经济区域角度来比较、分析 2014 年我国创业风险投资的运行状况，通过比较经济发达、有特色的地区与经济相对不发达、创投活动不活跃地区之间的差异，为我国创业风险投资今后发展起到一个指南针作用。

本节的区域划分，是根据经济发展的联系紧密程度以及发展特色，并参照国家现有的经济区域划分，本着研究的连续性来划分的。当前我国最为关注的几个经济区域增长带是珠三角、长三角地区以及围绕北京、天津这样的大型城市、具有知识高密度的京津冀等地区，同时还有正在重新振兴的东北三省老工业基地。因此本节划分的区域有：

（1）京津冀地区；

（2）长三角地区（包括浙江、上海、江苏）；

（3）珠三角地区：广东（深圳）；

（4）东北三省地区：辽宁、吉林、黑龙江；

（5）其他区域（福建省放在这个部分统计）。

本节选取这五个区域，出发点之一是前三个区域是中国目前经济发展最快，也是最有活力的区域，充分代表了当前我国创业风险投资的前沿面；东北三省是我国的老工业基地，国有企业比重大，现在正面临经济和产业转型，国外经验证明了创业风险投资可以鼓励民营和科技经济发展，有效提升产业转型和升级，因此把东北三省地区单独列出来。本节分析的目标是通过分析这些经济区域的创业发展，从一个方面来测量地区经济和创新发展的活力。

6.5.1 我国创业风险投资机构项目的区域分布

表 6-18 显示了我国不同区域内的创业风险投资在 2014 年投资项目的占比，显然，长三角地区仍然是国内创业风险投资最活跃的地区，2014 年投资的项目占全国项目总数的近一半，京津冀地区占比为 18.2%。值得注意的是，东北三省创业风险投资的项目占比只有 2.4%，位列最后，显示出这个地区经济活力有待加强。

表 6-18　2014 年中国创业风险投资项目的区域分布

单位：%

区　域	长三角	珠三角	京津冀	东北三省	其他地区
项目占比	47.7	10.0	18.2	2.4	21.7

6.5.2　我国不同区域创业风险投资的投资强度

表 6-19、图 6-8 显示了 2014 年中国各经济区域内创业风险投资的投资强度。2014 年，京津冀地区的投资强度跃升到第一位，达到 5357 万元/项，比 2013 年增加了一倍多；珠三角地区的排名下降一位，不过绝对值比 2013 年有所增加；东北三省创业风险投资的投资强度排第三位，比 2013 年增加了一倍多。值得注意的是，长三角地区的项目投资平均规模是最低的，只有 1188.8 万元/项，主要是因为该地区的创业风险投资项目而且是早期阶段的项目数量多。

表 6-19　2014 年中国创业风险投资强度的区域分布　　单位：万元/项

区　域	京津冀	珠三角	东北三省	其他地区	长三角
投资强度	5357.0	2720.2	2216.1	1227.7	1188.8

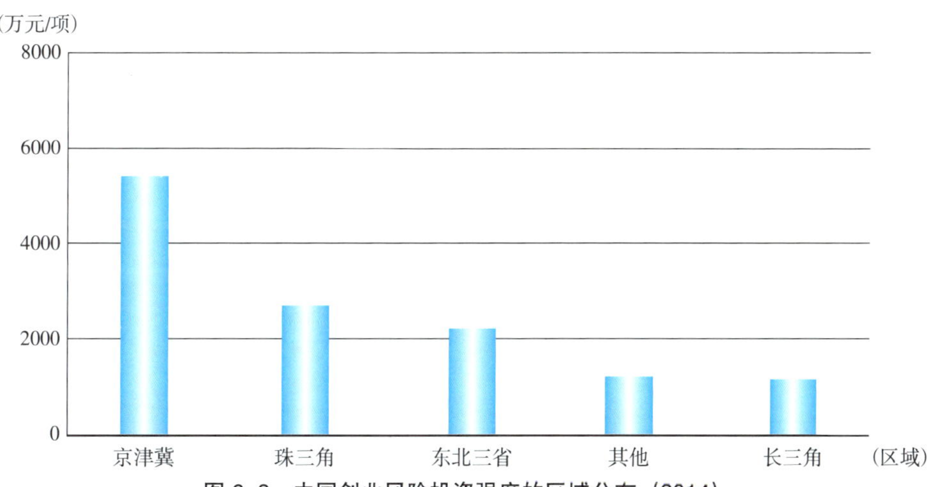

图 6-8　中国创业风险投资强度的区域分布（2014）

6.5.3　不同区域创业风险投资的持股结构

表 6-20、图 6-9 显示：2014 年，东北三省的创业风险投资机构在投资时，追求绝对控股的比例最高，达 10.2%，其余区域内持股比例≥50%都在 5%以下。与 2013 年相比，除了京津冀地区之外，其余区域内的创业风险投资机构持股比例≥50%的比例都有所下降，显示国内创投机构越来越重视联合投资的作用。

表 6-20　2014 年各经济区域创业风险投资的持股结构　　单位：%

区　域	东北三省	其他地区	京津冀	长三角	珠三角
持股比例≥50%	10.2	4.8	4.5	3.4	2.1
持股比例<50%	89.8	95.2	95.5	96.6	97.9

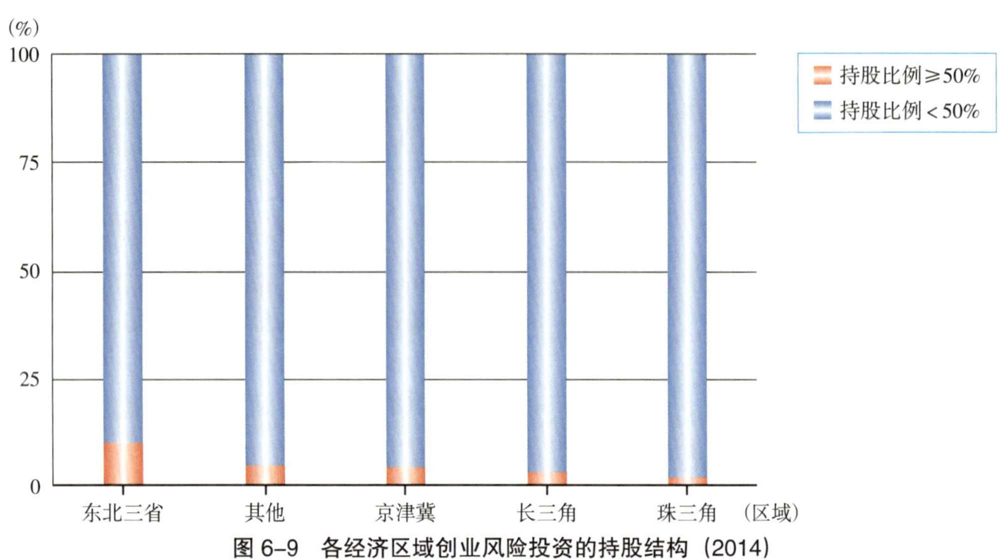

图 6-9 各经济区域创业风险投资的持股结构（2014）

6.5.4 不同经济区域创业风险投资项目所处阶段

表 6-21 和图 6-10 显示了 2014 年我国各个经济区域创业风险投资项目的阶段分布。

2014 年，珠三角地区创业风险投资机构投资于起步期的项目最多，占比为 45.19%；其次是成长（扩张）期的项目，占比为 33.47%；种子期的项目排在第三位，占比为 13.39%。东北三省和京津冀地区的项目所处阶段非常类似，基本是成长（扩张）期最多，起步期次之，两者合计占比都在 90%以上，种子期和成熟（过渡）期的比例基本相当。长三角地区的项目所处阶段与其他地区不同，种子期、起步期和成长（扩张）期的项目比例基本持平，显示该区域内创业风险投资对早期发展阶段的企业的重视。

表 6-21 2014 年各区域创业风险投资项目所处阶段 单位：%

区域 \ 所处阶段	种子期	起步期	成长（扩张）期	成熟（过渡）期	重建期
珠三角	13.39	45.19	33.47	7.95	—
东北三省	3.70	44.44	50.00	1.85	—
其他	19.96	35.50	34.66	9.45	0.42
长三角	29.91	31.64	31.46	6.64	0.36
京津冀	4.96	44.14	48.20	2.70	—

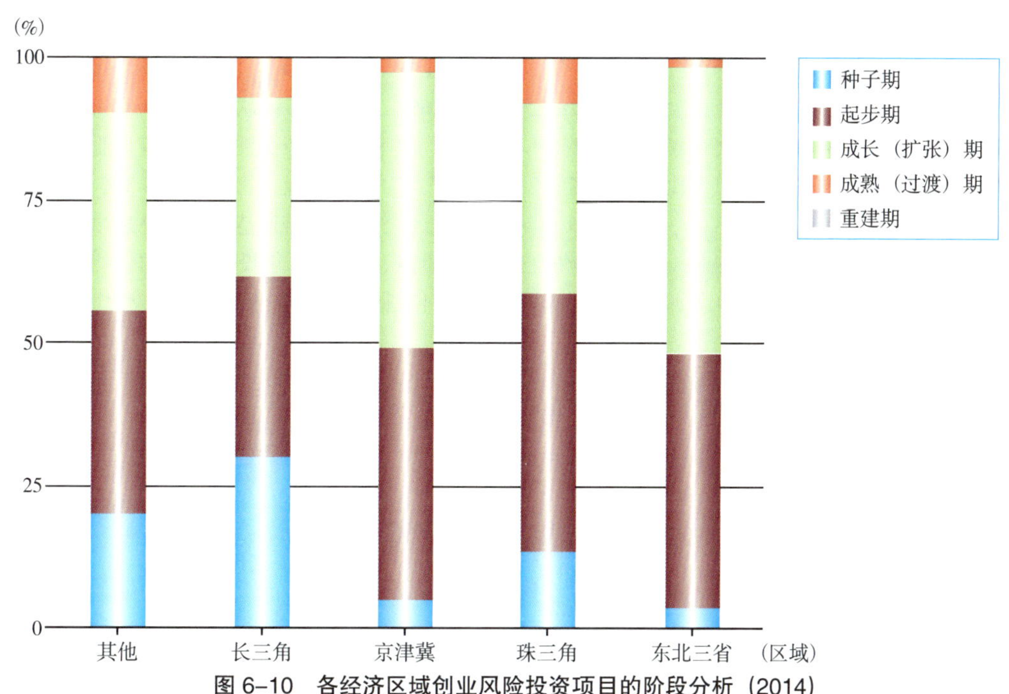

图 6-10　各经济区域创业风险投资项目的阶段分析（2014）

6.5.5　各经济区域创业风险投资项目的行业分布

图 6-11 至图 6-15 分别显示了 2014 年我国不同经济区域创业风险投资的行业分布。

图 6-11 显示：2014 年长三角地区的创业风险投资分布在 27 个行业，行业总数比 2013 年少 2 个；投资比例比

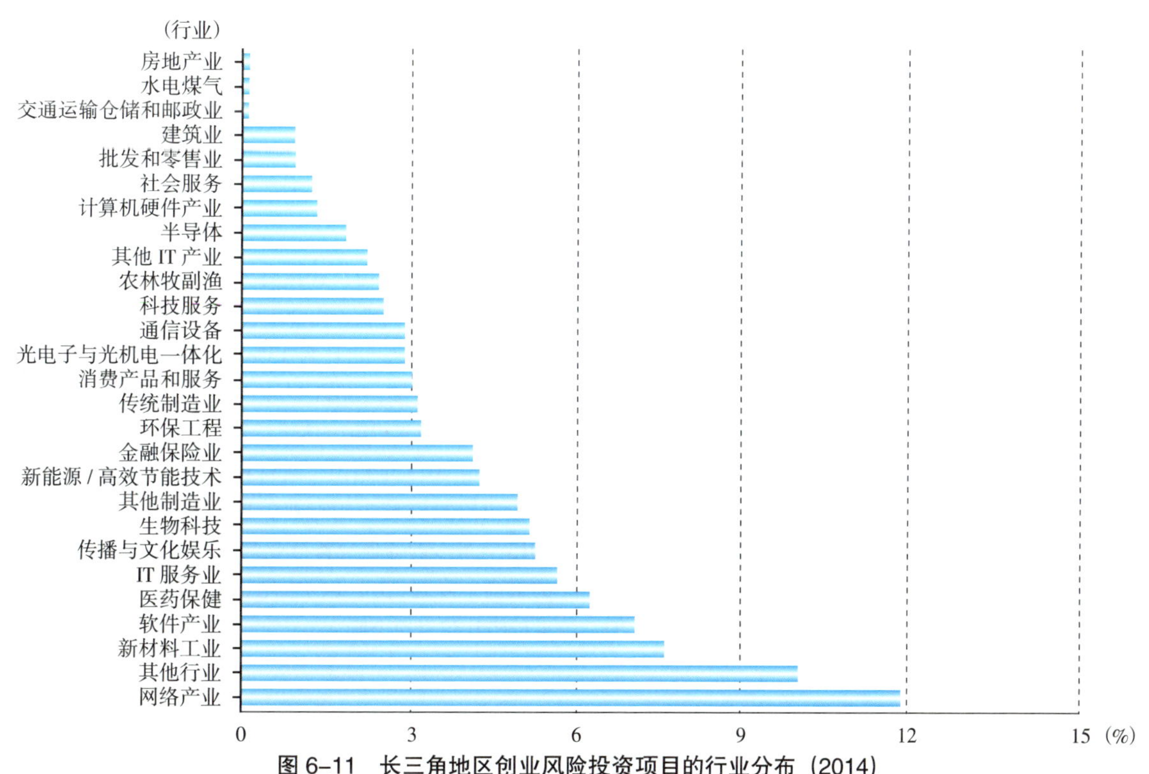

图 6-11　长三角地区创业风险投资项目的行业分布（2014）

较多的行业是网络产业、新材料产业、软件产业、医药保健、IT 服务业、传播与文化娱乐和生物科技。与 2013 年相比，网络产业一跃成为长三角地区创业风险投资最多的行业，医药保健、新材料工业、传播与文化娱乐、软件产业一直是该区域内投资较多的行业，项目占比下降较多的是新能源/高效节能技术、传统制造业。

图 6-12 显示：2014 年京津冀地区创业风险投资分布在 24 个行业，比 2013 年增加 1 个。2014 年非常明显的特点是，京津冀地区创业风险投资明显集中在通信设备和软件产业上，两者合计占比为 56.7%，其中最高的通信设备为 32.6%。另外，传统制造业、批发和零售业占比也相对较多，创业风险投资关注批发和零售业，显示京津冀一体化进入实质实施阶段，物流行业对于本地区十分重要。

软件产业和传统制造业一直是京津冀地区创业风险投资的重点，而 2013 年投资较多的新能源/高效节能技术、新材料工业，在 2014 年下降幅度较大。

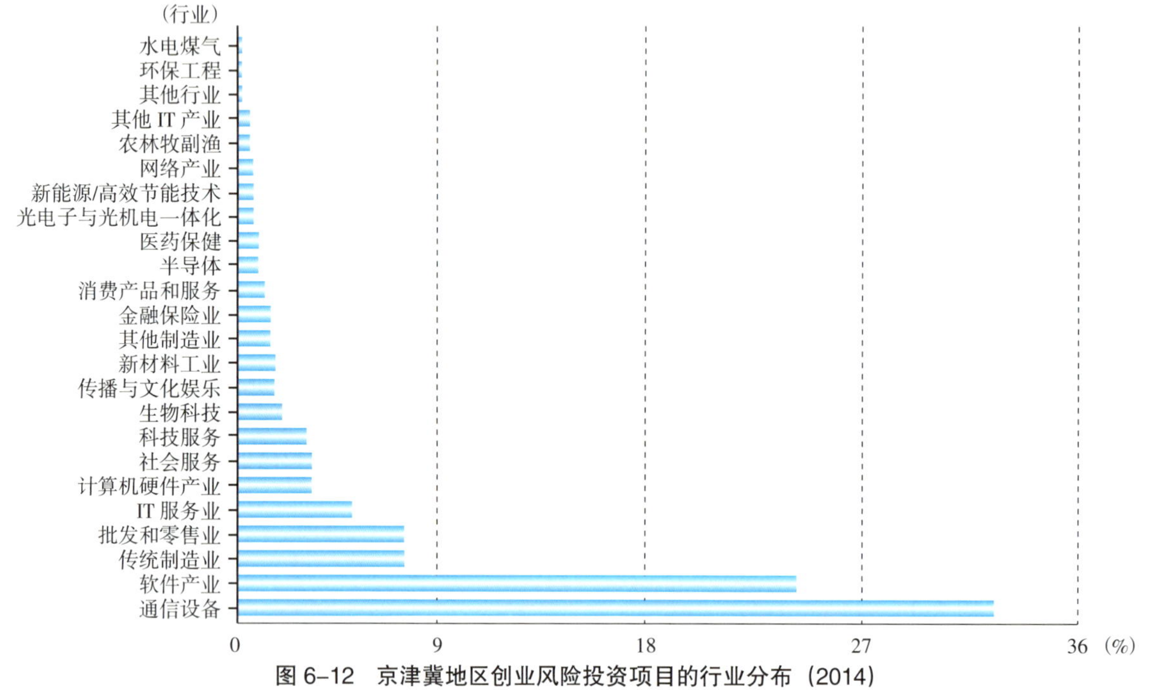

图 6-12 京津冀地区创业风险投资项目的行业分布（2014）

图 6-13 显示：2014 年珠三角地区创业风险投资分布在 24 个行业，比 2013 年少 2 个；投资较多的行业是网络产业、其他行业、IT 服务业、环保工程、医药保健、消费产品和服务、传播与文化娱乐，合计占比为 63.1%，其中最高的是网络产业，占比为 18.6%。

网络产业、医药保健、消费产品和服务、传播与文化娱乐一直是珠三角地区创业风险投资比较关注的行业。与 2013 年相比，网络产业占比上升较快，成为 2014 年的首选；而 2013 年投资最多的金融保险业，下降幅度很大，项目占比低于 1%；另外，生物科技行业的投资占比也在 2014 年有所下降。

从图 6-14 看出：2014 年东北三省地区的创业风险投资分布在 18 个行业，比 2013 年增加了 2 个行业；投资最多的是其他行业，占比为 13%，医药保健和新材料工业占比并列排第二位，达 11.1%；另外，投资相对较多的行业还有光电子与光机电一体化、新能源/高效节能技术、生物科技。与 2013 年相比，新材料工业一直是东北三省地区创业风险投资较多的行业，医药保健的项目比例上升，2013 年最多的通信设备行业则下降幅度很大，由 2013 年的最高下降到 2014 年的末尾，同时金融保险业、软件产业的占比也有所下降。

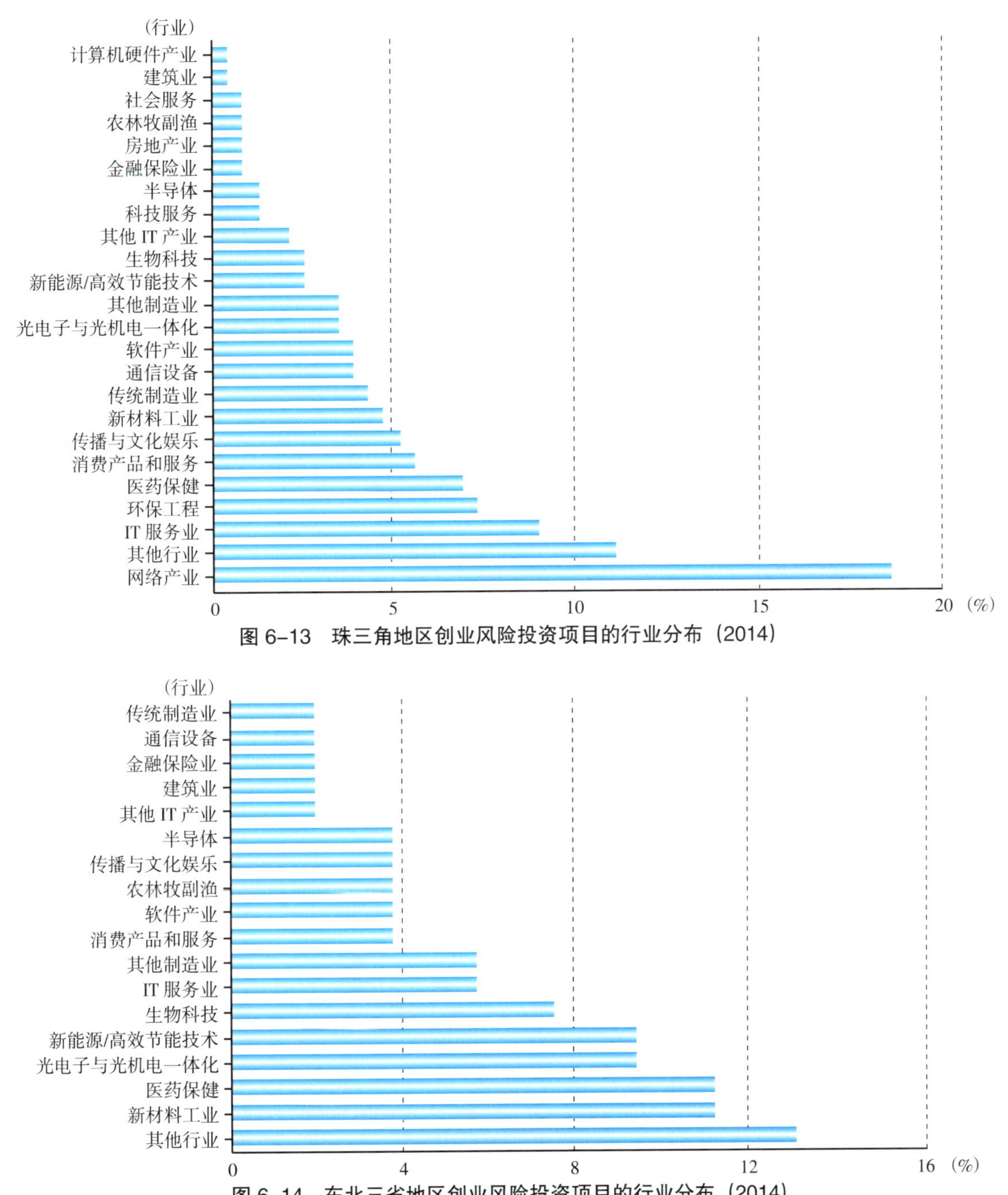

图 6–13　珠三角地区创业风险投资项目的行业分布（2014）

图 6–14　东北三省地区创业风险投资项目的行业分布（2014）

图 6–15 显示：2014 年其他区域的创业风险投资分布在 29 个行业，主要集中在其他行业、传统制造业、新能源/高效节能技术、新材料工业、农林牧副渔。与 2013 年相比，2014 年该区域内创业风险投资较多的行业变化不大，新能源/高效节能技术、传统制造业、医药保健、农林牧副渔一直是这些地区内创业风险投资比较关注的行业；典型差别是 2013 年投资最多的金融保险业项目占比下降幅度较大。

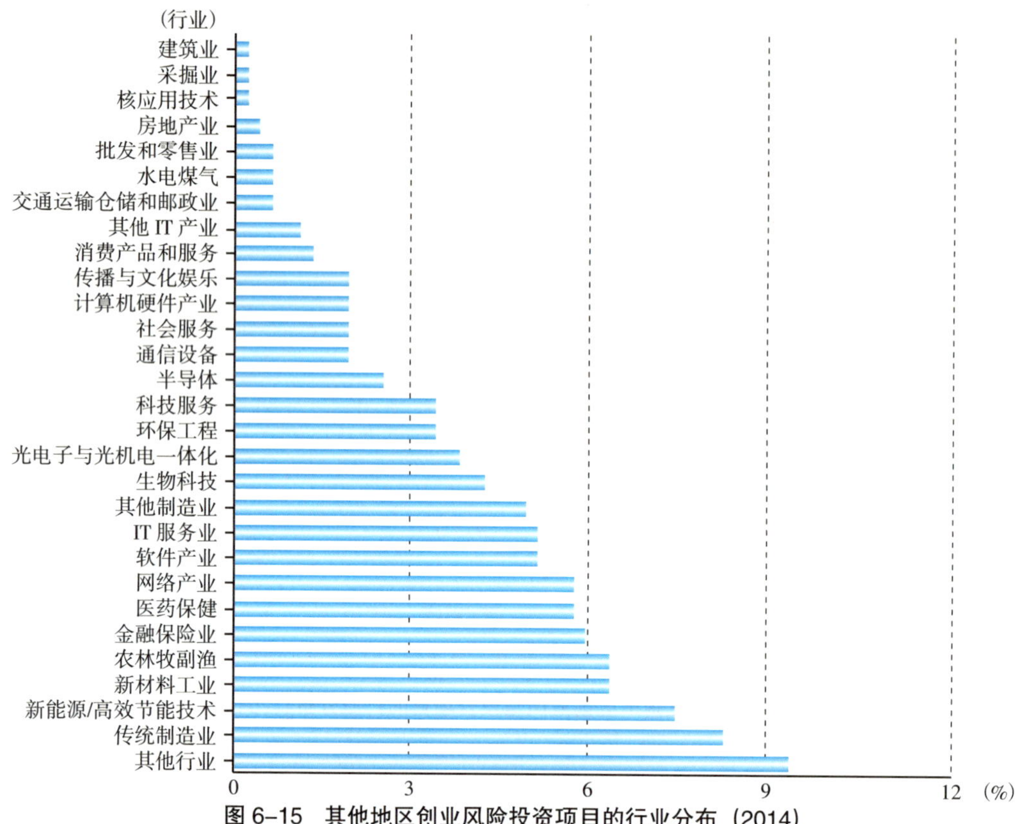

图 6-15 其他地区创业风险投资项目的行业分布（2014）

7 外资创业风险投资机构的运作

2014 年，外资创业风险投资机构与 2013 年相比呈现出一些新的特点：无论是从投资项目领域还是投资金额的角度，外资创业风险投资机构选择的投资项目行业分布更加倾向于新兴行业和业态，并且增加了对医疗、环保等高科技领域的关注；在投资强度方面，外资创业风险投资机构开始更加关注早前期项目，投资项目规模在 500 万元以下的占比增多；在选择项目信息来源时，外资创业风险投资机构更加倾向于有信誉担保的“股东推荐”、“朋友介绍”；更加重视从事创业风险投资人员的综合素质，对从业人员相关技术背景和技能要求的评估略有降低。

7.1 外资创业风险投资项目的行业分布

调查数据显示，2014 年外资创业风险投资机构的投资项目主要集中在 19 个领域（见表 7-1），其中，按投资金额所占比重分析，传播与文化娱乐、房地产业以及其他行业居前三位，分别占比 28.64%、11.26%和 9.9%；从投资项目所占比重分析，其他行业、传播与文化娱乐、医药保健居前三位，分别占比 15.29%、12.94 和 11.76%。此外，按投资金额和投资项目两方面分析，“光电子与光机电一体化”、“新材料工业”、“金融保险业”三个投资项目占比都较 2013 年有大幅下降，“生物科技”、“环保工程”、“IT 服务业”所占比重则有明显上升。这说明 2014 年我国外资创业风险投资机构的投资结构有了明显变化，从重视传统制造业等行业逐渐向新兴行业和业态转变，同时增加了对环保、医疗、文化等领域的关注。

表 7-1 外资创业风险投资项目的行业分布：投资项目与投资金额（2014） 单位：%

投资行业	投资金额所占比例	投资项目所占比例
传播与文化娱乐	28.64	12.94
房地产业	11.26	1.18
其他行业	9.90	15.29
医药保健	9.48	11.76
其他制造业	6.64	5.88
生物科技	5.27	3.53
环保工程	5.21	5.88
IT 服务业	5.01	7.06
新材料工业	4.92	8.24

续表

投资行业	投资金额所占比例	投资项目所占比例
新能源/高效节能技术	4.90	4.71
光电子与光机电一体化	2.35	3.53
金融保险业	1.46	3.53
传统制造业	1.46	3.53
其他 IT 产业	1.27	4.71
半导体	0.77	2.35
通信设备	0.60	1.18
软件产业	0.42	2.35
科技服务	0.24	1.18
网络产业	0.20	1.18

从具体行业分析来看，“传播与文化娱乐”成为 2014 年外资创业风险投资资金的主要投资方向（见图 7-1），较 2013 年的 16.61%上升了 12 个百分点，居投资金额分类中的第一位。与 2013 年相比，外资风险投资资金明显增加了对“房地产业”的投入，按资金分类所占比例由 2013 年的 0.54%上升至 2014 年的 11.26%。

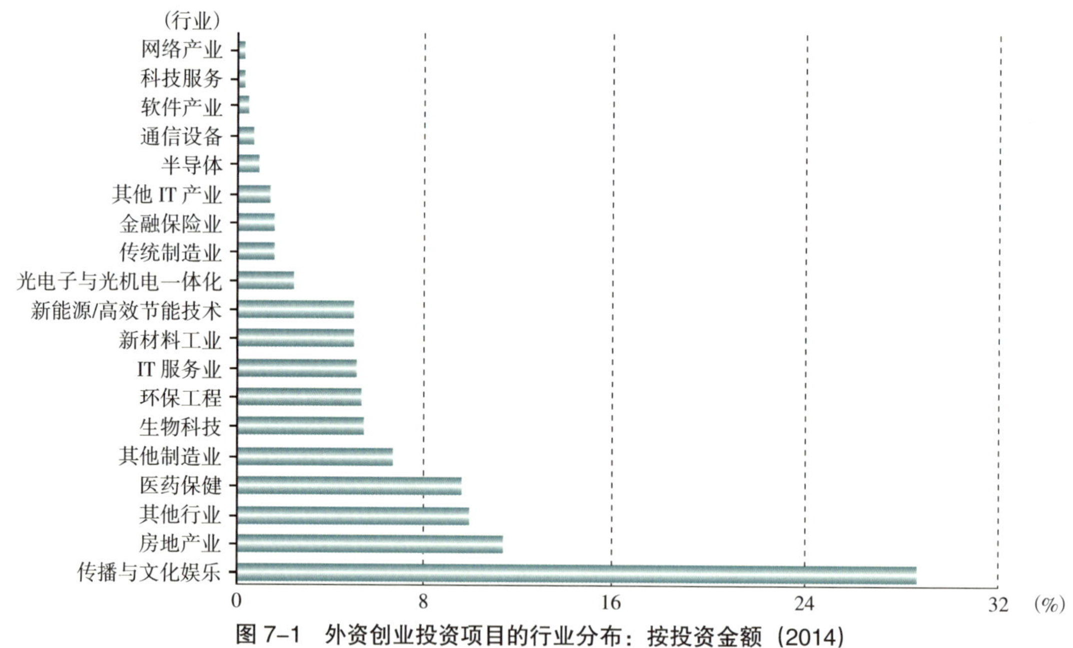

图 7-1 外资创业投资项目的行业分布：按投资金额（2014）

按投资项目对创业风险投资进行分类可以发现（见图 7-2），与 2013 年相比，外资创业风险投资机构可能存在资金相对分散、投资项目分类较广的情况，故 2014 年按投资项目分类中，其他行业所占比重要明显高于某一类具体项目，占比达到 15.29%。“传播与文化娱乐”所占比重较 2013 年有所下降，占比从 15.18%下降至 12.94%。

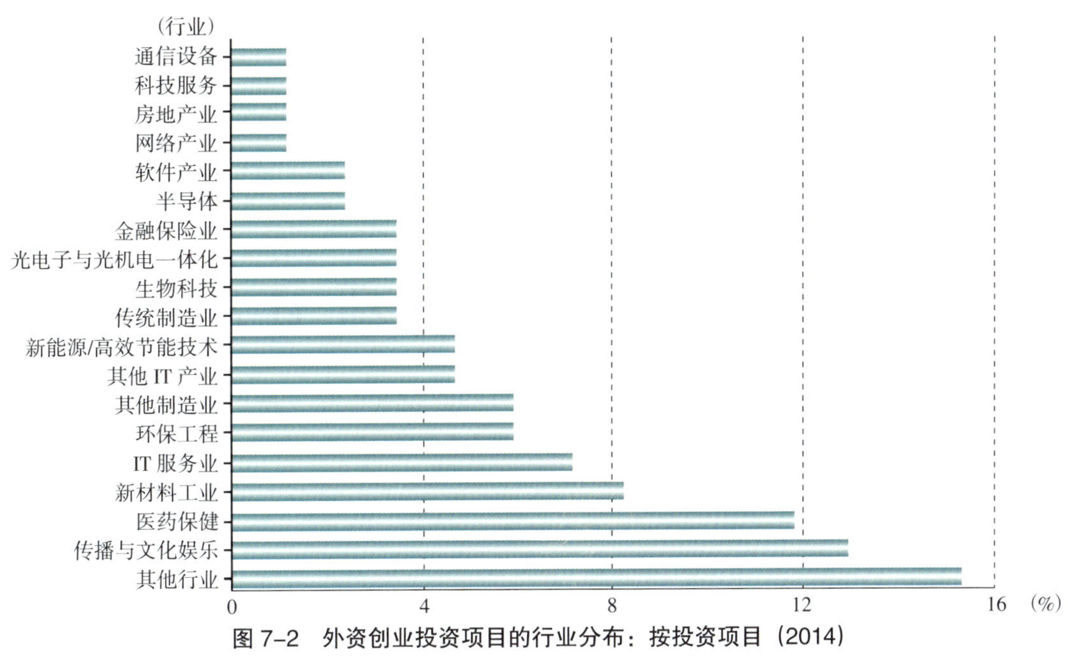

图 7-2　外资创业投资项目的行业分布：按投资项目（2014）

表 7-2 给出了 2014 年内资和外资创业风险投资项目前十大行业分布情况的对比，可以得出以下结论：

第一，内资、外资创业风险投资关注领域差异巨大。内资创业风险投资机构的投资金额主要集中在批发和零售业、通信设备行业、其他行业、传统制造业和软件产业。外资创业风险投资机构的关注焦点主要在传播与文化娱乐、房地产业、其他行业、医药保健和其他制造业。此外，外资创业风险投资对生物科技、环保工程、新材料工业以及新能源、高效节能技术也同样给予重视。并且，内资与外资创业风险投资机构共同关注的领域仅有传播与文化娱乐和新材料工业。由此可以看出，国内的创业风险投资机构对于投资的稳健性和收益可能会有较高的要求，而外资创业风险投资机构的关注重点多集中在与高科技有关的领域，能够对以创新和创造性为特点的小微企业给予资

表 7-2　内资、外资创业风险投资项目前十大行业分布：投资金额和投资项目（2014）　　单位：%

投资行业	内资		投资行业	外资	
	投资金额	投资项目		投资金额	投资项目
批发和零售业	22.5	2.0	传播与文化娱乐	28.6	12.9
通信设备	11.8	8.6	房地产业	11.3	1.2
其他行业	6.8	7.9	其他行业	9.9	15.3
传统制造业	6.5	5.0	医药保健	9.5	11.8
软件产业	6.3	9.7	其他制造业	6.6	5.9
医药保健	5.8	5.0	生物科技	5.3	3.5
计算机硬件产业	3.6	1.8	环保工程	5.2	5.9
网络产业	3.4	9.2	IT 服务业	5.0	7.1
传播与文化娱乐	3.2	3.5	新材料工业	4.9	8.2
新材料工业	2.9	5.8	新能源/高效节能技术	4.9	4.7

注：按“投资金额”占比排序。

金扶持。

第二，从投资项目和投资金额分析，外资创业风险投资机构投资的前十大行业均较 2013 年更为集中。与 2013 年相比，内资创业风险投资的前十大行业的投资金额占比从 70.6%上升至 72.8%，但投资项目所占比重略有下降，从 59.7%下降至 58.5%。与之相比，外资创业风险投资前十大行业分布的投资金额和投资项目占比均有所上升，其中投资金额占比从 2013 年的 81.5%大幅上升至 2014 年的 91.2%，投资项目占比由 2013 年的 71.4%上升至 2014 年的 76.5%。

7.2 外资创业风险投资项目所处阶段

通过对 2014 年外资创业风险投资项目所处阶段的调查发现（见图 7-3），无论是投资项目还是投资金额，外资对处于“成长（扩张）期”的项目依然有明显的投资偏好。但与之前相比，外资创业风险投资机构的投资阶段出现明显前移的状态。

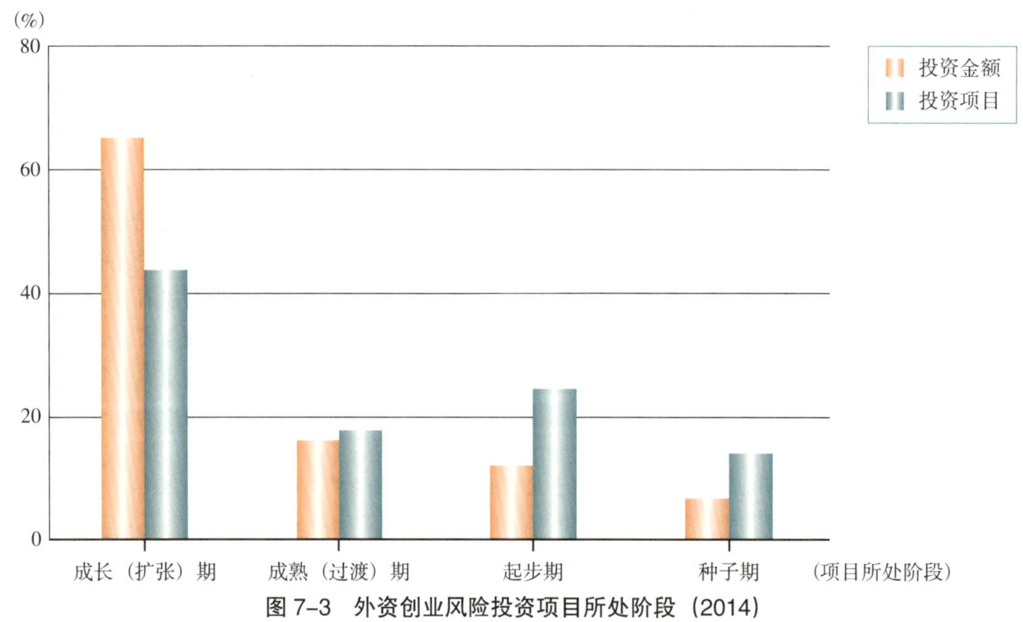

图 7-3 外资创业风险投资项目所处阶段（2014）

从投资金额角度分析，可以发现外资的资金较 2013 年更为集中，且主要集中在“成长（扩张）期”，所占比重由 2013 年的 52.8%上升至 2014 年的 65.5%。从投资项目来看，外资较 2013 年则相对分散，投资于“成长（扩张）期”和“起步期”的外资依然占主要地位但比重略有不同，其中成长（扩张）期所占比重比 2013 年下降了 9.2 个百分点，而投资于起步期的外资占比则由 2013 年的 23.4%上升至 24.7%，投资于种子期的外资所占比重也较 2013 年上升了 5.9 个百分点。

对比 2014 年内资和外资创业风险投资项目所处阶段（见表 7-3）可以发现以下异同点：

（1）与 2013 年相比，2014 年内资和外资创业风险投资机构开始更多地关注早前期的投资项目。其中，在“种子期”和“起步期”，内资机构投资的项目数量占比合计由 2013 年的 52.6%提升至 58%，而外资机构的投资项目数量占比累计也由 2013 年的 32.4%提升至 38.8%，分别提高了 5 个和 6 个百分点。

（2）从占比情况看，“成长（扩张）期”项目仍然是内资机构和外资机构关注的重点。与 2013 年相比，虽然内资和外资机构纷纷增加了对“种子期”和“起步期”项目的关注，但是按投资比重来看，处于“成长（扩张）期”的项目仍然得到了较多的支持。从具体数据看，2014 年，

表 7-3 内资和外资创业风险投资项目所处阶段（2014） 单位：%

投资阶段	投资项目		投资金额	
	内 资	外 资	内 资	外 资
种子期	21.0	14.1	4.5	6.6
起步期	37.0	24.7	21.2	12.0
成长（扩张）期	35.7	43.5	66.4	65.5
成熟（过渡）期	6.1	17.6	7.9	15.9
重建期	0.3	0.0	0.0	0.0

内资、外资创业风险投资机构对处于“成长（扩张）期”项目的投资金额显著增加，内资机构投资金额占比由 2013 年的 39.5%增加到 66.4%，外资机构投资金额占比由 2013 年的 52.8%增加到 65.5%。但是，从投资项目数量来看，内资、外资投资机构较 2013 年减少了对“成长（扩张）期”项目的投资。

（3）在投资项目和投资金额两方面，内资机构和外资机构对于“成长（扩张）期”的项目资金投入差距明显缩小。其中，投资项目占比差距从 2013 年的 15.8%缩小至 7.8%，投资金额占比差距从 2013 年的 13.3%缩减至 0.9%。此外，内资投资机构在“成长（扩张）期”的投资金额较 2013 年大幅提高，从 39.5%上升至 66.4%。

7.3 外资创业风险投资的投资强度

2014 年外资创业风险投资单项投资金额的分布情况依然延续 2011 年以来的状况（见表 7-4、图 7-4），即投资的单项资金规模仍然以 1000 万~2000 万元和 2000 万元以上为主，两者所占比重从 2013 年的 94.3%略微下降至 2014 年的 93.3%。其中，单项投资规模在 1000 万~2000 万元的项目比重略有上升，从 2013 年的 16.1%上升至 2014 年的 18.1%。此外，2014 年也出现了 0.1%的单笔投资金额在 100 万元项目以下的小型投资项目。然而，单笔投资金额在 1000 万元以下项目所占比重仍然很低，四个档位累计占比 6.7%。

表 7-4 外资创业风险投资单项投资金额的规模分布（2011~2014） 单位：%

投资金额分布（万元）/年份	100 以下	100~300	300~500	500~1000	1000~2000	2000 以上
2011	0.0	0.2	0.3	3.3	13.9	82.3
2012	0.4	0.4	1.4	9.7	24.5	63.7
2013	0.0	0.1	1.3	4.2	16.1	78.2
2014	0.1	0.4	0.9	5.3	18.1	75.2

通过对比内资和外资风险投资单项投资金额的规模分布（见表 7-5、图 7-5）可以发现，2000 万元以上的投资项目仍然是内资和外资创业风险投资机构的主要投资方向。其中，内资机构对 1000 万元以上的投资项目投资累计占比从 2013 年的 82.9%上升至 2014 年的 88.6%。而外资机构投资金额在 1000 万元以上项目的累计占比则从 2013 年的 94.3%下降了一个百分点至 93.3%。同时，与 2013 年相比，内资创业风险投资机构单笔投资在 2000 万元以上的项目占比明显提高，所占比重从 64.2%上升至 75.2%，与外资创业风险投资机构占比持平。此外，内资、

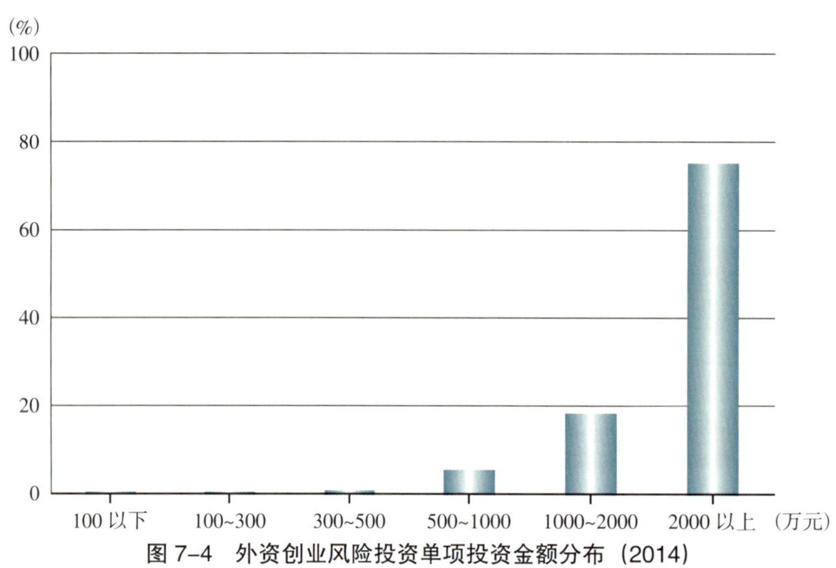

图 7-4 外资创业风险投资单项投资金额分布（2014）

外资创业风险投资机构单笔投资金额在 1000 万元以下的中小型项目占比与 2013 年相比也出现明显变化，其中，外资创业风险投资机构项目所占比重由 5.6%小幅提升至 6.7%，而内资创业风险投资机构的项目占比则下降了 5.6 个百分点，下降至 11.3%。

表 7-5 内资和外资创业风险投资单项投资金额的规模分布（2014） 单位：%

分布比例	100 万元以下	100 万~300 万元	300 万~500 万元	500 万~1000 万元	1000 万~2000 万元	2000 万元以上
外资	0.1	0.4	0.9	5.3	18.1	75.2
内资	0.3	1.9	2.7	6.4	13.4	75.2

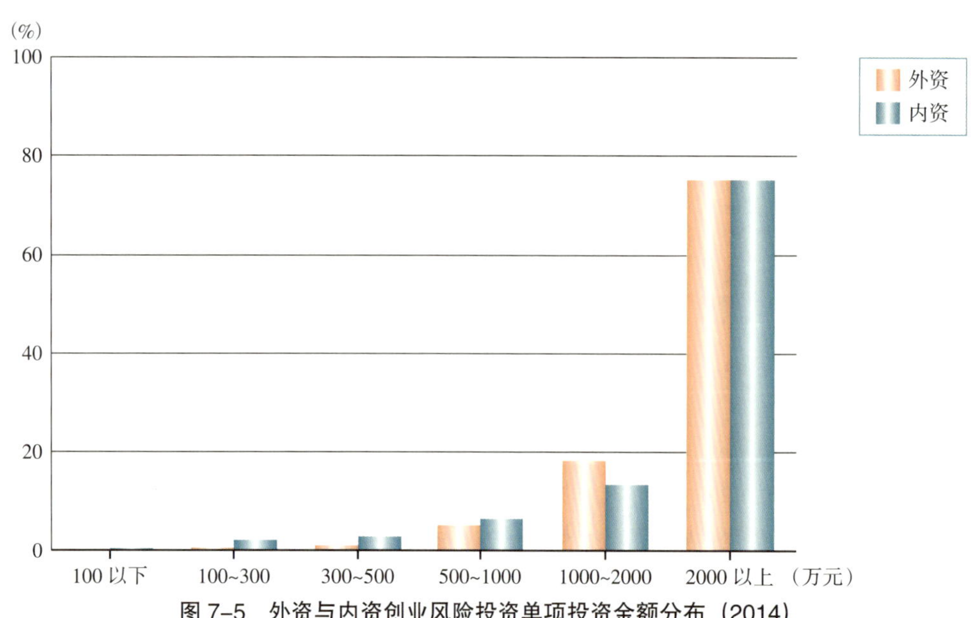

图 7-5 外资与内资创业风险投资单项投资金额分布（2014）

7.4 外资创业风险投资项目状况分析

7.4.1 创业风险投资项目的实收资本情况

与2013年相比，外资创业风险投资开始向早前期项目倾斜，实收资本规模分布情况也较2013年更为分散（见表7-6、图7-6）。其中，实收资本规模在500万元以下、1000万~3000万元的投资项目所占比重都有了明显的提升，所占比重分别从5.3%和15.8%上升至18.7%和25.3%；而实收资本规模在3000万元以上的项目占比则呈现出下降的状态，特别是实收资本规模在5000万元以上的项目所占比重从52.6%骤降至33.3%，下降了19.3个百分点；实收资本3000万~5000万元的项目占比则略下降至14.7%。从图7-6的外资创业风险投资项目实收资本规模分布的饼状图也可以更明显地看出外资创业风险投资机构的投资规模相对分散。

表7-6 外资创业风险投资项目实收资本的规模分布（2011~2014） 单位：%

年份 \ 实收资本（万元）	500以下	500~1000	1000~3000	3000~5000	5000以上
2011	9.3	5.9	27.1	16.9	40.7
2012	11.0	15.0	29.0	11.0	34.0
2013	5.3	8.8	15.8	17.5	52.6
2014	18.7	8.0	25.3	14.7	33.3

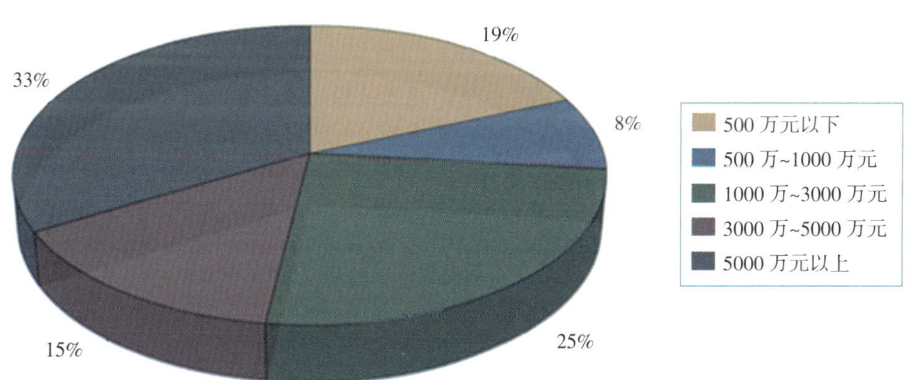

图7-6 外资创业风险投资项目实收资本的规模分布（2014）

2014年，外资创业风险投资机构主要的投资方向并没有发生改变，即实收资本在3000万元以上的投资项目依然是外资创业风险投资机构的主要选择。但投资金额所占比重与2013年相比有了明显变化：实收资本在5000万元以上的投资项目所占比重下降了19.3个百分点，而实收资本在1000万~3000万元的投资项目占比则上升了9.5个百分点，上升至25.3%；实收资本在500万元以下的投资项目占比则上涨至18.7%，较2013年上升了13.4个百分点。

另外，与2013年相比，内资创业风险投资机构最为明显的变化就是投资于实收资本在500万元以下的投资项目所占比重明显提升，由20.4%上升至36.2%。由此可见，2014年外资创业风险投资机构在中国的投资策略出现了投资阶段前移的趋势。而内资创业风险投资机构则主要关注投资金额在500万元以下的小型投资项目（见表7-7、图7-7）。

表 7-7 外资和内资创业风险投资项目实收资本的规模分布（2014） 单位：%

分布比例	500 万元以下	500 万~1000 万元	1000 万~3000 万元	3000 万~5000 万元	5000 万元以上
外资	18.7	8.0	25.3	14.7	33.3
内资	36.2	12.3	20.6	9.5	21.4

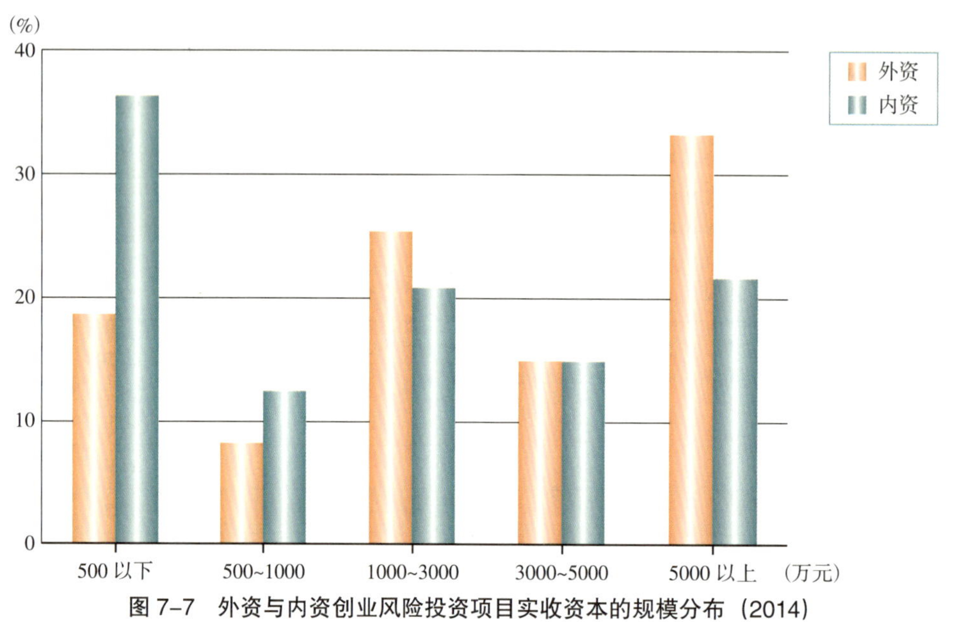

图 7-7 外资与内资创业风险投资项目实收资本的规模分布（2014）

7.4.2 创业风险投资项目的雇员情况

调查数据显示（见表 7-8、图 7-8），2014 年外资创业风险项目雇员人数分布基本保持稳定，其中，除投资项目雇员人数在 10~50 人和 100~150 人的规模分布较 2013 年有所上升外，其余雇佣人员规模分布都出现了不同程度的下降。

表 7-8 外资创业风险投资项目雇员人数分布（2011~2014） 单位：%

年份 \ 分布比例（人）	10 以下	10~50	50~100	100~150	150~200	200 以上
2011	3.6	13.4	8.9	14.3	13.4	46.4
2012	8.3	17.9	9.5	21.4	10.7	32.1
2013	13.3	13.3	16.7	10.0	6.7	40.0
2014	10.5	19.7	10.5	15.8	6.6	36.8

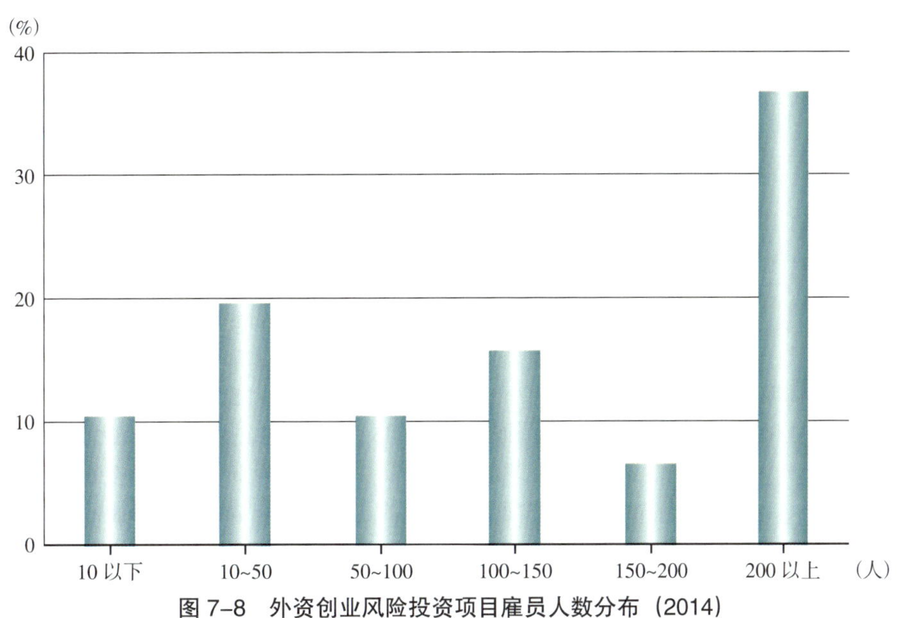

图 7-8 外资创业风险投资项目雇员人数分布（2014）

表 7-9、图 7-9 给出了 2014 年外资与内资创业风险投资项目雇员人数分布情况，其中外资创业风险投资机构更加倾向于投资雇员人数规模在 150 人及以下和 200 人以上的项目，前者占比之和为 56.5%；而从项目雇员人数规模分布情况，也同样能够得出内资创业风险投资机构更倾向于小型项目，这与投资项目的实收资本规模分析所得结论一致。此外，雇员人数在 200 人以上的大型投资项目占比仍然是内资和外资机构差异最大的一组，由 2013 年相差 16.8 个百分点提高到 2014 年的 17.6%，但所占比重均出现下降，其中外资机构占比由 2013 年的 40%下降至 2014 年的 36.8%，内资机构占比则由 23.2%下降至 19.2%。

表 7-9 外资与内资创业风险投资项目雇员人数分布（2014） 单位：%

分布比例（人）	10 以下	10~50	50~100	100~150	150~200	200 以上
外资	10.5	19.7	10.5	15.8	6.6	36.8
内资	19.1	33.3	15.1	8.3	5.0	19.2

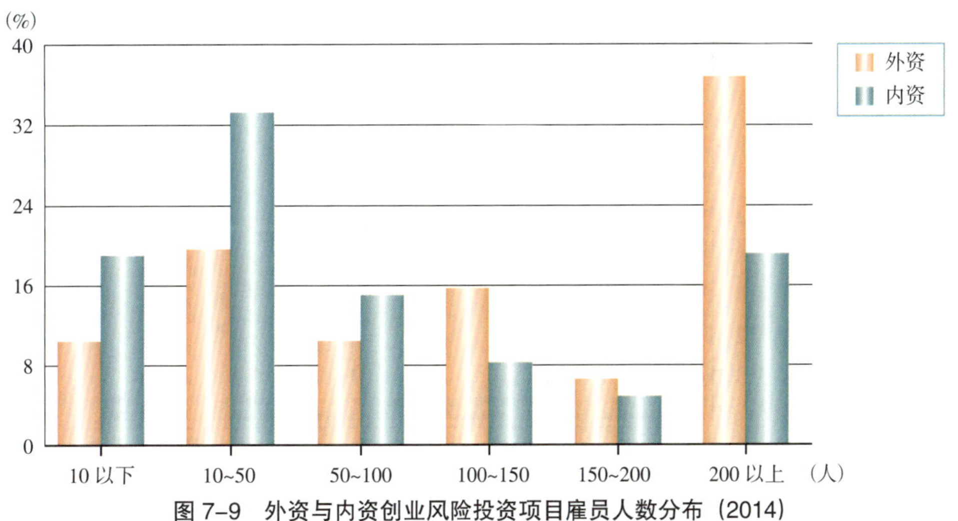

图 7-9 外资与内资创业风险投资项目雇员人数分布（2014）

7.5 外资创业风险投资项目的总体运作情况

表 7-10 和图 7-10 给出了截至 2014 年底外资创业风险投资项目运行的基本情况。通过调查发现，2014 年外资创业风险投资的整体投资周期较 2013 年和 2012 年有所延长，从侧面反映出外资创业风险投资机构开始关注早前期的投资项目。

（1）与 2013 年相比，2014 年“已上市”的投资项目占比明显下降，比重由 10.8%下降至 4.5%，下降了 6.3 个百分点。原因可能在于根据 2013 年对投资项目运行情况的调查，“准备上市”的项目仅占全部运作情况的 7%。此外，与 2013 年“准备上市”项目所占比重相比，2014 年有 15%的项目准备上市，所占比重连续三年上升。

（2）“被其他机构收购”项目所占比重上升，由 2013 年的 5.1%上升至 2014 年的 9.8%。其中相对而言，比重变化明显的是“被境外收购”的项目，占比由 0.2%上升至

表 7-10 截至 2014 年底外资创业风险投资项目运作情况 单位：%

投资项目运作情况	已上市		准备上市		被其他机构收购			原股东（创业者）回购	管理层收购	继续运行	清算
	境内上市	境外上市	境内上市	境外上市	境内上市公司收购	境内非上市公司或自然人收购	境外收购				
2012 年	10.7		6.2		6.0			6.5	0.7	68.8	1.1
	7.6	3.1	5.1	1.1	1.1	4.9	0.0				
2013 年	10.8		7.0		5.1			10.0	14.0	52.0	1.1
	7.4	3.4	6.5	0.5	0.8	4.1	0.2				
2014 年	4.5		15.0		9.8			4.0	0.0	70.6	0.9
	3.3	1.2	9.5	5.5	0.5	5.5	3.8				

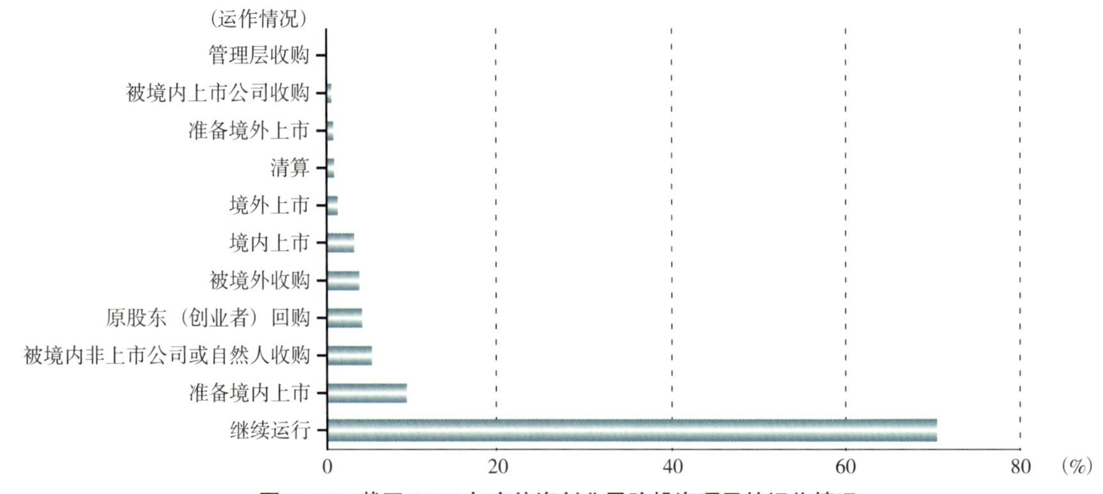

图 7-10 截至 2014 年底外资创业风险投资项目的运作情况

3.8%。

（3）2014 年“原股东（创业者）回购”的投资项目所占比例出现三年来新低，仅占 4%。而通过对 31 份样本调查发现 2014 年并未发生管理层收购情况。

（4）“继续运行”的投资项目仍然是外资创业风险投资项目最主要的运行情况，且所占比重较 2013 年有较大幅度上升，由 52%上升至 70.6%。这可能是外资创业风险投资机构开始转变投资策略，逐渐投资于早前期的项目所导致。

表 7-11、图 7-11 给出了截至 2014 年底外资与内资创业风险投资项目运作情况进行的对比，从表中可以看出内资机构和外资机构的投资项目运作情况并没有出现明显差异。其中，内资和外资“继续运行”的投资项目仍然占较大比重，且所占比重之间的差异进一步缩小，由 2013 年相差 15.9 个百分点下降到 2014 年仅相差 0.9 个百分点。此外，2014 年外资投资机构以“其他机构收购”退出的项目占比最高，而内资机构的投资项目则继续以上市为主要退出渠道。

表 7-11　截至 2014 年底外资与内资创业风险投资项目运作情况　单位：%

运作情况	继续运行	准备上市	其他机构收购	已上市	原股东（创业者）回购	清算	管理层收购
外资	70.6	10.2	9.7	4.5	4.0	0.9	0.0
内资	69.7	9.3	4.6	7.7	6.7	1.4	0.7

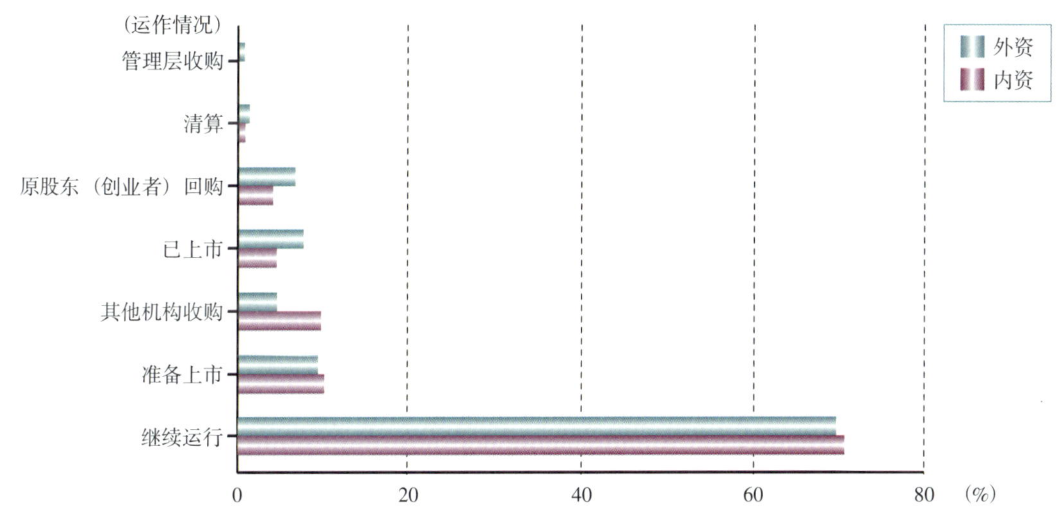

图 7-11　截至 2014 年底外资与内资创业风险投资项目的运作情况

7.6 影响外资创业风险投资机构投资决策的因素

2014 年影响外资创业风险投资机构投资决策的前三个主要因素分别是“市场前景”、“管理团队”以及“技术因素”（见图 7-12），分别占比 18.5%、16%和 12.3%。首先，与 2013 年相比，投资项目的“市场前景”成为影响外资创业风险投资机构是否进行投资以及如何对投资项目进行选择的最主要因素。其次，“管理团队”因素所占比重由

2013 年的 19.2%下降至 2014 年的 16%，成为 2014 年影响外资创业风险投资机构投资决策的第二个主要因素。最后，“技术因素”所占比重为 12.3%，超越“盈利模式”成为第三个影响外资创业风险投资机构投资决策的因素。

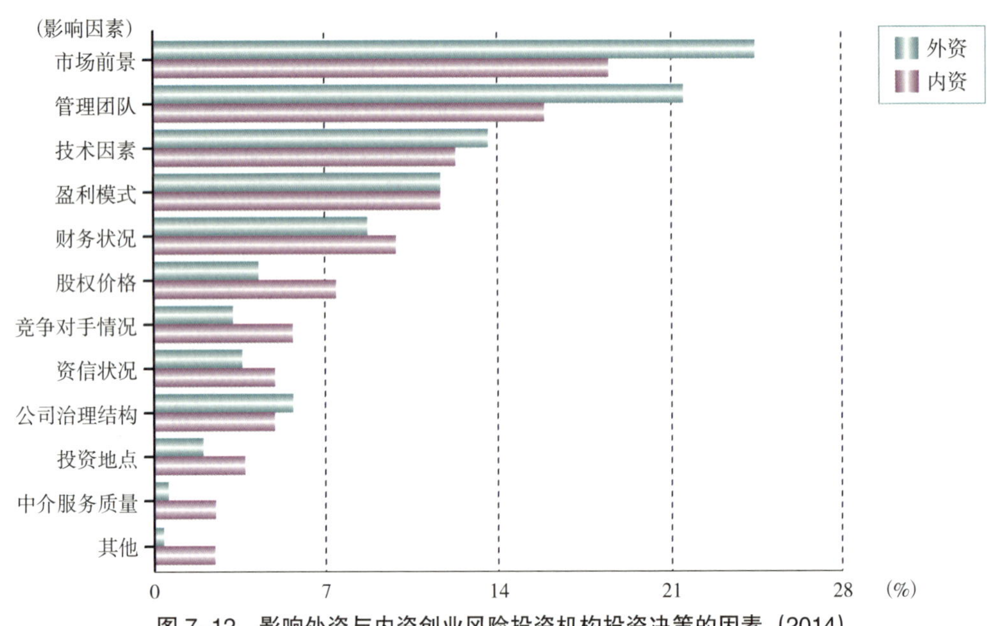

图 7-12 影响外资与内资创业风险投资机构投资决策的因素（2014）

对比 2014 年内资和外资创业风险投资机构决策要素可以发现，“市场前景”、“管理团队”、“技术因素”、“盈利模式”以及“财务状况”是影响内资和外资投资决策的前五个共同要素，所占比重合计分别为 80.2%和 68.4%。其中，内资创业风险投资机构对于“市场前景”和“管理团队”的重视程度分别以 24.5%和 21.6%的比重高于外资创业风险投资机构，所占比例分别相差了 6 个和 5.6 个百分点。

除了前五个最主要因素外，内资创业风险投资机构还比较看重投资项目的“公司治理结构”，其在影响内资和外资机构决策要素中所占比重分别为 5.6%和 4.9%，而外资创业风险投资机构更注重“股权价格”，其在影响内资和外资机构决策要素中所占比重分别为 7.4%和 4.3%。

7.7 外资创业风险投资机构获取信息的主要渠道

通过对内资和外资创业风险投资机构获取信息渠道的调查发现（见图 7-13），获取信息的主要渠道与 2013 年相比出现较大变化：

（1）“股东推荐”成为外资创业风险投资机构最主要的信息来源，排名由 2013 年的第五位上升至 2014 年的第一位，所占比重上升至 18.6%。

（2）“项目中介机构”的排名下降两位，所占比重由 2013 年的 20.6%下降至 2014 年的 16.9%。

（3）“政府部门推荐”的排名延续了 2013 年的下降态势，从 2012 年的 21.4%下降至 2013 年的 18.1%，到 2014 年进一步下降至 15.3%。

此外，与 2013 年相比，内资创业风险投资机构三个主要信息来源仍然是“政府部门介绍”、“项目中介机构”以及“朋友介绍”。但是，“项目中介机构”所占比重比

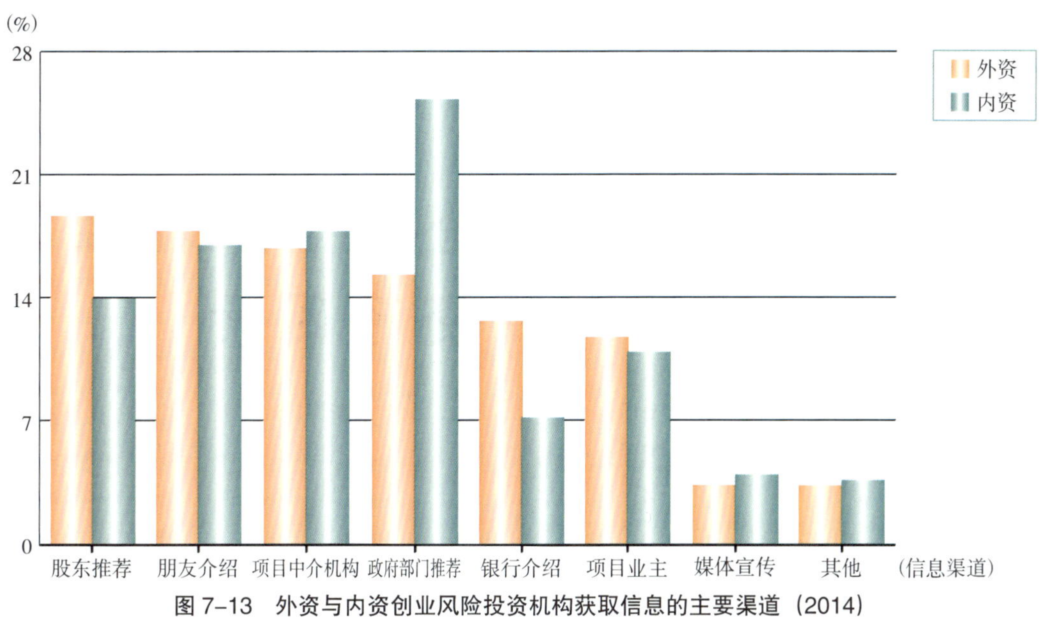

图 7-13　外资与内资创业风险投资机构获取信息的主要渠道（2014）

2013 年有所提高，成为内资创业风险投资机构的第二个主要信息来源，而“朋友介绍”所占比重有所下降，成为机构获取信息的第三个来源，因为内资机构在获取信息时往往比外资机构更具有优势，所以，外资机构更倾向于“股东推荐”、“朋友介绍”等熟人之间的信誉。

7.8 外资创业风险投资项目的监管模式

与 2013 年相比，2014 年外资创业风险投资项目的监管模式并没有发生比较明显的变化（见图 7-14），“提供管理咨询”、“董事会席位”和“财务咨询”仍然是外资创业风险投资机构投资项目的主要监管模式。“提供管理咨询”和“董事会席位”所占比重均为 33.3%，分别比 2013 年上升了 1.1 个和 0.1 个百分点。

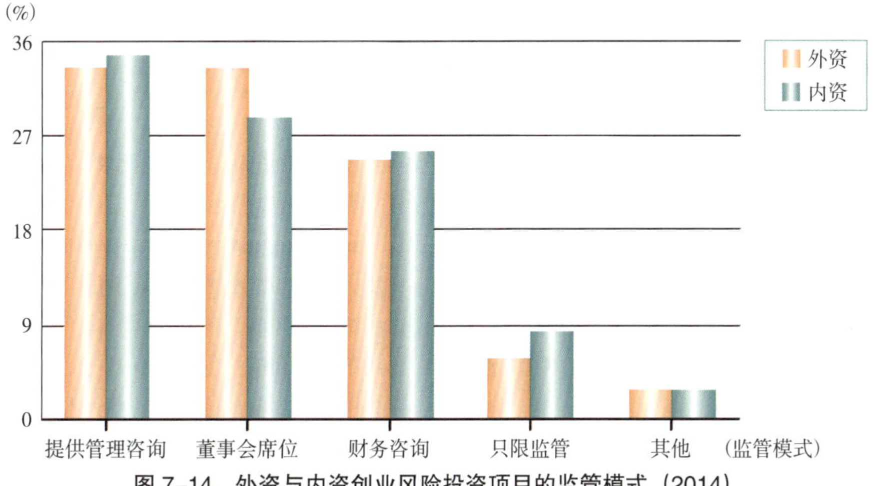

图 7-14　外资与内资创业风险投资项目的监管模式（2014）

对比内资和外资创业风险投资项目监管模式可以发现，内资创业风险投资机构“提供管理咨询”和“财务咨询”两个监管方式所占比重分别以 34.5%和 25.5%略微高于外资机构，而“董事会席位”的监管模式占比则低于外资机构 4.6 个百分点。

7.9 与外资创业风险投资机构经营有关的人力资源因素

本节从创业风险投资人员应该具备的基本素质以及我国从事创业风险投资人员缺乏的知识两方面开展了有关调查。可以发现与 2013 年相比，外资创业风险投资机构对相关从业人员的综合素质提出了更高的要求。

通过调查外资和内资创业风险投资机构对创业风险投资从业人员基本素质的要求发现（见图 7-15），2014 年外资机构对合格创业风险投资人员从业素质要求发生明显变化。与 2013 年相比，外资创业风险投资机构更加注重从业人员的“判断力和洞察力”，其所占比重较 2013 年上升了 2.1 个百分点，成为 2014 年合格的从业人员最应该具备的素质，在“判断力和洞察力”、“商务谈判能力”、“资本运作能力”、“财务管理能力”、“技术背景”、“人际关系网络”这几个重要因素中排名第一，“商务谈判能力”和“资本运作能力”的排名分别从 2013 年的第六位和第四位上升至 2014 年的第二位和第三位，所占比例均为 17.4%。

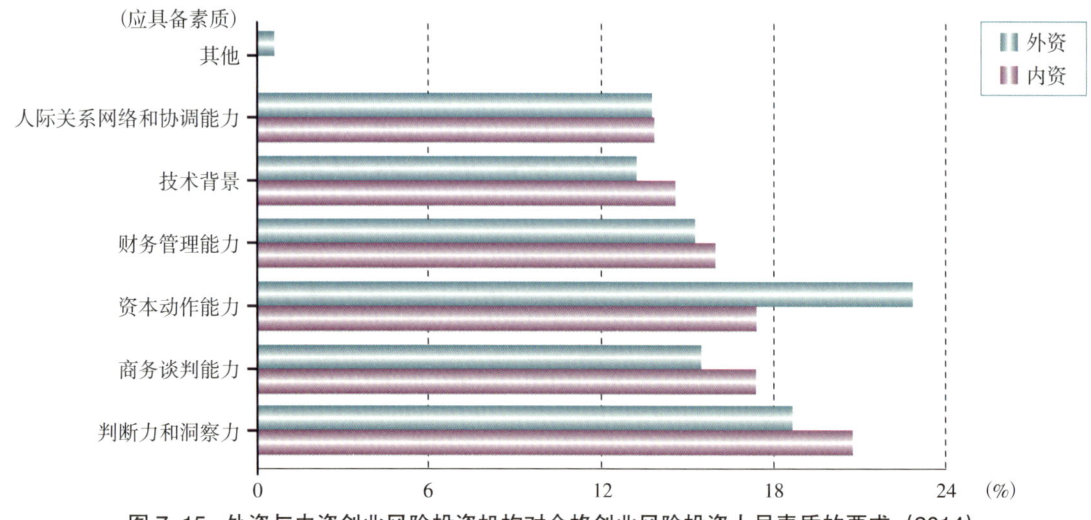

图 7-15 外资与内资创业风险投资机构对合格创业风险投资人员素质的要求（2014）

此外，通过对比内资和外资机构对于从事创业风险投资人员基本素质的要求能够发现，内资创业风险投资机构对于从业人员是否具备“资本运作能力”有更高期望，所占比重为 22.9%，而“判断力和洞察力”以 18.7%的比重成为第二个重要素质。

调查显示（见图 7-16），2014 年外资创业风险投资机构认为我国从事创业风险投资的相关人员最缺乏的是“项目识别”的相关知识，所占比重由 2013 年的第四位上升至第一位，“资本运作”从 2013 年的第五位上升至 2014 年的第二位，而“技术评估”和“技术背景”分别从 2013 年的第一位和第二位下降至第三位和第四位。这说明 2014 年我国从事创业风险投资的相关人员加强了技术层面的学习，但在综合素质方面，项目识别和资本运作等方面的知识仍然有待提高。

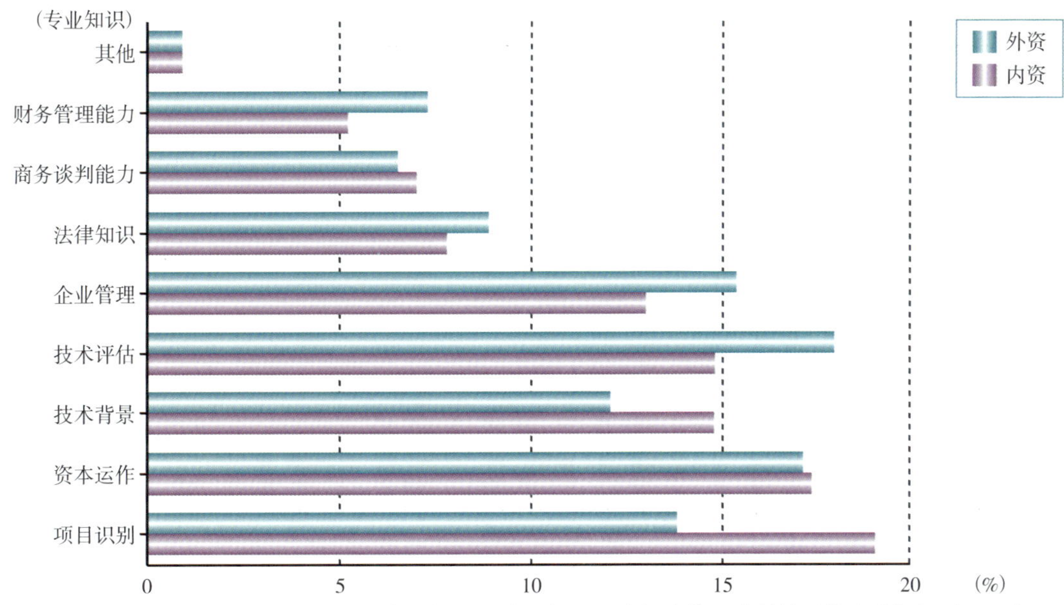

图 7-16 外资与内资创业风险投资机构认为我国创业风险投资从业人员缺乏的专业知识（2014）

对比内资、外资创业风险投资机构对于人才的要求，2014 年内资创业风险投资机构认为从业人员最缺乏的知识依然是“技术评估”和“资本运作”，所占比重分别是 18%和 17.2%。而外资机构认为从业人员最缺乏的“项目识别”技能，在内资创业风险投资机构认为我国创业风险投资从业人员缺乏的专业知识中排名第四，占比仅为 13.9%。

7.10 外资创业风险投资机构对总体发展环境的评价

创业风险投资主要的获利形式是通过市场退出机制将投入的资本由股权形态转化为资金形态，从而获得高收益。2014 年，作为创新主体的企业创新热情不高、企业缺乏创新动力。同时受到总体宏观经济环境影响，创业风险投资呈现出融资难、管理去投资化、投资项目去库存化等特点。

2014 年外资创业风险投资机构关于投资效果是否理想的调查显示（见图 7-17），“退出渠道不畅”仍然是外资创业风险投资机构认为导致投资效果不理想的最主要原因，所占比重由 2013 年的 28.2%上升至 31.4%。这说明我国创业风险投资的多层次资本市场、产权交易市场等支撑体系仍然有待进一步加强。

外资机构认为，与 2013 年相比，“市场竞争”成为第二个可能会影响创业风险投资效果的原因，所占比重由 2013 年的不到 8%上升至 2014 年的 17.1%。“政策环境变化”对我国创业风险投资效果的影响由第二位下降至第三位，比重由 28%下降至 14.3%。这说明了在我国创业风险投资快速发展的过程中，创业风险投资政策得到了不断优化和完善，给予了外资创业风险投资机构一定政策优惠和支持。

对比内资、外资机构对行业总体发展环境的评价（见图 7-17），“退出渠道不畅”也同样成为内资创业风险投资机构认为投资效果不理想的最重要因素。而内资机构认为影响投资效果的第二个因素则是“政策环境变化”。

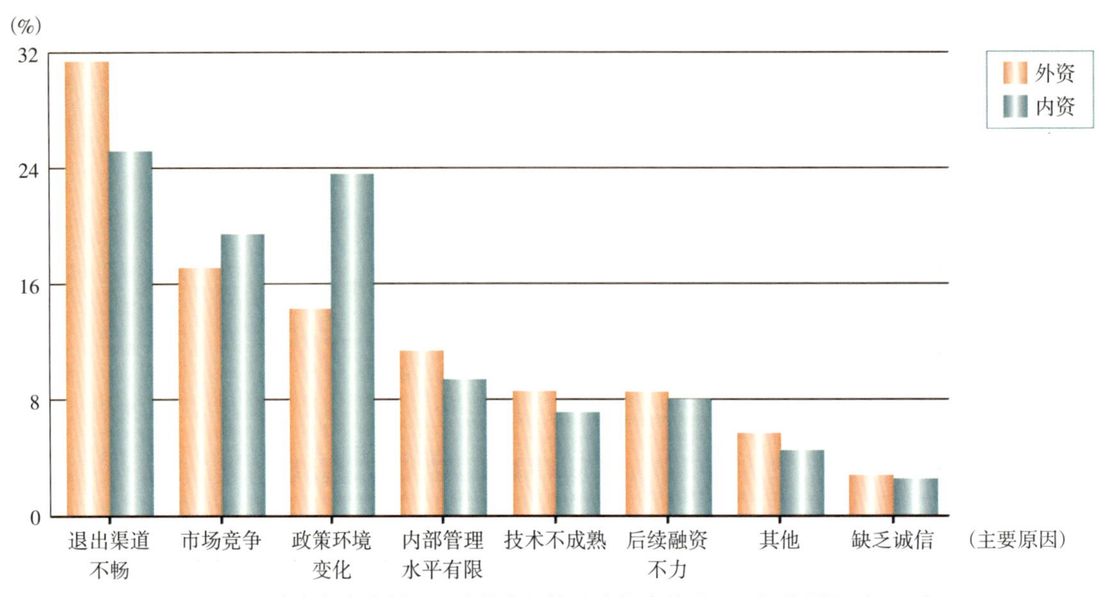

图 7-17 外资与内资创业风险投资机构认为投资效果不理想的原因（2014）

2014 年针对外资与内资创业风险投资机构面临的主要发展困难进行了判断，调查结果显示（见图 7-18），“多层次资本市场不完善”、“缺乏好项目”以及“政策不明朗”是外资创业风险投资机构认为发展过程中面临的三个困难，所占比重分别是 49.2%、34.3%和 20%。此外，与 2013 年较为不同的地方是，“企业管理水平”和“创业投资人员的素质低”不再是 2014 年阻碍外资创业风险投资机构发展水平的原因。

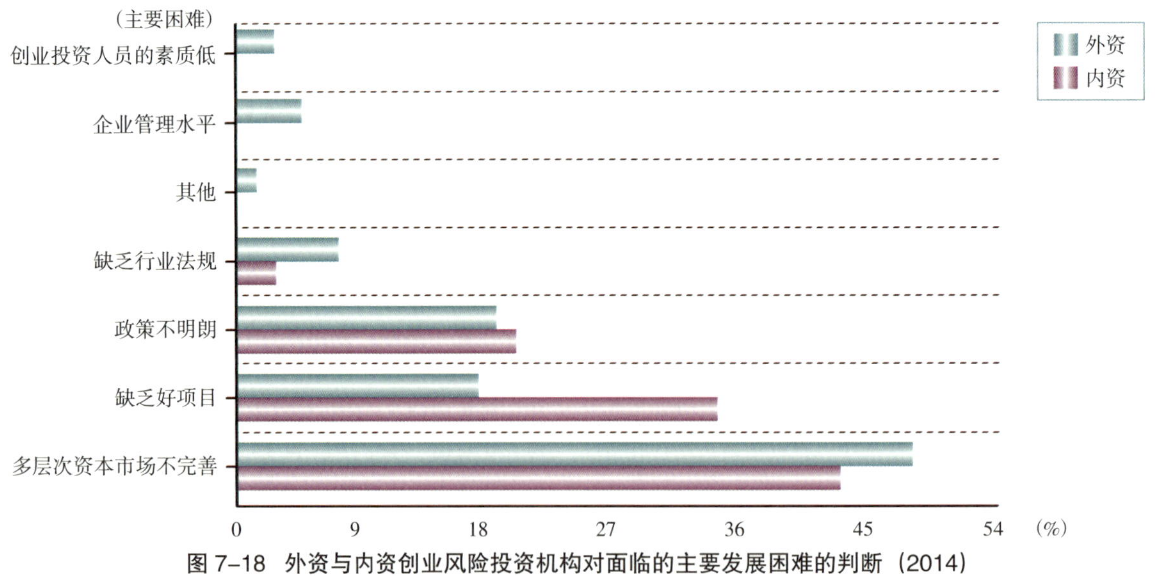

图 7-18 外资与内资创业风险投资机构对面临的主要发展困难的判断（2014）

对比内资和外资创业风险投资机构对环境的总体评价可以发现，“多层次资本市场不完善”成为内资和外资创业风险投资机构共同认定的主要障碍，但所占比重内资比外资高出 5.2 个百分点。而对内资机构而言，受“政策不明朗”困难的影响要大于“缺乏好项目”的影响。

8 中国创业风险投资发展环境

8.1 中国创业风险投资机构的政策环境

根据调研样本数据，本节将主要分析中国创业风险投资机构当前所处的政策环境，梳理中国创业风险投资机构最希望出台的有关政策等信息。

8.1.1 中国创业风险投资机构可以享受到的政府扶持政策

近年来，中央及地方都出台了一系列相关政策措施支持我国创业风险投资发展。2014 年调查显示，约有 20.2%的创业风险投资机构享受到政府资金支持，比例低于 2013 年的 22.0%，22.9%的创业风险投资机构享受到所得税减免政策优惠，低于 2013 年的 25.0%；29.1%的创业风险投资机构在信息交流方面得到了政府支持，13.4%的创业风险投资机构在人员培训方面得到了政府帮助（见图 8-1），都略高于 2013 年。可以看出，政府对创投机构在财税方面的直接支持在减少，但给予的间接服务支持比例在增加。

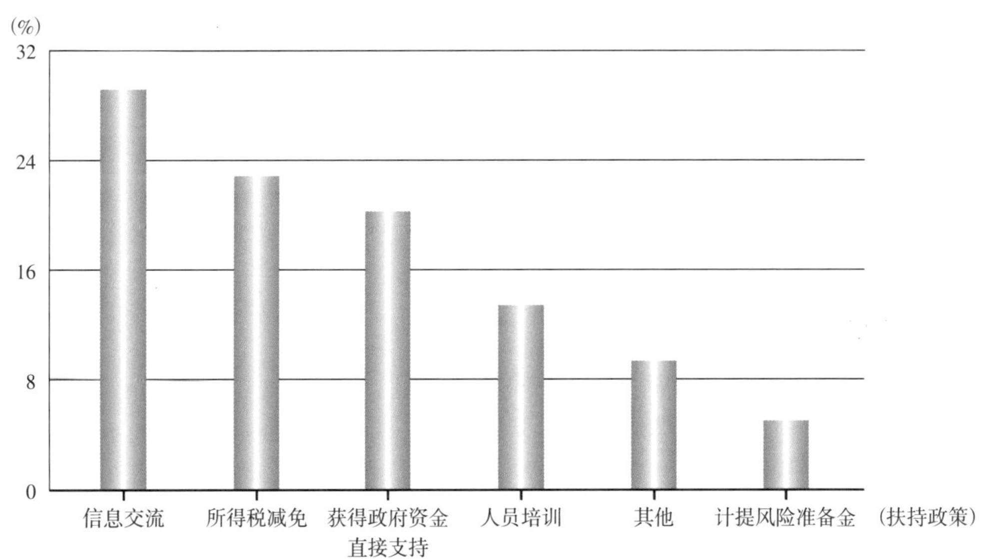

图 8-1 创业风险投资机构可以享受到的政府扶持政策（2014）

2014 年调查显示[①]，各地实施了多项政府扶持政策措施支持创业风险投资机构发展，北京、江苏等地区都有20%以上的创业风险投资机构获得政府资金支持，较往年有所下降，天津约有 48.15%的创业风险投资机构获得政府资金支持，相对占比较高。所得税减免依然是政府直接支持创业风险投资机构的主要措施，江西、浙江、新疆等地超过 30%的创业风险投资机构获得所得税减免；河北、甘肃等许多地区的创业风险投资机构可以计提风险准备金，降低了投资风险和成本；同时，各地普遍为创业风险投资机构提供了信息交流服务（见图 8-2），较往年有了较大比

①有效样本数为 1002 份。

例的增长。各项扶持政策的受惠面进一步扩大，为创业风险投资机构发展营造了良好的环境。

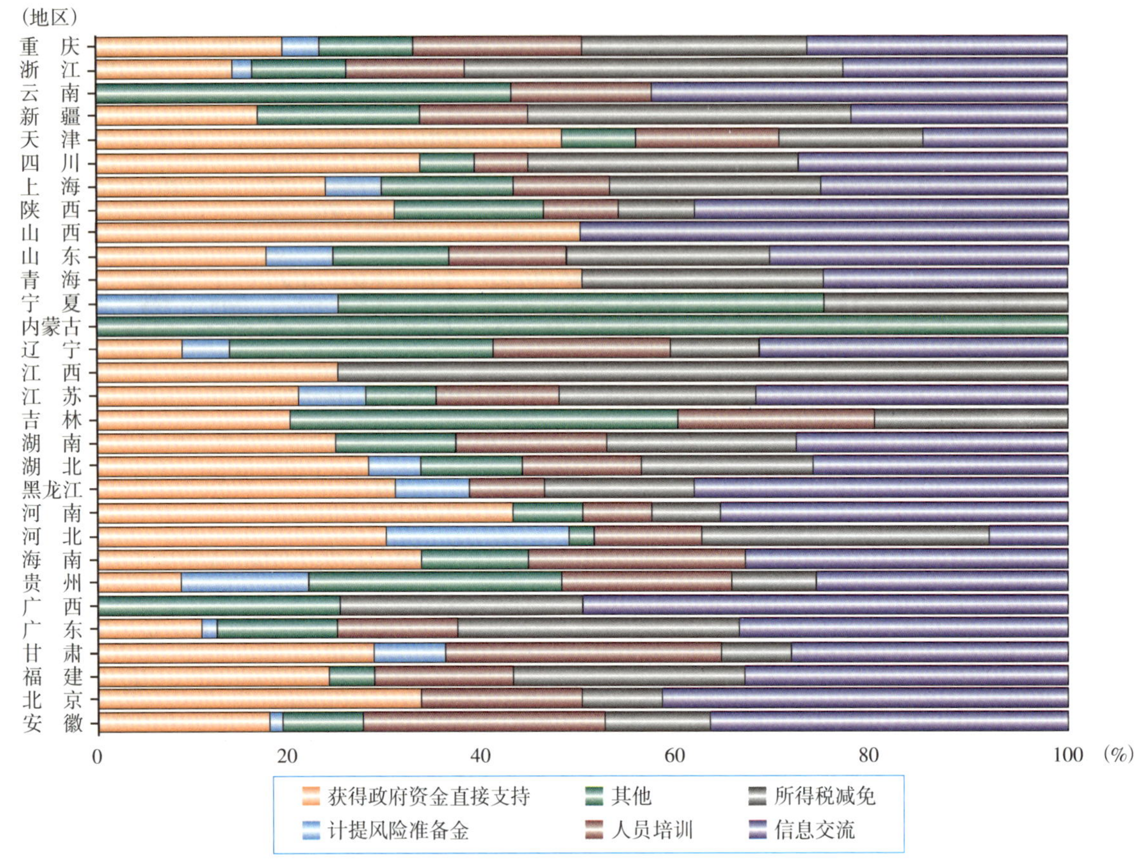

图 8-2 创业风险投资机构可以享受到的政府扶持政策（2014）

8.1.2 中国创业风险投资机构税收负担情况

2007 年财政部、国家税务总局出台了《关于促进创业投资企业发展有关税收政策的通知》（财税〔2007〕31 号），对创业风险投资机构实行税收优惠政策。《国家税务总局关于实施创业投资企业所得税优惠问题的通知》（国税发〔2009〕87 号）就创业风险投资企业所得税优惠的有关问题进行具体规定。

2014 年调查显示，56.3%的创业风险投资机构税收负担在 10%以下，17.9%的创业风险投资机构税收负担在 10%~20%，17.8%的创业风险投资机构税收负担在 20%~30%，仅 8.0%的创业风险投资机构承担着 30%以上的较高税负（见图 8-3）。与近几年相比，2014 年我国创业风险投资行业整体税收负担有所减少，高税收负担的创业风险投资机构占比略有下降。尽管绝大部分创业风险投资机构税收占比分布于 30%以下，但仍有一些地区税收优惠政策并未有效落实，在一定程度上影响创业风险投资行业发展。

8.1.3 中国创业风险投资机构希望的政府激励政策

2014 年调查样本显示，中国创业风险投资机构最希望出台的政府激励政策主要有以下几类（见图 8-4）：

（1）税收减免。根据调查，中国创业风险投资机构最希望出台的政府激励政策是税收减免类，占 25.5%，比 2013 年有所上升。

（2）设立政策类引导基金。根据调查，23.9%的调查对象希望设立政策性引导基金，并通过参股或融资担保等方式支持创业风险投资发展，占比较 2013 年略有提高。

（3）完善多层次资本市场。根据调查，17.2%的调查对象希望进一步完善中国多层次资本市场建设，占比较 2013 年略有下降，国内多层次资本市场的不断完善发挥了积极作用。

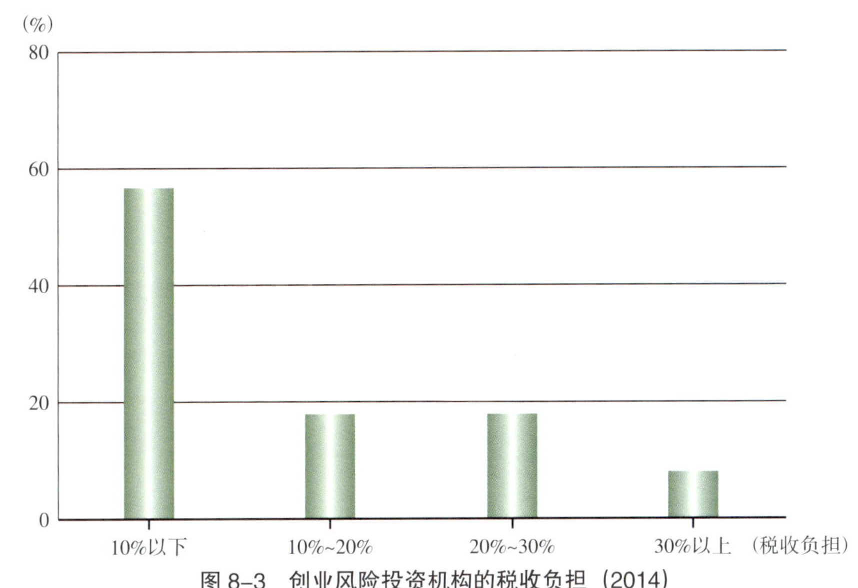

图 8-3 创业风险投资机构的税收负担(2014)

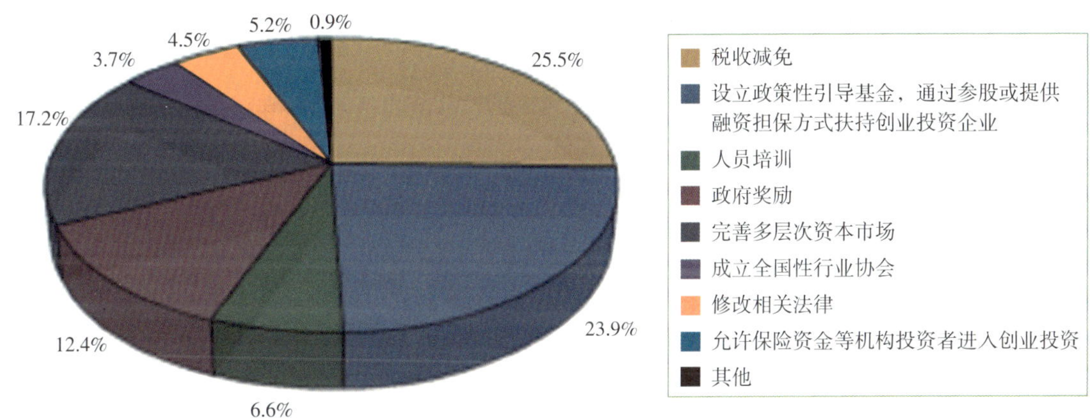

图 8-4 创业风险投资机构希望的政府激励政策(2014)

(4)政府奖励。根据调查,12.4%的创业风险投资机构希望能够出台相关政府奖励政策,鼓励创业风险投资发展,支持科技成果转化和科技型中小企业发展。

(5)扩大资金来源。5.2%的创业风险投资机构希望允许保险等机构投资者进入创业风险投资领域。但目前,由于受到《商业银行法》、《保险法》等限制,我国数十万亿的社会保险、银行、保险等机构资金还无法大规模进入创业风险投资领域。

8.2 国家科技计划支撑创业风险投资发展

8.2.1 国家科技计划对创业风险投资项目的支持情况

2014 年调查样本显示[①],中国创业风险投资项目中,约有 7%的项目获得了国家科技计划的支持,低于 2013 年的 10.2%,其中,2.18%创业风险投资项目获得了科技型中小企业技术创新基金支持,低于 2013 年的 3.08%;有

① 有效样本数为 2473 份。

0.65%和 0.57%创业风险投资项目分别受到“火炬”计划和“863 计划”的支持，约有 3.32%受到了其他国家级计划的支持（见图 8-5），较 2013 年减少了 13.09%，创业风险投资项目中获得国家科技计划项目的占比有一定幅度的减少。

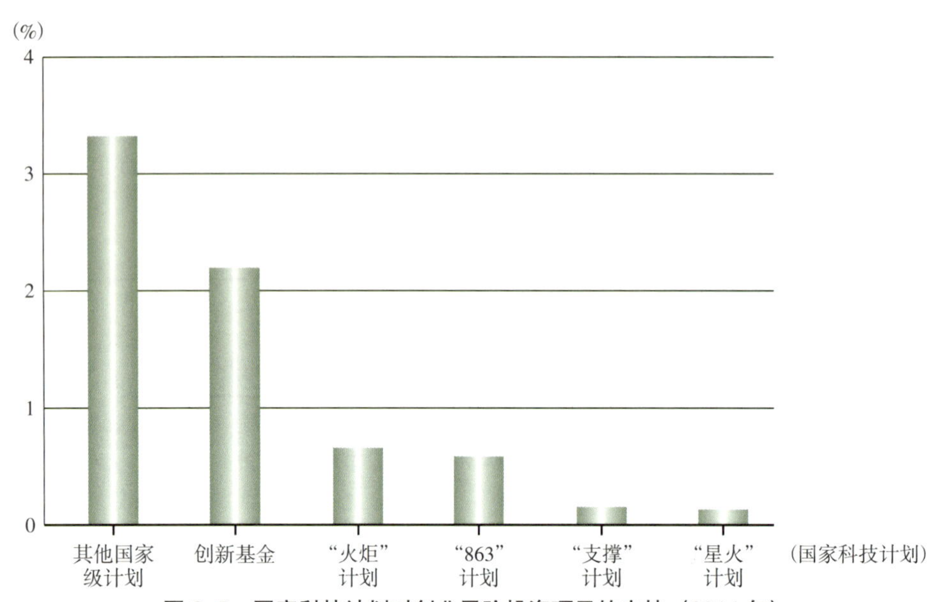

图 8-5 国家科技计划对创业风险投资项目的支持（2014 年）

8.2.2 国家科技计划与创业风险投资项目对接的关键因素

2014 年调查显示，36%的创业风险投资机构认为加大基础、应用和开发投入能够促进国家科技计划和创业风险投资项目的对接，比例高于 2013 年的 33.6%；22%的创业风险投资机构认为需要尽快设立科技型中小企业上市的绿色通道，较 2013 年略有减少；12%的创业风险投资机构认为应鼓励、资助创业风险投资与孵化器之间的合作；22%的创业风险投资机构认为应对创业风险投资项目给予直接资助（见图 8-6），高于 2013 年的 20.0%。仅 4%的创投机构要求加大科技项目信息的公开度，略低于 2013 年的 4.8%，这与近年来政府深化科技体制改革，加强政府信息透明度相关。

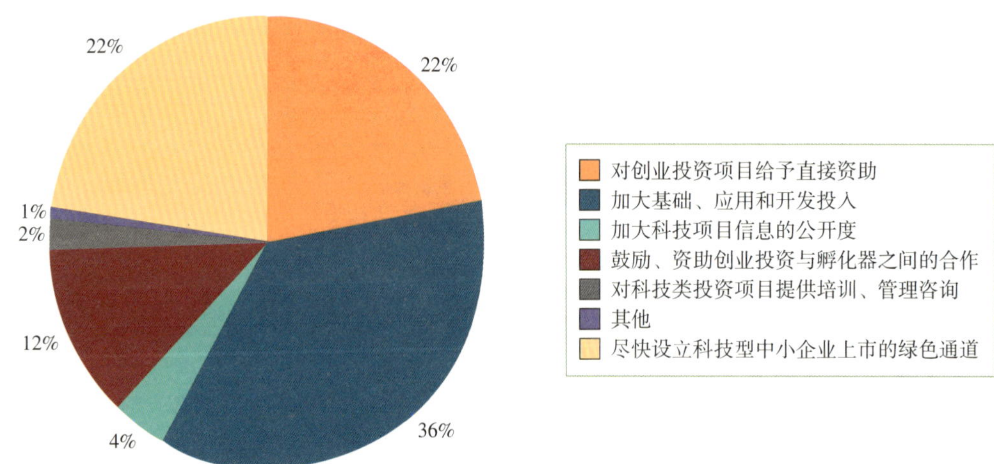

图 8-6 国家科技计划与创业风险投资良好对接的关键字

8.3 中国促进创业风险投资发展的主要政策

本节对中国促进创业风险投资发展出台的国家层面政策文件进行了梳理（见表 8-1），自 1999 年国务院办公厅转发科技部等七部门联合出台的《关于建立风险投资机制的若干意见》开始，我国各有关部门相继出台了支持创业风险投资发展的相关政策，涉及外商投资、监督管理、税收优惠、引导基金等方面，有效地推动了我国创业风险投资事业的快速健康发展。

表 8-1 中国促进创业风险投资发展的主要政策文件

文件名称	出台时间	出台组织及部门等	主要精神
《关于建立风险投资机制的若干意见》	1999 年	科技部、国家计委、国家经贸委、财政部、人民银行、税务总局、证监会	明确发展创业风险投资重要意义，并提出指导、规范我国创业风险投资发展的基本原则
《中华人民共和国信托法》	2001 年	第九届全国人民代表大会常务委员会第二十一次会议通过	明确了委托人和受托人之间的法律关系，为创业风险投资发展提供依据
《中华人民共和国中小企业促进法》	2002 年	第九届全国人民代表大会常务委员会第二十八次会议通过	提出通过税收政策鼓励各类依法设立的创业风险投资机构，增加对中小企业的投资
《外商投资创业投资企业管理规定》	2003 年	外经贸部、科技部、国家工商总局、国家税务总局、国家外汇管理局	为鼓励、规范外国公司、企业和其他经济组织或个人从事创业风险投资提供管理依据
《关于外商投资创业投资公司缴纳企业所得税有关税收问题的通知》	2003 年	国家税务总局	为外商投资创业风险投资企业组建为法人及非法人的创业风险投资企业明确了有关税收问题
《关于外商投资举办投资性公司的规定》	2004 年	商务部	对外商投资举办投资性公司的注册资本、组织形式、投资行为等提出了管理规定
《创业投资企业管理暂行办法》	2005 年	发改委、科技部、财政部、商务部、人民银行、税务总局、工商总局、银监会、证监会、国家外汇管理局	对创业风险投资企业实行备案管理，并对其经营范围、投资行为等进行了规定
《关于促进创业投资企业发展有关税收政策的通知》	2007 年	财政部、国家税务总局	对投资支持中小高新技术企业的创业风险投资企业给予税收优惠
《科技型中小企业创业投资引导基金管理暂行办法》	2007 年	财政部、科技部	开展设立科技型中小企业创业风险投资引导基金，支持引导创业风险投资机构向初创期科技型中小企业投资
《关于创业投资引导基金规范设立与运作的指导意见》	2008 年	发改委、财政部、商务部	对规范设立创业风险投资引导基金提出要求
《关于外商投资创业投资企业创业投资管理企业审批有关事项的通知》	2009 年	商务部	对总投资在 1 亿美元以下的外商投资创业风险投资企业、创业风险投资管理企业的审批权限等进行了下放
《关于加强创业投资企业备案管理严格规范创业投资企业募资行为的通知》	2009 年	发改委	明确创业风险投资企业备案条件，严控“募集有限合伙基金”和“从事代理业务”等名义的非法集资活动
《关于实施创业投资企业所得税优惠问题的通知》	2009 年	国家税务总局	对合伙企业、外商投资创业风险投资企业等有关问题明确了税收优惠政策

续表

文件名称	出台时间	出台组织及部门等	主要精神
《关于实施新兴产业创投计划、开展产业技术研究与开发资金参股设立创业投资基金试点工作的通知》	2009 年	发改委、财政部	扩大产业技术研发资金创业风险投资试点，推动利用国家产业技术研发资金，参股设立创业风险投资基金（即创业投资企业）试点工作
《首次公开发行股票并在创业板上市管理办法》	2009 年	证监会	创业板的推出为我国创业风险投资发展提供了良好的退出渠道，将进一步促进创业风险投资事业健康、快速发展
《关于豁免国有创业投资机构和国有创业投资引导基金国有股转持义务有关问题的通知》	2010 年	财政部	规避相关政策影响，提高了国有创业风险投资机构的积极性，鼓励和引导国有创业风险投资机构加大对中早期项目的投资
《科技型中小企业创业投资引导基金股权投资收入收缴暂行办法》	2010 年	财政部	明确了科技型中小企业创业投资引导基金收入的上缴办法及相关管理权责等事宜
《国家科技成果转化引导基金管理暂行办法》	2011 年	财政部、科技部	明确提出以政府创业风险投资引导基金模式运作支持科技成果转化的相关事宜
《新兴产业创投计划参股创业投资基金管理暂行办法》	2011 年	财政部、国家发改委	提出政府公共资金以直接投资或参股投资等方式支持战略性新兴产业发展的事宜
《关于促进科技和金融结合加快实施自主创新战略的若干意见》	2011 年	科技部、财政部、中国人民银行、国务院国资委、国家税务总局、中国银监会、中国证监会、中国保监会	八部委联合文件指导全国开展科技和金融结合工作，对于各级政府开展创业风险投资提出了指导建议
《关于促进股权投资企业规范发展的通知》	2011 年	发改委	对于股权投资企业的设立、募资、投资，以及风险控制、基本职责、信息披露等提出了要求
《非上市公众公司监督管理办法》	2012 年	证监会	将非上市公众公司纳入合法监管，有利于中小企业融资，对促进创业风险投资机构投资中小企业有积极意义
《全国中小企业股份转让系统有限责任公司管理暂行办法》	2013 年	证监会	进一步完善多层次资本市场建设，有利于创业风险投资机构股权退出
《中小企业发展专项资金管理办法》	2014 年	财政部、工业和信息化部、科技部、商务部	进一步完善科技型中小企业创业投资引导基金管理模式和支持方式
《私募投资基金监督管理暂行办法》	2014 年	证监会	将创投等以私募性质募集资金的投资基金纳入备案监管

2014 年，财政部、工信部、科技部、商务部联合发布了《中小企业发展专项资金管理办法》，整合开展了一系列面向中小企业创新发展的专项资金支持，其中，对 2007 年启动的科技型中小企业创业投资引导基金在管理模式和支持方式等方面进行了修订和完善，增加了亏损补偿等方式，进一步让利市场机构，降低投资风险，引导社会资本参与政府计划，支持初创期科技型企业发展。同年，证监会发布了《私募投资基金监督管理暂行办法》，对包括创投、证券投资基金等在内的以私募形式募集资金进行投资的基金行业进行了备案监管，目的在于进一步规范私募投资行为，促进资本市场健康发展。

9 中国创业风险投资引导基金发展情况

9.1 中国创业风险投资引导基金发展现状[①]

为贯彻落实创新驱动发展战略，进一步发挥市场机制积极作用，许多地方政府进一步改革创新财政投入方式，其中，通过创业风险投资引导基金的方式来配置财政资源成为许多地方政府的选择。

调查样本显示，截至 2014 年底，获得政府创业风险投资引导基金参股支持的创业风险投资机构数量累计达到 322 家，政府创业风险投资引导基金累计出资 363.27 亿元，引导带动的创业风险投资管理资金规模超过 1800 亿元。

2014 年调查样本显示：引导基金支持的创业风险投资机构平均管理资本规模达 50143.9 万元，略低于非引导基金支持的创业风险投资机构的 53544.8 万元，而非引导基金支持的创业风险投资机构管理资本规模较 2013 年大幅增长，可以看出，社会资本参与创业风险投资行业的规模日益增长（见图 9–1）。

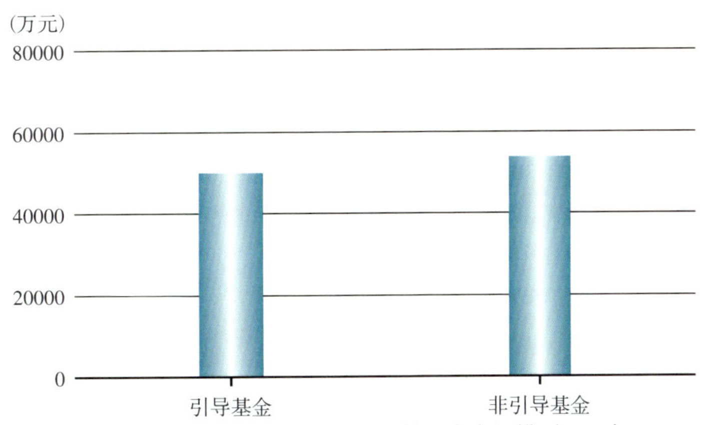

图 9–1 创业风险投资机构平均管理资本规模（2014）

从资本构成结构来看，有引导基金支持的创业风险投资机构资本构成中，12.5%来自于政府部门，20.9%来自于国有独资投资机构，35.2%来自非上市企业，与 2013 年相比，非上市公司出资占比有所下降，政府部门占比继续下降。而非引导基金支持的创业风险投资机构资本更多地来自于非上市企业、国有独资投资机构和个人，三者合计占到总资本的 74%（见图 9–2），较 2013 年有所下降。

① 有效样本数为 1254 份。

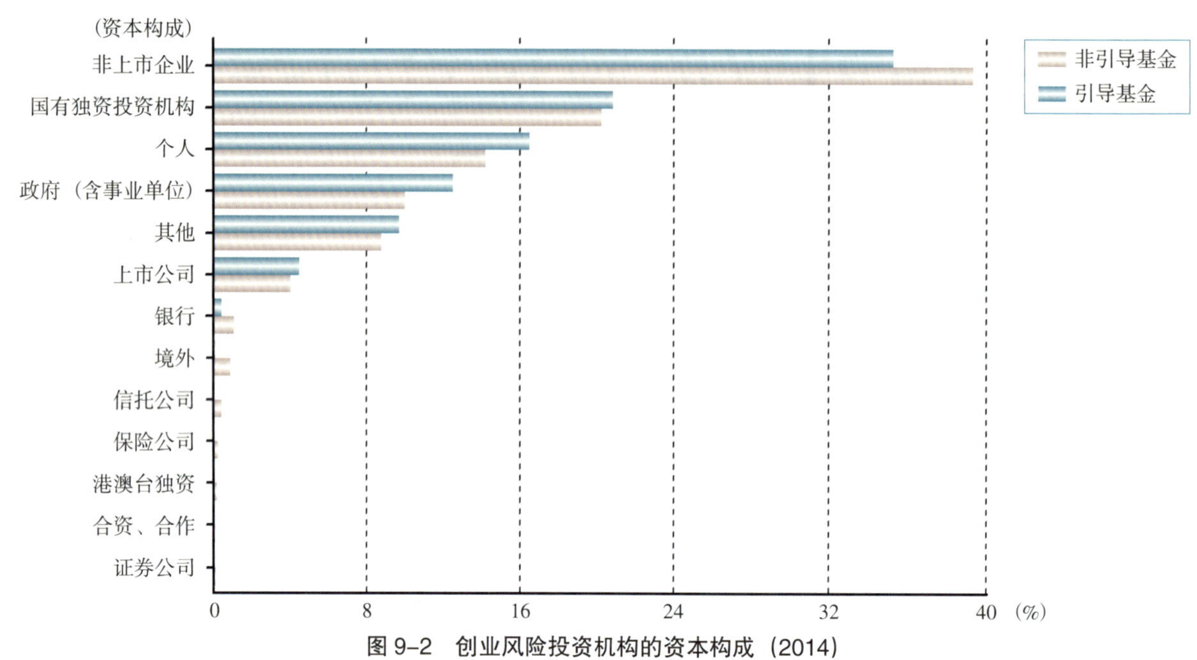

图 9-2　创业风险投资机构的资本构成（2014）

从国家层面来看，截至 2014 年底，由财政部、科技部设立的“科技型中小企业创业投资引导基金”采取风险补助、投资保障、阶段参股等方式，共投入财政资金 49.93 亿元。其中，出资 34.43 亿元以阶段参股方式参股了 100 家重点投资于科技型中小企业的创业投资企业，累计注册资本约 220 亿元；通过风险补助和投资保障方式共立项 1896 项，累计安排补助资金 15.5 亿元（见表 9-1）。

表 9-1　科技部科技型中小企业创业投资引导基金运行情况（2007~2014）

分类 年份	风险补助		投资保障（前、后）		共　计	
	数量（项）	资金（万元）	数量（项）	资金（万元）	数量（项）	资金（万元）
2007	50	7115	52	2885	102	10000
2008	77	6590	75	3410	152	10000
2009	55	4670	131	10330	186	15000
2010	66	4540	180	10460	246	15000
2011	56	4110	125	10890	181	15000
2012	87	7033	199	12967	286	20000
2013	96	9655	162	10345	258	20000
2014	142	13175	343	36825	485	50000
共计	629	56888	1267	98112	1896	155000

资料来源：科技部创新基金管理中心。

9.2 中国创业风险投资引导基金投资项目的行业分布[①]

从投资金额分布看，2014 年引导基金支持的创业风险投资机构有 11.7%的资金投向传统制造业，较 2013 年的 3.8%大幅提升；5.4%的资金投向新材料工业，较 2013 年大幅减少。此外，生物科技、网络产业、通信设备、软件产业的投资金额占比也较往年有了大幅增长。从投资项目数看，6.8%的资金投向新材料工业，较 2013 年大幅减少，而投向网络产业、通信设备、金融保险业、软件产业和 IT 服务业的项目数量，均较 2013 年明显增加。综合来看，2014 年有引导基金支持创业风险投资机构的投资领域更加分散，投向了许多热点新兴产业领域（见表 9–2）。

表 9–2 引导基金支持创业风险投资机构投资项目行业分布（2013~2014）[②] 单位：%

投资行业	投资金额		投资项目	
	2013 年	2014 年	2013 年	2014 年
新材料工业	11.6	5.4	10.1	6.8
传统制造业	3.8	11.7	5.9	4.7
其他制造业	4.9	4.1	4.8	4.2
其他行业	2.1	6.6	2.4	6.5
消费产品和服务	6.6	2.7	5.2	3.3
新能源/高效节能技术	6.8	3.9	7.2	4.5
生物科技	2.3	4.8	4.4	4.9
光电子与光机电一体化	6.3	4.4	5.0	3.6
农林牧副渔	4.6	2.3	4.1	2.7
医药保健	12.3	14.8	10.0	7.2
网络产业	2.8	4.7	5.5	11.5
通信设备	0.2	3.5	0.2	2.8
金融保险业	4.0	2.5	1.7	2.5
科技服务	1.4	2.2	2.4	2.6
半导体	2.5	2.7	3.3	2.7
软件产业	1.4	3.1	4.2	7.5
环保工程	2.4	2.2	3.1	3.2
IT 服务业	3.4	5.1	4.2	7.0
传播与文化娱乐	5.9	4.1	5.0	4.6
建筑业	1.4	0.3	1.1	0.3
批发和零售业	0.8	0.0	0.6	0.7

① 有效样本数：获引导基金支持创投 960 份，非引导基金支持创投 1350 份。
② 2014 年有效样本数为 960 份，2013 年有效样本数为 542 份。

续表

投资行业	投资金额		投资项目	
	2013 年	2014 年	2013 年	2014 年
其他 IT 产业	0.4	1.4	0.7	1.7
社会服务	0.9	1.6	1.1	1.7
计算机硬件产业	1.6	1.0	1.5	2.1
交通运输仓储和邮政业	5.0	0.1	1.5	0.2
核应用技术	0.1	0.2	0.2	0.1
水电煤气	0.3	0.3	0.4	0.2
采掘业	0.4	—	0.6	—
房地产	—	4.3	—	0.3

引导基金支持创业风险投资机构投资项目行业分布与非引导基金支持创业风险投资机构有一定差异（见图 9-3）。2014 年，有引导基金支持的创业风险投资机构倾向于投资网络产业、软件产业、医药保健等领域；非引导基金支持的创业风险投资机构更加倾向于投资通信设备、软件产业、网络产业等领域。

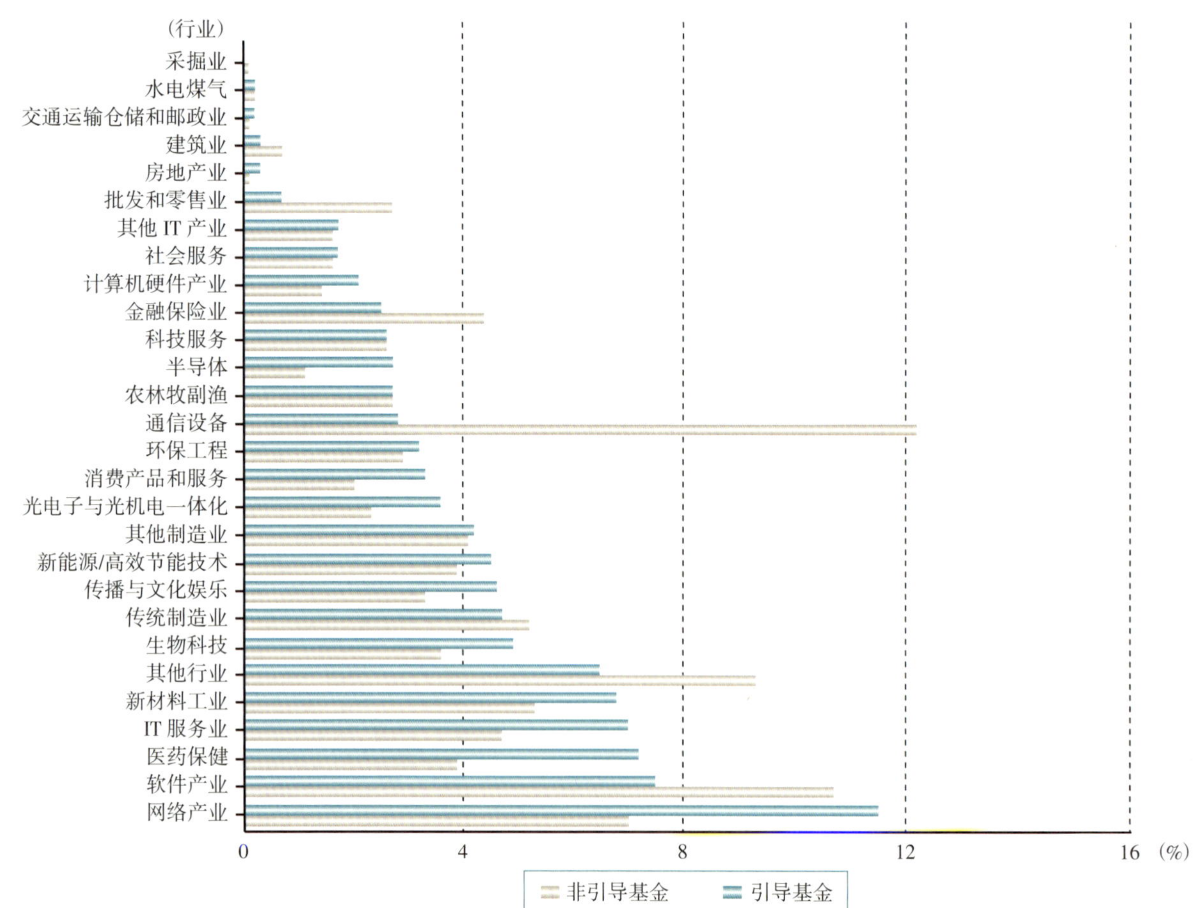

图 9-3　创业风险投资机构投资项目的行业分布（2014）

9.3 中国创业风险投资引导基金投资项目所处阶段[①]

2014 年，政府引导基金支持的创业风险投资机构主要投资处于种子期、起步期和成长（扩张）期的项目，投资金额分别占 6.6%、28.3%、52.6%，其中投资种子期的金额占比较上年下降 5 个百分点；投资项目数分别占 32.4%、32.4%、30.1%，与 2013 年相比，投资种子期的项目数量占比大幅上涨。从投资金额与投资项目的占比可以看出，2014 年有引导基金支持的创业风险投资机构投资行为有所转变，投资种子期的比例大幅增长（见图 9-4），符合政府引导基金政策目标。

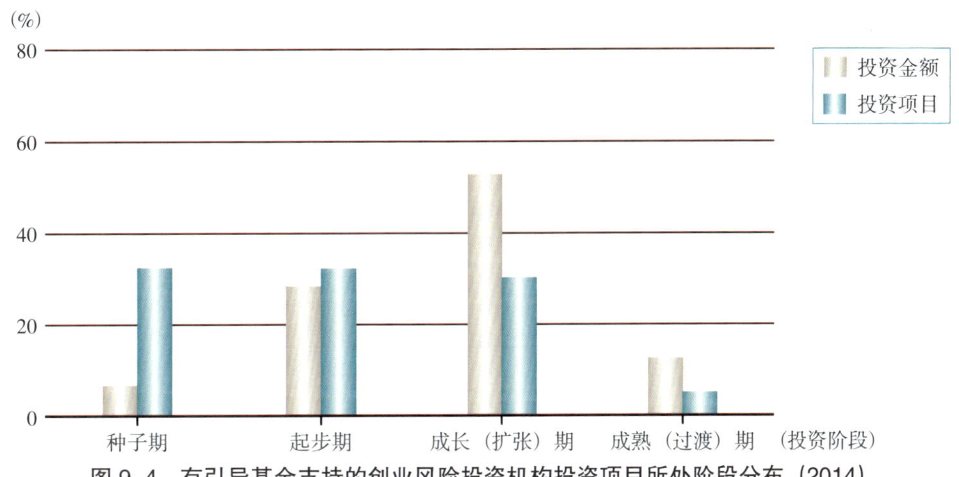

图 9-4 有引导基金支持的创业风险投资机构投资项目所处阶段分布（2014）

与非引导基金支持创业风险投资机构相比，2014 年，引导基金支持创业风险投资机构更加倾向于投资早前期企业，投资于早前期的企业资金占比明显高于非引导基金支持创业风险投资机构（见图 9-5）。

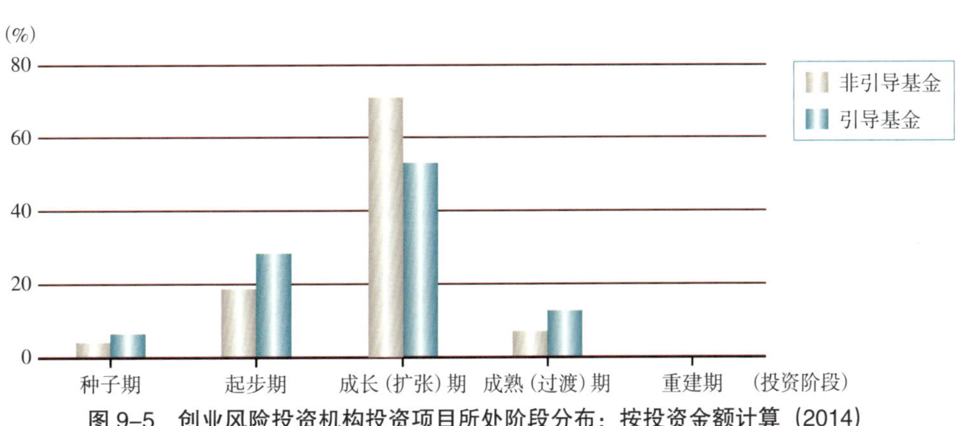

图 9-5 创业风险投资机构投资项目所处阶段分布：按投资金额计算（2014）

① 有效样本数：获引导基金支持创投 986 份，非引导基金支持创投 1362 份。

9.4 中国创业风险投资引导基金投资项目运作状况[①]

2014 年调查样本显示，有引导基金支持的创业风险投资机构与非引导基金支持的创业风险投资机构的投资强度没有明显差异，单笔投资金额在 1000 万元以上的占比超过 80%，单笔投资低于 500 万元的占比不足 8%，较非引导基金支持的创业风险投资机构高 3.9 个百分点，明显高于 2013 年。与 2013 年相比，投资超过 2000 万的占比有所下降（见表 9–3、图 9–6）。

表 9–3 创业风险投资机构的项目投资金额比较（2014） 单位：%

分布比例	100 万元以下	100 万~300 万元	300 万~500 万元	500 万~1000 万元	1000 万~2000 万元	2000 万元以上
引导基金支持的 VC	0.4	2.9	4.3	11.1	23.1	58.1
非引导基金支持的 VC	0.2	1.4	2.1	4.9	10.6	80.8

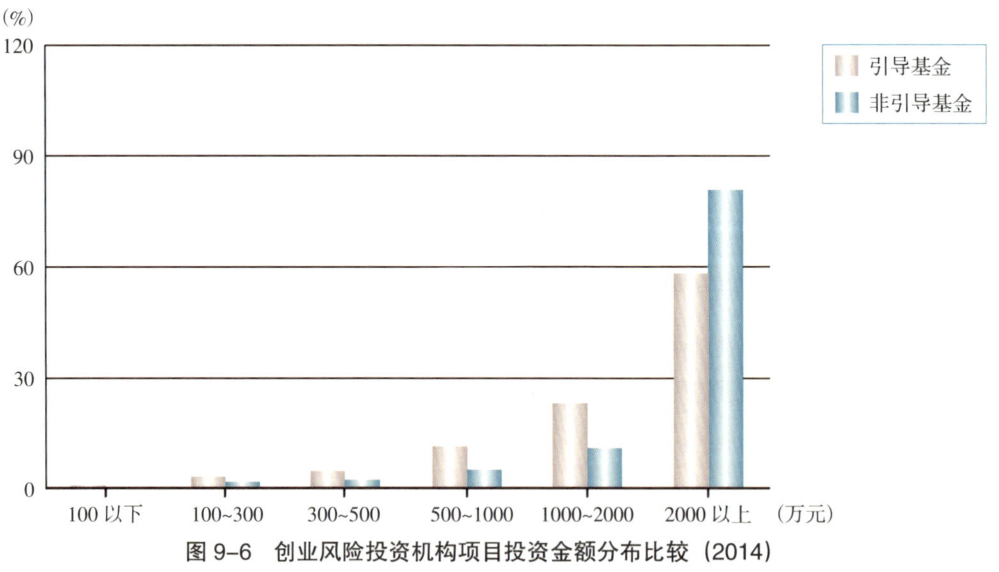

图 9–6 创业风险投资机构项目投资金额分布比较（2014）

2014 年调查样本显示，获引导基金支持的创业风险投资机构共计投资了 302 家高新技术企业，占总投资项目数的 29.8%；非引导基金支持的创业风险投资机构共计投资了 241 家高新技术企业，占总投资项目数的 16.5%；与 2013 年相比，获引导基金支持的创业风险投资机构投资高新技术企业的项目数比重明显下降，但平均投资金额较 2013 年有所上升（见表 9–4）。

① 有效样本数：获引导基金支持创投 1012 份，非引导基金支持创投 1362 份。

表 9-4　创业风险投资机构投资项目中投资高新技术企业的情况（2014）[①]

企业分类	投资高企数（家）	投资高企项目数占比（%）	平均投资金额（万元）
非引导基金支持的 VC	241	16.5	1589.6
引导基金支持的 VC	302	29.8	2066.2

注：投资项目中存在非引导基金和引导基金支持创投同时投资情况。

2014 年调查样本显示，获引导基金支持的创业风险投资机构投资项目与非引导基金支持的创业风险投资机构投资项目中继续运行、准备境内上市等比例相对较高，两类样本均有超过 60%的投资项目仍处于运行阶段。与 2013 年相比，由于 IPO 退出渠道不畅，大部分创业投资机构投资项目保持继续运作状态，但获引导基金支持的创业风险投资机构的准备上市项目比例有所提高，非引导基金支持的创业风险投资机构投资项目中准备上市项目比例较 2013 年有明显下降（见表 9-5、图 9-7）。

表 9-5　创业风险投资机构投资项目运作状况（2014）[②]　　单位：%

运作情况	继续运行	准备境内上市	已境内上市	原股东（创业者）回购	被境内非上市公司或自然人收购	已境外上市	清算	管理层收购	被境内上市公司收购	准备境外上市	被境外收购
引导基金支持的 VC	67.9	10.4	5.4	8.3	2.4	1.3	1.5	1.1	1.2	0.2	0.2
非引导基金支持的 VC	70.5	8.5	6.3	5.8	3.0	1.8	1.3	0.5	1.8	0.3	0.3

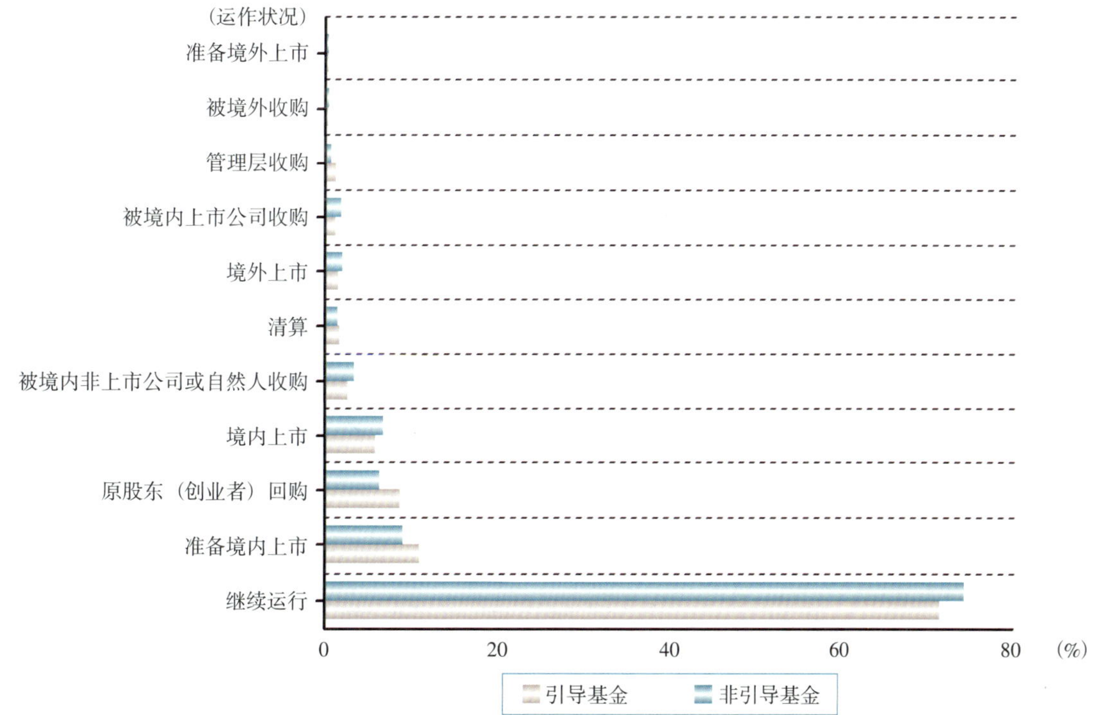

图 9-7　创业风险投资机构投资项目运作状况（2014）

① 有效样本数：获引导基金支持创投 302 份，非引导基金支持创投 241 份。
② 有效样本数：获引导基金支持创投 283 份，非引导基金支持创投 864 份。

附录 1 2014 年美国创业风险投资综述

一、总体概况

2014 年，对于美国创业风险投资行业而言是不平凡的一年。募资终于上升了，部分原因是过去几年长期投资者的比例增加，这些长期投资者将资本重新投入新基金中。投资水平飙升到泡沫时代的高度，尽管其中大多数都是外部资金参与投资一些大型、扩张期后期企业。IPO 市场的许多关键指标也创出千年新高。投资轮次总数和首轮融资数目与前几年基本持平，投资仍然以种子期和早期的公司为主。

良好的 IPO 市场继续包括了一些中等规模的交易，连续两年的退出行业主要来自于生物技术与制药行业。

随着行业近期持续萎缩，管理资本如预期那样继续下降。

一个健康的风险投资系统需要平衡各项标准，因此，虽然新的投资机会即交易量很高，最好的投资机会也得到了投资，但投资压力依然存在。其总体情况如表 1 所示。

表 1 美国创业风险投资（VC）总体情况统计

指标 \ 年份	1994	2004	2014
现存 VC 机构数量（家）	385	985	803
现存 VC 基金数量（家）	635	1803	1206
专业投资人数（人）	3735	8964	5680
首次 VC 基金募集数量（家）	25	36	32
当年募集资金的 VC 基金数量（家）	136	210	257
VC 当年募集的资本额（十亿美元）	7.6	17.6	29.9
VC 管理资本金额（十亿美元）	33.2	271.1	156.5
平均 VC 管理资本额（百万美元）	86.2	275.2	194.9
截至目前的 VC 基金平均规模（百万美元）	42.6	95.3	111
当年新增 VC 基金平均规模（百万美元）	55.9	83.8	116.3
截至目前最大 VC 基金募集额（百万美元）	1775	6300	6300

资料来源：亚洲创业基金期刊集团。

二、行业资源

目前，美国创业风险投资行业的活跃程度大概只有2000 年顶峰时的一半。例如，2000 年，1049 家机构投资规模都在 500 万美元以上，而 2014 年，虽然新机构和新基金都有所增加，但是只有 635 家机构投资规模在 500 万美元以上，其中，仅 195 家机构是首轮融资，197 家投资在生命科学领域。

正如预期的那样，截至 2014 年底，美国风险投资管理资本已减少到 1565 亿美元（见图 1）。其中，31 家机构管理了超过 10 亿美元的资本，360 家机构管理的资本在 500 万美元或以下。大型风险投资机构的地理位置也越来越集中，加州地区的机构管理了 54%的资本，较上年增加了 5 个百分点。这主要源于加州的投资机构募集规模较大，一些东海岸的投资机构也向西海岸搬迁。

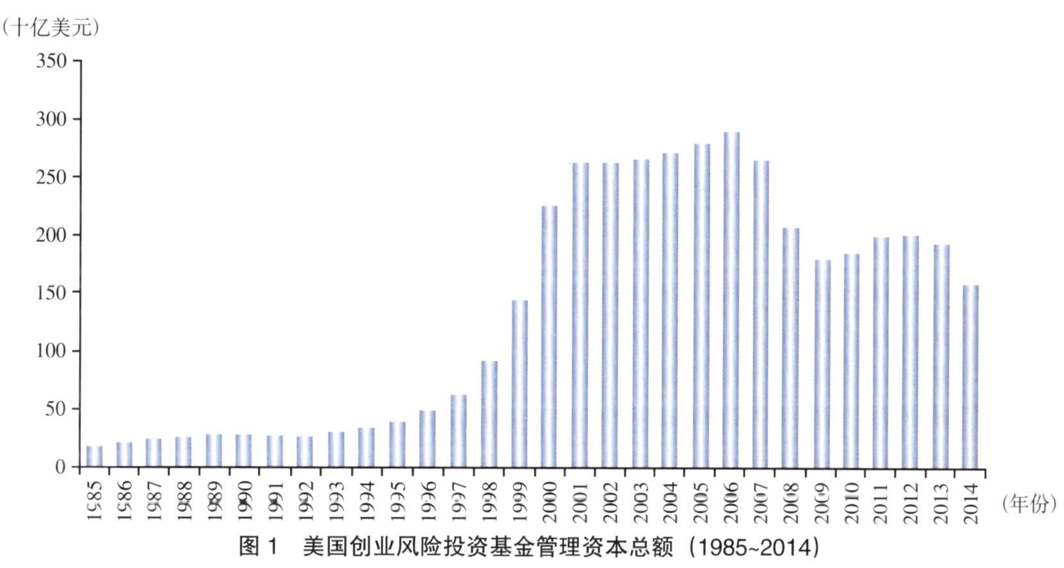

图 1　美国创业风险投资基金管理资本总额（1985~2014）

三、资金募集

2014 年，美国创业风险投资基金的新募基金出资承诺由 2013 年的 177 亿美元增长到 300 亿美元（见图 2），这主要源于 2012 年、2013 年和 2014 年强劲的 IPO 市场回馈了投资者长期投资资金，投资者能够将这些资金再投资于新募集的基金。2014 年共有 257 笔基金筹资，其募资额与 2013 年及更早的创业投资金额趋势相一致，接近千禧年之后的新高。

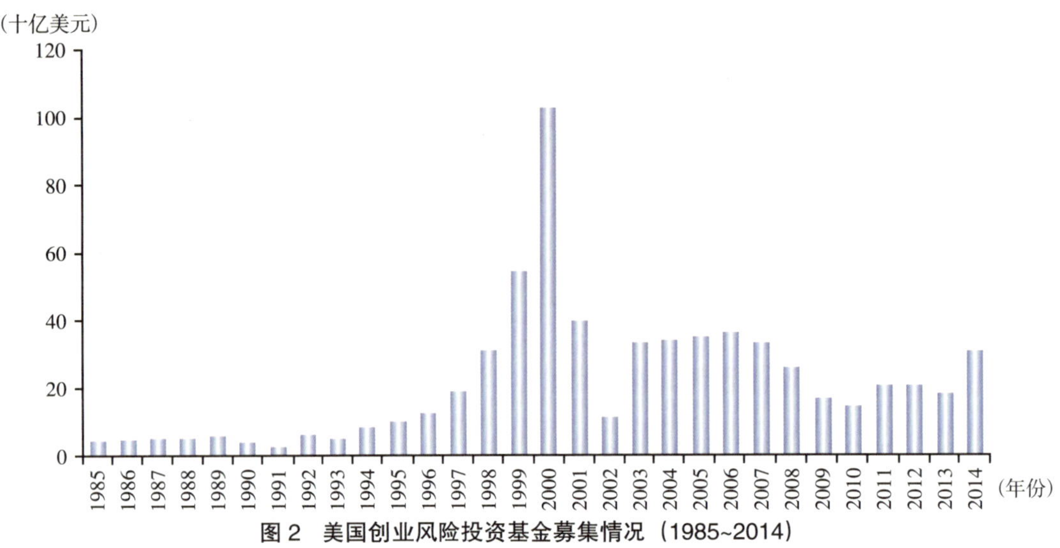

图 2　美国创业风险投资基金募集情况（1985~2014）

四、投资活动

2014 年美国创业风险投资行业的投资水平提升十分显著，达到 493 亿美元，是自 2000 年以来的最高金额，也是历年来第三高的年份（见图 3）。此前，从 2002 年开始到 2013 年，投资水平始终维持在 300 亿美元左右的投资金额。然而，2014 年的显著增长主要源于有十几家企业获得了巨额投资，如果把它们从总量中去除，数据与前几年相比基本持平。这些公司获得了很高的关注，正式投资者看到了公司的巨大潜力，具有颠覆性创新的公司在上市之前获得了巨额投资。

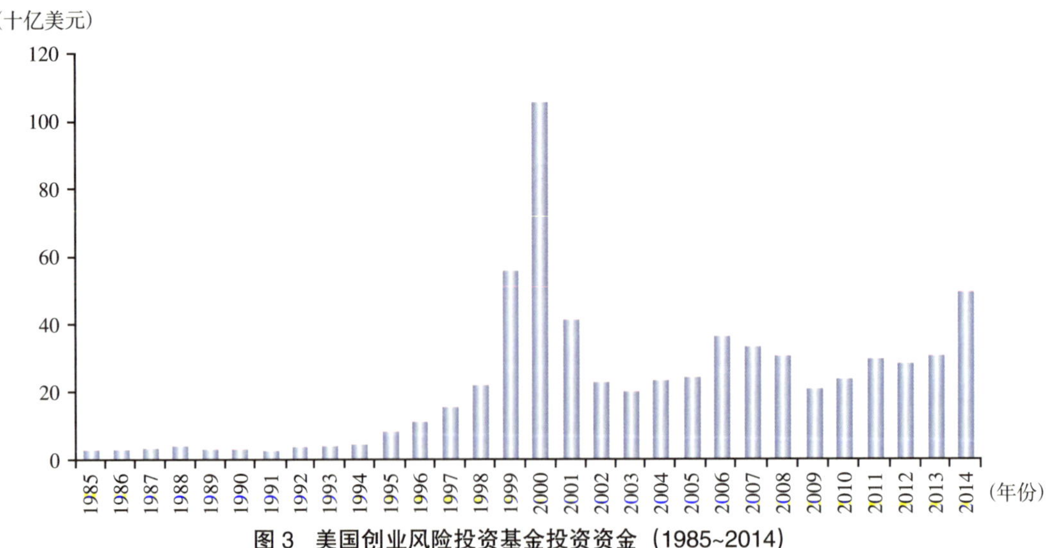

图 3　美国创业风险投资基金投资资金（1985~2014）

（一）投资行业

按照投资行业划分（见表 2、图 4），软件行业是 2014 年的主导产业，投资金额占 41%；位居第二的投资行业是生物技术，占总投资额的 12%；传媒和娱乐业，即社交网络涉及的产业目录，也获得了 12%的投资，而 IT 服务业获得了 7%的投资。

表 2 按行业分类统计的投资情况（2014）

行业分类	全部投资			首轮投资		
	企业数（家）	交易数（起）	投资数量（十亿美元）	企业数（家）	交易数（起）	投资数量（十亿美元）
信息技术	2611	3050	35.7	1059	1059	5.2
医学/健康学/生命科学	650	827	8.8	174	174	1.2
非高科技类	404	484	4.8	177	177	0.9
总数	3665	4361	49.3	1410	1410	7.3

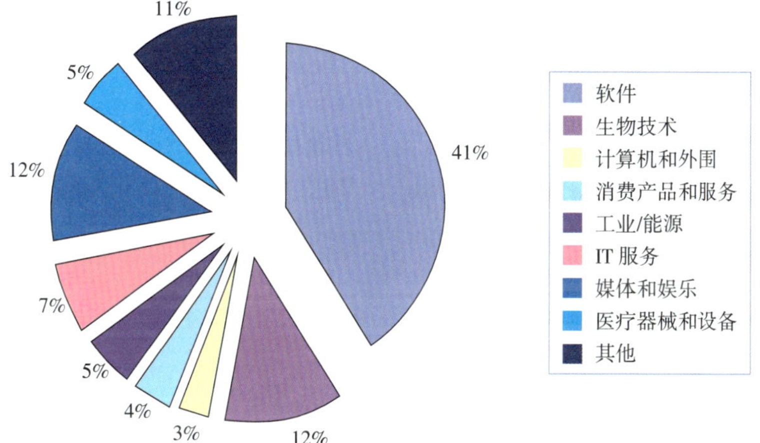

图 4 按行业部门统计的创业资本投资（2014）

（二）投资阶段

按投资金额划分投资阶段，2014 年种子期投资占 2%，早期投资占 32%，42%的项目投资在扩张期；而 2013 年投资在种子期的项目占 3.3%，早期投资占 34.4%，投资阶段略有后移（见图 5）。

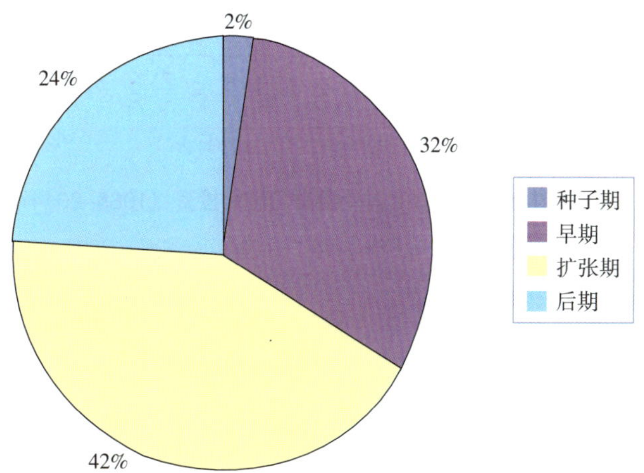

图 5 创业投资基金的投资阶段（按资金占比）(2014)

（三）投资地区

按投资地区划分，2014 年，美国创业风险投资有 42%的企业，57%的资金来自于加利福尼亚州，较 2013 年有所减少。排名前五位的地区（加利福尼亚、马萨诸塞州、纽约、德州和华盛顿）投资资金占总投资的 68%（见表 3），较 2013 年下降 10 个百分点，投资地区的集中度进一步下降。

表 3 按地区划分的风险资本投资（2014）

地　区	企业数量（家）	占比（%）	投资额（百万美元）	占比（%）
加利福尼亚州	1810	0.42	28103	0.57
马萨诸塞州	390	0.09	4639.5	0.09
纽约	438	0.10	4300.7	0.09
德州	188	0.04	1517.7	0.03
华盛顿	112	0.03	1241.2	0.03
合计	2938	0.68	39802.1	0.81

（四）投资轮次

从投资轮次分布来看，2014 年，美国风险创业投资中首轮投资金额仅 51 亿美元，占比 15%，较 2013 年下降 2.3 个百分点，419.15 亿美元用于后续投资（见图 6）。

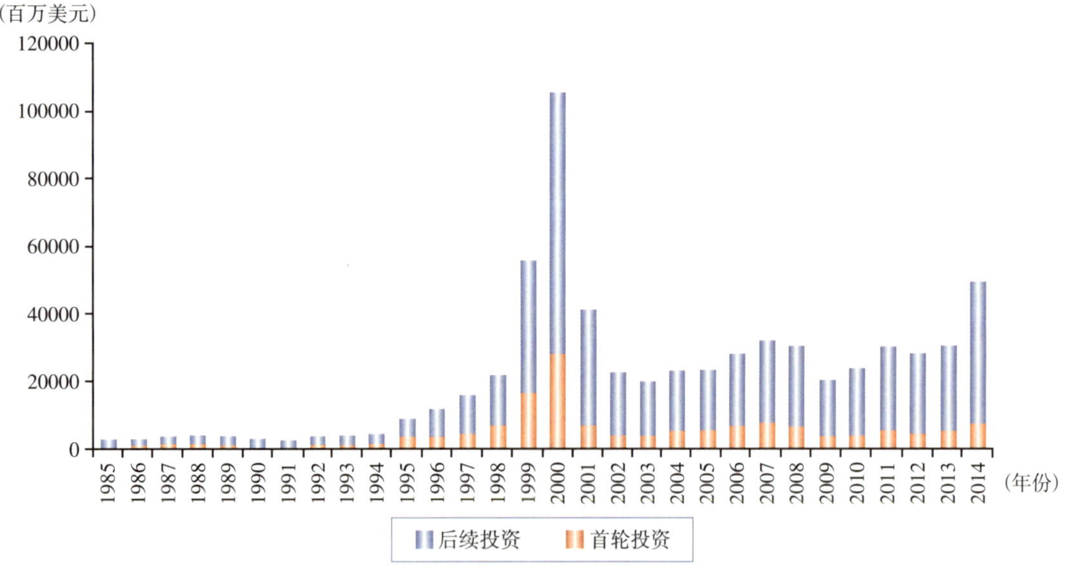

图 6 创业风险投资的首轮投资与后续投资（1985~2014）

五、投资退出

2014 年对于美国创业风险投资退出而言是不平凡的一年，IPO 市场和并购市场对初创企业和投资者的回报比近几年要好得多。2014 年，115 家具有创业风险投资背景的企业成功上市，是 2000 年以来上市最多的年份（见图 7），也是除 2012 年以外发行金额最高的年份，因为 2012 年有着 facebook 的 160 亿美元 IPO 的显著贡献。有趣的是，不同于 2013 年的反常情况，2014 年大多数新股发行又回归到了生物技术企业，且许多上市的生物技术公司都是中小规模。

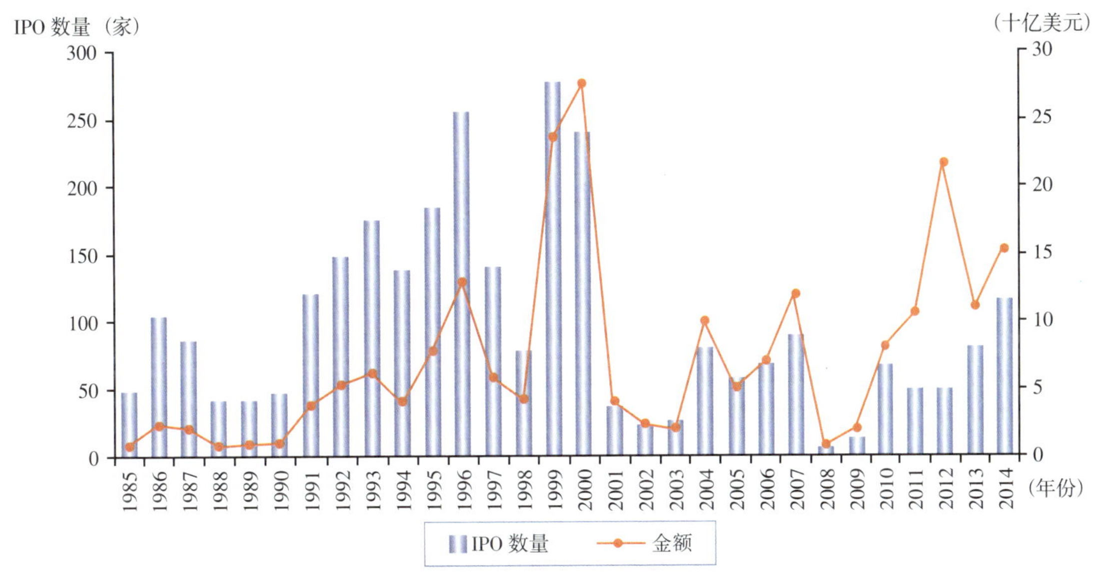

图 7　获得创业风险投资的 IPO 数量（1985~2014）

资料来源：数据由美国风险投资协会 National Venture Capital Association 提供。

尽管投资总额比前几年好，但是 IPO 市场的总体水平大大低于 20 世纪 90 年代，当时 14%的首轮融资企业最后都上市了。

2014 年被投资企业的上市估值总计 1211 亿美元，而投资于这些企业的创业风险投资总计约 138 亿美元。

2014 年 459 家被投资企业被收购，其中，137 家披露了价格，总计约 475 亿美元，基本上是上一年的 3 倍。

附录 2 2014 年欧洲创业风险投资回顾

2014 年，受全球经济复苏影响，欧洲创业风险投资行业总体状况有所回升，募资与投资均较上一年有所上升。投资的主要行业集中在生命科学、计算机和消费电子、通信业和能源环境产业等领域，投资以初创期项目占主导，全年共有 8 家风险投资资助的企业通过 IPO 实现退出。

一、资金募集

2014 年，整个欧洲股权投资募集的资金达到 446 亿欧元，在过去五年中排在第二位，与 2013 年相比，下降了 18%。从募集的基金数量而言，全年共新成立基金 298 只，达到近五年的高峰，较上一年增长 12%。其中，40%的机构投资者来自欧洲以外的地区；养老基金超过了 1/3；母基金占 12%，政府投资占 11%，保险资金占 10%。

风险投资的募集较 2013 年减少了 12%，仅为 41 亿欧元。其中，以早期阶段投资为主的基金增长了 32%，达到近六年以来的最高值。

并购基金募集减少了 23%，为 351 亿欧元。成长资本的募集量达到近年来的最高值，较 2013 年增长近 70%，达到 18 亿欧元（见表 1、图 1）。

表 1 欧洲股权投资市场募集资金主要特征（2014）

	所有股权类基金	风险投资	并购	成长资本
新募集基金额（十亿欧元）	44.6	4.1	35.1	1.8
新募集基金数（只）	298	120	89	25

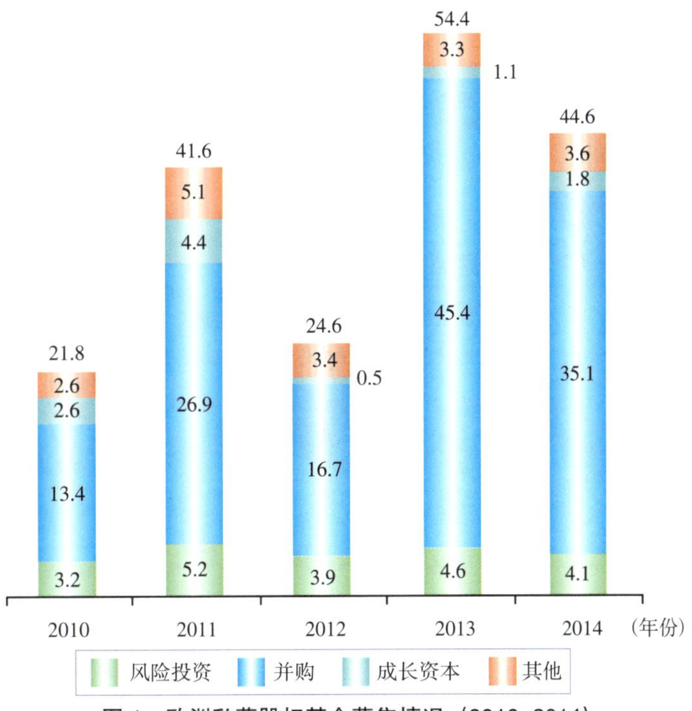

图 1　欧洲私募股权基金募集情况（2010~2014）

按资金来源划分，在整个欧洲股权投资市场中，养老基金一直是其最主要的资金来源，约占 1/3。对于创业风险投资资金募集而言，政府出资占主导，占比 35%，较 2013 年下降 3.3 个百分点（见图 2、图 3）。

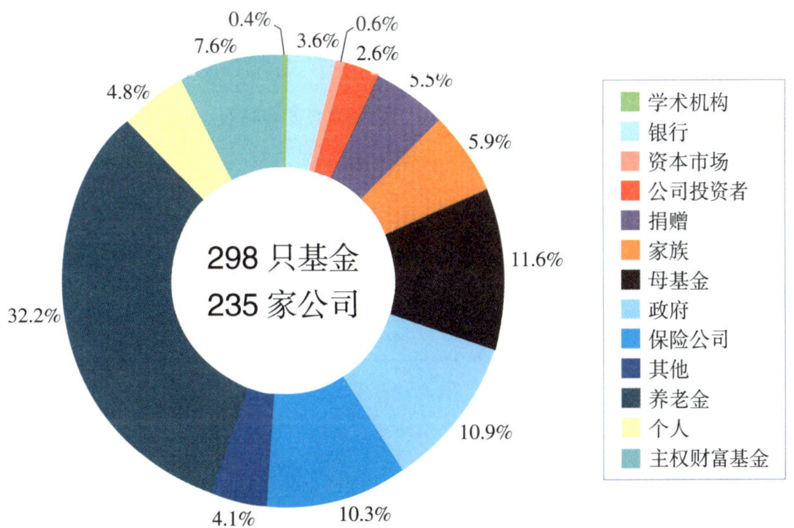

图 2　欧洲股权投资市场募集基金来源（2014）

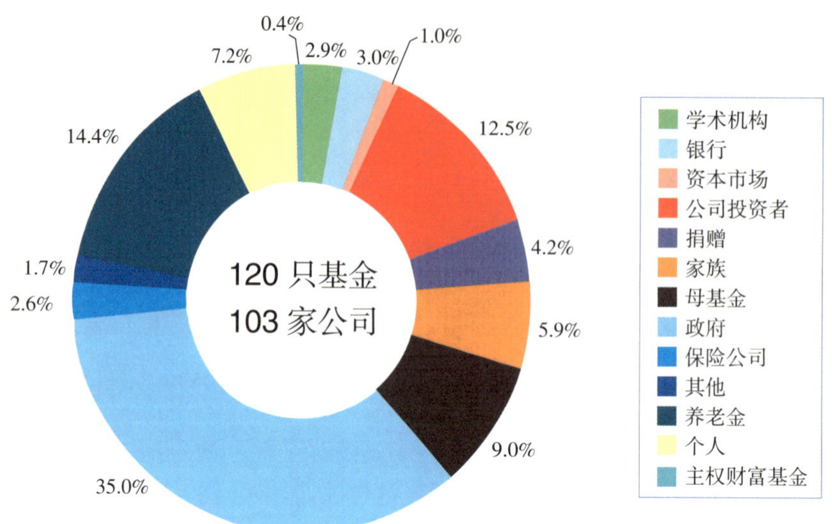

图 3 欧洲创业风险投资募集基金来源（2014）

二、投资活动

2014 年，欧洲整个私募股权市场投资额增长了 14%，达到 415 亿欧元。投资企业数量增长了 8%，达到了五年以来的峰值，共有 5500 家企业获得了股权投资，其中 80%的企业为中小企业。

其中，创业风险投资的投资金额增长了 6%，达到 36 亿欧元，超过 3200 家企业获得了风险投资资助；超过 900 家企业获得了并购投资，金额达到 313 亿欧元；成长资本投资增长了 56%，达到 56 亿欧元，投资的企业数量增长了 13%，达到 1270 家（见表 2、图 4）。

表 2 欧洲股权投资市场投资活动的主要特征（2014）

	所有股权类基金	风险投资	并 购	成长资本
投资金额（十亿欧元）	41.5	3.6	31.3	5.6
投资项目数（家）	5519	3209	945	1270
涉及的企业数（家）	1120	656	467	402
涉及的基金数（只）	1740	1010	631	584

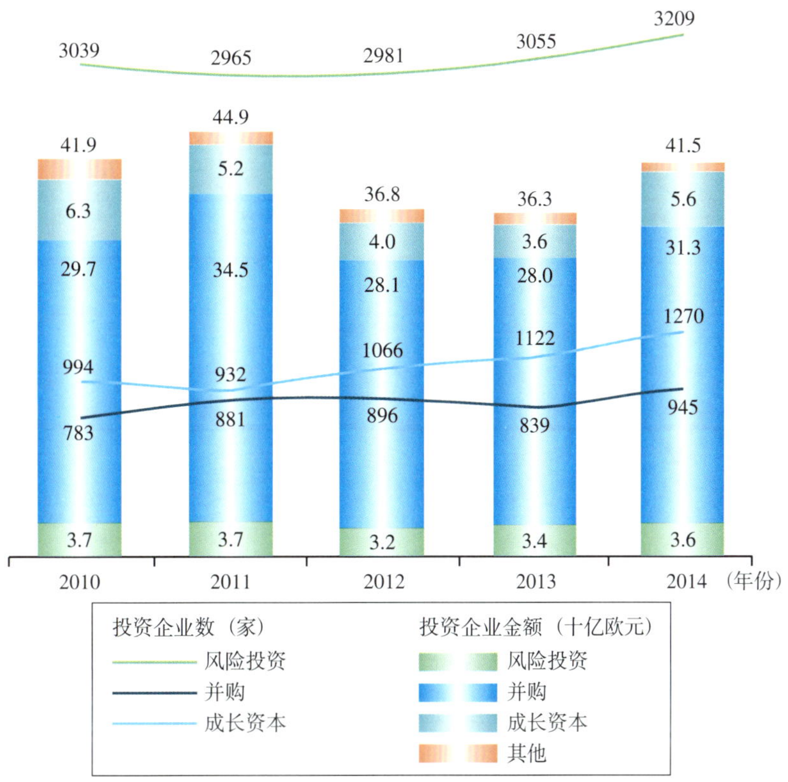

图 4　欧洲股权投资趋势（2010~2014）

总体而言，2000 年至今，整个欧洲股权投资市场投资金额占 GDP 的比重为 0.2%~0.6%。2014 年，欧洲股权投资市场投资金额占 GDP 的比重为 0.28%，较 2013 年提高 0.02 个百分点。其中，创业风险投资的投资金额占 GDP 的比重为 0.024%，丹麦创业风险投资占 GDP 的比重排在第一位，达到 0.076%（见图 5、图 6）。

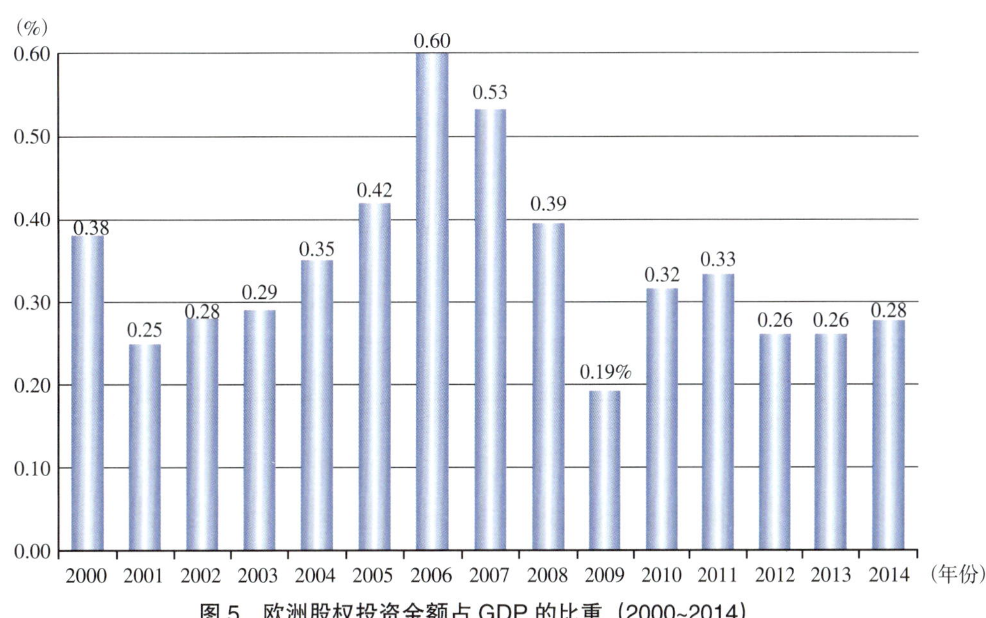

图 5　欧洲股权投资金额占 GDP 的比重（2000~2014）

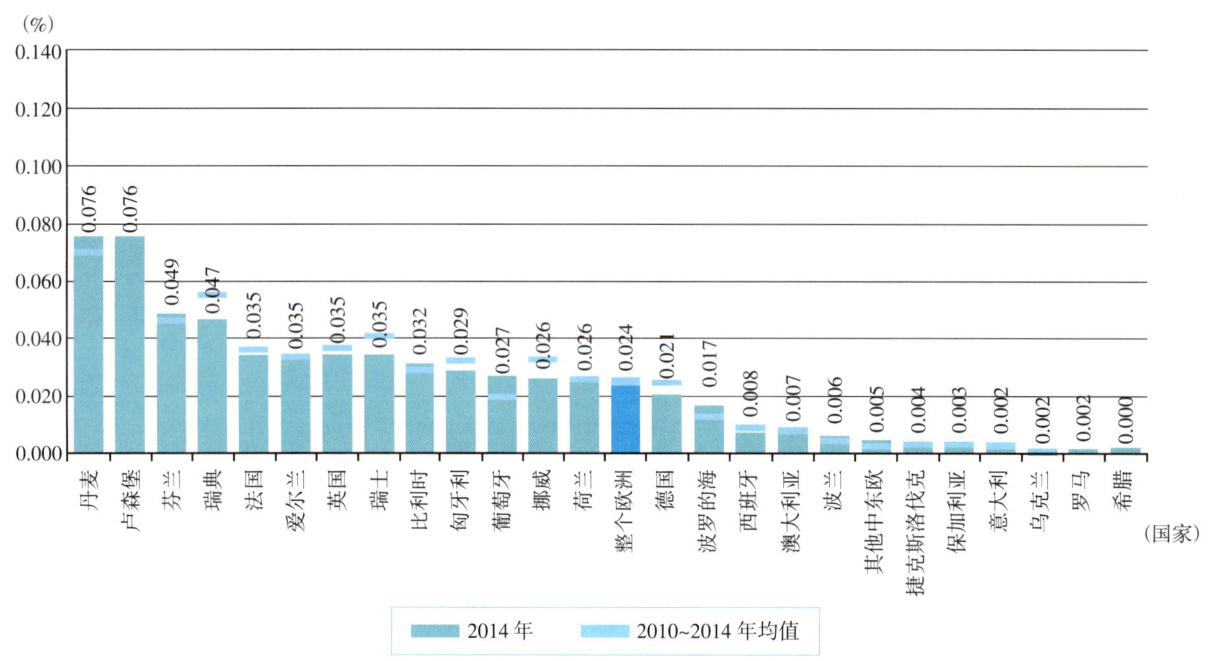

图 6　欧洲主要国家风险投资占 GDP 的比重（2014）

(一) 投资阶段分布

2014 年，创业风险投资金额共计 36 亿欧元，较 2013 年增加 2 亿欧元，其中，种子期的投资金额 1 亿欧元，占比 2.8%；起步期的投资金额 19 亿欧元，占比 52.8%；合计占比 55.6%，与 2013 年基本持平（见图 7）。

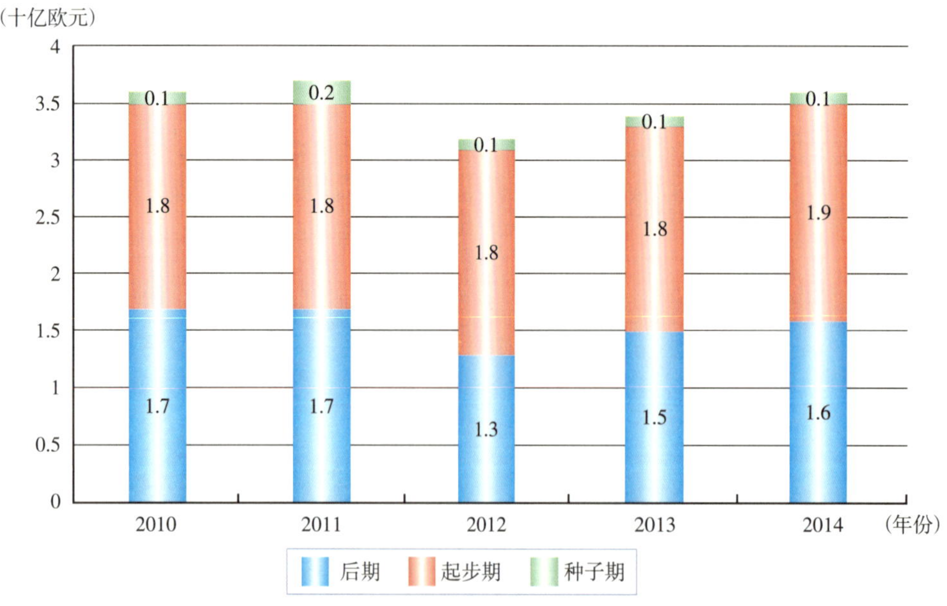

图 7　欧洲创业风险投资基金投资阶段（按投资金额）(2010~2014)

按照投资项目数划分，2014 年欧洲创业风险投资行业全年投资项目数共计 3209 家，较 2013 年增加 154 家，达到五年内峰值。其中，投资于种子期的项目数为 468 家，占比 14.6%；投资于起步期的项目数 1930 家，占比 60.1%；两者合计占比 74.7%（见图 8）。

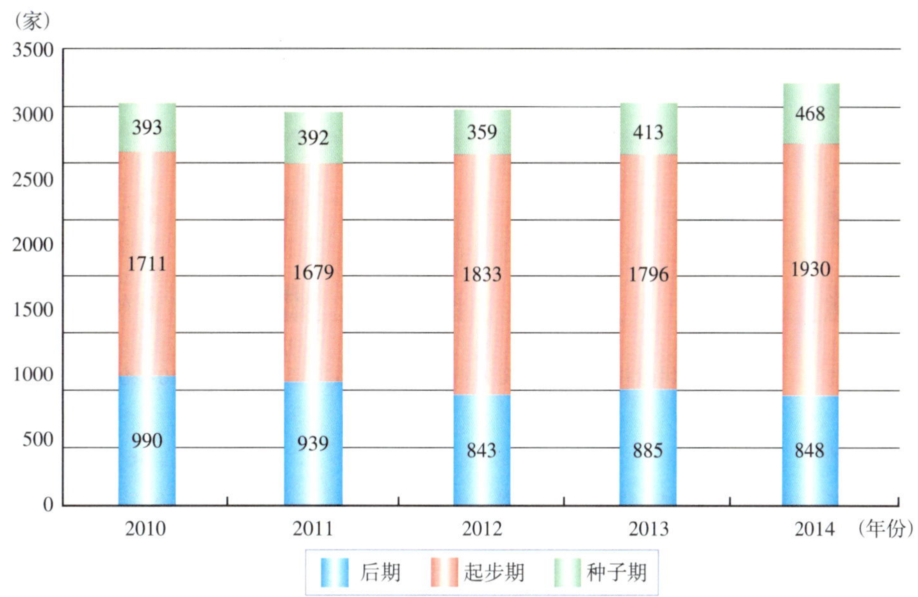

图 8　欧洲创业风险投资基金投资阶段（按投资项目数）(2010~2014)

（二）投资行业分布

按创业风险投资的投资行业划分，无论从投资金额还是投资项目的角度，生命科学、计算机和消费电子与通信业始终排在前三位。2014 年，生命科学、计算机和消费电子、通信业和能源环境产业获得了 70%的投资金额；按照投资项目数划分，工业产品投资项目数超过了能源投资，排在第四位（见图 9、图 10）。

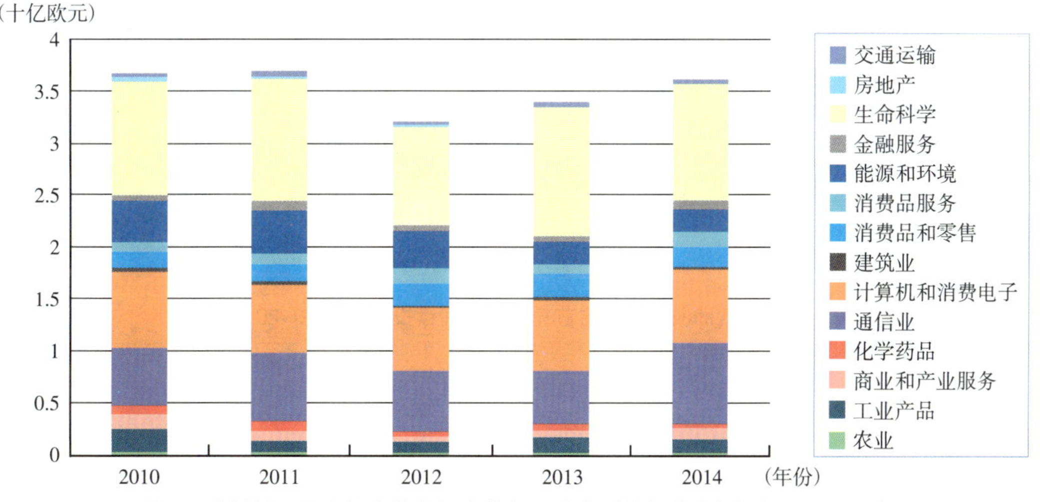

图 9　欧洲创业风险投资基金投资的行业分布（按投资金额）(2010~2014)

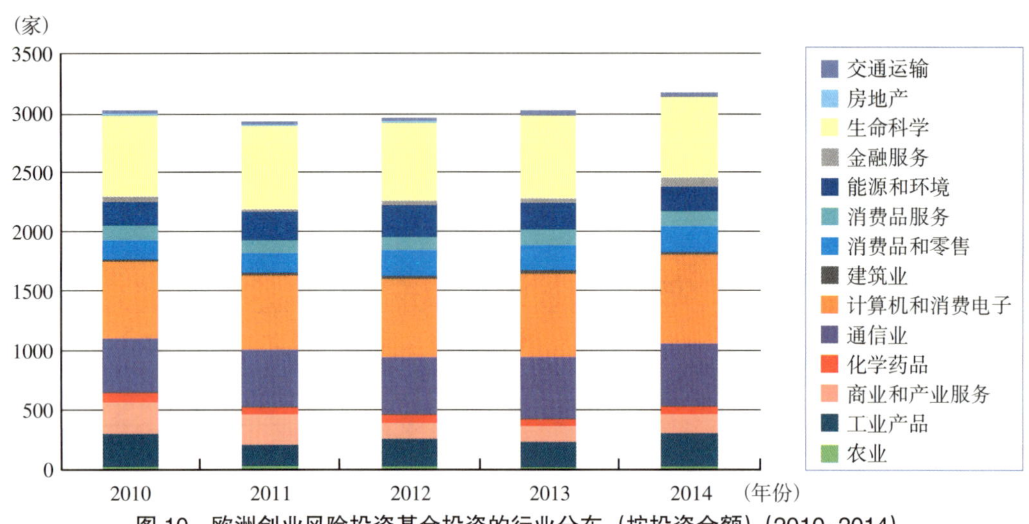

图 10 欧洲创业风险投资基金投资的行业分布（按投资金额）(2010~2014)

(三) 投资轮次分布

从投资轮次分布来看，欧洲股权投资市场的首轮投资与后续投资占比大致保持一致，首轮投资略少于后续投资。2014 年，首轮投资占 46%，后续投资占 54%（见图 11）。

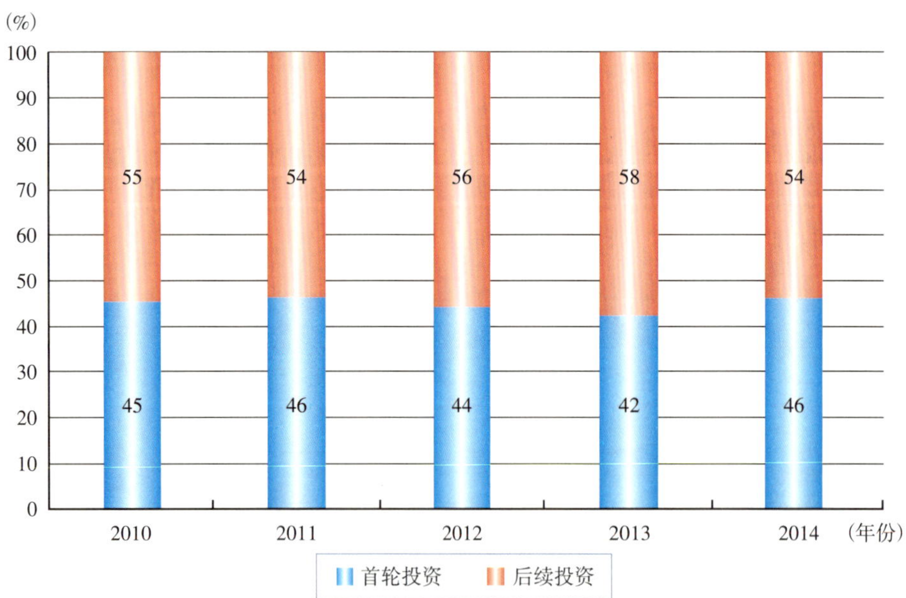

图 11 欧洲股权投资的首轮投资与后续投资（2010~2014）

三、退出活动

2014 年，整个欧洲股权投资市场共有 2400 家企业实现股权投资退出，退出金额达 378 亿欧元，达到了历史最高水平。与 2013 年相比，退出企业数上升了 5%，金额上升了 10%。其中，风险投资的企业退出数量占 42%，全年退出的企业超过 1000 家；退出金额仅占 5%，退出金额较 2013 年减少了 16%，达到 19 亿欧元。

表 3 欧洲股权投资市场退出活动的主要特征（2014）

	所有股权类基金	创业风险投资	并购	成长资本
退出金额（十亿欧元）	37.8	1.9	32.8	2.2
退出项目数（家）	2416	1003	776	611
涉及的企业数（家）	664	311	338	175
涉及的基金数（只）	1188	555	571	254

（一）退出方式

按退出金额划分，2014 年，欧洲股权投资的主要退出方式依次为贸易销售（占比 26%）、出售给其他 PE 公司（占比 24%），以及出售给公募基金（占比 10%）。2014 年，欧洲创业风险投资的主要退出方式依次为贸易销售（占比 45.3%）、清算（占比 18.0%）、出售给其他 PE 公司（占比 11.2%），全年通过 IPO 退出的企业仅占 1.7%（见图 12）。

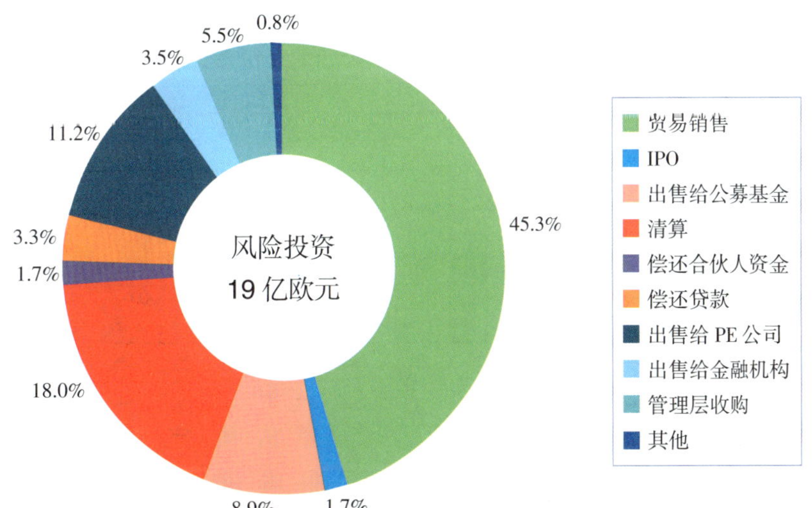

图 12 欧洲创业风险投资的主要退出方式（按金额划分）（2014）

按退出项目划分，2014 年，欧洲创业风险投资的主要退出方式依次为清算（占比 26.3%）、贸易销售（占比 21.7%）、偿还合伙人资金（占比 17.5%），全年通过 IPO 退出的企业共计 8 家，是 2013 年的 2 倍（见图 13）。

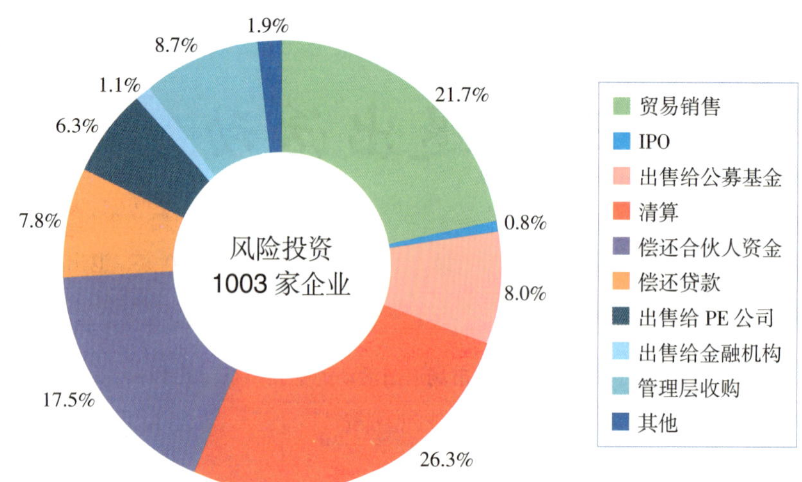

图 13 欧洲创业风险投资的主要退出方式（按项目划分）(2014)

（二）退出的行业划分

按退出项目数划分，2014 年，整个欧洲股权投资市场当年退出项目最多的行业依次为：商业工业产品（380 项）、计算机与消费电子（273 项）、消费品与零售业（268 项）、生命科学（235 项）、通信业（185 项）、消费品服务（130 项）等；按退出金额划分，当年实现退出的金额依次为通信业（56 亿欧元）、消费品与零售业（54 亿欧元）、生命科学（44 亿欧元）、商业工业产品（44 亿欧元）、商业工业服务（26 亿欧元）、计算机与消费电子（22 亿欧元）等（见图 14）。

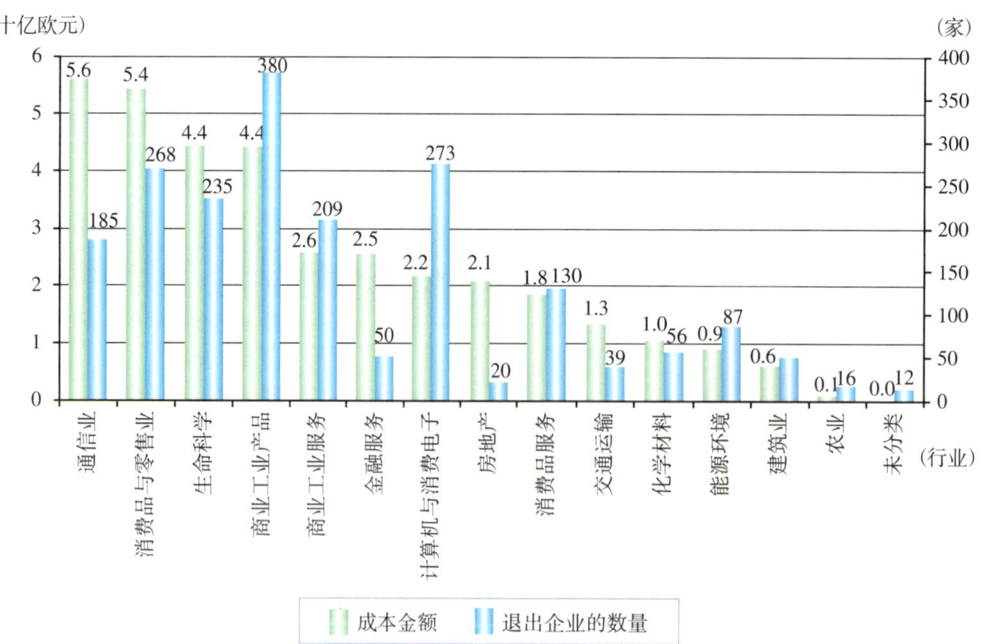

图 14 欧洲风险投资退出的主要行业分布（2014）

资料来源：数据由欧洲私募股权和风险投资协会 European Private Equity and Venture Capital Association 提供。

附录 3 2014 年韩国创业风险投资回顾

一、韩国创业风险投资市场概况

2014 年韩国经济缓慢增长，要实现全面复苏仍任重道远。2014 年韩国创业风险投资企业存量仅微幅上升为 103 家，但是仍未达到 2011 年水平；累计注册资本金额也有所上升，但是低于 2012 年的水平（见表 1）。

表 1 韩国创业风险投资公司概况（2005~2014）

指标 \ 年份	2005	2006	2007	2008	2009	2010	2011	2012	2013	2014
当年新注册数（注销数）	0（3）	13（11）	7（10）	5（9）	12（9）	13（10）	9（7）	6（6）	3（7）	6（4）
当年公司存量（家）	102	104	101	97	100	103	105	105	101	103
累计注册资本（十亿韩元）	1536.8	1553.7	1555.8	1475.8	1360.8	1383.8	1398.5	1445.5	1397.6	1422.2

截止到 2014 年底，韩国共有 103 家创业风险投资企业，管理着 481 只创业风险投资基金（见表 1、表 2、图 1）。当年新增注册基金公司 82 家，注销基金 37 只，创业风险投资企业注册资本为 14222 亿韩元，创业风险投资基金管理资本为 122168 亿韩元（见表 1、表 2）。

表 2 韩国创业风险投资基金概况（2005~2014）

指标 \ 年份	2005	2006	2007	2008	2009	2010	2011	2012	2013	2014
当年新注册数（只）	46	48	67	51	74	67	67	41	54	82
金额（十亿韩元）	945.4	861.7	1127.9	975.1	1420.9	1589.9	2286.1	772.7	1567.9	2570.4
当年注销数（只）	69	98	84	48	44	40	43	45	30	37
金额（十亿韩元）	433.7	741.8	929.4	406.3	491.7	550.4	440.0	858.6	504.6	832.9
当年存量（只）	400	350	333	336	366	393	417	431	431	481
累计金额（十亿韩元）	4757.6	4877.5	5076.0	5644.8	6574.0	7613.5	9460.0	9374.1	10479.3	12216.8

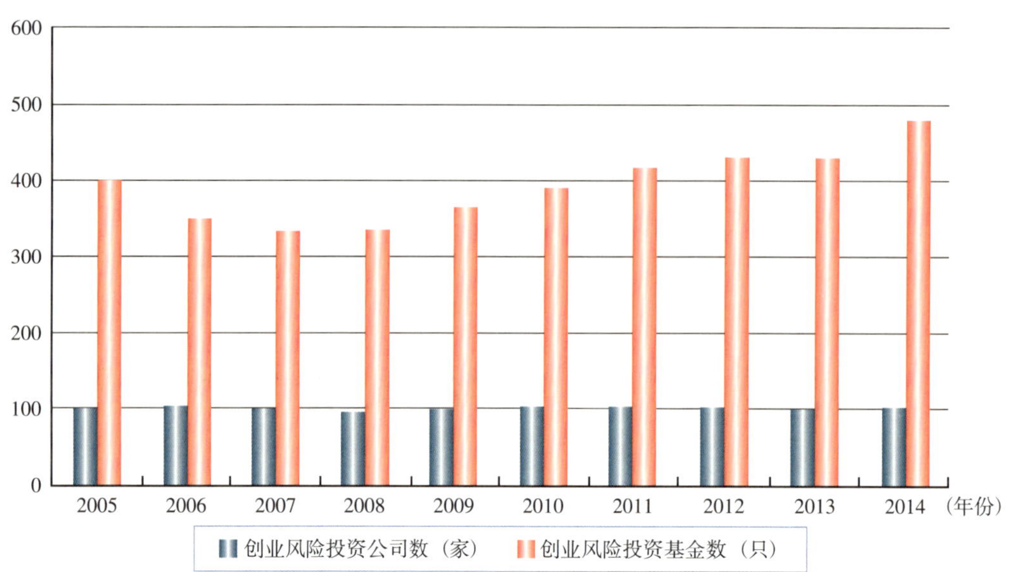

图 1 韩国创业风险投资市场概况（2005~2014）

二、韩国创业风险投资活动

表 3 韩国创业风险投资项目数及金额（2005~2014）

项目＼年份	2005	2006	2007	2008	2009	2010	2011	2012	2013	2014
新投资项目数（项）	635	617	615	496	524	560	613	688	755	901
新投资金额数（十亿韩元）	757.3	733.3	991.7	724.7	867.1	1091.0	1260.8	1233.3	1384.5	1639.3
投资强度（十亿韩元/项）	1.19	1.19	1.61	1.46	1.65	1.95	2.06	1.79	1.83	1.82

三、韩国创业风险投资行业分布

2014 年，从投资项目看，韩国创业风险机构的投资集中在图像/性能/存储、ICT 服务、游戏，三者占比分别为 21.6%、15.9%、14.3%；从投资金额看，排名前三的行业分别为生物/医药、图像/性能/存储、零售/服务，三者占比分别为 17.9%、17.0%、12.5%（见表 4、图 2）。

表 4 韩国创业风险投资行业分布（2014）

指标＼行业	ICT 制造	ICT 服务	电子/机器/设备	化工/材料	生物/医药	图像/性能/存储	游戏	零售/服务	其他
项目（项）	86	153	86	47	87	208	137	119	38
金额（十亿韩元）	195.1	191.3	156.0	82.7	292.8	279.0	176.2	204.6	61.6

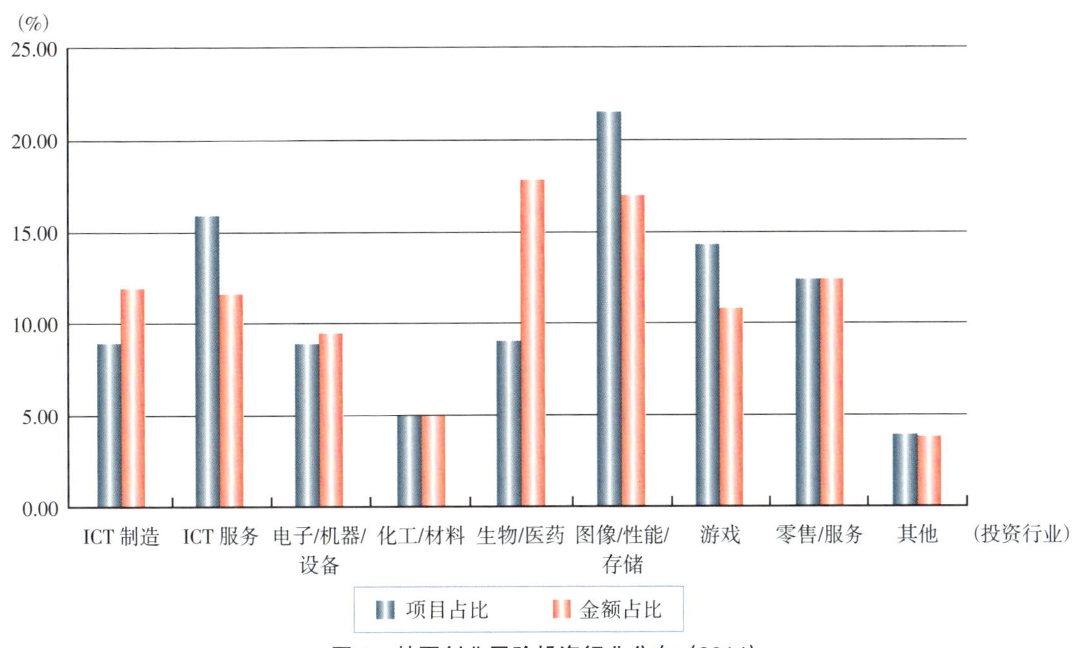

图 2 韩国创业风险投资行业分布（2014）

四、韩国创业风险投资阶段分布

从投资项目看，2014 年韩国创业风险投资项目主要集中在早期阶段，较上年有较大幅度上升；从投资金额看，仍然以扩展期为最多，所占比重为 44.4%，较上年稍微下降（见表 5、图 3、图 4）。

表 5 韩国创业风险投资阶段分布（2014）

阶 段	早 期	创建期	扩展期
项目（项）	438	231	266
金额（十亿韩元）	504.5	406.9	727.9

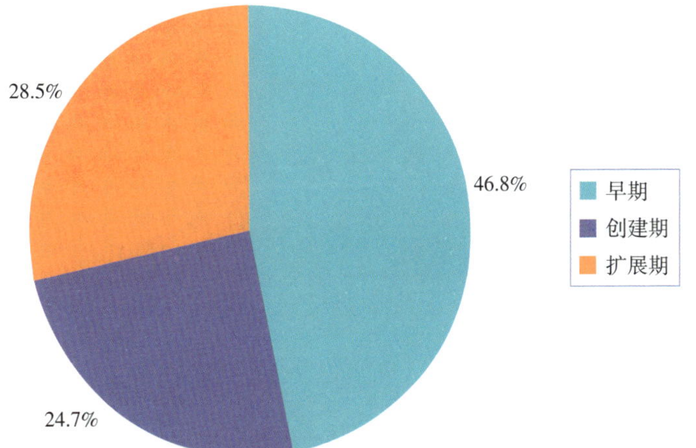

图 3 韩国创业风险投资阶段分布（按项目划分）(2014)

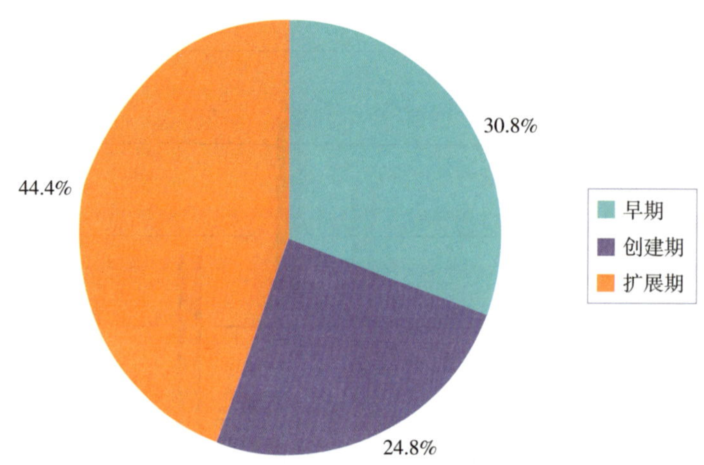

图 4　韩国创业风险投资阶段分布（按金额划分）(2014)

资料来源：数据由韩国风险投资协会 Korean Venture Capital Association 提供。

附录 4 2015 硅谷指数解读

硅谷是一个只关注“想法”与“将想法付诸实践”的地方，全球创业者纷至沓来，为硅谷的创新创业不断注入新鲜的血液。每年一季度，反映硅谷上一年发展的权威报告《硅谷指数》都会及时出版。自 1995 年开始，至今已出版 20 年。《2015 硅谷指数》的发布，带来了硅谷新的发展动向与趋势，为全球科技集聚提供了一份具有参考价值的硅谷年报。综合而言，硅谷创新创业方面呈现如下特点：

一、专利注册数持续增长，信息行业比重最大

2013 年，硅谷的专利注册数持续增长，共计 16975 件，较上年增加了 1910 件。其中，计算机、数据处理及信息存储行业的专利最多，占硅谷专利总数的 40%。其次是通信行业的专利注册量，占总数的 24%。硅谷和旧金山地区的专利注册数占加州和美国专利注册总数的比例分别增加到 52.3%和 13.8%。硅谷地区每十万人的专利授权数为 581 件，高于旧金山的 237 件和加州地区的 95 件。然而，2011~2013 年，旧金山和加州地区的人均专利注册量迅速增多，要高于硅谷地区，三者分别为 65.2%、26.8%和 22%。此外，旧金山人均专利注册量在 2013 年增长了 22.7%，是硅谷和加州地区增长率的两倍多。

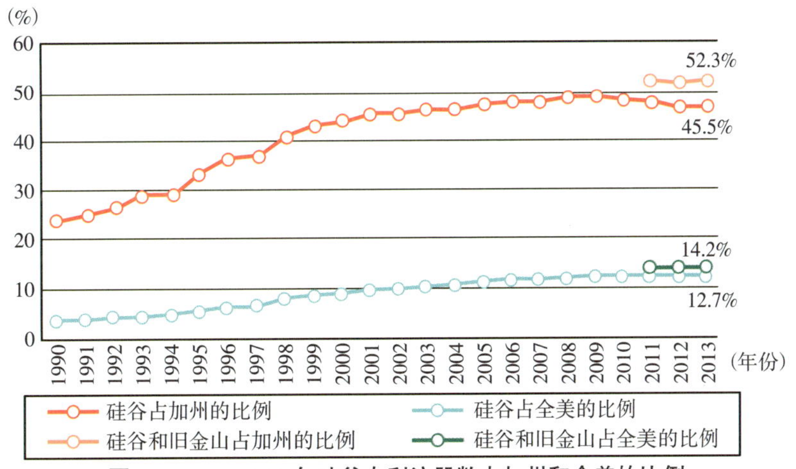

图 1 1990~2013 年硅谷专利注册数占加州和全美的比例

二、风险投资额猛涨，清洁技术行业达到历史最高值

2014 年，硅谷和旧金山地区的风险投资额猛涨，是 2000 年以来获得风险投资最多的一年，仅前三季度就达到 146 亿美元（其中旧金山 72 亿美元，硅谷 74 亿美元）。硅谷和旧金山地区的风险投资额占加州和全美总额的比例为 73.7%和 43%，分别增长了 1.5%和 7%。风险投资额的增长一方面来源于几笔大额的交易，主要包括优步公司（12 亿美元）和另外 5 家公司，另一方面是因为旧金山的企业获得的风险投资金额不断增多，比 2013 年全年增长了 68%。按行业分布来看，软件业在近 5 年内持续上升，成为吸引风险投资最多的行业，分别占硅谷和旧金山风险投资总额的 55%和 56%。其次是生物技术行业（10%）、娱乐媒体行业（8%）、医疗器械设备（8%）以及其他相关行业。值得一提的是，网络及设备行业获得的风险投资金额较 2002 年互联网泡沫时期的 19%大大下降，不足 1%。

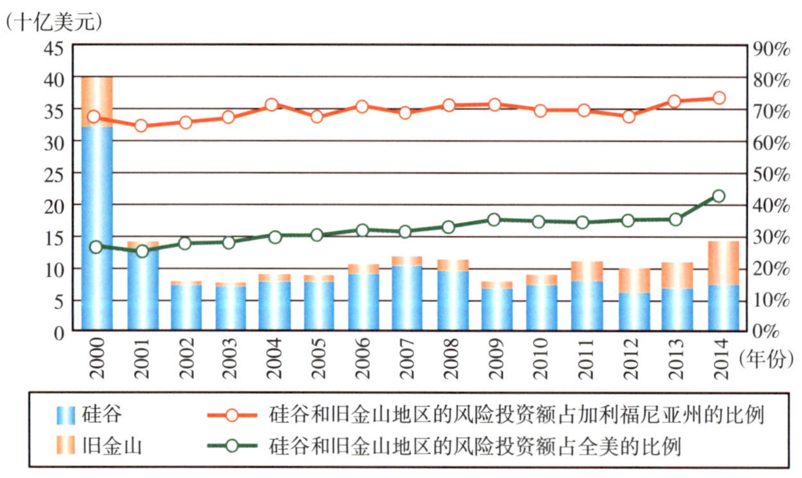

图 2 2000~2014 年硅谷风险投资额

同年，清洁技术行业的风险投资额急剧增长，达到历史最高值，为 32.7 亿美元。有 75%的风险投资额来自旧金山地区，该地区清洁技术行业的风险投资额比上年增长超过 300%。同样，硅谷和旧金山在清洁技术行业的风险投资总额占加州和全美清洁技术行业风险投资总额的比例也大大提高，分别为 80.2%和 53.1%。其中，节能技术获得了 40.6%的风险投资。太阳能方面的投资继连续三年的下跌后出现反弹，达到 14.8%。就风险投资交易数量来看，旧金山自 2003 年以来持续增加，而硅谷则较 2011 年出现了下跌，这说明风险投资的单笔金额逐渐增多。

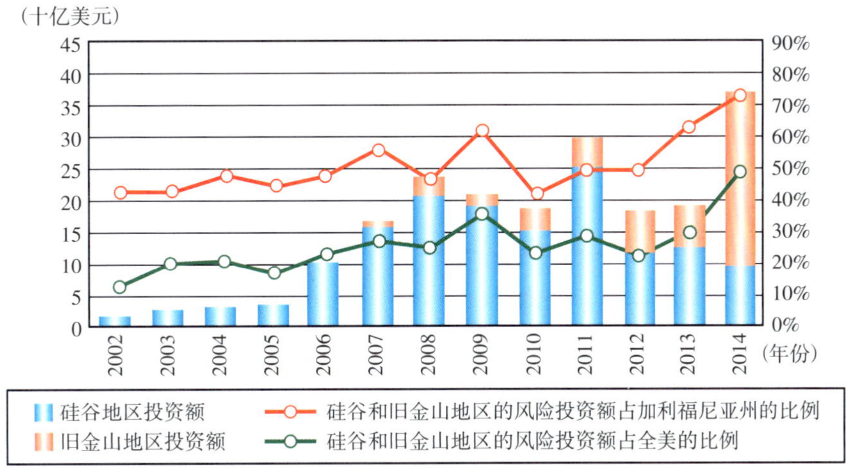

图 3　2002~2014 年硅谷清洁技术行业的风险投资情况

2014 年前三季度，硅谷的天使投资金额与上年基本持平，旧金山较上年有所增长。旧金山种子期企业获得的 A 轮融资投资额大幅增多，初创企业快速增长。整体上，上述两个地区的天使投资占加州天使投资总额的比例相对稳定（占 85%）。

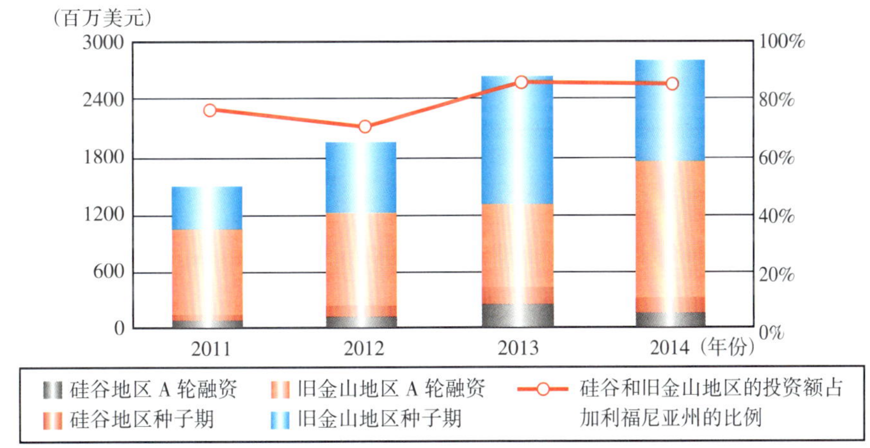

图 4　2011~2014 年硅谷、旧金山及加州天使投资情况

三、IPO 数量基本持平，旧金山兼并交易猛增

2014 年，全美 IPO 数量为 275 家，其中硅谷为 23 家（2013 年为 20 家）。而加州其他地区的增长更为明显，从上年的 23 家增加到 35 家，旧金山占了 5 家。另外，国内其他 IPO 数量为 151 家，增加了 9 家。在美国交易所上市的国际企业越来越多，这些企业来自中国（21%）、以色列（18%）、英国（11%）以及其他 19 个国家。虽然数量上增多，但是硅谷占加州上市总数下跌至 40%，占全美上市总数的比例略有增长，从 10.8%增长到 11%。

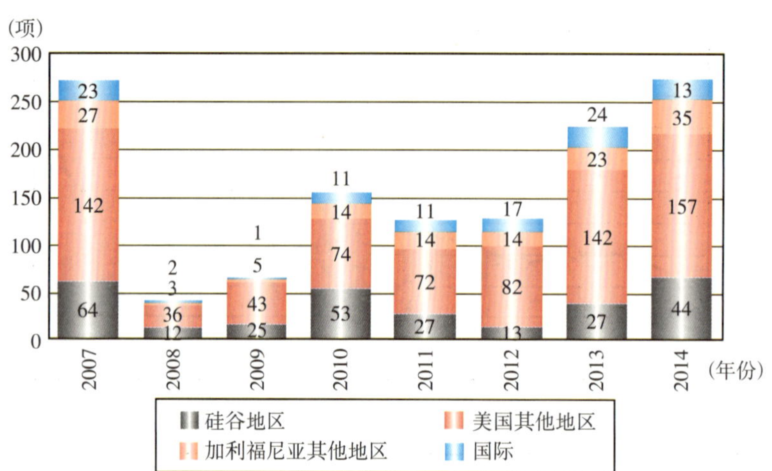

图 5 2007~2014 年全美 IPO 总数

截至 2014 年三季度，硅谷兼并活动数量为 560 件，与 2013 年基本持平，而旧金山的兼并活动数量为 403 件，超过了 2013 年全年水平。虽然总量上有所增加，但硅谷和旧金山占加州、全美并购活动的比例和去年相似，分别为 41%和 10%。此外，硅谷和旧金山地区收购方为本地的交易数量较上年都有所增长，分别为 58.6%和 53.8%。而收购双方均为本地的交易数量却分别下降了 4.3%和 3.2%。

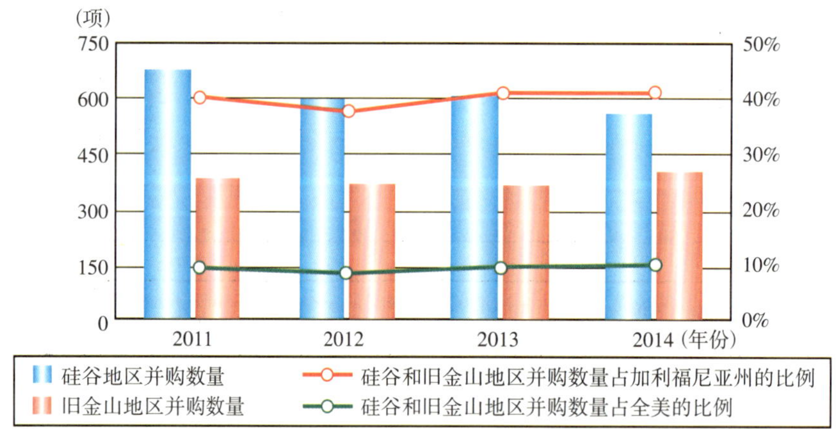

图 6 2011~2013 年硅谷、旧金山、加州及全美的并购数量

四、非雇主企业持续增多

2011~2012 年，非雇主企业（个人创业，没有员工的企业）数量持续增多，超过 19 万家。这期间，硅谷和旧金山的企业家们不断成立新公司，硅谷 2893 家，旧金山 1482 家。2012 年，硅谷 26%的非雇主企业涉及专业技术领域和科技服务行业。全美和加州范围内，只有 14%和 17.5%的非雇主企业从事该行业。这表明，硅谷非雇主企业更显专业。这种非雇主企业的统计指标在国内是没有的，而美国为何设定？其数量的增长有着怎样的内涵？尽管《硅谷指数》没有给出直接的回答，但这是值得我们关注的。

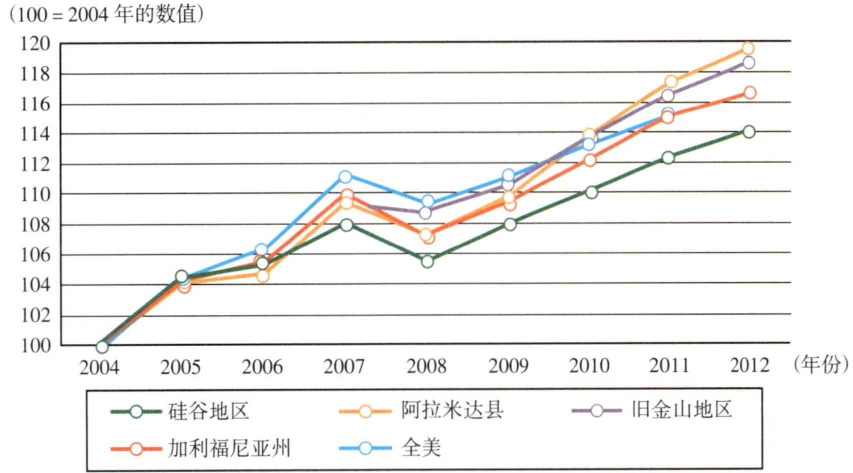

图 7　2004~2012 年硅谷、旧金山、加州及全美的非雇主企业情况

综合而言，《2015 硅谷指数》表明 2015 年硅谷地区就业形势好转，收入提高，失业率和贫困率下降。硅谷创新不断好转的同时也带动了旧金山地区的创新。风险投资、天使投资、专利注册以及并购活动迅速增多，这些使得硅谷的创新引擎全速发动，推动整个地区经济的快速发展。

（特别感谢杭州市科技信息研究院吕克斐供稿）

附录 5 关于印发《中小企业发展专项资金管理暂行办法》的通知

财企〔2014〕38 号

各省、自治区、直辖市、计划单列市财政厅（局）、中小企业主管部门、科技厅（委、局）、商务主管部门，新疆生产建设兵团财务局、工业和信息化委员会、科技局、商务局，有关中央所属单位：

为促进中小企业特别是小型微型企业健康发展，规范和加强中小企业发展专项资金的使用和管理，财政部会同工业和信息化部、科技部、商务部制定了《中小企业发展专项资金管理暂行办法》。现印发给你们，请遵照执行。

财政部　工业和信息化部　科技部　商务部

2014 年 4 月 11 日

中小企业发展专项资金管理暂行办法

第一章　总　则

第一条　为了规范中小企业发展专项资金的管理和使用，提高资金使用效益，根据《中华人民共和国预算法》、《中华人民共和国中小企业促进法》等有关规定，制定本办法。

第二条　本办法所称中小企业发展专项资金（以下简称专项资金），是指中央财政预算安排，用于支持中小企业特别是小微企业科技创新、改善中小企业融资环境、完善中小企业服务体系、加强国际合作等方面的资金。

第三条　专项资金的宗旨是，贯彻落实国家宏观政策和扶持中小企业发展战略，弥补市场失灵，促进公平竞争，激发中小企业和非公有制经济活力和创造力，促进扩大就业和改善民生。

第四条　专项资金的使用和管理遵循公开透明、突出重点、统筹管理、加强监督的原则，确保资金使用规范、安全和高效，并向中西部地区倾斜。

第五条　专项资金综合运用无偿资助、股权投资、业务补助或奖励、代偿补偿、购买服务等支持方式，采取市场化手段，引入竞争性分配办法，鼓励创业投资机构、担保机构、公共服务机构等支持中小企业，充分发挥财政资金的引导和促进作用。

第六条　专项资金建立部门共管、专家评审、项目公示、追踪问效的全过程协作管理机制，加强绩效评价及结果运用，实现资金分配的激励和约束。

第七条　专项资金由财政部会同工业和信息化部、科技部、商务部（以下统称相关部门）按照职责分工共同管理。

财政部负责专项资金的预算管理和资金拨付，会同相关部门制定资金分配方案，并对资金的使用和管理情况等开展绩效评价和监督检查。

相关部门会同财政部开展专项资金项目管理工作，确定年度支持重点，组织项目申报和评审，并对项目实施情况进行跟踪服务和监督检查。

第二章 支持科技创新

第八条 发挥财政资金对中小企业科技创新活动的引导作用，支持和鼓励科技型中小企业研究开发具有良好市场前景的前沿核心关键技术，借助创业投资机制促进中小企业科技创新，推动实施国家创新驱动战略。

第九条 专项资金安排专门支出支持中小企业围绕电子信息、光机电一体化、资源与环境、新能源与高效节能、新材料、生物医药、现代农业及高技术服务等领域开展科技创新活动（国际科研合作项目除外）。

第十条 专项资金运用无偿资助方式，对科技型中小企业创新项目按照不超过相关研发支出 40%的比例给予资助。每个创新项目资助额度最高不超过 300 万元。

第十一条 专项资金安排专门支出设立科技型中小企业创业投资引导基金（以下简称引导基金），用于引导创业投资企业、创业投资管理企业、具有投资功能的中小企业服务机构等（以下统称创业投资机构）投资于初创期科技型中小企业。

第十二条 引导基金运用阶段参股、风险补助和投资保障等方式，对创业投资机构及初创期科技型中小企业给予支持。

第十三条 阶段参股是指引导基金向创业投资企业进行股权投资，参股比例最高不超过创业投资企业募集资金总额的 25%，且不做第一大出资人，不参与创业投资企业的日常经营和管理。

引导基金参股期内，创业投资企业投资于初创期科技型中小企业的累积金额不低于引导基金出资额的 2 倍。

第十四条 引导基金参股股权经相关部门和财政部审核后，可按照以下方式退出：

（一）在约定期限内按照约定价格退出。引导基金参股 4 年内退出的，转让价格为引导基金原始投资额；参股 4 年以上 6 年以内退出的，转让价格为引导基金原始投资额及从第 5 年起按照转让时中国人民银行公布的 1 年期贷款基准利率计算的利息之和；参股满 6 年仍未退出的，将与其他出资人同股同权在存续期满后清算退出。

（二）先于保障出资人退出。引导基金参股前，确定一个或多个出资人作为引导基金参股本金回收的保障人（以下简称保障出资人）。引导基金参股后，创业投资企业如发生收益或清算分配，引导基金将先于保障出资人获得分配直至收回引导基金原始投资额及从第 5 年起按照当时中国人民银行公布的 1 年期贷款基准利率计算的利息之和，从而实现退出。

第十五条 引导基金股权投资收入上缴中央国库，纳入中央公共财政预算管理。

第十六条 风险补助是指引导基金对创业投资机构投资于年销售收入不超过 2000 万元的初创期科技型中小企业的投资项目给予一定比例的投资奖励和损失补偿。

（一）投资奖励：引导基金对投资项目，按照不超过实际投资额 5%的比例给予奖励，每个投资项目奖励额度最高不超过 100 万元，每家创业投资机构年度累计奖励额度最高不超过 500 万元。

（二）损失补偿：引导基金对创业投资机构已获得投资奖励支持的投资项目，按照不超过投资退出时实际损失额 50%的比例给予补偿，每个投资项目损失补偿额度最高不超过 200 万元。

第十七条 投资保障是指创业投资机构将正在进行高新技术研发、有投资潜力的，且年销售收入不超过 2000 万元的初创期科技型中小企业确定为“辅导企业”，引导基金对“辅导企业”给予投资前保障或投资后保障。

（一）投资前保障：引导基金给予每个项目投资前资助额度最高不超过 100 万元，用于补助“辅导企业”高新技术研发的费用支出。

（二）投资后保障：创业投资机构对“辅导企业”实施投资后，引导基金给予每个项目投资后资助额度最高不超过 200 万元，用于补助“辅导企业”高新技术产品产业化的费用支出。

第三章 改善融资环境

第十八条 发挥财政资金对信用担保机构等中小企业融资服务机构的激励作用，引导其提升业务能力、规范经营行为、加快扩大中小企业融资服务规模，缓解中小企业融资难问题。

第十九条 专项资金安排专门支出支持中小企业信用担保机构（以下简称担保机构）、中小企业信用再担保机构（以下简称再担保机构）增强资本实力、扩大中小企业融资担保和再担保业务规模。

第二十条 专项资金运用业务补助、增量业务奖励、资本投入、代偿补偿、创新奖励等方式，对担保机构、再担保机构给予支持。

（一）业务补助：专项资金对担保机构开展的中小企

业特别是小微企业融资担保业务，按照不超过年平均在保余额 2%的比例给予补助；对再担保机构开展的中小企业融资再担保业务，按照不超过年平均在保余额 0.5%的比例给予补助。

（二）增量业务奖励：专项资金对担保机构，按照不超过当年小微企业融资担保业务增长额 3%的比例给予奖励；对再担保机构，按照不超过当年小微企业融资再担保业务增长额 1%的比例给予奖励。

（三）资本投入：专项资金对中西部地区省级财政直接或间接出资新设或增资的担保机构、再担保机构，按照不超过省级财政出资额 30%的比例给予资本投入支持，并委托地方出资单位代为履行出资人职责。

（四）代偿补偿：中央和地方共同出资，设立代偿补偿资金账户，委托省级再担保机构实行专户管理，专项资金出资比例不超过 60%。

当省级再担保机构对担保机构开展的小微企业融资担保业务按照代偿额 50%以上的比例（含）给予补偿时，代偿补偿资金按照不超过代偿额 30%的比例对担保机构给予补偿。该代偿业务的追偿所得，按照代偿补偿比例缴回代偿补偿资金账户。

（五）创新奖励：专项资金对积极探索创新小微企业融资担保业务且推广效用显著的担保机构，给予最高不超过 100 万元的奖励。

第二十一条 经省级以上财政部门通过竞争性方式选定为从事政府采购信用担保业务的担保机构，可按本办法规定申请专项资金资助。

第二十二条 担保机构、再担保机构可以同时申请以上不限于一项支持方式的资助，但单个担保机构当年获得专项资金的资助额度最高不超过 2000 万元，单个再担保机构当年获得专项资金的资助额度最高不超过 3000 万元（资本投入方式除外）。

单个代偿补偿资金账户当年获得专项资金的出资额度最高不超过 3 亿元。

第四章 完善服务体系

第二十三条 发挥财政资金在构建完善多元化、多层次中小企业公共服务体系方面的激励作用，加快改善中小企业服务环境、提升服务水平，促进中小企业公平参与市场竞争。

第二十四条 专项资金安排专门支出支持各类中小企业公共服务平台和服务机构的建设和运行，增强服务能力、降低服务成本、增加服务种类、提高服务质量，为中小企业提供全方位专业化优质服务。重点支持以下内容：

（一）科技服务。包括技术咨询、研发设计、检验检测、技术转移、技术工程化、技术培训、科技企业孵化等服务。

（二）商贸服务。包括产品认证、市场宣传推介、品牌建设、电子商务、商业特许经营、商标注册等服务，以及参加各类重点展会、创新营销和商业模式、扩大信用销售、发展专业市场和特色商业街、推广现代流通方式等事项。

（三）综合性服务。包括中小企业运行监测、政策宣传、违法违规行为发布、风险预警、数据共享、产供销等信息服务，及管理咨询、创业辅导、创业基地、技术改造、产业升级、人才培训、财务会计、知识产权、工业设计、质量认证、仓储物流、法律咨询、投融资辅导、职业经理人建设等服务。

（四）其他促进中小企业发展的服务。

第二十五条 专项资金运用无偿资助、业务奖励、政府购买服务等方式，对中小企业公共服务平台和服务机构给予支持。

（一）无偿资助。专项资金对服务平台或机构实施的服务场地改造、软硬件设备及服务设施购置等提升服务能力的建设项目，按照不超过项目总投资额 30%的比例给予补助。每个建设项目补助额度最高不超过 500 万元。

专项资金对中小企业参加的重点展会，给予减收或免收展位费、布展费、展品运输费等费用补贴。

（二）业务奖励。专项资金对服务平台或机构开展的中小企业服务，综合考虑其服务中小企业数量、收费标准、客户总体满意度等因素，按照不超过年度实际运营成本 40%的比例给予奖励。每个项目奖励额度最高不超过 500 万元。

专项资金对保险机构面向中小企业开展的内贸信用险业务给予奖励支持。

（三）政府购买服务。专项资金向服务平台或机构购买中小企业发展迫切需要、市场供给严重不足的公共性服务。

第五章 促进国际合作

第二十六条 发挥中央财政资金在中小企业国际合作

中的统筹和协调作用，鼓励加快引进国际先进技术，避免盲目重复引进及恶性竞争。

第二十七条　专项资金安排专门支出支持国内中小企业与欧盟企业、研究单位等（以下简称欧方合作机构）在节能减排相关领域开展科研合作。

（一）促进国内中小企业与欧方合作机构联合研究开发国际尖端节能减排技术。重点支持有利于国内中小企业追踪国际技术发展方向，掌握关键核心技术，填补国内技术空白的研发项目。

（二）引导国内中小企业转化中欧节能减排先进技术合作成果。重点支持国内中小企业应用中欧联合研发成果，开展技术延伸研究及小试、中试等活动，推动技术成果产业化的研发项目。

（三）鼓励国内中小企业从欧方合作机构引进、消化吸收国际先进节能减排技术。重点支持国内中小企业引进适合我国国情的先进技术，进行消化吸收再创新或本土化改造，提升我国技术研发水平与推广应用能力的研发项目。

（四）推动国内中小企业与欧方合作机构加强节能减排技术交流与合作。重点支持国内中小企业参加欧方合作机构组织的与节能减排技术相关的国际会议、访问等交流项目。

第二十八条　专项资金运用无偿资助方式，对科研合作项目给予支持。研发项目按照不超过项目投资额40%的比例给予资助，每个项目资助额度最高不超过300万元。

交流项目按照不超过实际发生的国际差旅费（仅包括国际交通费、会议费）50%的比例给予资助，每个项目资助额度最高不超过30万元。

第六章　资金管理和工作组织

第二十九条　财政部综合考虑本年度专项资金预算规模、相关部门提出的年度工作计划、上年度预算执行情况、以前年度绩效评价结果等因素，确定各类支持方向的年度预算规模。

第三十条　相关部门分别会同财政部组织开展项目申报工作，在每年3月底前下发工作通知，明确专项资金支持重点、申报条件等事项。

各省、自治区、直辖市、计划单列市及新疆生产建设兵团中小企业主管部门、科技主管部门、商务主管部门（以下统称省级有关主管部门）会同同级财政部门、中央所属单位，按照本办法等规定，在工作通知下发40日内组织项目申报。

第三十一条　省级有关主管部门、财政部门应加强项目的筛选和核实工作，可通过政府购买服务方式引入第三方评估机制，确保申报材料真实可靠，提升项目层次和质量。

第三十二条　省级有关主管部门会同同级财政部门对本地区申请项目进行公示后上报相关部门和财政部。

第三十三条　相关部门会同财政部通过政府购买服务等方式建立项目储备、申报、跟踪管理系统，建立专家评审制度，组织专家对地方和中央所属单位的申请项目进行评审论证。

第三十四条　相关部门建立健全专家库，确保入库专家与评审专家在数量上保持合理比例，加强对入库专家能力、职业道德等素质的前置审核工作，建立比例淘汰机制。

第三十五条　相关部门严格实行专家随机抽取制度和回避制度，在评审过程中建立专家交叉评审、集中评审等相互监督机制，研究建立评审专家责任追究机制，强化对评审专家的责任约束。

第三十六条　相关部门建立健全与评审专家的联系沟通机制，避免部门人员擅自对评审专家施加影响。

第三十七条　相关部门会同财政部根据专家评审意见提出项目立项计划，并向社会公示，公示期不少于10个工作日。

第三十八条　对项目公示期内提出异议的项目，相关部门会同财政部及时组织调查核实。

项目公示期结束后，相关部门将公示期内没有异议的项目和经调查核实没有问题的项目列为立项项目，向财政部提出资金安排建议。

第三十九条　财政部根据当年预算安排情况，对资金安排建议进行审定，在全国人民代表大会批准预算后90日内将项目支出预算指标下达到省级财政部门和中央所属单位。专项资金的支付，按照财政国库管理制度的有关规定执行。

第七章　绩效评价

第四十条　财政部会同相关部门建立专项资金绩效评价制度，明确评价原则、组织实施、评价依据、评价内容、指标体系、分值权重、评分标准等内容。

第四十一条　财政部通过政府购买服务等方式，对专项资金分配使用、项目实施及效果等实施评价，在充分听取相关部门意见后形成绩效评价结果，并将其作为专项资金以后年度支持方向预算安排的重要依据。

第四十二条 财政部会同相关部门根据绩效评价结果，及时完善资金使用、项目组织等管理制度，不断改进专项资金管理机制。

第八章 监督检查

第四十三条 各级财政部门定期或不定期对专项资金使用情况进行监督检查，必要时可委托社会中介机构进行审计或评估。各级中小企业主管部门、科技主管部门和商务主管部门定期或不定期对项目实施情况进行监督检查。

第四十四条 专项资金应当用于规定的支持方向和重点。对违反规定使用、骗取资金的行为，该项目单位三年内不得申请专项资金扶持，并依照《财政违法行为处罚处分条例》等国家有关规定进行处理。

第九章 附 则

第四十五条 本办法由财政部会同相关部门负责解释。

第四十六条 本办法自发布之日起施行。《财政部 工业和信息化部关于印发〈中小企业发展专项资金管理办法〉的通知》（财企〔2012〕96 号）、《财政部 工业和信息化部关于印发〈中小企业信用担保资金管理办法〉的通知》（财企〔2012〕97 号）、《财政部关于印发〈地方特色产业中小企业发展资金管理办法〉的通知》（财企〔2013〕67 号）、《财政部关于印发〈西藏及四川云南甘肃青海四省藏区中小企业发展创业资金管理暂行办法〉的通知》（财企〔2010〕241 号）、《财政部 科技部关于印发〈科技型中小企业技术创新基金财务管理暂行办法〉的通知》（财企〔2005〕22 号）、《财政部 科技部关于印发〈科技型中小企业创业投资引导基金管理暂行办法〉的通知》（财企〔2007〕128 号）、《财政部 科技部关于印发〈中欧中小企业节能减排科研合作资金管理暂行办法〉的通知》（财企〔2011〕226 号）同时废止。

附录 6　科技部　财政部关于印发《国家科技成果转化引导基金设立创业投资子基金管理暂行办法》的通知

国科发财〔2014〕229 号

各省、自治区、直辖市及计划单列市科技厅（委、局）、财政厅（局），新疆生产建设兵团科技局、财务局，科技部、财政部各有关司（中心），各有关单位：

根据《国家科技成果转化引导基金管理暂行办法》（财教〔2011〕289 号），为规范国家科技成果转化引导基金设立创业投资子基金工作，科技部、财政部制定了《国家科技成果转化引导基金设立创业投资子基金管理暂行办法》。现予印发，请遵照执行。

科技部　财政部

2014 年 8 月 8 日

国家科技成果转化引导基金设立创业投资子基金管理暂行办法

第一章　总　则

第一条　为规范国家科技成果转化引导基金（以下简称引导基金）设立创业投资子基金（以下简称子基金），加强资金管理，根据《国家科技成果转化引导基金管理暂行办法》，制定本办法。

第二条　引导基金按照政府引导、市场运作、不以营利为目的的原则设立子基金。设立方式包括与民间资本、地方政府资金以及其他投资者共同发起设立，或对已有创业投资基金增资设立等。

第三条　科技部按照《国家科技成果转化引导基金管理暂行办法》和本办法规定的条件和程序批准出资设立子基金。

第二章　子基金的设立

第四条　子基金应当在中国大陆境内注册，募集资金总额不低于 10000 万元人民币，且以货币形式出资，经营范围为创业投资业务，组织形式为公司制或有限合伙制。

第五条　引导基金对子基金的参股比例为子基金总额的 20%~30%，且始终不作为第一大股东或最大出资人；子基金的其余资金应依法募集，境外出资人应符合国家相关规定。

第六条　子基金存续期一般不超过 8 年。在子基金股权资产转让或变现受限等情况下，经子基金出资人协商一致，最多可延长 2 年。

第七条　在中国大陆境内注册的投资企业或创业投资管理企业（以下统称投资机构）可以作为申请者，向科技部、财政部申请设立子基金。多家投资机构拟共同发起子基金的，应推举一家机构作为申请者。

科技部、财政部委托引导基金的受托管理机构受理子基金的设立申请。

第八条 申请者为投资企业的，其注册资本或净资产应不低于 5000 万元；申请者为创业投资管理企业的，其注册资本应不低于 500 万元。

第九条 申请者应当确定一家创业投资管理企业作为拟设立的子基金的管理机构。该管理机构应具备以下条件：

（一）在中国大陆境内注册，主要从事创业投资业务；

（二）具有完善的创业投资管理和风险控制流程，规范的项目遴选和投资决策机制，健全的内部财务管理制度，能够为所投资企业提供创业辅导、管理咨询等增值服务；

（三）至少有 3 名具备 5 年以上创业投资或相关业务经验的专职高级管理人员；在国家重点支持的高新技术领域内，至少有 3 个创业投资成功案例；

（四）应参股子基金或认缴子基金份额，且出资额不得低于子基金总额的 5‰；

（五）企业及其高级管理人员无重大过失，无受行政主管机关或司法机关处罚的不良记录。

第十条 申请者向受托管理机构提交的申请应包括以下材料：

（一）子基金组建或增资方案；

（二）主要出资人的出资承诺书或出资证明；

（三）会计师事务所出具的投资机构近期的审计报告；

（四）子基金管理机构的有关材料；

（五）其他应当提交的资料。

第十一条 受托管理机构收到申请后，应对申请材料进行初审。对于不符合要求的，应及时通知申请者补充完善；对于符合要求的，应在规定时间内组织开展尽职调查，形成调查报告，并向引导基金理事会提交调查报告和子基金设立方案。

受托管理机构按照理事会要求委托专业化的社会中介机构开展尽职调查等工作。

第十二条 引导基金理事会依据《国家科技成果转化引导基金理事会规程》的相关规定，对调查报告和子基金设立方案进行审核，形成审核意见。

第十三条 科技部根据引导基金理事会的审核意见，对子基金设立方案进行合规性审查。对于符合设立条件的，科技部商财政部同意后向社会公示，公示期为 10 个工作日；公示无异议的，批准出资设立子基金，并向社会公告。

第三章 投资管理

第十四条 科技部、财政部委托受托管理机构向子基金派出代表，依据法律法规和子基金章程或合伙协议等行使出资人职责，参与重大决策，监督子基金的投资和运作，不参与日常管理。子基金管理机构做出投资决定后，应在实施投资前 3 个工作日告知受托管理机构代表。

第十五条 子基金管理机构在完成子基金 70%的资金委托投资之前，不得募集其他基金。子基金的待投资金应存放托管银行或购买国债等风险低、流动性强的符合国家有关规定的金融产品。

子基金管理费由子基金出资人与子基金管理机构协商确定。

第十六条 子基金投资于转化国家科技成果转化项目库中科技成果的企业的资金应不低于引导基金出资额的 3 倍，且不低于子基金总额的 50%；其他投资方向应符合国家重点支持的高新技术领域；所投资企业应在中国大陆境内注册。

第十七条 子基金不得从事以下业务：

（一）投资于已上市企业（所投资企业上市后，子基金所持股份未转让及其配售部分除外）；

（二）从事担保、抵押、委托贷款、房地产（包括购买自用房地产）等业务；

（三）投资于股票、期货、企业债券、信托产品、理财产品、保险计划及其他金融衍生品；

（四）进行承担无限连带责任的对外投资；

（五）吸收或变相吸收存款，以及发行信托或集合理财产品的形式募集资金；

（六）向任何第三方提供资金拆借、赞助、捐赠等；

（七）其他国家法律法规禁止从事的业务。

第十八条 引导基金以出资额为限对子基金债务承担责任。子基金清算出现亏损时，首先由子基金管理机构以其对子基金的出资额承担亏损，剩余部分由引导基金和其他出资人按出资比例承担。

第十九条 出现下列情况之一时，引导基金可选择退出，且无需经由其他出资人同意：

（一）子基金方案获得科技部批准后，未按规定程序完成设立手续超过一年的；

（二）引导基金向子基金账户拨付资金后，子基金未开展投资超过一年的；

（三）子基金投资项目不符合本办法规定的政策目标的；

（四）子基金未按照章程或合伙协议约定投资的；

（五）子基金管理机构发生实质性变化的。

第二十条 子基金存续期内，鼓励子基金的股东（出资人）或其他投资者购买引导基金所持子基金的股权或份额。同等条件下，子基金的股东（出资人）优先购买。

对于发起设立的子基金，注册之日起 4 年内（含 4 年）购买的，以引导基金原始出资额转让；4 年至 6 年内（含 6 年）购买的，以引导基金原始出资额及从第 5 年起按照转让时中国人民银行公布的 1 年期贷款基准利率计算的利息之和转让；6 年以上仍未退出的，将与其他出资人同股同权在存续期满后清算退出。

对于增资设立的子基金的，上述年限从子基金完成变更登记手续之日起计算。

第二十一条 子基金存续期结束时，子基金出资各方按照出资比例或相关协议约定获取投资收益。子基金的年平均收益率不低于子基金出资时中国人民银行公布的一年期贷款基准利率的，引导基金可将其不超过 20%的收益奖励子基金管理机构。

第四章 托管银行

第二十二条 科技部、财政部通过招标等方式确定若干家银行作为子基金的托管银行，并向社会公布。托管银行应当符合以下条件：

（一）成立时间在 5 年以上的全国性股份制商业银行；

（二）具有专门的基金托管机构和创业投资基金托管经验；

（三）无重大过失以及受行政主管机关或司法机关处罚的不良记录。

第二十三条 子基金应在科技部、财政部公布的银行名单中选择托管银行，签订资产托管协议，开设托管账户。托管银行与子基金主要出资人、子基金管理机构之间不得有股权和亲属等关联及利害关系。

第二十四条 托管银行负责托管子基金资产，按照托管协议和投资指令负责子基金的资金往来，定期向受托管理机构报告资金情况。受托管理机构负责对托管银行履行职责情况进行考核。

第二十五条 子基金存续期内产生的股权转让、分红、清算等资金应进入托管账户，不得循环投资。

第五章 收入收缴

第二十六条 引导基金投资子基金的收入包括引导基金退出时应收回的原始投资及应取得的收益、子基金清算时引导基金应取得的剩余财产清偿收入等。

上述原始投资及应取得的收益，按照引导基金的实际出资额以及引导基金股权或份额转让协议等确定；应取得的剩余财产清偿收入根据有关法律程序确定。

第二十七条 引导基金投资子基金的所得收入上缴中央国库，纳入中央公共财政预算管理。收入收缴工作由受托管理机构负责，按照国库集中收缴有关规定执行。

第二十八条 引导基金投资子基金的收入按以下程序上缴：

（一）受托管理机构与子基金其他出资人等商议股权或份额退出、收益分配及清算等事宜，并对子基金实施情况的专项审计报告、受让子基金股权或份额申请以及确认收入所依据的相关资料等进行审核；

（二）受托管理机构根据商议及审核结果，提出引导基金退出及收入收缴实施方案，报科技部、财政部审定；

（三）受托管理机构根据科技部、财政部的审定意见，办理股权或份额转让、收入收缴等手续，向有关缴款单位发送缴款通知；

（四）缴款单位在收到缴款通知后的 30 日内，将应缴的引导基金投资子基金收入缴入引导基金在托管银行开设的指定账户。

第六章 管理与监督

第二十九条 受托管理机构应建立子基金管理信息系统，实施子基金设立及运作的过程管理，并采取投资告知、定期报告、专项审计等方式，加强对子基金的管理和监督。

第三十条 受托管理机构应向科技部、财政部定期提交子基金运作情况和引导基金投资子基金收入上缴情况，及时报告子基金法律文件变更、资本增减、违法违规事件、管理机构变动、清算与解散等重大事项。

第三十一条 科技部、财政部委托引导基金理事会对子基金运作情况定期开展绩效评价，对受托管理机构改进工作提出建议。

第三十二条 受托管理机构不能有效履行职责、发生重大过失或违规行为等造成恶劣影响的，科技部、财政部视情况给予约谈、批评、警告直至取消其受托管理资格的处理。处理结果可向社会公告。

第三十三条 任何单位和个人不得隐瞒、滞留、截留、挤占、挪用引导基金投资子基金的收入。一经发现和查实前述行为，除收回有关资金外，按照《财政违法行为处罚处分条例》（国务院令第 427 号）的规定处理。

第七章 附 则

第三十四条 本办法规定的相关事项应在子基金章程或合伙协议等文件中载明。

第三十五条 本办法由科技部、财政部负责解释。

第三十六条 本办法自发布之日起 30 日后施行。

附录 7 私募投资基金监督管理暂行办法

中国证券监督管理委员会令

第 105 号

第一章 总 则

第一条 为了规范私募投资基金活动，保护投资者及相关当事人的合法权益，促进私募投资基金行业健康发展，根据《证券投资基金法》、《国务院关于进一步促进资本市场健康发展的若干意见》，制定本办法。

第二条 本办法所称私募投资基金（以下简称私募基金），是指在中华人民共和国境内，以非公开方式向投资者募集资金设立的投资基金。私募基金财产的投资包括买卖股票、股权、债券、期货、期权、基金份额及投资合同约定的其他投资标的。非公开募集资金，以进行投资活动为目的设立的公司或者合伙企业，资产由基金管理人或者普通合伙人管理的，其登记备案、资金募集和投资运作适用本办法。证券公司、基金管理公司、期货公司及其子公司从事私募基金业务适用本办法，其他法律法规和中国证券监督管理委员会（以下简称中国证监会）有关规定对上述机构从事私募基金业务另有规定的，适用其规定。

第三条 从事私募基金业务，应当遵循自愿、公平、诚实信用原则，维护投资者合法权益，不得损害国家利益和社会公共利益。

第四条 私募基金管理人和从事私募基金托管业务的机构（以下简称私募基金托管人）管理、运用私募基金财产，从事私募基金销售业务的机构（以下简称私募基金销售机构）及其他私募服务机构从事私募基金服务活动，应当恪尽职守，履行诚实信用、谨慎勤勉的义务。私募基金从业人员应当遵守法律、行政法规，恪守职业道德和行为规范。

第五条 中国证监会及其派出机构依照《证券投资基金法》、本办法和中国证监会的其他有关规定，对私募基金业务活动实施监督管理。设立私募基金管理机构和发行私募基金不设行政审批，允许各类发行主体在依法合规的基础上，向累计不超过法律规定数量的投资者发行私募基金。建立健全私募基金发行监管制度，切实强化事中事后监管，依法严厉打击以私募基金为名的各类非法集资活动。建立促进经营机构规范开展私募基金业务的风险控制和自律管理制度，以及各类私募基金的统一监测系统。

第六条 中国证券投资基金业协会（以下简称基金业协会）依照《证券投资基金法》、本办法、中国证监会其他有关规定和基金业协会自律规则，对私募基金业开展行业自律，协调行业关系，提供行业服务，促进行业发展。

第二章 登记备案

第七条 各类私募基金管理人应当根据基金业协会的规定，向基金业协会申请登记，报送以下基本信息：

（一）工商登记和营业执照正副本复印件；

（二）公司章程或者合伙协议；

（三）主要股东或者合伙人名单；

（四）高级管理人员的基本信息；

（五）基金业协会规定的其他信息。基金业协会应当在私募基金管理人登记材料齐备后的 20 个工作日内，通过网站公告私募基金管理人名单及其基本情况的方式，为私募基金管理人办结登记手续。

第八条 各类私募基金募集完毕，私募基金管理人应当根据基金业协会的规定，办理基金备案手续，报送以下基本信息：

（一）主要投资方向及根据主要投资方向注明的基金

类别。

（二）基金合同、公司章程或者合伙协议。资金募集过程中向投资者提供基金招募说明书的，应当报送基金招募说明书。以公司、合伙等企业形式设立的私募基金，还应当报送工商登记和营业执照正副本复印件。

（三）采取委托管理方式的，应当报送委托管理协议。委托托管机构托管基金财产的，还应当报送托管协议。

（四）基金业协会规定的其他信息。

基金业协会应当在私募基金备案材料齐备后的 20 个工作日内，通过网站公告私募基金名单及其基本情况的方式，为私募基金办结备案手续。

第九条 基金业协会为私募基金管理人和私募基金办理登记备案不构成对私募基金管理人投资能力、持续合规情况的认可；不作为对基金财产安全的保证。

第十条 私募基金管理人依法解散、被依法撤销，或者被依法宣告破产的，其法定代表人或者普通合伙人应当在 20 个工作日内向基金业协会报告，基金业协会应当及时注销基金管理人登记并通过网站公告。

第三章 合格投资者

第十一条 私募基金应当向合格投资者募集，单只私募基金的投资者人数累计不得超过《证券投资基金法》、《公司法》、《合伙企业法》等法律规定的特定数量。投资者转让基金份额的，受让人应当为合格投资者且基金份额受让后投资者人数应当符合前款规定。

第十二条 私募基金的合格投资者是指具备相应风险识别能力和风险承担能力，投资于单只私募基金的金额不低于 100 万元且符合下列相关标准的单位和个人：

（一）净资产不低于 1000 万元的单位；

（二）金融资产不低于 300 万元或者最近三年个人年均收入不低于 50 万元的个人。

前款所称金融资产包括银行存款、股票、债券、基金份额、资产管理计划、银行理财产品、信托计划、保险产品、期货权益等。

第十三条 下列投资者视为合格投资者：

（一）社会保障基金、企业年金等养老基金，慈善基金等社会公益基金；

（二）依法设立并在基金业协会备案的投资计划；

（三）投资于所管理私募基金的私募基金管理人及其从业人员；

（四）中国证监会规定的其他投资者。

以合伙企业、契约等非法人形式，通过汇集多数投资者的资金直接或者间接投资于私募基金的，私募基金管理人或者私募基金销售机构应当穿透核查最终投资者是否为合格投资者，并合并计算投资者人数。但是，符合本条第（一）、（二）、（四）项规定的投资者投资私募基金的，不再穿透核查最终投资者是否为合格投资者和合并计算投资者人数。

第四章 资金募集

第十四条 私募基金管理人、私募基金销售机构不得向合格投资者之外的单位和个人募集资金，不得通过报刊、电台、电视、互联网等公众传播媒体或者讲座、报告会、分析会和布告、传单、手机短信、微信、博客和电子邮件等方式，向不特定对象宣传推介。

第十五条 私募基金管理人、私募基金销售机构不得向投资者承诺投资本金不受损失或者承诺最低收益。

第十六条 私募基金管理人自行销售私募基金的，应当采取问卷调查等方式，对投资者的风险识别能力和风险承担能力进行评估，由投资者书面承诺符合合格投资者条件；应当制作风险揭示书，由投资者签字确认。私募基金管理人委托销售机构销售私募基金的，私募基金销售机构应当采取前款规定的评估、确认等措施。投资者风险识别能力和承担能力问卷及风险揭示书的内容与格式指引，由基金业协会按照不同类别私募基金的特点制定。

第十七条 私募基金管理人自行销售或者委托销售机构销售私募基金，应当自行或者委托第三方机构对私募基金进行风险评级，向风险识别能力和风险承担能力相匹配的投资者推介私募基金。

第十八条 投资者应当如实填写风险识别能力和承担能力问卷，如实承诺资产或者收入情况，并对其真实性、准确性和完整性负责。填写虚假信息或者提供虚假承诺文件的，应当承担相应责任。

第十九条 投资者应当确保投资资金来源合法，不得非法汇集他人资金投资私募基金。

第五章 投资运作

第二十条 募集私募证券基金，应当制定并签订基金合同、公司章程或者合伙协议（以下统称基金合同）。基金合同应当符合《证券投资基金法》第九十三条、第九十四条规定。募集其他种类私募基金，基金合同应当参照《证券投资基金法》第九十三条、第九十四条规定，明确约定各方当事人的权利、义务和相关事宜。

第二十一条 除基金合同另有约定外，私募基金应当由基金托管人托管。基金合同约定私募基金不进行托管的，应当在基金合同中明确保障私募基金财产安全的制度措施和纠纷解决机制。

第二十二条 同一私募基金管理人管理不同类别私募基金的，应当坚持专业化管理原则；管理可能导致利益输送或者利益冲突的不同私募基金的，应当建立防范利益输送和利益冲突的机制。

第二十三条 私募基金管理人、私募基金托管人、私募基金销售机构及其他私募服务机构及其从业人员从事私募基金业务，不得有以下行为：

（一）将其固有财产或者他人财产混同于基金财产从事投资活动；

（二）不公平地对待其管理的不同基金财产；

（三）利用基金财产或者职务之便，为本人或者投资者以外的人牟取利益，进行利益输送；

（四）侵占、挪用基金财产；

（五）泄露因职务便利获取的未公开信息，利用该信息从事或者明示、暗示他人从事相关的交易活动；

（六）从事损害基金财产和投资者利益的投资活动；

（七）玩忽职守，不按照规定履行职责；

（八）从事内幕交易、操纵交易价格及其他不正当交易活动；

（九）法律、行政法规和中国证监会规定禁止的其他行为。

第二十四条 私募基金管理人、私募基金托管人应当按照合同约定，如实向投资者披露基金投资、资产负债、投资收益分配、基金承担的费用和业绩报酬、可能存在的利益冲突情况以及可能影响投资者合法权益的其他重大信息，不得隐瞒或者提供虚假信息。信息披露规则由基金业协会另行制定。

第二十五条 私募基金管理人应当根据基金业协会的规定，及时填报并定期更新管理人及其从业人员的有关信息、所管理私募基金的投资运作情况和杠杆运用情况，保证所填报内容真实、准确、完整。发生重大事项的，应当在 10 个工作日内向基金业协会报告。私募基金管理人应当于每个会计年度结束后的 4 个月内，向基金业协会报送经会计师事务所审计的年度财务报告和所管理私募基金年度投资运作基本情况。

第二十六条 私募基金管理人、私募基金托管人及私募基金销售机构应当妥善保存私募基金投资决策、交易和投资者适当性管理等方面的记录及其他相关资料，保存期限自基金清算终止之日起不得少于 10 年。

第六章 行业自律

第二十七条 基金业协会应当建立私募基金管理人登记、私募基金备案管理信息系统。基金业协会应当对私募基金管理人和私募基金信息严格保密。除法律法规另有规定外，不得对外披露。

第二十八条 基金业协会应当建立与中国证监会及其派出机构和其他相关机构的信息共享机制，定期汇总分析私募基金情况，及时提供私募基金相关信息。

第二十九条 基金业协会应当制定和实施私募基金行业自律规则，监督、检查会员及其从业人员的执业行为。会员及其从业人员违反法律、行政法规、本办法规定和基金业协会自律规则的，基金业协会可以视情节轻重，采取自律管理措施，并通过网站公开相关违法违规信息。会员及其从业人员涉嫌违法违规的，基金业协会应当及时报告中国证监会。

第三十条 基金业协会应当建立投诉处理机制，受理投资者投诉，进行纠纷调解。

第七章 监督管理

第三十一条 中国证监会及其派出机构依法对私募基金管理人、私募基金托管人、私募基金销售机构及其他私募服务机构开展私募基金业务情况进行统计监测和检查，依照《证券投资基金法》第一百一十四条规定采取有关措施。

第三十二条 中国证监会将私募基金管理人、私募基金托管人、私募基金销售机构及其他私募服务机构及其从业人员诚信信息记入证券期货市场诚信档案数据库；根据私募基金管理人的信用状况，实施差异化监管。

第三十三条 私募基金管理人、私募基金托管人、私募基金销售机构及其他私募服务机构及其从业人员违反法律、行政法规及本办法规定，中国证监会及其派出机构可以对其采取责令改正、监管谈话、出具警示函、公开谴责等行政监管措施。

第八章 关于创业投资基金的特别规定

第三十四条 本办法所称创业投资基金，是指主要投资于未上市创业企业普通股或者依法可转换为普通股的优先股、可转换债券等权益的股权投资基金。

第三十五条 鼓励和引导创业投资基金投资创业早期的小微企业。享受国家财政税收扶持政策的创业投资基金，其投资范围应当符合国家相关规定。

第三十六条 基金业协会在基金管理人登记、基金备案、投资情况报告要求和会员管理等环节，对创业投资基金采取区别于其他私募基金的差异化行业自律，并提供差异化会员服务。

第三十七条 中国证监会及其派出机构对创业投资基金在投资方向检查等环节，采取区别于其他私募基金的差异化监督管理；在账户开立、发行交易和投资退出等方面，为创业投资基金提供便利服务。

第九章 法律责任

第三十八条 私募基金管理人、私募基金托管人、私募基金销售机构及其他私募服务机构及其从业人员违反本办法第七条、第八条、第十一条、第十四条至第十七条、第二十四条至第二十六条规定的，以及有本办法第二十三条第一项至第七项和第九项所列行为之一的，责令改正，给予警告并处三万元以下罚款；对直接负责的主管人员和其他直接责任人员，给予警告并处三万元以下罚款；有本办法第二十三条第八项行为的，按照《证券法》和《期货交易管理条例》的有关规定处罚；构成犯罪的，依法移交司法机关追究刑事责任。

第三十九条 私募基金管理人、私募基金托管人、私募基金销售机构及其他私募服务机构及其从业人员违反法律法规和本办法规定，情节严重的，中国证监会可以依法对有关责任人员采取市场禁入措施。

第四十条 私募证券基金管理人及其从业人员违反《证券投资基金法》有关规定的，按照《证券投资基金法》有关规定处罚。

第十章 附 则

第四十一条 本办法自公布之日起施行。

附录 8 国务院关于进一步促进资本市场健康发展的若干意见

国发〔2014〕17 号

各省、自治区、直辖市人民政府，国务院各部委、各直属机构：

进一步促进资本市场健康发展，健全多层次资本市场体系，对于加快完善现代市场体系、拓宽企业和居民投融资渠道、优化资源配置、促进经济转型升级具有重要意义。20 多年来，我国资本市场快速发展，初步形成了涵盖股票、债券、期货的市场体系，为促进改革开放和经济社会发展作出了重要贡献。但总体上看，我国资本市场仍不成熟，一些体制机制性问题依然存在，新情况新问题不断出现。为深入贯彻党的十八大和十八届二中、三中全会精神，认真落实党中央和国务院的决策部署，实现资本市场健康发展，现提出以下意见。

一、总体要求

（一）指导思想。

高举中国特色社会主义伟大旗帜，以邓小平理论、“三个代表”重要思想、科学发展观为指导，贯彻党中央和国务院的决策部署，解放思想，改革创新，开拓进取。坚持市场化和法治化取向，维护公开、公平、公正的市场秩序，维护投资者特别是中小投资者合法权益。紧紧围绕促进实体经济发展，激发市场创新活力，拓展市场广度深度，扩大市场双向开放，促进直接融资与间接融资协调发展，提高直接融资比重，防范和分散金融风险。推动混合所有制经济发展，完善现代企业制度和公司治理结构，提高企业竞争能力，促进资本形成和股权流转，更好发挥资本市场优化资源配置的作用，促进创新创业、结构调整和经济社会持续健康发展。

（二）基本原则。

资本市场改革发展要从我国国情出发，积极借鉴国际经验，遵循以下原则：

一是处理好市场与政府的关系。尊重市场规律，依据市场规则、市场价格、市场竞争实现效益最大化和效率最优化，使市场在资源配置中起决定性作用。同时，更好发挥政府作用，履行好政府监管职能，实施科学监管、适度监管，创造公平竞争的市场环境，保护投资者合法权益，有效维护市场秩序。

二是处理好创新发展与防范风险的关系。以市场为导向、以提高市场服务能力和效率为目的，积极鼓励和引导资本市场创新。同时，强化风险防范，始终把风险监测、预警和处置贯穿于市场创新发展全过程，牢牢守住不发生系统性、区域性金融风险的底线。

三是处理好风险自担与强化投资者保护的关系。加强投资者教育，引导投资者培育理性投资理念，自担风险、自负盈亏，提高风险意识和自我保护能力。同时，健全投资者特别是中小投资者权益保护制度，保障投资者的知情权、参与权、求偿权和监督权，切实维护投资者合法权益。

四是处理好积极推进与稳步实施的关系。立足全局、着眼长远，坚定不移地积极推进改革。同时，加强市场顶层设计，增强改革措施的系统性、针对性、协同性，把握好改革的力度、节奏和市场承受程度，稳步实施各项政策措施，着力维护资本市场平稳发展。

（三）主要任务。

加快建设多渠道、广覆盖、严监管、高效率的股权市场，规范发展债券市场，拓展期货市场，着力优化市场体系结构、运行机制、基础设施和外部环境，实现发行交易方式多样、投融资工具丰富、风险管理功能完备、场内场外和公募私募协调发展。到 2020 年，基本形成结构合理、功能完善、规范透明、稳健高效、开放包容的多层次资本市场体系。

二、发展多层次股票市场

（四）积极稳妥推进股票发行注册制改革。建立和完善以信息披露为中心的股票发行制度。发行人是信息披露第一责任人，必须做到言行与信息披露的内容一致。发行人、中介机构对信息披露的真实性、准确性、完整性、充分性和及时性承担法律责任。投资者自行判断发行人的盈利能力和投资价值，自担投资风险。逐步探索符合我国实际的股票发行条件、上市标准和审核方式。证券监管部门依法监管发行和上市活动，严厉查处违法违规行为。

（五）加快多层次股权市场建设。强化证券交易所市场的主导地位，充分发挥证券交易所的自律监管职能。壮大主板、中小企业板市场，创新交易机制，丰富交易品种。加快创业板市场改革，健全适合创新型、成长型企业发展的制度安排。增加证券交易所市场内部层次。加快完善全国中小企业股份转让系统，建立小额、便捷、灵活、多元的投融资机制。在清理整顿的基础上，将区域性股权市场纳入多层次资本市场体系。完善集中统一的登记结算制度。

（六）提高上市公司质量。引导上市公司通过资本市场完善现代企业制度，建立健全市场化经营机制，规范经营决策。督促上市公司以投资者需求为导向，履行好信息披露义务，严格执行企业会计准则和财务报告制度，提高财务信息的可比性，增强信息披露的有效性。促进上市公司提高效益，增强持续回报投资者能力，为股东创造更多价值。规范上市公司控股股东、实际控制人行为，保障公司独立主体地位，维护各类股东的平等权利。鼓励上市公司建立市值管理制度。完善上市公司股权激励制度，允许上市公司按规定通过多种形式开展员工持股计划。

（七）鼓励市场化并购重组。充分发挥资本市场在企业并购重组过程中的主渠道作用，强化资本市场的产权定价和交易功能，拓宽并购融资渠道，丰富并购支付方式。尊重企业自主决策，鼓励各类资本公平参与并购，破除市场壁垒和行业分割，实现公司产权和控制权跨地区、跨所有制顺畅转让。

（八）完善退市制度。构建符合我国实际并有利于投资者保护的退市制度，建立健全市场化、多元化退市指标体系并严格执行。支持上市公司根据自身发展战略，在确保公众投资者权益的前提下以吸收合并、股东收购、转板等形式实施主动退市。对欺诈发行的上市公司实行强制退市。明确退市公司重新上市的标准和程序。逐步形成公司进退有序、市场转板顺畅的良性循环机制。

三、规范发展债券市场

（九）积极发展债券市场。完善公司债券公开发行制度。发展适合不同投资者群体的多样化债券品种。建立健全地方政府债券制度。丰富适合中小微企业的债券品种。统筹推进符合条件的资产证券化发展。支持和规范商业银行、证券经营机构、保险资产管理机构等合格机构依法开展债券承销业务。

（十）强化债券市场信用约束。规范发展债券市场信用评级服务。完善发行人信息披露制度，提高投资者风险识别能力，减少对外部评级的依赖。建立债券发行人信息共享机制。探索发展债券信用保险。完善债券增信机制，规范发展债券增信业务。强化发行人和投资者的责任约束，健全债券违约监测和处置机制，支持债券持有人会议，维护债权人整体利益，切实防范道德风险。

（十一）深化债券市场互联互通。在符合投资者适当性管理要求的前提下，完善债券品种在不同市场的交叉挂牌及自主转托管机制，促进债券跨市场顺畅流转。鼓励债券交易场所合理分工、发挥各自优势。促进债券登记结算机构信息共享、顺畅连接，加强互联互通。提高债券市场信息系统、市场监察系统的运行效率，逐步强化对债券登记结算体系的统一管理，防范系统性风险。

（十二）加强债券市场监管协调。充分发挥公司信用类债券部际协调机制作用，各相关部门按照法律法规赋予的职责，各司其职，加强对债券市场准入、信息披露和资信评级的监管，建立投资者保护制度，加大查处债券市场虚假陈述、内幕交易、价格操纵等各类违法违规行为的力度。

四、培育私募市场

（十三）建立健全私募发行制度。建立合格投资者标准体系，明确各类产品私募发行的投资者适当性要求和面向同一类投资者的私募发行信息披露要求，规范募集行为。对私募发行不设行政审批，允许各类发行主体在依法合规的基础上，向累计不超过法律规定特定数量的投资者发行股票、债券、基金等产品。积极发挥证券中介机构、资产管理机构和有关市场组织的作用，建立健全私募产品发行监管制度，切实强化事中事后监管。建立促进经营机构规范开展私募业务的风险控制和自律管理制度安排，以及各类私募产品的统一监测系统。

（十四）发展私募投资基金。按照功能监管、适度监管的原则，完善股权投资基金、私募资产管理计划、私募集合理财产品、集合资金信托计划等各类私募投资产品的监管标准。依法严厉打击以私募为名的各类非法集资活动。完善扶持创业投资发展的政策体系，鼓励和引导创业投资基金支持中小微企业。研究制定保险资金投资创业投资基金的相关政策。完善围绕创新链需要的科技金融服务体系，创新科技金融产品和服务，促进战略性新兴产业发展。

五、推进期货市场建设

（十五）发展商品期货市场。以提升产业服务能力和配合资源性产品价格形成机制改革为重点，继续推出大宗资源性产品期货品种，发展商品期权、商品指数、碳排放权等交易工具，充分发挥期货市场价格发现和风险管理功能，增强期货市场服务实体经济的能力。允许符合条件的机构投资者以对冲风险为目的使用期货衍生品工具，清理取消对企业运用风险管理工具的不必要限制。

（十六）建设金融期货市场。配合利率市场化和人民币汇率形成机制改革，适应资本市场风险管理需要，平稳有序发展金融衍生产品。逐步丰富股指期货、股指期权和股票期权品种。逐步发展国债期货，进一步健全反映市场供求关系的国债收益率曲线。

六、提高证券期货服务业竞争力

（十七）放宽业务准入。实施公开透明、进退有序的证券期货业务牌照管理制度，研究证券公司、基金管理公司、期货公司、证券投资咨询公司等交叉持牌，支持符合条件的其他金融机构在风险隔离基础上申请证券期货业务牌照。积极支持民营资本进入证券期货服务业。支持证券期货经营机构与其他金融机构在风险可控前提下以相互控股、参股的方式探索综合经营。

（十八）促进中介机构创新发展。推动证券经营机构实施差异化、专业化、特色化发展，促进形成若干具有国际竞争力、品牌影响力和系统重要性的现代投资银行。促进证券投资基金管理公司向现代资产管理机构转型，提高财富管理水平。推动期货经营机构并购重组，提高行业集中度。支持证券期货经营机构拓宽融资渠道，扩大业务范围。在风险可控前提下，优化客户交易结算资金存管模式。支持证券期货经营机构、各类资产管理机构围绕风险管理、资本中介、投资融资等业务自主创设产品。规范发展证券期货经营机构柜台业务。对会计师事务所、资产评估机构、评级增信机构、法律服务机构开展证券期货相关服务强化监督，提升证券期货服务机构执业质量和公信力，打造功能齐备、分工专业、服务优质的金融服务产业。

（十九）壮大专业机构投资者。支持全国社会保障基金积极参与资本市场投资，支持社会保险基金、企业年金、职业年金、商业保险资金、境外长期资金等机构投资者资金逐步扩大资本市场投资范围和规模。推动商业银行、保险公司等设立基金管理公司，大力发展证券投资基金。

（二十）引导证券期货互联网业务有序发展。建立健全证券期货互联网业务监管规则。支持证券期货服务业、各类资产管理机构利用网络信息技术创新产品、业务和交易方式。支持有条件的互联网企业参与资本市场，促进互联网金融健康发展，扩大资本市场服务的覆盖面。

七、扩大资本市场开放

（二十一）便利境内外主体跨境投融资。扩大合格境外机构投资者、合格境内机构投资者的范围，提高投资额度与上限。稳步开放境外个人直接投资境内资本市场，有序推进境内个人直接投资境外资本市场。建立健全个人跨境投融资权益保护制度。在符合外商投资产业政策的范围内，逐步放宽外资持有上市公司股份的限制，完善对收购兼并行为的国家安全审查和反垄断审查制度。

（二十二）逐步提高证券期货行业对外开放水平。适时扩大外资参股或控股的境内证券期货经营机构的经营范围。鼓励境内证券期货经营机构实施“走出去”战略，增强国际竞争力。推动境内外交易所市场的连接，研究推进境内外基金互认和证券交易所产品互认。稳步探索B股市场改革。

（二十三）加强跨境监管合作。完善跨境监管合作机制，加大跨境执法协查力度，形成适应开放型资本市场体系的跨境监管制度。深化与香港、澳门特别行政区和台湾地区的监管合作。加强与国际证券期货监管组织的合作，积极参与国际证券期货监管规则制定。

八、防范和化解金融风险

（二十四）完善系统性风险监测预警和评估处置机制。建立健全宏观审慎管理制度。逐步建立覆盖各类金融市场、机构、产品、工具和交易结算行为的风险监测监控平台。完善风险管理措施，及时化解重大风险隐患。加强涵盖资本市场、货币市场、信托理财等领域的跨行业、跨市场、跨境风险监管。

（二十五）健全市场稳定机制。资本市场稳定关系经济发展和社会稳定大局。各地区、各部门在出台政策时要充分考虑资本市场的敏感性，做好新闻宣传和舆论引导工作。完善市场交易机制，丰富市场风险管理工具。建立健全金融市场突发事件快速反应和处置机制。健全稳定市场预期机制。

（二十六）从严查处证券期货违法违规行为。加强违法违规线索监测，提升执法反应能力。严厉打击证券期货违法犯罪行为。完善证券期货行政执法与刑事司法的衔接机制，深化证券期货监管部门与公安司法机关的合作。进一步加强执法能力，丰富行政调查手段，大幅改进执法效率，提高违法违规成本，切实提升执法效果。

（二十七）推进证券期货监管转型。加强全国集中统一的证券期货监管体系建设，依法规范监管权力运行，减少审批、核准、备案事项，强化事中事后监管，提高监管能力和透明度。支持市场自律组织履行职能。加强社会信用体系建设，完善资本市场诚信监管制度，强化守信激励、失信惩戒机制。

九、营造资本市场良好发展环境

（二十八）健全法规制度。推进证券法修订和期货法制定工作。出台上市公司监管、私募基金监管等行政法规。建立健全结构合理、内容科学、层级适当的法律实施规范体系，整合清理现行规章、规范性文件，完善监管执法实体和程序规则。重点围绕调查与审理分离、日常监管与稽查处罚协同等关键环节，积极探索完善监管执法体制和机制。配合完善民事赔偿法律制度，健全操纵市场等犯罪认定标准。

（二十九）坚决保护投资者特别是中小投资者合法权益。健全投资者适当性制度，严格投资者适当性管理。完善公众公司中小投资者投票和表决机制，优化投资者回报机制，健全多元化纠纷解决和投资者损害赔偿救济机制。督促证券投资基金等机构投资者参加上市公司业绩发布会，代表公众投资者行使权利。

（三十）完善资本市场税收政策。按照宏观调控政策和税制改革的总体方向，统筹研究有利于进一步促进资本市场健康发展的税收政策。

（三十一）完善市场基础设施。加强登记、结算、托管等公共基础设施建设。实现资本市场监管数据信息共享。推进资本市场信息系统建设，提高防范网络攻击、应对重大灾难与技术故障的能力。

（三十二）加强协调配合。健全跨部门监管协作机制。加强中小投资者保护工作的协调合作。各地区、各部门要加强与证券期货监管部门的信息共享与协同配合。出台支持资本市场扩大对外开放的外汇、海关监管政策。地方人民政府要规范各类区域性交易场所，打击各种非法证券期货活动，做好区域内金融风险防范和处置工作。

（三十三）规范资本市场信息传播秩序。各地区、各部门要严格管理涉及资本市场的内幕信息，确保信息发布公开公正、准确透明。健全资本市场政策发布和解读机制，创新舆论回应与引导方式。综合运用法律、行政、行业自律等方式，完善资本市场信息传播管理制度。依法严肃查处造谣、传谣以及炒作不实信息误导投资者和影响社会稳定的机构、个人。

国务院

2014 年 5 月 8 日

附录9 国务院办公厅关于多措并举着力缓解企业融资成本高问题的指导意见

国办发〔2014〕39号

各省、自治区、直辖市人民政府，国务院各部委、各直属机构：

当前，我国经济形势总体向好，但仍存在不稳定因素，下行压力依然较大，结构调整处于爬坡时期，解决好企业特别是小微企业融资成本高问题，对于稳增长、促改革、调结构、惠民生具有重要意义。当前企业融资成本高的成因是多方面的，既有宏观经济因素又有微观运行问题，既有实体经济因素又有金融问题，既有长期因素又有短期因素，解决这一问题的根本出路在于全面深化改革，多措并举，标本兼治，重在治本。金融部门和金融机构要认真贯彻落实国务院第49次、第57次常务会议精神，采取综合措施，着力缓解企业融资成本高问题，促进金融与实体经济良性互动。经国务院同意，现提出以下意见：

一、保持货币信贷总量合理适度增长

继续实施稳健的货币政策，综合运用多种货币政策工具组合，维持流动性平稳适度，为缓解企业融资成本高创造良好的货币环境。优化基础货币的投向，适度加大支农、支小再贷款和再贴现的力度，着力调整结构，优化信贷投向，为棚户区改造、铁路、服务业、节能环保等重点领域和"三农"、小微企业等薄弱环节提供有力支持。切实执行有保有控的信贷政策，对产能过剩行业中有市场有效益的企业不搞"一刀切"。进一步研究改进宏观审慎管理指标。落实好"定向降准"措施，发挥好结构引导作用。（人民银行负责）

二、抑制金融机构筹资成本不合理上升

进一步完善金融机构公司治理，通过提高内部资金转移定价能力、优化资金配置等措施，遏制变相高息揽储等非理性竞争行为，规范市场定价竞争秩序。进一步丰富银行业融资渠道，加强银行同业批发性融资管理，提高银行融资多元化程度和资金来源稳定性。大力推进信贷资产证券化，盘活存量，加快资金周转速度。尽快出台规范发展互联网金融的相关指导意见和配套管理办法，促进公平竞争。进一步打击非法集资活动，维护良好的金融市场秩序。（人民银行、银监会、证监会、保监会、工业和信息化部等负责）

三、缩短企业融资链条

督促商业银行加强贷款管理，严密监测贷款资金流向，防止贷款被违规挪用，确保贷款资金直接流向实体经济。按照国务院部署，加强对影子银行、同业业务、理财业务等方面的管理，清理不必要的资金"通道"和"过桥"环节，各类理财产品的资金来源或运用原则上应当与实体经济直接对接。切实整治层层加价行为，减少监管套利，引导相关业务健康发展。（人民银行、银监会、证监会、保监会、外汇局负责）

四、清理整顿不合理金融服务收费

贯彻落实《商业银行服务价格管理办法》，督促商业银行坚决取消不合理收费项目，降低过高的收费标准。对于直接与贷款挂钩、没有实质服务内容的收费项目，一律予以取消；对于发放贷款收取利息应尽的工作职责，不得再分解设置收费项目。严禁"以贷转存"、"存贷挂钩"等变相提高利率、加重企业负担的行为。规范企业融资过程中担保、评估、登记、审计、保险等中介机构和有关部门的收费行为。在商业银行和相关中介机构对收费情况进行全面深入自查的基础上，在全国范围内加强专项检查。对于检查发现的违规问题，依法依规严格处罚。（银监会、发展改革委等负责）

五、提高贷款审批和发放效率

优化商业银行对小微企业贷款的管理，通过提前进行

续贷审批、设立循环贷款、实行年度审核制度等措施减少企业高息“过桥”融资。鼓励商业银行开展基于风险评估的续贷业务，对达到标准的企业直接进行滚动融资，优化审贷程序，缩短审贷时间。对小微企业贷款实施差别化监管。（银监会、人民银行负责）

六、完善商业银行考核评价指标体系

引导商业银行纠正单纯追逐利润、攀比扩大资产规模的经营理念，优化内部考核机制，适当降低存款、资产规模等总量指标的权重。发挥好有关部门和银行股东的评价考核作用，完善对商业银行经营管理的评价体系，合理设定利润等目标。设立银行业金融机构存款偏离度指标，研究将其纳入银行业金融机构绩效评价体系扣分项，约束银行业金融机构存款“冲时点”行为。（银监会、财政部负责）

七、加快发展中小金融机构

积极稳妥发展面向小微企业和“三农”的特色中小金融机构，促进市场竞争，增加金融供给。优化金融机构市场准入，在加强监管前提下，加快推动具备条件的民间资本依法发起设立中小型银行等金融机构。积极稳妥培育立足本地经营、特色鲜明的村镇银行，引导金融机构在基层地区合理布局分支机构和营业网点。（银监会负责）

八、大力发展直接融资

健全多层次资本市场体系，继续优化主板、中小企业板、创业板市场的制度安排。支持中小微企业依托全国中小企业股份转让系统开展融资。进一步促进私募股权和创投基金发展。逐步扩大各类长期资金投资资本市场的范围和规模，按照国家税收法律及有关规定，对各类长期投资资金予以税收优惠。继续扩大中小企业各类非金融企业债务融资工具及集合债、私募债发行规模。降低商业银行发行小微企业金融债和“三农”金融债的门槛，简化审批流程，扩大发行规模。（证监会、人民银行、发展改革委、财政部、银监会、保监会等负责）

九、积极发挥保险、担保的功能和作用

大力发展相关保险产品，支持小微企业、个体工商户、城乡居民等主体获得短期小额贷款。积极探索农业保险保单质押贷款，开展“保险+信贷”合作。促进更多保险资金直接投向实体经济。进一步完善小微企业融资担保政策，加大财政支持力度。大力发展政府支持的担保机构，引导其提高小微企业担保业务规模，合理确定担保费用。（保监会、财政部、银监会、工业和信息化部负责）

十、有序推进利率市场化改革

充分发挥金融机构利率定价自律机制作用，促进金融机构增强财务硬约束，提高自主定价能力。综合考虑我国宏微观经济金融形势，完善市场利率形成和传导机制。（人民银行负责）

从中长期看，解决企业融资成本高的问题要依靠推进改革和结构调整的治本之策，通过转变经济增长方式、形成财务硬约束和发展股本融资来降低杠杆率，消除结构性扭曲。围绕使市场在资源配置中起决定性作用和更好发挥政府作用，继续深化政府职能转变，推进国有企业改革和财税改革，简政放权，打破垄断，硬化融资主体财务约束，提高资金使用效率。落实对小微企业的税收支持政策，切实增强小微企业核心竞争力和盈利能力。引导小微企业健全自身财务制度，提高经营管理水平。各地区、各部门要高度重视降低企业融资成本的相关工作，加强组织领导和分工协作，注重工作实效。对各项任务落实要有布置、有督促、有检查。国务院办公厅对重点任务落实情况进行跟踪督查。各部门有关落实进展情况，由人民银行定期汇总后报国务院。

国务院办公厅

2014 年 8 月 5 日

附录 10 中国创业风险投资机构名录

公司名称	成立时间	网址	传真
安徽鼎信创业投资有限公司	2012-06-05	—	0551-65319112
安徽丰创生物技术产业创业投资有限公司	2013-04-02	—	0552-4093180
安徽高科创业投资有限公司	2010-01-28	www.ahgoco.com	0551-65319112
安徽国安创业投资有限公司	2010-09-15	—	0551-65732844
安徽国耀创业投资有限公司	2013-11-28	—	—
安徽国元创投有限责任公司	2010-06-13	www.ahgyct.com	0551-63699700
安徽红土创业投资有限公司	2010-08-10	www.szvc.com.cn	0551-65666025
安徽华文创业投资管理有限公司	2003-06-04	—	0551-63533281
安徽徽商产业投资基金管理有限公司	2008-03-18	www.hygcapital.com	0551-5844598
安徽汇智富创业投资有限公司	2013-03-26	—	0551-65383158
安徽火花科技创业投资有限公司	2013-06-25	—	—
安徽昆冈创业股权投资合伙企业（有限合伙）	2010-08-17	—	—
安徽联华盈创投资管理有限公司	2013-09-05	—	0551-65367330
安徽省安庆发展投资（集团）有限公司	2004-07-19	www.aqfztz.com	0556-5595212
安徽省创投资本基金有限公司	2010-07-27	—	0551-65773880
安徽省创业投资有限公司	2008-07-09	—	0551-63677130
安徽省高新创业投资有限责任公司	2009-12-23	—	—
安徽省科创投资管理咨询有限责任公司	2000-10-31	—	0551-66195765
安徽省科技产业投资有限公司	1999-07	www.ahkjtz.com.cn	0551-66195708
安徽西格玛壹号投资合伙企业（有限合伙）	2013-05-24	—	—
安徽兴皖创业投资有限公司	2010-08-20	—	0551-63677130
安庆百科担保资产监管有限公司	2006-03-03	—	0556-5323311
安庆发投创业投资有限公司	2012-09-28	—	—
蚌埠市科技创业投资有限公司	2008-06-26	—	0552-3186802
蚌埠市远大创新创业投资有限公司	2010-09-28	—	0551-63186678
蚌埠皖北金牛创业投资有限公司	2011-05-17	—	0552-4129773
蚌埠中城创业投资有限公司	2009-03-16	—	0552-3183880

公司名称	成立时间	网址	传真
滁州浚源创业投资中心（有限合伙）	2011-06	jycapital.cn	010-82661938
合肥高特佳创业投资有限责任公司	2010-04-19	www.szgig.com	0551-65310817
合肥高新科技创业投资有限公司	2012-10-19	gxkt.hfgxjt.com	0551-65326509
合肥广电投资有限责任公司	2003-08-06	www.hfbtv.com	0551-63509205
合肥赛富合元创业投资中心（有限合伙）	2011-01-13	—	—
合肥世纪创新投资有限公司	2002-09-11	—	0551-66195765
合肥市创新科技风险投资有限公司	2000-08-28	www.hfgk.com	0551-62675471
合肥市高科技风险投资有限公司	2000-04-18	—	—
合肥同安创业投资基金行	2010-09	—	0551-63677135
合肥智鼎创业投资管理有限公司	2009-11-10	www.qyzyw.com	0551-64651822
华晟创业投资管理有限公司	2012-05-14	—	0551-63533681
淮南市创业风险投资有限公司	2011-11-26	—	0554-6679199
汇智创业投资有限公司	2009-04-29	—	0551-65321476
六安高科创业投资有限公司	2011-10-20	—	0564-3323933
陕西西科天使投资管理有限公司	2014-10-31	—	—
铜陵天源股权投资集团有限公司	2007-02-01	—	0562-2885077
芜湖达成创业投资中心（有限合伙）	2010-04-28	—	—
芜湖富海浩研创业投资基金	2012-12-27	—	0551-65844598
芜湖奇瑞科技有限公司	2001-11-21	www.mychery.com	0553-5922267
芜湖瑞建汽车产业创业投资有限公司	2010-07-01	—	0553-3812768
芜湖瑞业股权投资基金（有限合伙）	2009-12-21	—	021-64151936
芜湖市科技创业投资有限公司	2004-05-28	www.whkctz.com	0553-5846386
芜湖市世纪江东创业投资中心（有限合伙）	2009-08-18	www.jd-capital.cn	0553-5772022
芜湖远大创业投资有限公司	2009-04-23	—	0553-5992133
襄阳市国泰华稳盈产业投资基金中心（有限合伙）	2014-09-01	—	—
宣城富国银洋投资中心（有限合伙）	2014-12-02	—	—
浙江华睿蓝石创业投资有限公司	2014-09-02	—	—
IBM 雷曼中国投资基金管理公司	2006-10-30	—	—
IDG 资本	1992-08-01	www.idgvc.com	010-65260624
北京博瑞盛德创业投资有限公司	2009-11-09	—	—
北京长电创新投资管理有限公司	2008-02-27	—	—
北京晨光创业投资有限公司	2000-12-25	www.chgvc.com	010-69709488
北京晨光宏盛中小企业创业投资有限公司	2009-03-11	www.bjcghs.com	010-89710922
北京厚持投资管理有限公司	2011-12-12	www.holchcapital.com	—
北京厚德科创科技孵化器有限公司	2012-07-04	www.hdcxg.com	010-62607776
北京厚生投资管理中心（有限合伙）	2010-03-01	—	010-65676011
北京华创盛景投资管理有限公司	2010-01-26	—	—
北京华汇通创业投资管理有限公司	2007-07-01	www.bjhhtvc.com	010-82158765

公司名称	成立时间	网址	传真
北京华商盈通投资有限公司	2008-03-07	—	—
北京汇金立方投资管理中心（有限合伙）	2008-05-01	—	—
北京惠通九鼎投资管理有限公司	—	—	—
北京加华伟业资本管理有限公司	2006-07-01	www.scharvestcap.com	010-58252171
北京金沙江创业投资管理有限公司	2004-10-01	www.gsrventures.com	010-3317950
北京联想之星创业投资有限公司	—	www.legendstar.com.cn	010-62560980
北京普凯瑞盛股权投资管理中心（有限合伙）	2011-09-06	—	—
北京普思投资有限公司	2009-12-04	www.pusicapital.com	010-65818551
北京青云创业投资管理有限公司	2001-07-13	www.cefund.com	010-56815712
北京盛达瑞丰投资管理有限公司	2007-07-24	—	—
北京盛世景投资管理有限公司	2006-09-11	www.sensegain.com	010-88580834
北京顺为创业投资有限公司	2011-05-17	www.shunwei.com	010-59851443
北京沃衍资本管理中心（有限合伙）	2011-03-01	www.richlandcap.com	010-85187550
北京新安财富资本投资有限公司	2000-08	www.acvc.com.cn	010-63972281
北京正润创业投资有限责任公司	2007-11-19	www.prope.com.cn	010-88568807
北京中关村青年科技创业投资有限公司	2000-01	www.bjcvc.com.cn	010-68118842
北京中瀚海联资产管理有限公司	—	—	—
北京中经瑞益投资管理有限公司	2000-08-01	www.real-capital.cn	—
贝塔斯曼亚洲投资基金	2008-01-01	www.baifund.com	—
创新工场	2009-09-01	www.chuangxin.com	—
大河资本管理有限公司	2005-01-01	—	—
德同（北京）投资管理有限公司	2009-11-01	—	—
鼎晖创业投资	2006-01-01	www.cdhfund.com	010-65815654
泛海投资股份有限公司	1995-07-01	www.oceanwidecapital.com	010-85114112
福建劲达创业投资有限公司	—	www.jindavc.com	010-68364555
富达国际风险投资（香港）有限公司	1994-09-01	www.fidelitygrowthpartners.cn	010-25089519
高捷资本	2006-01-01	ecc-capital.com	010-65678439
国投创新投资管理（北京）有限公司	2009-01-01	www.sdicfund.com	010-88006339
红土嘉智投资管理顾问（北京）有限公司	2009-04-02	—	—
厚朴投资管理公司	2007-11-01	—	010-51819556
华控汇金投资管理有限公司	2003-09-01	www.thcapital.com.cn	010-59761104
建信（北京）投资基金管理有限公司	2011-03-24	www.ccbtpe.comindex.aspx	010-67596590
金陵华软投资集团	2010-09-21	www.chinakinglink.com	010-65535484
金石投资有限公司	2007-10-01	www.goldstone-investment.com	010-60837823
经纬创投中国基金	2008-01-28	www.matrixpartners.com.cn	010-64999990
君联资本	2001-04-01	www.legendcapital.com.cn	010-62509024
开信创业投资管理有限公司	2008-01-01	www.kaixininvestment.com	010-58023920
昆吾九鼎投资管理有限公司	2007-07-27	www.jdcapital.com	010-63221112
蓝山中国资本	2006-03-01	—	010-65308763

公司名称	成立时间	网址	传真
联想控股有限公司	1984-04-01	www.legendholdings.com.cn	010-62560980
启迪创业投资管理（北京）有限公司	2001-03-30	www.tsinghua-vc.com	010-62705133
天津裕丰股权投资管理有限公司	2009-09-01	www.avicfund.com	010-65675125
新奥投资基金管理（北京）有限公司	2011-07-15	—	—
新奥资本管理有限公司	2006-10-01	www.capital.enn.cn	010-58256930
银河创新资本管理有限公司	2009-10-21	yhcxzb.chinastock.com.cn	010-83574014
英诺天使基金	2013-01-01	www.innoangel.com	—
永威投资有限公司	1995-10-01	www.asiavest.com	010-65687382
招商致远资本投资有限公司	2009-08-28	—	—
中发君盛（北京）投资管理有限公司	2009-12-12	—	—
中国创业投资有限公司	—	www.chinavest.com	010-63293886
中国高新投资集团公司	1989-04-19	www.gaoxin-china.com.cn	010-63288530
中金创新（北京）国际投资管理顾问有限公司	—	—	—
重庆麒厚西海股权投资管理有限公司	1998-04-01	www.changancap.com	023-84002640
福建北辰星投资管理有限公司	2014-12-12	www.poritarcap.com	—
福建红桥创业投资管理有限公司	2007-08-29	hqcapital.com.cn	0592-2278628
福建华兴创业投资有限公司	2000-12-26	www.fjhxvc.com	0591-87858275
福建省乐助投资有限公司	2011-04-25	—	—
福建迅成创业投资有限公司	2007-07-31	www.chancevc.com	0591-22855397
福州开发区富屯新城投资管理有限公司	2014-07-01	www.fzftxc.com	—
南安市红桥创业投资有限公司	2010-08-13	www.hqcapital.com.cn	0595-86392990
泉州市红桥创业投资有限公司	2010-02-22	www.hqcapital.com.cn	0595-28292990
厦门创翼创业投资有限公司	2008-06-20	—	0592-2360798
厦门创翼德晖股权投资合伙企业（有限合伙）	2011-02-11	www.divinecapital.com.cn	0592-2915616
厦门高新技术风险投资有限公司	1998-12-28	—	0592-2102861
厦门高新科创天使创业投资有限公司	2013-03-11	www.xmibi.com	0592-3923999
厦门国海坚果投资管理有限公司	2013-03-28	www.capitalnuts.com	0592-2577217
厦门红土创业投资有限公司	2010-06-08	—	0592-5778290
厦门华登创业投资有限公司	2008-08-13	www.xmerqing.com	0592-2219232
厦门京道联萃创业投资管理有限公司	2012-02-24	—	0592-8269533
厦门七匹狼创业投资有限公司	2009-07-03	www.sw-gh.complatform-3.html	0592-5377752
厦门七匹狼节能环保产业创业投资管理有限公司	2012-12-28	—	0592-5377752
厦门松涛风险投资股份有限公司	2000-04-28	www.songtao.com.cn	0592-6093926
厦门永红创业投资有限公司	2006-12-19	—	0592-5058092
甘肃省科技发展投资有限责任公司	1993-04-22	—	0931-8730629
甘肃省科技风险投资有限公司	2001-08	—	0931-8537887
甘肃现代农业产业创业投资基金有限公司	2012-12-25	—	0931-4890588
兰州高科创业投资担保有限公司	2003	—	0931-8711879
兰州天键投资咨询服务有限公司	2006	—	—

公司名称	成立时间	网址	传真
深圳市分享投资合伙企业（有限合伙）	2007-08-27	—	0755-86331909
广东创华投资有限公司	2010-12-22	—	020-87112133
广东启程青年创业投资合伙企业	2013-11-15	www.tsinghua-vc.com	020-31001286
广东融易创业投资有限公司	2011-02-14	www.ry168.cn	0769-23075503
广东粤科钜华创业投资有限公司	2010-10-11	—	0757-26331688
广东粤科润华创业投资有限公司	2012-10-18	—	0750-3882739
广东中大粤科投资有限公司	2009-10-10	—	020-84110011
国信弘盛创业投资有限公司	2008-08-08	hs.guosen.com.cn	0755-25472415
君盛投资管理有限公司	2003-01-13	www.junsancapital.com	0755-82571198
鲁证创业投资有限公司	2010-05-21	—	0755-82798613
融石创业投资管理（深圳）有限公司	2008-02-04	www.rockstead.com	0755-82991769
深圳创富成长创业投资有限公司	2009-05-20	—	0755-26994531
深圳大石资本管理有限公司	2013-09-27	www.gemvc.com	023-88653504
深圳东方赛富投资有限公司	2010-05-06	www.esaif-capital.com	0755-88315925
深圳国成世纪创业投资有限公司	2003-04-16	www.ciamvc.com	0755-82967097
深圳力合创业投资有限公司	1999-08-31	www.leaguer.com.cn	0755-26551372
深圳力合清源创业投资管理有限公司	2010-04-28	www.leaguercapital.com	0755-86363823
深圳清华力合创业投资有限公司	1999-08-31	www.leaguer.com.cn	0755-26551372
深圳市保中太创业投资有限公司	2007-04-06	—	0755-83264501
深圳市博叡创业投资有限公司	2010-03-18	www.boricapital.com	0755-83562711
深圳市创东方投资有限公司	2007-08-21	www.cdfcn.com	0755-88316231
深圳市创新投资集团有限公司	1999-08-26	www.szvc.com.cn	0755-8291880
深圳市达晨财智创业投资管理有限公司	2008-12-15	—	0755-83515115
深圳市达晨创业投资有限公司	2000-04	www.fortunevc.com	0755-83515115
深圳市大正元股权投资基金管理有限公司	2010-04-16	www.tdrcap.com	0755-33371191
深圳市东方富海投资管理有限公司	2006-10-10	www.ofcapital.com	0755-83475799
深圳市孚威创业投资有限公司	2007-10-15	—	0755-25771505
深圳市富坤创业投资有限公司	2008-04-11	www.rlequities.com	0755-88311638-8019
深圳市高特佳投资集团有限责任公司	2001-03-02	www.szgig.com	0755-86332710
深圳市高新投创业投资有限公司	1994-12-29	www.szhti.com.cn	0755-82852555
深圳市国成科技投资有限公司	1997-09-08	www.szgcvc.com	0755-83516944
深圳市红岭创投股权投资基金管理有限公司	2012-03-22	—	0755-82038849
深圳市佳利泰创业投资有限公司	2009-07-20	www.jialitai.com	0755-25312056
深圳市君丰创业投资基金管理有限公司	2009-09-30	www.jfamc.com	0755-82823397
深圳市年利达创业投资有限公司	2007-09-20	—	0755-23993622
深圳市鹏德创业投资有限公司	2010-07-19	www.pengdecapital.com	—
深圳市山海创业投资管理有限公司	2005-08-29	www.sunhighvc.com	0755-26077778
深圳市松禾资本管理有限公司	2007-04-26	www.pinevc.com.cn	0755-83290622
深圳市天图创业投资有限公司	2002-04-11	www.tiantu.com.cn	0755-36909834

公司名称	成立时间	网址	传真
深圳市同创伟业创业投资有限公司	2000-06-26	www.cowincapital.com.cn	0755-82879025
深圳市同威创业投资有限公司	2008-03-02	www.copowerpe.com	0755-26935161
深圳市倚锋创业投资有限公司	2007-08-22	www.efung.cc	0755-88308601
深圳市悦享资本管理有限公司	2010-08-06	www.szyxzbgl.com	0755-23819923
深圳市中金石创业投资有限公司	2009-09-18	—	0755-82876373
银河粤科（广东）产业投资基金（有限合伙）	2013-12-16	—	020-87687938
盈富泰克创业投资有限公司	2000-04-20	www.infovc.com	0755-82966479
招商局科技集团有限公司	1995-12-20	www.cmtech.net	0755-26888628
肇庆市粤科金瑞投资管理有限公司	2010-08-19	—	0758-2321528
肇庆市粤科金叶创业投资有限公司	2010-10-18	—	0758-2321528
珠海高新技术创业服务中心	2004-08-25	www.zhhbi.com	0756-3629998
珠海红杉资本股权投资中心（有限合伙）	2010-03-26	—	0756-3629900
珠海金控高新产业投资中心（有限合伙）	2014-04-23	—	—
珠海金控高新创业投资有限公司	2013-11-19	—	0756-2992888
珠海领先互联高新技术产业投资中心（有限合伙）	2014-12-02	—	0756-3333838
珠海招商银科股权投资中心（有限合伙）	2012-01-21	—	0755-26677220
广西海东科技创业投资有限公司	2010-04-14	—	022-59852168
广西中小企业创业投资有限公司	2009-08-12	gxfi.net	0771-5586630
柳州开元创业投资有限公司	2011-12-30	—	0771-5715238
鼎信博成创业投资有限公司	2010-08-26	—	0851-5806514
贵阳创新天使投资基金有限公司	2014-03-01	—	0851-85806514
贵阳高科创业投资有限责任公司	2009-09-03	www.guiyanggk.com	0851-88255917
贵阳高新创业投资有限公司	2011-04-27	—	0851-82203995
贵阳花溪技创业投资有限公司	2011-07-19	—	0851-3863159
贵阳市创业投资有限公司	2010-12-28	www.gyiig.com	0851-84757198
贵阳市星火现代服务业创业投资有限公司	2014-05-13	—	—
贵州鼎信博成投资管理有限公司	2009-09-16	www.gztvc.net	0851-5806514
贵州鼎信卓越创业投资有限公司	2013-12-06	—	—
贵州国喜投资有限公司	2011-09-06	—	0851-82264888
贵州经开创业投资管理有限公司	2012-06-01	www.gzjkct.com	0851-3890646-804
贵州经开创业投资有限公司	2012-08-21	—	0851-3890646-804
贵州省科技风险投资有限公司	1998-12	www.gztvc.net	0851-5806514
贵州中鼎投资管理有限公司	2004-09-04	www.gzzd.cn	0851-86824648
六盘水市科技创业投资有限公司	2011-11-04	—	—
铜仁梵净山科技创业投资有限公司	—	—	—
遵义科技创业投资有限公司	2010-11-05	—	0851-28922337
海口市创新产业投资有限公司	2008-03-18	www.haikouvc.com	0898-66738612
海南恒星创业投资管理有限公司	2007-09-24	—	0898-66836117
海南华棋科技创业投资管理有限公司	2009-09-09	—	0898-68581383

公司名称	成立时间	网址	传真
海南宣辰科技创业投资管理有限公司	2008-09-25	—	0898-66836105
保定高新技术创业服务中心	1994-11-01	—	0312-3326988
保定市创元科技风险投资有限公司	2008-12-22	—	0312-5902519
保定市科锐特创业投资有限公司	2006-02-27	www.krtvc.com	0312-3371336
邯郸高新创业投资有限公司	2009-12-17	—	0310-5100033
河北金冀达创业投资有限公司	2009-08-31	—	0311-85961613
河北科技投资集团有限公司	2001-02-15	www.hebvc.com	0311-85961613
河北省环海股权投资基金股份有限公司	2011-04-06	—	—
河北天鑫创业投资有限公司	2011-07-04	—	—
河北兴石创业投资有限公司	2009-12-21	—	—
河北燕郊燕胜创业投资有限公司	2011-05-27	—	0316-3357676
廊坊市高科创新创业投资有限公司	2006-10-19	—	0316-2235613
秦皇岛燕大产业集团有限公司	1996-12-23	www.ysusp.com.cn	0335-8500962
石家庄高新区科发投资有限公司	2010-03-23	—	0311-66699013
石家庄高新区蓝狐投资有限公司	2009-06-26	sjzchenhuiasd.163.com	0311-66685159
石家庄科技创业投资有限公司	2002-09-19	—	0311-66685160
唐山高新创业投资有限公司	2007-07-02	—	0315-3858385
唐山科技发展投资管理有限责任公司	2009-04-22	—	—
安阳惠通高创新材料创业投资基金合伙企业（有限合伙）	2012-07-25	—	0371-86615676
河南宝祥民营科技创业投资有限公司	2012-12-05	—	0371-55011760
河南秉鸿生物高新技术创业投资有限公司	2012-11-05	www.beyondfund.com	010-82483542
河南创业投资股份有限公司	2002-08	www.hnvc.cn	0371-67897012
河南德瑞恒通高端装备创业投资基金有限公司	2013-05-15	—	0371-55698755
河南华祺节能环保创业投资有限公司	2013-06-20	www.haiyuqi.com	0371-86684801
河南华夏海纳创业投资集团有限公司	2009-06-18	www.huaxiahn.com	0371-86068196
河南西亚斯咨询服务有限公司	2013	—	—
河南中以科技投资中心（有限合伙）	2014-04-15	www.infinity-equity.com	—
哈尔滨创新投资有限公司	2002-06-28	—	0451-84686552
哈尔滨创业投资集团有限公司	2009-02-26	www.hrbvc.com.cn	0451-84858002
哈尔滨哈以孵化器管理有限公司	2011-04-07	www.harbin-incubator.com	—
哈尔滨市科技风险投资中心	1998-05	—	0451-84686552
哈尔滨市天琪股权投资基金管理企业（有限合伙）	2014	tqtz.com.cn	0451-82287805
哈尔滨以哈投资管理有限公司	2012-01-06	—	—
黑龙江红土科力创业投资有限公司	2011-07-11	—	0451-55553193
黑龙江省科力高科技产业投资有限公司	2003-06-25	www.hljkl.com	0451-51920801
楚商领先（武汉）创业投资基金管理有限公司	2013-06-25	www.chushang-invest.cc	027-87750827
湖北高富信创业投资有限公司	2013-02-18	—	—

公司名称	成立时间	网址	传真
湖北高和创业投资管理有限公司	2009-12-08	—	027-86659549
湖北红土创业投资有限公司	2009-12	www.szvc.com.cn	027-87339809
湖北九派创业投资有限公司	2010-09-09	www.9pvc.com	027-59339178
湖北科创天使投资有限公司	2014-07-11	—	027-87440849
湖北量科高投创业投资有限公司	2010-11-26	—	027-87440551
湖北善盈投资有限公司	2014-09-02	www.sying.cc	027-85699731
湖北省高新技术产业投资有限公司	2005-10-25	www.cnhbgt.com	027-87440849
湖北盛世高金创业投资有限公司	2011-03-24	—	027-87440849
湖北新能源投资管理有限公司	2010-08-18	—	027-65796340
华人创新集团有限公司	2000-03-06	www.hrjt.net.cn	027-87138855
科华银赛创业投资有限公司	2009-07-30	www.khysct.com	027-59817318
武汉承胜创业投资有限公司	2012-06-26	—	027-82920839
武汉东湖长瑞投资管理有限公司	2012-12-27	www.donghu-pe.comindex.html	—
武汉公牛创业投资有限公司	2011-11-12	—	—
武汉固德银赛创业投资管理有限公司	2009-04-21	www.gdysct.com	027-59817377
武汉硅谷天堂阳光创业投资有限公司	2009-03-18	—	027-84842228
武汉华工创业投资有限责任公司	2000-09-11	www.hustvc.com.cn	027-81338733
武汉华工科技企业孵化器有限责任公司	2003-04-09	www.whbi.com.cn	027-87522800
武汉华工科技投资管理有限公司	2011-02-28	—	027-87180149
武汉火炬科技投资有限公司	2000-12-01	—	027-85766665
武汉君慧投资管理有限公司	2011-06-10	www.legendcapital.com.cn	027-87159916
武汉科技创新朝阳创业投资有限公司	2010-12-22	—	027-81706081
武汉科技创新投资有限公司	2005-03-31	—	027-81706081
武汉科技投资有限公司	1992-05-06	—	027-65692512
武汉启迪东湖创业投资有限公司	2013-05-20	—	—
武汉融和创新投资有限公司	2013-01-28	—	027-87575508
武汉市洪山科技创业种子资金管理有限公司	2002-10-16	—	027-87526590
武汉市科创天使投资基金管理有限公司	2013-06-06	—	—
武汉天一医药科技投资有限公司	2002-06-11	—	027-87291037
武汉一道创业投资有限公司	2009-03-16	—	027-87056266
襄阳博润股权投资基金中心	2012-07-08	—	—
襄阳创新资本创业投资有限公司	2008-09-18	—	—
襄阳创新资本管理有限公司	2008-10-23	—	—
襄阳华鸿嘉和投资管理有限公司	2011-10-09	—	—
襄阳融汇通投资有限公司	2011-01	xyrht.kenyalong.net	0710-3344973
襄阳中广股权投资有限公司	2012-04-15	—	—
长沙高新技术创业投资管理有限公司	2000-09-09	www.cshvc.com	0731-88286898
长沙市科技风险投资管理有限公司	2000-05-18	www.csvcc.cn	0731-88286892
长沙通和投资管理咨询有限公司	2010-01-21	—	0731-89852729

公司名称	成立时间	网址	传真
长沙先导创业投资有限公司	2009-05-15	www.cpih.cn	0731-88768823
常德沅澧产业投资控股有限公司	2014-01-22	—	0736-7133995
常德中科芙蓉创业投资有限责任公司	2011-01-12	—	0736-7703079
湖南财富同超创业投资管理股份有限公司	2010-07-19	—	0731-82567348
湖南财富同超创业投资有限公司	2010-10-10	—	0731-82567348
湖南财信创业投资有限责任公司	2001-01-17	www.hncxvc.com	0731-5196822
湖南达晨财鑫创业投资有限公司	2011-03-28	—	0736-7133995
湖南高科发创智能制造装备创业投资有限公司	2013-02-05	—	0731-28665293
湖南高新创业投资管理有限公司	2011-03-10	—	0731-85165395
湖南海捷投资有限公司	2010-04-09	www.hiyield.cn	0731-88780198
湖南海捷先进装备创业投资有限公司	2013-05-08	www.hiyield.cn	0731-88780198
湖南湖大海捷津杉创业投资有限公司	2011-04-29	www.hiyield.cn	0731-88780100
湖南华菱津杉投资管理有限公司	2010-03-25	—	—
湖南摩根信通投资有限公司	2014-09-25	www.mgxtinvest.com	0731-84166383
湖南瑞驰丰和创业投资管理有限公司	2008-02-28	www.hnrichfund.com	0731-82768320
湖南三羊中小企业融资担保有限公司	2009-10-16	—	0731-88920778
湖南省广信创业投资基金有限公司	2012-06-05	—	0731-88737722
湖南湘投高科技创业投资有限公司	2000-02-23	www.hnhvc.com	0731-85188649
湖南新能源创业投资基金企业（有限合伙）	2010-05-14	—	0731-82768320
湖南兆富投资控股（集团）有限公司	2009-08-24	www.zaffer.cn	0731-88737722
湖南浙商嘉立创业投资有限公司	2010-08-06	—	0731-85696977
湖南臻泰股权投资管理合伙企业（有限合伙）	2012-12-27	—	—
邵阳市思考投资有限公司	2014-09-16	—	0739-5026767
湘潭火炬创业投资有限公司	2012-04-20	—	0731-55567188
永州潇商投资中心	2014-03-17	—	0746-8666671
株洲南车时代高新投资担保有限责任公司	2003-05-12	www.timesinvest.cn	0731-22877368
株洲市世富投资有限公司	2009-12-14	www.zzsafer.com	0731-22727013
株洲兆富成长企业创业投资有限公司	2010-10-13	—	0731-88737722
长春经开科技风险投资有限公司	2000-11-20	www.jlsme.com	0431-86711708
长春市科技发展中心	1997-06-06	www.ccfengxian.com	0431-81284582
吉林省高新技术创业投资有限公司	2009-12-10	—	0431-89684088
苏州深蓝创业投资有限公司	2007-09-04	—	0512-69211368
滨海沿海创业投资有限公司	2010-03	—	—
博辰创业投资管理（苏州）有限公司	2007-11-26	—	0512-66969661
长汉共同合作基金	2007-09-18	—	025-66009900
长三角创业投资企业	2008-01-07	—	021-53835998
常创（常州）创业投资合伙企业（有限合伙）	2013-09-03	—	0519-85220338
常熟博瀚创业投资有限公司	2009-11-23	—	0512-52351556
常熟高捷投资管理有限公司	2011-01-15	www.ecc-capital.com	010-65678515

公司名称	成立时间	网址	传真
常熟金茂创业投资管理有限公司	2010-11	www.jolmo.com	025-84730375
常熟经济开发区高新技术创业投资有限公司	2009-06	—	0512-52292926
常熟科华创业投资中心（有限合伙）	2011	www.nypcapital.com	—
常熟市国发创业投资有限公司	2010-11-25	—	0512-52876487
常州常荣创业投资有限公司	2009-09-08	—	0519-89816672
常州常以创业投资管理有限公司	2009-12-31	—	0519-89629972
常州常以创业投资中心（有限合伙）	2010-01-12	—	0519-89629972
常州德丰杰清洁技术创业投资中心（有限合伙）	2009-12	www.dfjcompass.com	0519-89182227
常州德丰杰投资管理有限公司	2009-12	www.dfjcompass.com	0519-89182227
常州德丰杰正道创业投资中心（有限合伙）	2012-03	www.dfjcompass.com	0519-89182227
常州德丰杰正道投资管理有限公司	2012-02-20	www.dfjcompass.com	0519-89182227
常州蜂鸟创业投资合伙企业（有限合伙）	2012-06-21	—	0519-81231818
常州高睿创业投资管理有限公司	2007-09-24	—	0519-85150557
常州高投创业投资有限公司	2008-07-22	—	0519-85150557
常州高新创业投资有限公司	2012-01-18	www.czhti.com.cn	0519-81235008
常州高新技术风险投资有限公司	2000-12-22	www.cz-vc.com	0519-85150557
常州和泰股权投资有限公司	2001-10-29	—	0519-85176186
常州和裕创业投资有限公司	2011-04	—	0519-85176186
常州华软投资管理有限公司	2010-07-07	—	010-65505560
常州金陵华软创业投资合伙企业（有限合伙）	2010-08-05	—	—
常州金码创业投资管理合伙企业（有限合伙）	2011-11-30	www.jolmo.net	025-84730211
常州金茂经信创业投资管理企业（有限合伙）	2013-12-31	www.jolmo.net	025-84730211
常州金茂新兴产业创业投资合伙企业（有限合伙）	2011-09	www.jolmo.net	025-84730211
常州力合创业投资有限公司	2008-10-10	www.leaguer.com.cn	0519-86220118
常州力合投资管理有限公司	2008-08	www.leaguercapital.com	0519-86220118
常州牡丹江南创业投资有限责任公司	2010-03-15	—	0519-68866908
常州青年创业投资中心（有限合伙）	2012-12-20	—	0519-85220338
常州青企联合创业投资合伙企业（有限合伙）	2013-01-05	—	0519-85220338
常州睿泰创业投资中心（有限合伙）	2012	—	—
常州赛富高新创业投资中心（有限合伙）	2009-12	www.sbaif.com	0519-89606122
常州市久益股权投资中心（有限合伙）	2010-07-30	www.nd-invest.cn	0519-89816672
常州市巨凝创业投资有限公司	2008-04	—	—
常州市民生投资中心（有限合伙）	2007-11-15	—	0519-85164197
常州武进红土创业投资有限公司	2008-08-19	www.szvc.com.cn	0519-86318682
常州武岳峰创业投资管理有限公司	2011-03-03	www.summitviewcapital.com	0519-86620218
常州武岳峰创业投资合伙企业（有限合伙）	2011-03-23	www.summitviewcapital.com	0519-86220218
常州信辉创业投资有限公司	2007-05-11	—	0519-88129050
常州钟楼红土创业投资有限公司	2013-08-23	www.szvc.com.cn	0519-86318682
丹阳市高新技术创业投资有限公司	2010-12-31	—	0511-86922610

公司名称	成立时间	网址	传真
高投名力成长创业投资有限公司	2007-04-29	www.mcgf.com.cn	021-62889166
高瞻（无锡）创业投资有限公司	2011-04	www.tallwoodvc.com	0510-81814997
高瞻（无锡）企业管理有限公司	2011-05	www.tallwoodvc.com	0510-81814997
光控（海门）创业投资有限公司	2012-11-30	—	—
国润创业投资（苏州）管理有限公司	2008-05	www.guorun.com	0512-62998663
海安峰融创业投资有限公司	2014-12-18	—	—
海安峰融投资管理有限公司	2014-10-15	—	—
海安知己基石创业投资有限公司	2014-09-05	—	—
海得汇金创业投资江阴有限公司	2011-03-03	www.head-capital.cn	0510-81602235
海门东翔创业投资有限公司	2012-12-19	—	—
海门时代伯乐股权投资合伙企业（有限合伙）	2014-09-26	—	—
海门市东洲创业投资有限公司	2011-12-28	—	0513-82212931
红塔创新（昆山）创业投资有限公司	2008-07-09	—	010-58555666
洪泽英飞尼迪创业投资中心（有限合伙）	2011-05	—	0517-83361705
华软创业投资宜兴合伙企业（有限合伙）	2010-08-28	www.csinvestmentgroup.com	—
华穗食品创业投资企业	2009-04-13	—	021-62898817
华映光辉投资管理（苏州）有限公司	2010	www.meridiancapital.com.cn	0512-68327950
淮安平衡股权投资基金中心（有限合伙）	2013-10-25	—	025-51889757
建湖县建科创业投资有限公司	2010-12	4408499.czvv.com	0515-86153863
江苏艾利克斯投资有限公司	2006-01-19	—	0511-86900801
江苏滨海高石创业投资有限公司	2011-08	—	—
江苏博硕高新技术产业投资发展有限公司	2011-09-18	—	0512-88880863
江苏昌盛阜创业投资有限公司	2008-08-22	—	0512-69560268
江苏诚行投资管理有限公司	2011 03 16		
江苏澄辉创业投资有限公司	2008-12-30	—	0512-66183052
江苏大丰众成科技创业投资有限公司	2010-04	—	0515-83855826
江苏大行临港产业投资有限公司	2012-12-26	—	0511-88224055
江苏鼎鸿创业投资有限公司	2008-03	—	0513-85159991
江苏鼎信咨询有限公司	1998-04-27	www.do-think.com	025-86586939
江苏东恒空港高新技术产业园有限公司	2011-08-26	—	025-52327675
江苏多良创业投资有限公司	2008-03-31	—	0519-83872660
江苏高成创业投资有限公司	2010-08-09	—	0512-56793680
江苏高达创业投资有限公司	1998-08-03	www.goodvc.cn	025-83153546
江苏高鼎科技创业投资有限公司	2007-08-31	www.js-vc.com	025-51889757
江苏高弘投资管理有限公司	2006-09	—	025-52313062
江苏高晋创业投资有限公司	2008-06-12	—	0519-85150557
江苏高科技投资集团有限公司	1992-07-30	www.js-vc.com	025-85529999
江苏高胜科技创业投资有限公司	2006-12-27	www.js-vc.com	025-51889757
江苏高投邦盛创业投资合伙企业（有限合伙）	2014-05-09	—	—

公司名称	成立时间	网址	传真
江苏高投成长创业投资有限公司	2008-01	—	025-66009900
江苏高投成长价值股权投资合伙企业（有限合伙）	2011-05	—	025-66009900
江苏高投创新价值创业投资合伙企业（有限合伙）	2011-05	—	025-66009900
江苏高投创新科技创业投资合伙企业（有限合伙）	2011-04	—	025-66009900
江苏高投创新天使创业投资合伙企业（有限合伙）	2013-11-30	—	025-66009900
江苏高投创新中小发展创业投资合伙企业（有限合伙）	—	—	025-66009900-9651
江苏高投创业投资管理有限公司	1999-01-29	—	025-85529999
江苏高投发展创业投资有限公司	2010-07-16	—	025-66009900
江苏高投科贷创业投资合伙企业（有限合伙）	2013-12-31	—	025-66009900-9651
江苏高投宁泰创业投资合伙企业（有限合伙）	2012-01-30	—	025-66009900-9651
江苏高投润泰创业投资合伙企业（有限合伙）	2012-02-14	—	025-66009900-9651
江苏高投鑫海创业投资有限公司	2011-04	—	0514-87876609
江苏高投中小企业创业投资有限公司	2009-05	—	025-66009900
江苏高新创业投资管理有限公司	2005-01-14	www.js-vc.com	025-51889757
江苏高新创业投资有限公司	2005-08-15	www.js-vc.com	025-51889757
江苏格瑞石墨烯创业投资有限公司	2012-04-10	—	0519-81085951
江苏汎渡投资有限公司	2009-07-15	—	0510-87822121
江苏国投衡盈创业投资中心（有限合伙）	2010-11-22	—	021-62785808
江苏海为创业投资有限公司	2010-12-03	—	0523-86239598
江苏恒凯投资有限公司	2013-10-24	—	—
江苏弘瑞科技创业投资有限公司	2002-09	—	025-52313062
江苏红黄蓝创业投资有限公司	2014-02-19	—	025-88869883
江苏华成华利创业投资有限公司	2009-10-21	—	0512-67161932
江苏华创医药研发平台管理有限公司	2007-06	—	—
江苏华控创业投资有限公司	2008-07-10	www.huakongpe.com	025-87716620-801
江苏华控投资管理有限公司	2008-01-15	—	025-87716220-801
江苏华全创业投资有限公司	2013-01-05	—	0523-80959672
江苏华睿投资管理有限公司	2010-06-12	—	—
江苏华厦创业投资有限公司	2006-09-30	—	0514-86569000
江苏汇鸿创业投资有限公司	2004-07-06	—	025-84572097
江苏嘉睿创业投资有限公司	2008-03-28	—	025-88160137
江苏金茂低碳产业创业投资有限公司	2010-11-19	www.jolmo.net	025-84730375
江苏金炻创业投资有限公司	2012-05-25	—	0515-82342000
江苏津通创业投资有限公司	2007-06-25	www.jinton.com	0519-86226016
江苏九洲投资集团创业投资有限公司	2007-09-19	www.jiuzhouinvest.com	0519-85220338
江苏巨能投资集团有限公司	2010-08-23	—	025-86716841
江苏巨业投资有限公司	2014-04-02	—	0513-87611102
江苏聚融创业投资有限公司	2011-11-16	—	0511-87899196

公司名称	成立时间	网址	传真
江苏科泉高新创业投资有限公司	2012-10-31	www.kequanvc.com	025-85589174
江苏旷达创业投资有限公司	2007-06	—	0519-86546893
江苏蓝色动力投资管理有限公司	2010-09-26	—	0517-80850098
江苏联发创业投资有限公司	2011-12-13	—	0513-88869069
江苏隆鑫创业投资有限公司	2006-06	—	025-84401201
江苏迈新创业投资有限公司	2009-08-17	—	0519-87195666
江苏人才创新创业投资合伙企业（有限合伙）	2014-03-25	—	—
江苏如东高新创业投资有限公司	2014-05-05	—	0513-88158132
江苏瑞明创业投资管理有限公司	2009-12-30	jsrm2009@yeah.net	025-83172132
江苏瑞庭投资管理有限公司	2013-09-27	—	51385158550
江苏桑夏投资有限公司	2010-04-28	—	—
江苏省高科技产业投资有限公司	1997	www.jsvc.com.cn	025-83317551
江苏省高新技术创业服务中心	1996-10	www.jsbi.cn	025-83232021
江苏省苏港创业投资有限公司	2010-08	www.sgct.com.cn	0515-83289299
江苏省苏高新风险投资股份有限公司	2000-03-31	www.sz-vc.com	0512-68243439
江苏晟华创业投资有限公司	2009-04-09	www.shct1688.com	0516-83897897
江苏盛泉创业投资有限公司	2007-06	www.vc-century.com	025-58071508
江苏盛宇丹昇创业投资有限公司	2008-10-28	—	0511-86929333
江苏思佰益投资管理有限公司	2013-07-02	—	0510-81766568
江苏苏大天宫创业投资管理有限公司	2010-10-08	sdkjy.suda.edu.cn	0512-62925790
江苏苏大投资有限公司	2001-02	—	0512-67504016
江苏苏豪投资集团有限公司	1999-05-06	—	—
江苏天氏创业投资有限公司	2005	—	025-87752270
江苏通顺创业投资有限公司	2009-08-25	—	0512-69560268
江苏同兴财富投资管理有限公司	2008-05	—	0512-69560268
江苏拓达创业投资有限责任公司	2012-11-26	—	0516-68005601
江苏威望创业投资有限公司	2009-10-14	—	—
江苏橡树资本投资有限公司	2009-06-23	—	0510-85183628
江苏新材料产业创业投资企业（有限合伙）	2013-11-13	www.jolomo.net	025-84730375
江苏新创投资有限公司	2007-10-17	—	0523-84623002
江苏新海连创业投资有限公司	2010-04-27	—	—
江苏鑫澳创业投资有限公司	2009-02-17	—	0512-58165929
江苏信泉创业投资管理有限公司	2006-12-30	—	025-58071508
江苏兴科创业投资有限公司	2007-08-20	www.jsxinkect.com	0519-86302628
江苏学府科技创业园有限公司	2010-06-08	—	0511-84405258
江苏毅达并购成长股权投资基金（有限合伙）	2014-11-26	—	—
江苏毅达股权投资基金管理有限公司	2014-02-18	—	—
江苏鹰能创业投资有限公司	2007-08-28	—	025-66009900
江苏镇江京口工业园区高创中心	2011-03-16	www.kingkj.cn	0511-85345150

公司名称	成立时间	网址	传真
江苏中科华艺创业投资有限公司	2007-03-30	—	0513-88869883
江苏中科物联网科技创业投资有限公司	2010-07-14	www.casiot.com	0510-85380859
江苏卓创创业投资有限公司	2013-12-12	—	0513-80559909
江苏紫金文化产业二期投资基金（有限合伙）	2014-09-16	—	—
江苏紫金文化产业发展基金（有限合伙）	2010-03-15	—	025-66009900
江阴市高新技术创业投资有限公司	2007-02-06	—	0510-81602090
姜堰市高新实业投资有限公司	2010-12-23	—	0523-88279301
靖江市高新技术创业投资有限公司	2010-03	—	0523-89181480
句容市高新技术创业服务中心	2013-04-01	—	0511-87272670
凯风创业投资有限公司	2006-10-30	—	0512-66969533
昆山红土创业投资管理有限公司	2012-08-08	—	0512-36607933
昆山红土高新创业投资有限公司	2012-07-13	—	0512-3660732
昆山市国科创业投资有限公司	2001-08-31	—	0512-57367277
昆山中科昆开创业投资有限公司	2011-05	—	0512-36821078
连云港金海创业投资有限公司	2006-07-19	www.lygjhvc.com	0518-85523512
连云港市润财创业投资发展有限公司	2010-10-22	—	0518-85523920
连云港中科黄海创业投资有限公司	2010-03-22	www.csm-inv.com	0518-85807928
南京创业投资管理有限公司	2008-11-26	www.nj-vc.com	025-86579660
南京高科新创投资有限公司	2008-04-24	—	—
南京高新创业投资有限公司	2012-06-01	—	025-58696594
南京红土创业投资有限公司	2010-05-31	www.szvc.com.cn	025-58867560
南京科建创业投资有限公司	2007-02	—	025-86989717
南京科源投资管理有限公司	2012-08-22	—	025-85589174
南京栖霞科技发展投资有限公司	2012-03-16	—	—
南京市高新技术风险投资股份有限公司	2001-02-24	www.nj-vc.com	025-86599660
南京市栖霞区科技创业投资有限公司	2009-07-31	—	025-85566570
南京外滩明珠创业投资有限公司	2011-03-17	—	025-89669155
南京文化创业投资有限公司	2011-02	—	025-86579660
南京协立创业投资有限公司	2009-05-11	—	025-86816826
南京中成创业投资有限公司	2009-08	—	025-86579660
南京中原创业投资有限公司	2010-12-17	—	025-86579660
南京紫金创投基金管理有限责任公司	2011-09-02	—	025-86579655
南京紫金科技创业投资有限公司	2011-08-08	www.njzjkc.com	025-86579616
南通阿斯旺股权投资中心	2014-09-11	—	0513-87533223
南通爱福七龙投资中心（有限合伙）	2014-09-12	—	—
南通创源科技园发展有限公司	2013-05-07	www.innospring.net	0513-55018010
南通创源投资有限公司	2012-09	—	0513-86268555
南通得一投资中心（有限合伙）	2012-08-10	—	021-64178726
南通高胜成长创业投资有限公司	2008-09-10	www.js-vc.com	025-51889757

公司名称	成立时间	网址	传真
南通高特佳汇金投资合伙企业（有限合伙）	2013-05-24	—	—
南通国泰创业投资有限公司	2006-10-20	www.ntgtvc.com	0513-85288204
南通恒富创业投资合伙企业（有限合伙）	2013-12-16	—	0513-86126133
南通红土创新资本创业投资有限公司	2007-09	—	0513-83562508
南通红土伟达创业投资管理有限公司	2014-04-21	www.szvc.com.cn	0513-83562508
南通红土伟达创业投资有限公司	2014-04-21	www.szvc.com.cn	0513-83562508
南通金谷投资有限公司	2013-06-28	—	0513-88695186
南通金玖锐信投资管理有限公司	2013-12-09	www.shzhj.cn	0513-87169080
南通科创创业投资管理有限公司	2013-04-23	—	0513-85728713
南通科技创业投资有限公司	2011-04-22	—	0513-81500791
南通蓝海投资有限公司	2010-11-11	—	0513-86639999
南通磊泽投资有限公司	2011-09-07	—	0513-80113560
南通灵源投资中心（有限合伙）	2012-11-20	—	0513-81806183
南通玛叶娅股权投资基金管理有限公司	2012-02-28	www.myygqtz.com	0513-87513900
南通如意物联网产业投资基金管理中心（有限合伙）	2010-09-09	—	0513-87300528-815
南通杉杉创业投资中心（有限合伙）	2012-06-08	—	021-51561587
南通松禾创业投资合伙企业（有限合伙）	2009-01	—	0513-85507237
南通松禾创业投资中心（有限合伙）	2011-08-01	—	0513-85517915
南通松禾资本管理有限公司	2009-01-05	—	0513-85507237
南通通光投资中心（有限合伙）	2014-07-01	—	—
南通五水投资发展有限公司	2013-06-17	—	0513-85609598
农银国联无锡投资管理有限公司	2011-09-30	—	0510-85199103
邳州市高新区科创园投资发展有限公司	2014-07-18	—	—
日亚创业投资企业	2009-01-06	—	021-61976299
软库博辰创业投资企业	2008-03-03	—	0512-66969661
三角洲创业投资管理（苏州）有限公司	2007-10-16	—	021-53835998
苏州创东方富诚投资企业（有限合伙）	2010-09-20	—	0512-68322281
苏州创禾创业投资管理有限公司	2014-10-21	—	0512-63493186
苏州创元高投创业投资管理有限公司	2010-08-27	—	0512-68322738
苏州创元高新创业投资有限公司	2010-11-15	—	0512-68322738
苏州达泰创业投资管理有限公司	2010-05	www.delta-capital.cn	0512-66969930
苏州达泰创业投资中心（有限合伙）	2010-08	www.delta-capital.cn	0512-66969930
苏州德睿亨风创业投资有限公司	2010-04-21	—	0512-66969727
苏州德晟亨风创业投资合伙企业（有限合伙）	2011	—	0512-66969533
苏州东方汇富创业投资企业（有限合伙）	—	—	—
苏州方广创业投资管理合伙企业（有限合伙）	2012-05-28	—	021-54245723
苏州方广创业投资合伙企业（有限合伙）	2012-09-25	—	021-54245723
苏州福马创业投资有限公司	2009-10	—	0512-62821808

公司名称	成立时间	网址	传真
苏州富丽东方能源股权投资企业（有限合伙）	2011-07-28	—	0512-68322281
苏州富丽高新投资企业（有限合伙）	2010-11-10	—	0512-68322281
苏州富丽明康投资企业（有限合伙）	2011-07-26	—	0512-68322281
苏州富丽启康投资企业（有限合伙）	2011-07-25	—	0512-68322281
苏州富丽泰泓投资企业（有限合伙）	2010-12-24	—	0512-68322281
苏州富丽投资有限公司	2010-07-29	www.fuli-capital.com	0512-68322281
苏州高华创业投资管理有限公司	2009-09-08	—	0512-68313889
苏州高锦创业投资有限公司	2009-03-27	—	0512-68243439
苏州高铨创业投资企业（有限合伙）	2011-11	—	0512-68243439
苏州高投创业投资管理有限公司	2007-01	—	0512-68059096
苏州高新创业投资集团融联管理有限公司	2012-02-08	—	0512-68081156
苏州高新创业投资集团新麟管理有限公司	2008-12-04	—	0512-68762955
苏州高新创业投资集团有限公司	2008-07-30	www.sndvc.com	0512-68311200
苏州高新风投创业投资管理有限公司	2009-02-23	—	0512-68243439
苏州高新国发创业投资有限公司	2009-05-22	—	0512-65126380
苏州高新华富创业投资企业	2010-01-08	—	0512-68313889
苏州高新明鑫创业投资管理有限公司	2010-12-29	www.sndvc.com	0512-68313889
苏州高新启源创业投资有限公司	2011-05	www.sndvc.com	0512-68311200
苏州高新区创业科技投资管理有限公司	2003-03-03	—	0512-68323009
苏州高新新联创业投资管理有限公司	2009-06-24	—	0512-68313585
苏州高新友利创业投资有限公司	2010-04-28	—	0512-68313585
苏州高远创业投资有限公司	2007-03	—	0512-68059096
苏州高钺创业投资管理有限公司	2011	—	0512-68243439
苏州工业园区弘丰创业投资有限公司	2010-04	—	0512-69560268
苏州工业园区华穗创业投资管理有限公司	2008-07	—	021-62898817
苏州工业园区南凯创业投资有限公司	2011-03	—	0512-69560268
苏州工业园区启纳创业投资有限公司	2011-07	—	0512-69993999
苏州工业园区易联创业投资基金有限公司	2010-03	—	0512-669669938
苏州工业园区易联投资管理有限公司	2010	www.easternlink.com	0516-66969938
苏州工业园区易联投资中心（有限合伙）	2011-10-31	www.easternlinkcapital.com	0512-66969938
苏州工业园区原点创业投资有限公司	2008-03-26	—	0512-66969998
苏州工业园区原点正则壹号创业投资企业（有限合伙）	2013-11-19	—	0512-66969533
苏州国发创富创业投资企业（有限合伙）	2010-07-14	—	0512-65126380
苏州国发创新资本管理有限公司	2007-01-16	www.szvc.com.cn	0512-65168830
苏州国发创新资本投资有限公司	2007-01-12	—	0512-36607933
苏州国发创业投资控股有限公司	2008-05-08	www.sidvc.com	0512-65126380
苏州国发东方创业投资管理有限公司	2008-11-14	—	0512-65126380
苏州国发服务业创业投资企业（有限合伙）	2012-04-23	—	0512-65126380

公司名称	成立时间	网址	传真
苏州国发高铁文化创业投资管理有限公司	2013-08-19	—	—
苏州国发高铁文化创业投资中心（有限合伙）	2013-09-29	—	—
苏州国发高新创业投资管理有限公司	2008-12-17	—	0512-65126380
苏州国发宏富创业投资企业（有限合伙）	2011-04	—	0512-65126380
苏州国发建富创业投资企业（有限合伙）	2010-06-30	—	0512-65126380
苏州国发聚富创业投资有限公司	2010-03-25	—	0512-65126380
苏州国发黎曼创业投资有限公司	2010-05-19	—	0512-65126380
苏州国发融富创业投资管理企业（有限合伙）	2009-12-28	—	0512-65126380
苏州国发融富创业投资企业（有限合伙）	2010-01-20	—	0512-65126380
苏州国发天使创业投资企业（有限合伙）	2011-06	—	0512-65126380
苏州国发添富创业投资企业（有限合伙）	2012-05-09	—	0512-65126380
苏州国发文化产业创业投资企业（有限合伙）	2012-12-17	—	—
苏州国发涌富创业投资企业（有限合伙）	2011-06	—	0512-65126380
苏州国发源富创业投资企业（有限合伙）	2011-01	—	0512-65126380
苏州国发智富创业投资企业（有限合伙）	2010-03	—	0512-65126380
苏州国发众富创业投资企业（有限合伙）	2010-03-17	—	0512-65126380
苏州国润创业投资发展有限公司	2008-07	—	0512-62998663
苏州国润瑞祺创业投资企业（有限合伙）	2011-07	www.guorunpe.com	0512-62998663
苏州合盈创业投资管理有限公司	2010	www.renhua.cc	0512-67060338
苏州华创赢达创业投资基金企业（有限合伙）	2012	—	0512-63936955
苏州华映文化产业投资企业（有限合伙）	2010-09-20	www.meridiancapital.com.cn	0512-68327950
苏州辉宏原油股权投资企业（有限合伙）	2011-07-28	—	0512-68322281
苏州汇利华创业投资有限公司	2010-08-27	www.js-central.com	0512-68079590
苏州金林创业投资中心（有限合伙）	2008-01-03	www.jolmo.net	025 84730375
苏州金茂创业投资管理企业（有限合伙）	2011-05	www.jolmo.net	025-84730375
苏州金茂投资管理有限公司	2007-12-27	www.jolmo.net	025-84730211
苏州金茂新兴产业创业投资企业（有限合伙）	2011-06	www.jolmo.net	025-84730375
苏州君玄创业投资中心（有限合伙）	2011	—	025-86816826
苏州卡贝高登创业投资中心（有限合伙）	2011-01	www.kbgfund.com	0512-69572911
苏州卡贝金牛投资管理有限公司	2011-01	www.kbgfund.com	0512-69572911
苏州科技城创业投资有限公司	2007-12-24	—	0512-66899465
苏州科技创业投资公司	1993-07	—	0512-69330076
苏州科嘉创业投资中心	2011-05	www.kbgfund.com	0512-69572911
苏州科荣创业投资中心（有限合伙）	2011-07-04	—	—
苏州科盛投资管理有限公司	2011-09-29	www.kbgfund.com	—
苏州蓝贰创业投资有限公司	2010-01	—	0512-62725933
苏州蓝壹创业投资有限公司	2008-03	—	0512-62725933
苏州龙瑞创业投资管理有限公司	2009-12	—	0512-66969306
苏州龙跃投资中心（有限合伙）	2010-01	—	0512-66969306

公司名称	成立时间	网址	传真
苏州绿原大成投资管理有限公司	2011-03-04	—	0512-62990952
苏州明鑫高投创业投资有限公司	2011-02	www.sndvc.com	0512-68313889
苏州农发创业投资中心（有限合伙）	2010-04	—	0512-62990952
苏州启明创智股权投资合伙企业（有限合伙）	2011-10-17	www.qimingvc.com	—
苏州清商成长创业投资企业（有限合伙）	2011-09	—	0512-62621310
苏州仁华创业投资有限公司	2010-04	www.renhua.cc	0512-67060338
苏州融联创业投资企业（有限合伙）	2012-03-15	—	0512-68081156
苏州瑞璟创业投资企业（有限合伙）	2010-11-17	—	0512-68326637
苏州瑞曼投资管理有限公司	2010-03-17	—	0512-68326637
苏州盛泉百涛创业投资管理有限公司	2010-12-15	—	025-58071508
苏州盛泉海成创业投资合伙企业（有限合伙）	2014-10-23	—	025-58071508
苏州盛泉万泽创业投资合伙企业（有限合伙）	2011-03-03	—	025-58071508
苏州市澄和创业投资有限公司	2008-08	xcchfof.com	0512-66183052
苏州市吴江创业投资有限公司	2008	—	0512-63493186
苏州市吴中创业投资有限公司	2007-01-12	—	0512-66356670
苏州市相城创业投资管理有限责任公司	2009-01-16	—	0512-65808803
苏州市相城创业投资有限责任公司	2008	—	0512-65808803
苏州市相城高新创业投资有限责任公司	2009-03-12	—	0512-65808803
苏州蔚蓝投资管理有限公司	2008-03-07	—	0512-62725933
苏州吴中国发创业投资管理有限公司	2008-08-28	—	0512-65126380
苏州吴中国发创业投资有限公司	2008-08-28	—	0512-65126380
苏州吴中科技创业投资有限公司	2012-10-26	—	0512-65855966
苏州相城经济开发区相发投资有限公司	2011-08	—	0512-66183052
苏州香塘创业投资有限责任公司	2007	—	0512-53560126
苏州协立投资管理有限公司	2011-03	—	—
苏州新麟创业投资有限公司	2009-01-22	—	0512-68762955
苏州新麟二期创业投资企业（有限合伙）	2011-11	—	0512-68762955
苏州新协创业投资有限公司	2006-05	—	0512-62620019
苏州信慧成创业投资管理有限公司	2014-07-28	—	025-58071508
苏州亿和创业投资有限公司	2009-12-29	—	0512-68635705
苏州亿文创新资本管理有限公司	2007-12-03	—	0512-68635705
苏州亿文投资有限公司	2007-12-17	—	0512-68635705
苏州银基创业投资有限公司	2006-05-10	—	0512-67156968
苏州银基美林创业投资管理有限公司	2012-09-03	—	0512-67156968
苏州银基美林创业投资合伙企业（有限合伙）	2012-10-23	—	0512-67156968
苏州元风创业投资有限公司	2007-04	—	0512-66969998
苏州元禾控股有限公司	2001-11-28	www.oriza.com.cn	0512-66969998
宿迁国发创业投资企业（有限合伙）	2011-07-22	—	0527-81686002
宿迁科技创业投资有限公司	2012-03-23	—	0527-87031252

公司名称	成立时间	网址	传真
宿迁市开创创业投资有限公司	2010-09-07	—	0527-88859676
睢宁县天使创业投资有限责任公司	2013-03-06	—	0516-88037115
太仓高新创业投资有限公司	2013-05-17	www.tcaccelerator.com	0512-53206165
太仓生物医药创业投资有限公司	2012-09-20	bip.taicang.gov.cn	0512-33019923
太仓市科技创业投资有限公司	2008-08	—	0512-53739159
泰州华诚高新技术投资发展有限公司	2005	www.tzibi.com	0523-86196007
泰州华健创业投资有限公司	2007-06-08	—	—
泰州华盛投资开发有限公司	2007	—	0523-86200146
泰州健鑫创业投资有限公司	2012-12-14	—	—
泰州融众创业投资有限公司	2008-12	—	0523-86999080
泰州市创业风险投资有限公司	2001-08	—	0523-86196199
泰州市高港高新区开发投资有限责任公司	2010-08	—	0523-86118800
泰州市高科创业投资有限公司	2010-08-25	—	0523-86966047
泰州市环晟创业投资有限公司	2011-11	—	—
泰州中国医药城融健达创业投资有限公司	2013-04	—	—
无锡 TCL 创动投资有限公司	2009-04	—	0510-82800509
无锡 TCL 创业投资合伙企业（有限合伙）	2010-07	—	—
无锡创业投资集团有限公司	2000-10-26	www.wxvcg.com	0510-82700936
无锡高德创业投资管理有限公司	2006-09-30	—	0510-81813011
无锡高德创业投资有限公司	2006-09-06	—	0510-81813011
无锡高新技术风险投资股份有限公司	2000-08	www.wxvc.com.cn	0510-85226431
无锡国弘尚理投资管理有限公司	2010-03-19	—	0510-85213378
无锡国联创业投资有限公司	2006-09-21	www.glgc.com.cn	0510-82830598
无锡国联浚源创业投资中心（有限合伙）	2010-04-16	www.jycapital.cn	0510-82700340
无锡红杉恒业股权投资合伙企业（有限合伙）	2010-12-03	—	010-84475669
无锡红杉兴业股权投资合伙企业（有限合伙）	2010-10-21	—	010-84475669
无锡厚泽成长创业投资企业（有限合伙）	2011-07-08	—	—
无锡厚泽创新创业投资企业（有限合伙）	2011-06-28	—	0510-81816802
无锡花样日升创业投资中心（有限合伙）	2012-05-02	—	—
无锡江南大学国家大学科技园有限公司	2009-04-03	www.j-park.jiangnan.edu.cn	0510-85189107
无锡江南仁和新能源产业投资中心（有限合伙）	2012-03-01	—	0510-82695355
无锡均衡创业投资有限公司	2007-11-14	—	0510-86216256
无锡力合创业投资有限公司	2008-11	www.leaguercapital.com	0510-83590286
无锡力合清源创业投资合伙企业（有限合伙）	2011-09-09	www.leaguercapital.com	0510-83590296
无锡力合投资管理咨询有限公司	2009-04-17	www.leaguercapital.com	0510-83590296
无锡领峰创业投资有限公司	2009-12-11	—	0510-85213378
无锡瑞明博创业投资有限公司	2010-12-15	—	025-83172132
无锡世铭国联创业投资企业	2010-05-13	—	021-53752208
无锡市金惠创业投资有限责任公司	2006-11	—	0510-83590162

公司名称	成立时间	网址	传真
无锡市锡山创业投资有限公司	2007-08	—	0510-88705868
无锡市新区科技金融创业投资集团有限公司	2008-01-31	www.wxvc.com.cn	0510-85226431
无锡新区领航创业投资有限公司	2009-08-03	www.wxvc.com.cn	0510-85226431
无锡源生高科技投资有限责任公司	2006	—	0510-85342727-8102
无锡正海联云投资企业（有限合伙）	2012-12-04	—	—
无锡中科汇盈创业投资有限责任公司	2008-03-07	—	0510-85383122
无锡中科汇盈二期创业投资有限责任公司	2010-04-07	—	0510-85383122
无锡中美科技创新创业投资有限公司	2014-04-22	—	0510-85226431
吴江东方创富创业投资企业（有限合伙）	2008-11	—	—
吴江东方国发创业投资有限公司	2008-11-11	—	0512-65126380
吴江东方融富创业投资管理企业（有限合伙）	—	—	—
吴江东运创业投资有限公司	2008-06-24	www.dyvc.net	0512-63960764
吴江海博科技创业投资有限公司	2010-08-20	www.haiboinvestment.net	0512-63010566
吴江科祥创业投资中心（有限合伙）	2011	—	—
新沂市钟吾股权投资管理有限公司	2012-10	—	0516-81639533
兴化市高新投资有限公司	2010-07-16	—	0523-83242633
徐州高新创业投资有限公司	2010-02-24	—	0516-85906737
徐州国盛鸿运创业投资有限公司	2014-01-21	—	—
徐州淮创投资有限责任公司	2014-01-20	—	—
徐州淮海红土创业投资有限公司	2014-01-14	—	—
徐州支点创业投资合伙企业（有限合伙）	2012-11	—	0516-66690376
盐城高投创业投资有限公司	2010-08	—	025-85529999
盐城市恒利风险投资有限公司	2002-08-06	—	0515-88580802
盐城中小企业创业投资实业有限公司	2007-12	—	—
扬中创业投资有限公司	2011-05-01	www.yzgxct.com	0511-88126366
扬州长盛创业投资有限公司	2014-11-25	—	—
扬州高投创业投资管理有限公司	2011-01-13	www.js-vc.com	0514-87876609
扬州海圣创业投资中心（有限合伙）	2012-07-09	—	0514-87991537
扬州经济技术开发区高科创业投资有限公司	2012-11-22	—	0514-87962257
扬州经信新兴产业创业投资中心（有限合伙）	2013-01	www.jolmo.net	025-84730375
扬州平衡宜创创业投资基金中心（有限合伙）	2014-12-22	—	025-51889757
扬州平衡资本管理中心（有限合伙）	2014-11-25	—	025-51889757
扬州市富海永成股权投资合伙企业（有限合伙）	2014-09-22	—	021-50581867
扬州英飞尼迪创业投资管理有限公司	2010-11-08	—	0514-87785512
宜兴环保科技创新创业投资有限公司	2010-11-24	—	0510-87061315
宜兴杰宜投资管理有限公司	2012-12-14	—	0510-87880198-888
张家港市金茂创业投资有限公司	2008-04-15	—	0512-58157063
镇江高科创业投资有限公司	2012-03-16	—	0511-80822821
镇江高投创业投资有限公司	2008-07	—	025-66009900

公司名称	成立时间	网址	传真
镇江高新创业投资有限公司	2010-06-11	—	0511-83179317
镇江国投创业投资有限公司	2011-10-05	—	0511-85213636
镇江红土创业投资有限公司	2011-04-22	—	0511-85988773
镇江金山银河股权投资合伙企业（有限合伙）	2013-08-02	—	—
镇江京口高新技术创业服务中心	2006-09	—	0511-88793155
镇江君鼎协立创业投资有限公司	2013-02-04	—	025-86816826
镇江康成亨创业投资管理有限公司	2013-07-23	—	—
镇江康成亨创业投资合伙企业（有限合伙）	2013-08-12	—	—
镇江力合天使创业投资企业（有限合伙）	2012-12-13	—	0511-88884035
镇江绿洲创业园发展有限公司	2009-09-28	www.glnenergy.cn	0511-83999880
镇江乾鹏创业投资基金企业（有限合伙）	2012-11-20	—	0511-80896166
镇江市创业风险投资有限责任公司	2001-12-01	www.jszjvc.cn	0511-85015808
镇江新区高新技术产业投资有限公司	2009-07-16	www.zjxqjf.com	0511-83179317
镇江亿致能源科技孵化器有限公司	2010-10-18	—	0511-85630166
镇江银河创业投资有限公司	2012-06-11	—	—
镇江中安绿色投资管理有限公司	2013-08-09	—	0511-88890873
镇江中科金山创业投资企业（有限合伙）	2011-08-24	www.csm-inv.com	0510-85383122
镇江中小电子电器产业集聚创新服务中心	2007-09-13	—	0511-85936077
镇江中以景润创业投资管理有限公司	2013-10-12	—	—
中节能南通合同环境管理投资基金中心（有限合伙）	2013-04-03	—	—
中沃创业投资海安有限公司	2014-05-19	www.h8888.net	—
中新苏州工业园区创业投资有限公司	2001-11-28	—	0512-66969998
江西高技术产业投资股份有限公司	2002-03	www.jxvc.com.cn	0791-88110252
江西立达新材料产业创业投资中心（有限合伙）	2011-08-03	www.reitercapital.com	0791-83851565
南昌创业投资有限公司	2005-12	www.ncct.com.cn	0791-8193130
南昌新世纪创业投资有限责任公司	2009-02-24	www.xsjvc.com	0791-86757668
成大沿海产业（大连）基金管理有限公司	2011-09-28	—	0411-82691256
大连北部资产经营有限公司	1997-08	www.bbachina.com	0411-82520525
大连港航产业基金管理有限公司	2011-07-01	www.chnpsf.com	0411-86768576
大连高端装备制造业创业投资基金（有限合伙）	2012-06-20	—	0411-82536160
大连海融高新创业投资管理有限公司	2008-02-18	—	0411-84821325
大连海融高新创业投资基金有限公司	2007-12-29	—	0411-84821325
大连金东瑞达财富管理中心（有限合伙）	2014-05-06	—	0411-88079959
大连精石文化产业投资有限公司	2014-04-28	—	0411-83792186
大连赛伯乐创业投资中心（有限合伙）	2013-09-23	—	4006761188-1037
大连天使创业投资有限公司	2006-04-14	—	0411-84753186
大连万融天使投资有限公司	2010-11-30	—	0411-84821325
大连网信创业投资管理有限公司	1999-06-28	—	0411-82859969
大连银信创业投资有限公司	2006-09-13	—	0411-84802259-8001

公司名称	成立时间	网址	传真
大连装备创新投资有限公司	2009-10-29	—	—
德晟创业投资有限公司	2011-03-09	—	0411-82779477
联合创业集团有限公司	2005-07-07	—	0411-88009300
辽宁和元资产管理有限公司	2010-04	—	0411-82530155
辽宁科技创业投资有限责任公司	2000-02-28	www.lnvc.com.cn	024-23244922
沈阳科技风险开发事业中心（沈阳市中试服务中心）	1992-06-02	—	024-22791108
沈阳科技风险投资有限公司	1998-11-04	—	024-22791108
煜华尚和投资管理（大连）有限公司	2014-07-01	www.yuhuashanghe.com	0411-33985508
内蒙古自治区科技风险基金管理办公室	1998	www.fengxianjijin.com	0471-6280827
宁夏嘉润宝股权投资基金管理有限公司	2013-07-22	—	0951-5673359
宁夏银控科技创业投资有限公司	2002	—	0951-6199333
宁夏中财高新投资管理有限公司	2013-04-17	www.nxzcgx.com	0951-8507997
青海国科创业投资基金（有限合伙）	2013-10-23	—	0971-6152307
青海华控科技创业投资基金（有限合伙）	2013-02-21	—	—
青海欧瑞科技发展投资基金（有限合伙）	2012-03-27	—	010-59002776
德州市创业投资有限公司	2009-12-31	—	0534-2230518
东营经济开发区斯博特创业投资有限公司	2012-06-04	—	0546-8300909
东营市黄河三角洲投资中心（有限合伙）	2009-07-07	—	0546-7768881
东营市金凯高新投资有限公司	2009-02-16	—	0546-8300909
黄河三角洲投资管理有限公司	2009-04-03	—	0546-7768881
黄蓝创业投资有限公司	2012-08-06	—	—
济南华科创业投资合伙企业（有限合伙）	2013-11-12	—	0531-88816112
济南科技风险投资有限公司	2010-04	www.jnvc.com.cn	0531-88879277
济南云海创业投资有限公司	2013-05-24	—	0531-85106246
济宁博大创业投资有限公司	2009-10-27	—	—
济宁共创投资有限公司	2013-09-29	—	—
济宁鲁宁创业投资管理有限公司	2012-12-24	—	0537-2269315
济宁市惠达财丰创业投资有限公司	2014-03-11	www.huidatouzi.com	—
济宁市珑瑜惠达创业投资中心（有限合伙）	2012-11-16	—	0537-5667269
济宁银丰财盈医药产业创业投资中心（有限合伙）	2013-01-31	—	0537-5667269
济宁英飞尼迪创业投资管理公司	2010-12-22	www.infinity-equity.com	0537-3281509
济宁英飞尼迪创业投资中心（有限合伙）	2011-04-21	www.infinity-equity.com	0537-3281505
莱芜创业投资有限公司	2009-12-28	—	0634-8891182
莱芜科融投资管理合伙企业（有限合伙）	2013-08-16	—	0531-88982881
美世联合创业投资有限公司	2007-04-04	—	0543-3185686
青岛安芙兰创业投资有限公司	2006-01-12	www.vcpe.hk	0532-88018557
青岛迪凯投资管理有限公司	2014-11-27	—	—
青岛高创投资管理有限公司	2009-12-25	—	0532-88727626

公司名称	成立时间	网址	传真
青岛海尔赛富智慧家庭创业投资中心（有限合伙）	2014-09-01	—	010-65630251
青岛里程碑创业投资管理有限公司	2011-05-20	—	0532-80931757
青岛连科股权投资基金合伙企业（有限合伙）	2014-10-29	—	0532-55678701
青岛清控高创投资管理有限公司	2013-06-18	—	0532-88890577
青岛市科技风险投资有限公司	2000-08-17	www.qdstvc.com	0532-85063780
日照华和科技创业投资有限责任公司	2010-05-28	—	0633-8339288
山东德泰创业投资有限公司	2010-03-29	www.sddetai.cn	0535-3942685
山东多盈节能环保产业创业投资有限公司	2014-01-07	—	—
山东恒发创业投资有限公司	2012-02-28	—	0543-5077698
山东弘利创业投资有限公司	2009-12-31	—	0539-8385619
山东红桥创业投资有限公司	2011-12-22	—	0531-88982881
山东红土创业投资有限公司	2012-01-19	—	—
山东华天科技创业投资有限公司	2012-07-30	—	—
山东汇益创业投资有限公司	2014-01-13	—	0531-82912988
山东江诣创业投资有限公司	2010-08-12	—	0535-6719638
山东科创投资有限公司	2010-10-22	—	0537-3292806
山东蓝色经济创业投资有限公司	2011-02-16	www.sdoi.cn	0531-68610333
山东利泰投资有限公司	2009-03-24	—	—
山东齐星创业投资有限公司	2007-01-30	—	0543-4309019
山东省方正创业投资有限责任公司	2010-10-29	—	0543-6782271
山东天齐创业投资有限公司	2010-03-24	—	0533-3598500
山东同瑞大成创业投资有限公司	2012-07-03	—	—
潍坊市国信创业投资有限公司	2012-07-17	—	—
潍坊万通创业投资有限公司	2009-09-28	—	0536-8101018
烟台蓝桉投资中心	2014-04-23	—	—
烟台鲁创恒富创业投资中心（有限合伙）	2012-06-06	—	—
烟台盈智创业投资有限公司	2014-03-11	—	0535-6291105
烟台源创科技投资中心（有限合伙）	2014-07-17	—	010-58143806
淄博高新技术风险投资股份有限公司	2003-07-10	www.zbvc.net	0533-3586969
淄博市高新技术创业投资有限公司	2007-07-25	—	0533-6206621
山西省高新技术创业中心	1992-07	www.sxbi.orj	0351-2209903
山西省科技基金发展总公司（山西省风险投资协会）	1993-06	www.sxstfdc.com	0351-2026370
顶华创业投资管理（西安）有限公司	2009-03-12	—	029-88319611
顶华通路价值创业投资（西安）企业	2009-03-23	—	029-88319611
陕西高端装备高技术创业投资基金（有限合伙）	2013-06-28	—	0917-3322919
陕西航天红土创业投资有限公司	2010-06-24	—	029-89195163
陕西科技创业投资管理有限公司	2012-09-18	www.cycn.net	029-88443083
陕西省新材料高技术创业投资基金	2014-03-21	—	—

公司名称	成立时间	网址	传真
陕西天健君合投资管理有限公司	2008-07-11	www.shxtjjh.com	029-88785306
陕西西科天使企业管理合伙企业（有限合伙）	2013-01-18	—	029-88887557
陕西源丰投资发展有限公司	2009-03-24	—	029-68255896
陕西中福联融资担保有限公司	2010-09-21	www.zfldb.com	0917-3154888
西安创新投资管理有限公司	2001-07	—	029-88348867
西安高新技术产业风险投资有限公司	1999-02-01	www.capitech.com.cn	029-65690878
西安关天西咸投资管理有限公司	2012-03-08	—	029-88854188
西安红土创新投资有限公司	2008-06-24	—	—
西安迈朴投资发展有限公司	2002-01-08	—	029-89561001
西安西旅创新投资管理有限公司	2008-06-24	—	029-8919563
西安信实投资有限公司	2003-12-26	—	029-88351275
海硅（上海）创业投资合伙企业（有限合伙）	2011-08-05	—	021-65650817
上海遨问创业投资管理有限公司	2009-11-23	www.chinamaterialia.com	021-35322133
上海遨问创业投资合伙企业（有限合伙）	2012-09-14	www.chinamaterialia.com	021-35322133
上海博辰创业投资管理合伙企业（有限合伙）	2011-03-10	—	—
上海漕河泾创业投资有限公司	2002-05-22	—	021-64951721
上海晨晖创业投资管理有限公司	2013-10-23	www.chvc.com.cn	021-51355918
上海德丰杰龙升创业投资合伙企业（有限合伙）	2012-11-01	www.dfjdragon.com	021-62800585
上海复旦创业投资有限公司	2000-11-09	—	021-65642533
上海富欣创业投资有限公司	1999-04-08	sh-fortune.com.cn	021-20599098
上海嘉定创业投资管理有限公司	2011-08-01	www.jdsam.com	021-59521950
上海爵安股权投资基金有限公司	2014-10-10	www.shanghaijuean.com	021-51333589
上海科技创业投资股份有限公司	1993-06-30	www.sstic.com.cn	021-64330776
上海力合清源创业投资合伙企业（有限合伙）	2012-08-22	www.leaguercapital.com	021-62370021
上海联创永钦创业投资企业（有限合伙）	2011-08-31	www.newmargin.com	021-62123900
上海联升创业投资有限公司	2010-04-09	www.atlas-venture.com	021-64718011
上海南风股权投资管理有限公司	2009-09-28	www.southwindequity.com	021-52383372
上海磐石商联创业投资管理有限公司	2012-08-17	—	021-60938290
上海浦东新星纽士达创业投资有限公司	2009-06-19	—	021-50276385
上海汽车创业投资有限公司	2001-06-19	—	021-22011669
上海睿立投资管理有限公司	2009-09-11	www.realpe.com.cn	021-68862093
上海商投创业投资有限公司	2001-06-05	—	021-65650916
上海上实创业投资有限公司	2011-11-30	www.siicfm.com	021-39533976
上海时空五星创业投资管理有限公司	2009-11-18	—	021-61218707
上海市北科技创业投资有限公司	2011-11-23	—	021-62505267
上海天地人和创业投资有限公司	2008-10-13	www.tdgrowth.com	021-58791661
上海信息技术创业投资有限公司	2001-09-18	—	021-62720218
上海徐汇科技创业投资有限公司	1998-12-02	www.xhvc.net	021-33680013
上海寅福创业投资有限公司	2010-05-06	—	021-65650817

公司名称	成立时间	网址	传真
上海寅嘉创业投资管理有限公司	2010-06-22	www.incufortune.com	021-65650817
上海银闵创业投资企业（有限合伙）	2011-04-19	—	—
上海闸北创业投资有限公司	2011-11-09	—	021-62505267
上海张江创业投资有限公司	2000-07-12	www.zj-vc.com	021-50801918
上海兆丰创业投资有限公司	2003-12-18	—	021-64336311
上海真金创业投资管理有限公司	2011-08-26	www.shgenuine.com	021-50663716
上海真金高技术服务业创业投资中心（有限合伙）	2012-11-12	—	021-50663716
上海正海聚弘创业投资中心（有限合伙）	2014-08-21	—	021-50937905
上海正海资产管理有限公司	2008-01-31	www.royalsea-capital.com	021-50937905
上海正赛联创业投资管理有限公司	2011-01-31	www.cacfund.com	021-64275106
上海正赛联创业投资有限公司	2010-10-22	www.cacfund.com	021-64275106
成都成创汇智创业投资有限公司	2009-12-16	—	028-85337115
成都创新风险投资有限公司	2001-06-08	www.cd-vc.com.cn	028-85337115
成都德同银科创业投资合伙企业（有限合伙）	2010-03-03	www.dtcap.com	028-85231897
成都德同银科锦程创业投资合伙企业（有限合伙）	2013-11-19	www.dtcap.com	028-85231897
成都国泰光华投资有限公司	2010-08-16	—	—
成都汇金立方投资管理有限公司	2012-04-26	—	—
成都科创动力投资发展有限公司	2001-06-15	—	028-65575920
成都生产力促进中心	1997-07	www.cdppc.cn	028-65575920
成都天河中西医科技保育有限公司	2001-07-24	www.sc-tianhe.com	028-66070666
成都银科创业投资有限公司	2009-03-18	www.ykvc.cn	028-85336380
成都纵任创业投资有限公司	2010-08-16	—	028-65938919
双流聚源创业投资有限公司	2009-10-28	—	028-85810763
四川中物创业投资有限公司	2007-02-01	www.caep-vc.com	028-85311576
天创博盛（天津）股权投资基金合伙企业（有限合伙）	2011-10-18	—	022-58909386
天津滨海财富股权投资基金有限公司	2007-08-21	www.behycapital.com	022-23374077
天津滨海天创众鑫股权投资基金有限公司	2010-02-04	—	022-28408686
天津滨海天使创业投资有限公司	2006-09-11	—	022-58909386
天津创业投资有限公司	2001-03-30	www.tjvc.com.cn	022-58909386
天津迪恩投资管理有限公司	2012-06-13	—	022-59385952
天津歌子创业投资发展有限公司	2011-06-29	—	022-23357945-603
天津海泰科技投资管理有限公司	1997-05-08	www.hitech-investment.com	022-83715773
天津虹联创业投资有限公司	2009-12-28	—	022-26530257
天津火石信息服务业创业投资合伙企业（有限合伙）	2013-02-06	—	022-59385952
天津科技投资集团有限公司	1997-12	www.stic.com.cn	022-86430531-804
天津锟桥创业投资有限公司	2003-08-07	www.kqvc.com	022-87893441
天津软银博辰股权投资基金合伙企业（有限合伙）	2009-12-17	—	—

公司名称	成立时间	网址	传真
天津软银博欣股权投资基金合伙企业（有限合伙）	2011-03-18	—	—
天津软银欣创股权投资基金合伙企业（有限合伙）	2009-12-23	—	—
天津市中汇盈信投资管理有限公司	2010-05-24	www.zhyxifm.com	022-23352297
天津水星创业投资有限责任公司	2010-05-10	—	022-59852168
天津泰达科技投资股份有限公司	2000-10-13	www.tedavc.com.cn	022-66297288
天津天保成长创业投资有限公司	2007-03-06	—	022-58909386
天津天创盈讯创业投资合伙企业（有限合伙）	2011-09-26	—	022-58909386
天津天富创业投资有限公司	2007-12-04	—	022-58909386
天津天维创业投资合伙企业（有限合伙）	2012-04-26	—	—
天津天以生物医药股权投资基金有限公司	2010-11-25	—	022-28408686
天津天英创业投资管理有限公司	2010-06-22	—	022-58909386
天津燕山科技创业投资有限公司	2011-04-20	—	010-59782234
博汇源创业投资有限合伙企业	2009-05-26	—	0755-27821988
乌鲁木齐高新技术融资担保有限公司	2007-05-09	www.uhdz.gov.cn	0991-3834189
新疆创投资本管理有限责任公司	2010-07-15	www.xjvc.net	0991-3682873
新疆合赢成长股权投资有限合伙企业	2011-05-23	—	020-87553579
新疆火炬创业投资有限公司	2012-08-09	—	0991-3678085
新疆融汇鑫创业投资管理有限公司	2011-11-30	—	0991-6990026
新疆瑞景股权投资合伙企业（普通合伙）	2011-07-11	—	0991-3651290
新疆赛科森投资咨询有限责任公司	2002-04	—	0991-6611966
新疆新科源科技风险投资管理有限公司	2004-08	—	0991-3680756
新疆益通投资有限合伙企业	2011-03-01	—	0571-63431799
新疆浙新股权投资有限合伙企业	2011-11-02	—	—
新疆至诚股权投资有限责任公司	2011-05-17	—	0991-7842043
新疆中企股权投资管理有限公司	2010-11-02	www.xjinvest.com	0991-3827299
新疆中小企业创业投资股份有限公司	2010-01-26	www.xjvc.cn	0991-4583310
红塔创新投资股份有限公司	2000-06-15	—	010-58555666
昆明创业投资有限责任公司	2010-07-07	—	—
深圳市凯誉实业发展集团有限公司大理分公司	2014-07-24	www.overflyhk.com	0872-2428321
云南大顺股权投资基金管理有限公司	2012-04-23	—	—
云南和易创业投资有限公司	2008-07-30	—	0871-68038440
云南科技创业投资有限公司	2007-12-19	—	—
云南宁祥春融股权投资基金（有限合伙）	2013-08-07	—	0871-68358445-601
云南省林业投资有限公司	2009-05-27	www.cnynfi.com	0871-68338729
云南亿富达股权投资基金管理有限公司	2012-10-12	—	0871-67170098
云南越弘创业投资有限公司	2011-05-26	—	0871-65399198
安丰创业投资有限公司	2008-02-28	—	0571-87633580
长兴惠宏投资合伙企业（有限合伙）	2012-05-28	—	—
长兴科威创业投资合伙企业（有限合伙）	2014-12-30	—	—

公司名称	成立时间	网址	传真
东方星空创业投资有限公司	2008-10-29	—	0571-85058016
海宁海创创新投资合伙企业（有限公司）	2011-09-23	—	0571-87960022
海宁中新力合科金创业投资合伙企业（有限合伙）	2012-12-24	—	0571-89939766
杭州葆光投资管理有限公司	2012-10-18	—	0571-85455412
杭州长江创业投资有限公司	1996-01-06	—	0571-86624323
杭州诚和创业投资有限公司	2006-06-01	—	0571-88999278
杭州创东方富邦创业投资企业（有限合伙）	2010-12-19	—	0571-89716640
杭州创业加速器亚盈投资合伙企业（有限合伙）	2011-10-28	—	—
杭州德同创业投资合伙企业（有限合伙）	2010-07-08	—	0571-86690981
杭州德同投资管理有限公司	2010-04-21	—	0571-86690981
杭州敦和创业投资有限公司	2011-04-11	www.dunhevc.com	0571-87789050
杭州枫惠投资管理有限公司	2006-07-14	—	0571-89939631
杭州蜂窝投资管理有限公司	2013-12-16	—	0571-87203596
杭州富海银涛投资管理合伙企业（有限合伙）	2011-07-27	—	0571-28280180
杭州高特佳股权投资管理有限公司	2010-12	—	—
杭州高特佳龙之海脉投资管理合伙企业（有限合伙）	2011-06-15	—	—
杭州高新风险投资有限公司	2005-12-29	—	0571-88212247
杭州高盈创业投资合伙企业（有限合伙）	2010-06-28	—	—
杭州高盈蓝驰投资有限公司	2009-08-25	—	0571-87960022
杭州广润创业投资有限公司	2007-11-28	—	0571-86951902
杭州海邦投资管理有限公司	2010-12-10	www.hbvc.com.cn	0571-81022997
杭州海邦新湖人才创业投资合伙企业（有限合伙）	2013-08-02	www.hbvc.com.cn	0571-81022997
杭州海邦引智投资管理有限公司	2012-06-01	www.hbvc.com.cn	0571-81022997
杭州杭商宝石创业投资合伙企业（有限合伙）	2011-01-10	—	0571-86586927
杭州好望角启航投资合伙企业（有限合伙）	2011-09-21	—	0571-89719513
杭州好望角投资管理有限公司	2007-08-22	—	0571-89719513
杭州好望角引航投资合伙企业（有限合伙）	2014-05-55	—	0571-89719513
杭州好望角越航投资合伙企业（有限合伙）	2014-12-25	—	0571-89719513
杭州浩盈创业投资合伙企业（有限合伙）	2010-11-12	—	—
杭州合全投资管理有限公司	2006-11-20	www.hequangroup.com	0571-85300782
杭州恒岩股权投资合伙企业（有限合伙）	2012-04-25	—	021-32585857
杭州厚初创业投资合伙企业（有限合伙）	2014-05-22	—	0571-87988858
杭州华旦投资管理合伙企业（有限合伙）	2014-09-19	—	—
杭州吉成创业投资有限公司	2010-04-02	—	0571-87988858
杭州金色未来创业投资有限公司	2009-11-25	www.hzjswl.com.cn	0571-87923723
杭州金永信创业投资合伙企业（有限合伙）	2009-12-21	—	—
杭州金永信润禾创业投资合伙企业（有限合伙）	2010-05-04	—	0571-85279925
杭州金永信天时创业投资合伙企业	2010-04-07	—	0571-85279925

公司名称	成立时间	网址	传真
杭州锦聚投资管理有限公司	2014-07-21	—	—
杭州经济技术开发区创业投资有限公司	2008-10-09	—	0571-56638083
杭州科发创业投资合伙企业（有限合伙）	2013-01-09	www.zdkfcapital.com	0571-88250427
杭州兰德润广投资管理有限公司	2010-12-20	—	0571-86963977
杭州兰德优势创业投资合伙企业（有限合伙）	2011-07-07	—	—
杭州立元创业投资有限公司	2006-12-08	www.cnlyjt.com	0571-87769018
杭州灵峰赛伯乐创业投资合伙企业（有限合伙）	2008-12-10	—	0571-88085123
杭州灵琰投资合伙企业（有限合伙）	2013-06-03	—	0571-85455412
杭州钱江浙商创业投资合伙企业（有限合伙）	2009-06-03	—	0571-89922221
杭州如山创业投资有限公司	2007-08	—	0571-87896213
杭州润琰投资合伙企业（有限合伙）	2013-04-08	—	0571-85455412
杭州赛伯乐晨星投资合伙企业（有限合伙）	2010-09-21	—	0571-88085123
杭州赛硅银投资合伙企业 （有限合伙）	2014-04-11	www.cybernaut.com.cn	0571-89939834
杭州赛智创业投资有限公司	2009-03-13	—	0571-88085123
杭州市高科技投资有限公司	2000-08	—	0571-87024904
杭州万豪碧扬投资合伙企业（有限合伙）	2012-03-15	—	—
杭州万豪绵汐投资合伙企业（有限合伙）	—	—	—
杭州万豪培汕投资合伙企业（有限合伙）	2012-03-15	—	—
杭州万豪投资管理有限公司	2006-01-09	—	0571-88129640
杭州下城区创业投资有限公司	2008-06-10	www.hzxcgt.com	0571-85383218
杭州协诚慈德投资发展有限公司	2014-04-08	—	0571-57162991
杭州英维投资管理有限公司	2007-07-03	—	0571-28280180
杭州盈开投资管理有限公司	2009-06-23	www.incapital.cn	0571-87960022
杭州盈翔创业投资合伙企业（有限合伙）	2011-03-04	—	—
杭州浙科汇庆创业投资合伙企业（有限合伙）	2013-04-10	—	—
杭州浙科友业投资管理有限公司	2011-11	—	0571-88869550
湖州市创业投资有限责任公司	2008-09	—	0572-2212918
嘉兴华睿布谷鸟创业投资合伙企业（有限合伙）	2014-08-14	—	—
嘉兴天禀投资合伙企业（有限合伙）	2014-05-16	—	—
嘉兴天浩投资管理有限公司	2014-12-10	—	—
嘉兴天玑创业投资合伙企业（有限合伙）	2014-04-04	—	—
嘉兴天澜投资合伙企业（有限合伙）	2014-11-17	—	—
嘉兴天禄投资合伙企业（有限合伙）	2014-12-22	—	—
金华中呼股权投资管理有限公司	2011-08-17	—	0579-82056869
宁波安丰和众创业投资合伙企业（有限合伙）	2011-03-10	—	0571-87633580
宁波安丰汇群创业投资合伙企业（有限合伙）	2011-08-12	—	0571-87633580
宁波安丰汇盈创业投资合伙企业（有限合伙）	2011-08-12	—	0571-87633580
宁波安丰领先创业投资合伙企业（有限合伙）	2011-04-26	—	0571-87633580
宁波安丰添富创业投资合伙企业（有限合伙）	2012-07-13	—	0571-87633580

公司名称	成立时间	网址	传真
宁波安丰众盈创业投资合伙企业（有限合伙）	2010-04-27	—	0571-87633580
宁波科发海鼎创业投资合伙企业（有限合伙）	2014-05-30	www.zdkfcapital.com	0571-88250427
宁波市科发二号股权投资基金合伙企业（有限合伙）	2012-09-18	www.zdkfcapital.com	0571-88250427
宁波市科发股权投资基金合伙企业（有限合伙）	2012-03-01	www.zdkfcapital.com	0571-88250427
宁波天堂硅谷合众股权投资合伙企业（有限合伙）	2012-02-16	—	0571-86483535
宁波天堂硅谷和慧创业投资合伙企业（有限合伙）	2013-01-15	—	0571-87089718
宁波天堂硅谷融信股权投资合伙企业（有限合伙）	2013-11-07	—	0571-87089718
宁波天堂硅谷融正股权投资合伙企业（有限合伙）	2014-01-08	—	0571-87089718
宁波浙科汇聚创业投资合伙企业（有限合伙）	2014-07-16	—	—
衢州赛伯乐创业投资有限公司	2010-04-06	—	0574-88085123
绍兴凯泰投资管理有限公司	2010-11-26	—	0571-88129634
绍兴龙山赛伯乐创业投资有限公司	2008-09-03	—	0575-85156989
通联创业投资股份有限公司	2000-11	www.tonglianvc.com	0571-87153792
五都投资有限公司	2008-04-03	—	0571-87633677
浙江安丰进取创业投资有限公司	2009-03-25	—	0571-87633580
浙江安丰稳健创业投资有限公司	2009-07-08	—	0571-87633580
浙江博通创业投资有限公司	2007-07	—	0571-87087810
浙江春晖创业投资有限公司	2007-10-17	—	0575-82150888
浙江大学创新技术研究院有限公司	2012-09-29	www.zjuiti.com	0571-58122629
浙江大学创业投资有限公司	2001-01-03	—	0571-87382889
浙江大学科技创业投资有限公司	2008-10-29	—	0571-87397929
浙江东翰高投长三角股权投资合伙企业（有限合伙）	2010-09-20	—	025-66009900
浙江富国创新投资有限公司	2010-08-12	—	0571-88068369
浙江富国创业投资有限公司	2007-04-29	—	0571-88068369
浙江富国金溪创业投资合伙企业（有限合伙）	2011-07-25	—	0571-88068369
浙江富国投资管理有限公司	2010-07-13	—	0571-88068369
浙江富鑫创业投资有限公司	2008-02-03	www.zfinvest.com	0571-88352033
浙江国信创业投资有限公司	2003-03	—	0571-85069200
浙江海邦人才创业投资合伙企业（有限合伙）	2011-12	www.hbvc.com.cn	0571-81022997
浙江海帆股权投资管理有限公司	2013-03-05	—	—
浙江海洋经济创业投资有限公司	2010-01-19	—	0580 - 2036865
浙江浩誉创业投资有限公司	2011	—	0571-5689322
浙江合力创业投资有限公司	2011-03-09	—	0571-87988858
浙江恒岚股权投资合伙企业（有限合伙）	2011-11-03	—	021-32585857
浙江红石创业投资有限公司	2007-11-27	—	—
浙江华瓯创业投资有限公司	2007-11-16	www.hovc.cn	0571-87988858
浙江华瓯股权投资管理有限公司	2011-05-17	—	0571-87988858

公司名称	成立时间	网址	传真
浙江华睿德银创业投资有限公司	2010-05-04	—	0571-88163180
浙江华睿点金创业投资有限公司	2009-08-10	—	—
浙江华睿点石投资管理有限公司	2007-11-14	—	0571-88163180
浙江华睿富华创业投资合伙企业（有限合伙）	2012-07-03	—	—
浙江华睿海越光电产业创业投资有限公司	2009-12-23	—	—
浙江华睿海越投资有限公司	2009-07-20	—	—
浙江华睿海越现代服务业创业投资有限公司	2010-01-28	—	0571-88163180
浙江华睿弘源智能产业创业投资有限公司	2010-03-22	—	0571-88163180
浙江华睿互联投资有限公司	2010-10-20	—	0571-88163180
浙江华睿庆余创业投资有限公司	2013-12-30	—	—
浙江华睿如山创业投资有限公司	2010-12-07	—	0571-88163180
浙江华睿如山装备投资有限公司	2009-10-13	—	—
浙江华睿睿银创业投资有限公司	2007-03-28	—	—
浙江华睿盛银创业投资有限公司	2009-08-11	—	—
浙江华睿泰信创业投资有限公司	2008-07-21	—	—
浙江华睿投资管理有限公司	2002-08	www.sinowisdom.cn	0571-88163180
浙江华睿祥生环境产业创业投资有限公司	2010-11-15	—	0571-88163180
浙江华睿兴华股权投资合伙企业（有限合伙）	2012-12-24	—	—
浙江华睿医疗创业投资有限公司	2011-01-24	—	0571-88163180
浙江华睿中科创业投资有限公司	2010-07-05	—	0571-88163180
浙江嘉海创业投资有限公司	2010-01-13	—	0571-89922221
浙江嘉庆投资有限公司	2010-06-29	—	0571-86821212
浙江嘉银投资有限公司	2006-05-24	—	0571-88163180
浙江金桥创业投资有限公司	2007-08-14	www.jinqiaojituan.com	0571-89283995
浙江金永信投资管理有限公司	2005-03-24	—	0571-85279925
浙江君亚创业投资合伙企业（有限合伙）	2012-05-21	—	0571-86751630
浙江蓝石创业投资有限公司	2008-05-15	—	—
浙江临海永强股权并购投资中心（有限合伙）	2014-11-24	—	—
浙江隆德创业投资管理有限公司	2009-04-01	www.team-china.com	0571-87750989
浙江美林创业投资有限公司	2008-07-11	www.merrillcapital.cn	0571-85455412
浙江瓯联创业投资有限公司	2009-05-12	—	0571-87988858
浙江瓯盛创业投资有限公司	2008-06-03	—	0571-87988858
浙江瓯信创业投资有限公司	2009-04-02	—	0571-87988858
浙江普永泽股权投资合伙企业（有限合伙）	2010-08-24	—	021-32585857
浙江如山成长创业投资有限公司	2008-08-18	www.chinadunan.com	0571-87896213
浙江如山高新创业投资有限公司	2010-11-10	www.chinadunan.com	0571-87896213
浙江如山投资管理有限公司	2010-09-26	www.chinadunan.com	0571-87896213
浙江如山新兴创业投资有限公司	2012-09-11	—	0571-87896213
浙江若溪投资合伙企业（有限合伙）	2014-08-14	—	—

公司名称	成立时间	网址	传真
浙江赛伯乐投资管理有限公司	2008-06-16	www.zjcybernaut.com	0571-88085123
浙江赛康创业投资有限公司	2010-04-20	—	0571-88085123
浙江省创业投资集团有限公司	2000-09-30	www.zjvc.cn	0571-88259222
浙江省科技风险投资有限公司	1993-06	www.zvc-zj.com	0571-88869550
浙江省天堂硅谷创业创新投资服务中心有限公司	2008-05	www.vcpes.com	0571-86483535
浙江省浙创启元创业投资有限公司	2012-12-31	—	0571-88259222
浙江泰银创业投资有限公司	2007-10-26	—	—
浙江天使湾创业投资有限公司	2010-09-29	tisiwi.com	0571-89715708
浙江天堂硅谷长泰股权投资合伙企业（有限合伙）	2011-07-15	—	0571-86483535
浙江天堂硅谷长盈股权投资合伙企业（有限合伙）	2011-05-11	—	0571-86483535
浙江天堂硅谷朝阳创业投资有限公司	2007-04-16	—	0571-86483535
浙江天堂硅谷晨曦创业投资有限公司	2007-10-16	—	0571-86483535
浙江天堂硅谷大康股权投资合伙企业（有限合伙）	2012-08-21	—	0571-86483535
浙江天堂硅谷海天汇缘创业投资合伙企业（有限合伙）	2013-03-04	—	0571-86483535
浙江天堂硅谷合丰创业投资有限公司	2009-10-13	—	0571-86483535
浙江天堂硅谷合胜创业投资有限公司	2009-10-20	—	0571-87089718
浙江天堂硅谷合众创业投资有限公司	2007-10-24	—	0571-86483523
浙江天堂硅谷恒通创业投资有限公司	2008-05-26	—	0571-86483535
浙江天堂硅谷恒裕创业投资有限公司	2008-01-03	—	0571-86483535
浙江天堂硅谷汇通股权投资合伙企业（有限合伙）	2011	—	0571-86483535
浙江天堂硅谷久和股权投资合伙企业（有限合伙）	2012-03-01	—	0571-86483535
浙江天堂硅谷久鸿股权投资合伙企业（有限合伙）	2013	—	0571-86483535
浙江天堂硅谷久融股权投资合伙企业（有限合伙）	2011	—	0571-86483535
浙江天堂硅谷久晟股权投资合伙企业（有限合伙）	2011	—	0571-87089718
浙江天堂硅谷久盈股权投资合伙企业（有限合伙）	2012-02-13	—	0571-86483535
浙江天堂硅谷鲲诚创业投资有限公司	2006-12-01	—	0571-86483535
浙江天堂硅谷鲲鹏创业投资有限公司	2009-06-26	—	0571-86483535
浙江天堂硅谷七弦股权投资合伙企业（有限合伙）	2011	—	0571-86483535
浙江天堂硅谷台州合盈股权投资有限公司	2011	—	0571-86483535
浙江天堂硅谷阳光创业投资有限公司	2006-06-20	—	0571-86483535
浙江天堂硅谷银嘉股权投资合伙企业（有限合伙）	2010-11-16	—	0571-86483523
浙江天堂硅谷银泽股权投资合伙企业（有限合伙）	2010-10-19	—	0571-86483523
浙江天堂硅谷盈丰股权投资合伙企业（有限合伙）	2010-07-30	—	0571-87089718
浙江天堂硅谷盈通创业投资有限公司	2010-06-01	—	0571-86483535
浙江天堂硅谷元金创业投资合伙企业（有限合伙）	2013-03-20	—	0571-86483535
浙江天堂硅谷资产管理集团有限公司	2000-11-11	www.ttgg.com.cn	0571-86483535
浙江维科创业投资有限公司	2008-02-28	—	0571-87207613
浙江新安创业投资有限公司	2011	—	0571-88050547

公司名称	成立时间	网址	传真
浙江信德丰创业投资有限公司	2010-05-27	—	0571-87215866
浙江亚欧创业投资有限公司	2010-12-27	—	0571-89880002
浙江亿都创业投资有限公司	2007-11	—	0571-85310058
浙江盈瓯创业投资有限公司	2010-11-05	—	0571-87988858
浙江元飞投资有限公司	2012-07-01	—	—
浙江浙大科发股权投资管理有限公司	2003-11-11	www.zdkfcapital.com	0571-88250427
浙江浙华投资有限公司	2005-06-18	www.zhinvest.com.cn	0573-82582626
浙江浙科汇丰创业投资有限公司	2010-09	—	—
浙江浙科汇利创业投资有限公司	2010-05	—	—
浙江浙科汇涛创业投资合伙企业（有限合伙）	2011-05-09	—	—
浙江浙科汇盈创业投资有限公司	2009-08	—	—
浙江浙科美林创业投资有限公司	2011-04	—	—
浙江浙科升华创业投资有限公司	2010-10	—	—
浙江浙科银江创业投资有限公司	2010-10-14	—	—
浙江浙商长海创业投资合伙企业（有限合伙）	2010-12-14	—	0571-89922221
浙江浙商创业投资股份有限公司	2007-11	www.zsvc.com.cn	0571-89922221
浙江浙商创业投资管理集团有限公司	2007-11	www.zsvc.com.cn	0571-89922221
浙江浙商海鹏创业投资合伙企业（有限合伙）	2008-06-03	—	0571-89922221
浙江浙商诺海创业投资合伙企业（有限合伙）	2010-04-14	—	0571-89922221
浙江支汇股权投资合伙企业（有限合伙）	2010-08-24	—	021-32585857
浙江中大集团投资有限公司	2002-09-19	www.zhongda.com	0571-85777239
浙江中新力合科技金融服务有限责任公司	2011-09-29	—	0571-89939766
诸暨鼎信创业投资有限公司	2008-07-29	—	0571-87896213
诸暨贵银创业投资有限公司	2014-05-14	—	—
诸暨华睿嘉银创业投资合伙企业（有限合伙）	2014-11-21	—	—
昊云重庆股权投资基金管理有限公司	2012-11-23	www.howinfund.com	023-67511558
英飞尼迪（重庆）股权投资基金合伙企业（有限合伙）	2011-09-29	www.infinity-equity.com	023-63051585
圆基（重庆）股权投资基金管理有限公司	2010-02-05	—	023-63329022
重庆贝信投资有限公司	2014-02-21	—	023-88730291
重庆德同创业投资中心（有限合伙）	2010-04-01	—	023-67889905
重庆德同领航创业投资中心（有限合伙）	2014-04-30	—	023-67889905
重庆德同投资管理有限公司	2009-12-29	—	023-67889905
重庆富坤创业投资中心（有限合伙）	2009-09-22	www.rlequities.com	023-67030600
重庆富坤智通投资管理有限公司	2013-12-31	www.rlequities.com	023-67030600
重庆高新创业投资有限公司	2007-08	—	023-67308830
重庆汉能科技创业投资中心（有限合伙）	2011-05-16	www.hinagroup.com.cn	010-85889001
重庆恒锐源股权投资基金管理有限公司	2009-12-23	www.chinahry.com	023-86798500
重庆鸿曜股权投资基金管理有限公司	2014-12-29	—	—

公司名称	成立时间	网址	传真
重庆华犇创业投资管理有限公司	2010-04-16	www.chinarunvc.com	023-63318955
重庆开创高新技术创业投资有限公司	2005-03-25	—	023-68601100
重庆科技创业风险投资引导基金有限公司	2009-07-17	www.cqvcgf.com	023-67516108
重庆科技风险投资有限公司	1993-01-16	www.cqkjvc.com	023-67516883
重庆科兴乾健创业投资有限公司	2011-12-01	—	—
重庆两江新区创新创业投资发展有限公司	2011-09-26	www.chinaljcapital.com	023-88283537
重庆两江新区创业六环科技发展有限公司	2013-04-24	www.6link.cn	028-88722899-8055
重庆芃瑞股权投资基金管理有限公司	2013-07-30	www.prpe.cn	023-88601266
重庆赛卓股权投资基金管理有限公司	2015-07-08	www.sunzro.com	—
重庆三屋领秀创业投资有限公司	2012-11-22	—	023-62611660
重庆三屋投资有限公司	2009-12-02	www.cqswtz.com	023-62611660
重庆实友投资有限公司	2013-05	—	—
重庆市大渡口区科技产业创业投资有限公司	2013-01-21	—	023-67516108
重庆顺势创行股权投资基金管理有限公司	2010-09-02	—	—
重庆泰豪晟大股权投资基金管理中心（有限合伙）	2011-08-06	—	023-63022990
重庆泰豪渝晟股权投资基金中心（有限合伙）	2011-08-05	—	023-63022990
重庆泰然天合股权投资基金管理有限公司	2014-01-24	www.tairantianhe.com	023-67767660
重庆天承易果投资集团有限公司	2013-07-10	—	—
重庆天使科技创业投资有限公司	2010-01-25	—	023-67516883
重庆天毅伟业医药投资管理中心（有限合伙）	2014-02-18	—	023-88537630
重庆西证渝富股权投资基金管理有限公司	2012-05-10	—	023-67760963
重庆新天泽股权投资基金管理有限公司	2013-04-17	www.xtzfund.com	023-61667055-222
重庆新天泽华立股权投资基金合伙企业（有限合伙）	2014-01-09	—	023-61667055-222
重庆鑫山股权投资基金管理有限公司	2011-12-07	www.x-shan.com	023-67517660
重庆兴农股权投资基金管理有限公司	2014-05-07	—	—
重庆兴农资产经营管理有限公司	2013-08-28	—	023-88733896
重庆易一天使投资有限公司	2013-06-08	www.yiyitianshi.com	023-86788098
重庆英飞尼迪创业投资中心（有限合伙）	2011-08-16	www.infinity-equity.com	023-63051585
重庆英飞尼迪投资管理有限公司	2011-11-11	www.infinity-equity.com	023-63051585
重庆永盟股权投资基金管理有限公司	2012-05-25	www.chinavcbi.com	—
重庆圆基新能源创业投资基金合伙企业（有限合伙）	2011-01-27	—	023-63329022
重庆中福创新股权投资基金管理有限公司	2014-03-17	www.cftfund.com	023-63420250
重庆中昊股权投资基金管理有限公司	1999-08-17	www.hexuncn.com	023-63839988
重庆中景商业管理有限公司	2014-04-01	—	023-81303680